The State's Sexuality

ASIA PACIFIC MODERN

Takashi Fujitani, Series Editor

See series list at end of book.

The State's Sexuality

PROSTITUTION AND POSTCOLONIAL
NATION BUILDING IN SOUTH KOREA

Park Jeong-Mi

UNIVERSITY OF CALIFORNIA PRESS

University of California Press
Oakland, California

Library of Congress Cataloging-in-Publication Data

Names: Park, Jeong-Mi, 1976– author.
Title: The state's sexuality : prostitution and postcolonial nation building in
    South Korea / Park Jeong-Mi.
Other titles: Asia Pacific modern ; 20.
Description: Oakland, California : University of California Press, [2024] |
    Series: Asia pacific modern ; 20 | Includes bibliographical references and
    index.
Identifiers: LCCN 2024003724 (print) | LCCN 2024003725 (ebook) |
    ISBN 9780520396456 (cloth) | ISBN 9780520396463 (paperback) |
    ISBN 9780520396470 (epub)
Subjects: LCSH: Prostitution—Korea (South)—History—20th century. | Sex
    workers—Political aspects—Korea (South)—20th century. | Prostitution—
    Government policy—Korea (South)—20th century. | Prostitution—Law and
    legislation—Korea (South)—20th century.
Classification: LCC HQ248.A5 P37 2024 (print) | LCC HQ248.A5 (ebook) |
    DDC 306.74095195—dc23/eng/20240206
LC record available at https://lccn.loc.gov/2024003724
LC ebook record available at https://lccn.loc.gov/2024003725

33 32 31 30 29 28 27 26 25 24
10 9 8 7 6 5 4 3 2 1

The publisher and the University of California Press Foundation gratefully acknowledge the generous support of the Philip E. Lilienthal Imprint in Asian Studies, established by a major gift from Sally Lilienthal.

For Kim Yeon-Ja and You Youngnim

CONTENTS

ILLUSTRATIONS

FIGURES

TABLES

ACKNOWLEDGMENTS

This book is based on my PhD dissertation, submitted to Seoul National University in 2011. Almost two decades have passed from when I decided to write a dissertation on prostitution to the publication of this book. This journey, which has taken much longer than I anticipated, was full of adventures, sometimes difficult but more often exciting, joyful, and rewarding. Thanks to the many people I have encountered on my path, I have been able to keep forging ahead and finish this journey.

I cannot remember when I first became interested in prostitution. It seems that the issue has been near me from the moment I realized that I am not only a person but also a woman. To be a proper woman in Korea meant not to be a prostitute. Nobody taught me this idea explicitly, but I perceived it just from the atmosphere, probably since my early teens. In contrast, I vividly remember exactly when I determined to study prostitution: one summer night in 2005 when I read Kim Yeon-Ja's autobiography. At the time I was undecided about which subject to choose for my dissertation. While prostitution was a strong interest, I was hesitant to write about the topic since it was, and still is, "a difficult issue [even] for feminists," as Priscilla Alexander wrote in 1987. Then, when I read Kim's book, which narrated her life story from her time as a "comfort woman" for the U.S. military to becoming an activist struggling for the rights of her fellow sex workers, I resolved to tackle the subject head on. I felt that this powerful text spoke directly to me and compelled me to explore and make widely known what social conditions circumscribed the lives of women like Kim, a goal I have humbly attempted to achieve through this book. In addition, Kim was gracious enough to grant me an interview in 2018, which is included in chapter 4. I deeply appreciate her for her ceaseless bravery and the kindness she has constantly shown me.

While Kim's life story inspired my research, You Youngnim not only helped me complete my dissertation but also encouraged me to continue researching the theme after my graduation. As a director of the Durebang, a counseling center for the comfort women engaged by American servicemen (see chapter 5), she willingly shared with me, an unknown PhD candidate, the valuable materials that the center housed. I sent the Durebang two copies of my dissertation to express my gratitude. A few months later she called me. She said that she had read my work and invited me to present it at a colloquium. So, on June 3, 2011, I delivered a presentation in front of the activists of the Solidarity for Human Rights of Camptown Women, and it was the start of my involvement in the lawsuit filed by the comfort women for the U.S. military against the Korean government (something I address further in the introduction and epilogue). As part of this engagement, I explained the peculiar legal structure of Korean prostitution policies to the lawyers who prepared the lawsuit, provided them with a diverse selection of official documents that I had found as evidence, and testified in court as an expert witness for the plaintiffs. In turn, my research was greatly enriched by the lawsuit. I was provided with the opportunity to deliberate on the further range of issues discussed during the proceedings, which greatly motivated me to continue my work on the topic. Perhaps most importantly, I was able to interview some of the plaintiffs thanks to the introductions provided by You Youngnim (see chapter 4). I dedicate my book to Kim Yeon-Ja and You Youngnim, two warmhearted grandmothers and pioneering feminists.

I am also very grateful to the 122 plaintiffs, including Park Yeongja, Han Min-Ju (pseudonym), and Yang Hye-Sun (pseudonym), who granted me interviews; the feminist activists who stood by the plaintiffs, including Woo Soon Duk, Ahn Kim JeongAe, Kim Tae-Jung, Kim Eunjin, Joyce Kim, Ko You-kyŏng, Ryu In Kyoung, and Lee Ko Woon; and the lawyers who represented them, including Ha Ju-Hee, Kim Jin, and Cha Hye-Ryeong. I also thank Lee Ock-jeong, a director of the Magdalena Community, a shelter for women engaged in prostitution, for sharing her experiences with me through an interview (see chapters 4 and 5). Feminist activists and scholars based in the United States also expressed great interest in the lawsuit and solidarity with the plaintiffs and activists. Here I would like to thank Margo Okazawa-Rey, Gwen Kirk, Deborah Lee, Suzy Kim, Hosu Kim, Martha M. Matsuoka, Thomas Kim, and other activists and scholars of the Women for Genuine Security, Rutgers University, the Nodutdol, Scripps College, and Mills College, for organizing serial colloquia (April 18–25, 2019) under the title "Korean 'Comfort Women' for U.S. Troops: History and Significance of the Survivors' Lawsuit against the Korean Government" and welcoming speakers from Korea, including me.

This book is not only a fruit of feminist solidarity but also, of course, a scholarly work. The Department of Sociology, Seoul National University, where I earned my BA, MA, and PhD, was the womb that nurtured my growth as a sociologist. My supervisor, Chung Chin Sung, who specialized in Japanese colonial injustice, including the history of Japanese military comfort women, taught me the significance of accounting for the experience of the oppressed in sociological studies. Jung Keun-Sik constantly encouraged me to explore new areas, perspectives, and methodologies, and it was only after I participated in field research in Okinawa under his supervision that I realized my identity as a historical sociologist and the joys of delving into piles of old documents to uncover how events, ideas, and discourses from the forgotten past continue to profoundly shape society today. I learned feminist jurisprudence from Yang Hyunah, who taught me that it is important not only to investigate how women are discriminated against in the legal system but also to analyze how gendered subjects are constituted by law. From Bae Eun-Kyung I gained the perspective that women are not merely held in social structures but flexibly navigate them according to their desires, thanks to the example of her study on birth control in Korea. The late Kim Chin Kyun, forever a young sociologist at heart, was a great teacher who gave me faith that the mission of sociology is to contribute to making the world freer, more egalitarian, and more democratic. I would also like to thank all the other teachers who taught me at SNU—the late Kim Chae-Yoon, Kim Kyong-Dong, Shin Yong-Ha, Kwon Tae-Hwan, Hong Doo-Seung, Han Sang-Jin, Lim Hyun-Chin, Song Ho-Keun, Park Myoung-Kyu, Chang Kyung-Sup, Yee Jaeyeol, Suh Yi-Jong, Park Keong-Suk, Kim Hong-Jung, Hwang Jung-Mee, and Joo Eunwoo—for all their sociological knowledge and insights. My graduate friends vitalized my life with their passion, humor, and friendship, and I am particularly thankful to Oh Hyeon-Mi, Choi Jong-Sook, Jeon Yoon-Jeong, Ku Mi-Jin, Yu Jin, Kang Inhwa, Yi Jung-Yeon, Jeong Young Sin, Yoo Hyung-geun, Hyun Min, Lee Sun Hyoung, Eum Hye Jin, Chung In-Kyoung, and Kim Wonjung.

The Research Institute for Comparative History and Culture, Hanyang University, offered me my first job as well as a very new, productive environment in which to interact with scholars from diverse disciplines, including history, memory studies, sociology, and law. Its director, Lim Jie-Hyun, a champion of transnational perspectives through his pioneering critiques of nationalism and his active cooperation with numerous global scholars, provided me with wonderful opportunities to access international academia via a series of conferences, lectures, and colloquia. Yun Hae-dong, an exemplary critical historian who explores the opaque, gray areas of Japanese colonial rule, has also always been highly supportive and immensely encouraging. Kim Sang-Hyun enriched my research with his sharp comments and inspired me to expand my theoretical scope to consider Foucault's notions of biopolitics and governmentality. Last but not least, Hong Yang Hee and So Hyunsoog gave me the pleasure of their company and inspired me to deliberate closely upon the continuities between the colonial and postcolonial legal systems.

The John W. Kluge Center was an ideal place to develop my dissertation into a book. Thanks to a generous Kluge Fellowship, I was able to investigate the rich archives at the Library of Congress, the National Archives and Records Administration at College Park (NACP), and the Wilson Center for eleven months, sites that I could not access while writing my dissertation in Korea. The materials I collected during this period helped me reveal the role that the U.S. government and its military in Korea played in the formation of Korean prostitution policies, something I highlight in chapters 1 and 2. I deeply appreciate the help of Robert Gallucci, the director of the Kluge Center; the wonderful staff at the center, including Mary Lou Reker, JoAnne Kitching, Jason Steinhauer, and Travis Hensley; the devoted librarians at the Library of Congress; and above all, the anonymous reviewers of my proposal who allowed me this great chance to research in Washington, D.C. At the Kluge Center, I also enjoyed the pleasure of interacting with other Kluge Fellows, including Julia G. Young, Theo Christov, Anna T. Brown Ribeiro, Rachel Sheldon, and Andrew Devereux. Inspired by their achievements and support, I first dreamed of publishing my book at a U.S. university press. I am also grateful to Eric Van Slander and James Person for assisting me in finding valuable resources at NACP and the Wilson Center respectively, and to Katharine H. S. Moon for her pioneering study on U.S.-military-oriented prostitution and the donation of her documents to the Wilson Center (the Kathy Moon Papers). I thank Jisoo Kim and Gregg Brazinsky of the Institute for Korean Studies, George Washington University, Jason Yoon of the Peace and Prosperity Forum, and Jung-Sil Lee of the Washington Coalition for Comfort Women for showing their interest in my study and for offering me the opportunity to present my work. I am indebted to independent researchers Yu Chong Park and Mi Sook Yun Kim and Shin Jae-Ho of the National Institute of Korean History for helping me discover various materials at NACP. Thanks to Lee Dongheon, Park Myounghye, Oh Eunjeong, Son Jemin, and Jeongyeon Shim, my family and I were able to successfully adapt to life in America and enjoy our first long stay overseas.

The past and present professors of the Department of Sociology, Chungbuk National University, warmly greeted me as their colleague. I want to thank Min Kyonghee, Kang Hee-Kyung, Seo Gwan-mo, Nam Chae-Bong, Hurh Seok-ryol, Lee Hang-Woo, Lee Hae-Jin, Hong Deok-Hwa, Seo Seonyoung, and Kim Hyun Woo. Following the critical and cordial academic tradition that they built and continue, I was able to embark on writing my book. Chung Il Joon of Korea University taught me the importance of archival research at the NACP and has always supported my research. Thanks to the excellent works of Park Jung Ae and Kim Joohee, I could understand more clearly the colonial prostitution regime and the current sex industry. Kim Joohee also kindly invited me to participate in the anthology *Decriminalization* (*Pulchŏbŏl*, 2022), and it was my honor to work together with members of the Human Rights Action for Women in Prostitution Eloom, including Hwang Yu Na, Choi Byeol, and Noh Hyejin, and all the other related contributors who made this book possible. Another joint research project on camptown women in Gyeonggi Province helped me concretely address their status as *homo sacer*, borrowing from Georgio Agamben, and I would like to thank Jung Hey-Won, Ahn Taeyoon, and Lim Hae Kyoung, the coauthors of that project report. I also appreciate KBS journalist Noh Yun-Jeong for readily sharing with me the primary sources that she collected and digitalized.

As a scholar who has been educated only in Korea, it was not easy to decide to publish a book in English. I was fortunate to take an English writing class from Han Eunkyeong at the Language Education Institute, SNU, whose encouragement was crucial in enabling me to take this first step. Minjeong Kim of San Francisco State University and Todd A. Henry of the University of California, San Diego, have been wonderful mentors who gladly shared precious advice on getting a book published. Kenneth Rosenberg kindly helped me prepare my public lecture at the Library of Congress, presented on July 28, 2016, which developed into chapter 2, and Luke Houston, as my first reader, offered a lot of useful feedback and meticulously edited the whole manuscript. I would like to express my special appreciation to Takashi Fujitani for recognizing my work as worthy of publishing in his series.

I also thank the two anonymous reviewers for their time and energy in reading my initial manuscript and giving me valuable comments, not to mention the wonderful editorial staff of the University of California Press for helping me to complete this book. In particular, my editor Enrique Ochoa-Kaup counseled me through the whole process of publishing with his kind and detailed guidance.

My undergraduate friends Lee Ka Eun, Shim Jungshuk, Cho Seung Yon, and Jun Jung Hyon have long been supporters of this book even before I conceived it. I bet that they will buy this book to check their names in the acknowledgments. I thank Kim Chung-kang and Lee Soyoung, my closest colleagues and comrades, for sharing almost every joy and sorrow we encountered on the path from PhD to becoming tenure-track professors. I must also thank Heo Eun, who must have been my twin sister in a previous life. It was only thanks to her willingness to share her heartfelt support and mindful advice that I was able to get through the adventure of this project successfully. Finally, I would like to express my deepest appreciation to my family. The best fortune in my life is that I met Jiwon as my husband and Suhyun as my son. Jiwon has always stood by me since my early twenties with his warm love, witty humor, and wise advice, and Suhyun continues to light up our lives with all the joys he has been bringing to us. I pray that Suhyun will be always as happy as now, loving life, in the world that Jiwon is dreaming of.

Throughout the long process of its completion and thanks to all the people I have mentioned, this book has gradually taken shape. Over this period, various elements of the manuscript have been previously published in several Korean journal articles and book chapters, as well as two English-language articles.[1] However, the manuscript before you is an entirely rewritten work, containing more material and a nuanced, in-depth analysis specifically oriented to readers unfamiliar with Korean history in the English-speaking world. On that note, my final thought is to acknowledge the reader. I am very excited about meeting you through my book. Thank you for joining me here.

NOTE ON ROMANIZATION

For the romanization of names of Korean people, terms, and publications, I utilized the McCune-Reischauer system in general. In cases where an alternative spelling has been widely used or I could check people's own romanized names, I followed those versions and put the McCune-Reischauer romanization in parentheses—for example, Rhee Syngman (Yi Sŭng-Man) and Kim Yeon-Ja (Kim Yŏn-Ja). In referring to Korean people, I put their surnames first, according to the Korean standard. When Korean authors have already chosen and used their own romanized names in English-language publications or English abstracts of Korean-language articles, theses, and dissertations, I have followed these precedents in the text and endnotes and put the McCune-Reischauer romanization in parentheses in the bibliography. For the names of Korean places, in particular major cities and provinces, I followed the Revised Romanization Principle established by the National Institute of Korean Language in 2000—for instance, Seoul, Busan, and Gyeonggi.

Introduction

WEAVING PROSTITUTION INTO
THE NARRATIVE OF THE NATION-STATE

"STATELESS PATRIOTS" AND THEIR GREAT NATION

On December 21, 2017, Park Yeongja (Pak Yŏng-Ja), a sixty-two-year-old woman, stood in front of the Seoul High Court. She had engaged in prostitution for American servicemen from the 1970s to the mid-1990s in Dongducheon and Uijeongbu, South Korea (hereafter Korea). Park and 121 other women who had endured similar experiences filed a lawsuit on June 25, 2014, to demand reparations from the Korean government for violating their human rights. It was the final day of arguments in the appeal trial, and her testimony was as follows:

Dear honorable judge,
   Some of us are illiterate, and most of us were daughters abandoned by poor families. Despite this, for our families, or our better life, we tried to find a job at state-approved employment agencies, but they trafficked us to camptowns [the specially designated entertainment and commercial districts surrounding U.S. military bases]. This was against our will. We were trafficked because of our ignorance. Most of us were minors. There were no adults who would help the teenage girls in camptowns. . . .
   We were stateless people. When we asked police officers to help us escape, they brought us back to the brothel owners. Public health clinics kept on implementing the painful and humiliating sexually transmitted infection testing twice a week. Moreover, when we were arbitrarily apprehended through crackdowns or contact tracing, we were incarcerated in the same clinics, and administered with unpleasant penicillin shots even though we did not have STIs. No matter how sick we were because of diseases other than STIs, they didn't give us any injections or drugs.
   We think the state is responsible for building the camptowns and neglecting [the illegal activities inside] these areas. If the state created the

camptowns, it should have monitored what occurred within and intervened. *Even though the state praised us as patriots*, it did not punish vicious brothel owners, not to mention the GIs frequently committing violence against us. . . . Honorable judge, please pay attention to our suffering! I earnestly beg you to reach the right decision. [emphasis added][1]

On February 8, 2018, nearly fifty days after Park testified, the appeals court recognized that Korea's past authoritarian government administrations had constructed, operated, and managed the camptowns, justified and facilitated prostitution within such areas even though it had long been prohibited by law, and performed vicious and forced methods of STI control.[2] Based on these facts, the appeals court decided that the Korean government should pay compensation of 3 million KRW (around US$3,000) to all the plaintiffs and additional compensation of 4 million KRW (around US$4,000) to seventy-four plaintiffs who testified to their experience of being forcefully quarantined and treated in STI facilities. In response, both the plaintiffs and the defendant appealed to the Supreme Court, and on September 29, 2022, the Supreme Court finalized the appeals court's decision.[3] With this verdict, the camptown women finally triumphed against their national government, eight years and three months after the proceedings were first initiated. During this period twenty-four plaintiffs passed away and three others lost contact with the legal team, also presumed to be deceased.

This unprecedented legal struggle on the part of one of the most disenfranchised, persecuted female groups in Korea was a milestone not only for Korean feminism but also for Korean democracy. The 122 brave women stepped forward to testify to their painful experience on behalf of all the women who had provided sexual services to U.S. troops. The Korean judiciary was compelled to listen to their voices and finally accepted their testimony as the truth alongside other supporting evidence, although the courts ultimately decided upon only a small and symbolic amount of compensation compared to the huge trauma these women had endured. The feminist activists at the counseling centers and shelters, who had stood by the camptown women since the late 1980s, prepared the lawsuit and persuaded the survivors to litigate. The thirty-six pro bono lawyers from the MINBYUN-Lawyers for a Democratic Society presented their case, and experts such as a doctor, a photographer, and two academic researchers testified as expert witnesses. I was honored to be one of these witnesses. My PhD dissertation, which provided the foundation for this book, and the official documents

I uncovered were cited in the rulings as evidence to prove the Korean government's intrinsic role in the making of the camptowns and their draconian policing of the plaintiffs relative to STI control. Nevertheless, my contribution was only a tiny part of the whole body of evidence presented at the trial, where the lawyers submitted nearly 550 evidentiary documents to prove the case.

This lawsuit functioned as a sort of revelatory public sphere to encourage people to confront and reflect on the neglected, oppressed, and forgotten history of the camptown women. Among the vast body of evidence presented at the trial, I highlight the quoted passage from Park Yeongja's testimony. It was plainly constructed out of her suffering, independent of any conceptual or rhetorical pretense. However, it raises profound theoretical questions. What was the importance of these women to the state, and what was the precise intention of the state in the creation and perpetuation of their circumstances? Why did the state deploy such harsh measures to control them, while suspending the constitutional rights that might have served to protect them? In other words, how could these women come to justifiably consider themselves "stateless people" externalized from citizenship, while still being seen as belonging to the nation and even being interpellated as "patriots" by the state at the same time? What laws and regulations did the Korean state utilize to circumscribe them as "stateless patriots," and how have the laws and regulations changed over time? And then, ultimately, what were the effects of such policies on the nation-state?

The State's Sexuality seeks to unpack the enigmatic relationship that stateless patriots like Park Yeongja have had with the state of Korea. The purpose of this book is not merely to provide a detailed analysis of how the state controlled such women. Rather, it attempts to elucidate how this control over these women, or more accurately, how constituting them as targets for state intervention, and maximizing their utility while suppressing their presumed threat, contributed to the making of Korea as a nation-state. To this end, the focus of this book is primarily on the policies deployed toward prostitution in Korea. Through such legal and administrative measures, the Korean state has historically sought to identify, classify, and discipline prostitutes or sex workers, created institutional apparatuses, and positioned agents that they encounter. Thus, prostitution policies function as the crucial initial point of mediation between the state and the women, and their substance contains numerous features to help critically clarify the relationship between the two.

Thus, *The State's Sexuality* illuminates how prostitution and the women involved in it are constitutive and contradictory components of Korea's postcolonial nation-state, included and excluded at once by what Ann Laura Stoler has called "interior frontiers." Inspired by Étienne Balibar, Stoler has discussed these interior frontiers primarily in relation to racist governance, which differentiates white, proper citizens ("us") from improper citizens or "subcitizens," colonial subjects, *métissage*, or inassimilable immigrants ("them"), and thereby disenfranchises the latter as "internal enemies" and excludes them from legal protection.[4] Stoler further argues that such internal borders are "not always raced" but foster other forms of discrimination and violence against those seemingly "destroying normality or deviating from it."[5] Here, I expand this concept of interior frontiers to help us grasp the gender politics that constitute female others deviant and/or expelled from a "normal," "moral" community buttressed by a culturally authorized gender/sexual order, and who therefore are considered dangerous to society: in this case, prostitutes. However, simultaneously and conversely, prostitutes in postcolonial Korea not only were deemed internal enemies who posed a moral and pathological threat to the nation. They also were framed as patriots, that is, those crucial to the survival, development, and prosperity of the nation.

Through the lens of prostitution relative to this paradoxical context, this book examines the unique trajectory of Korea's postcolonial national construction. As have other countries, the nation-state of Korea has been subject to continuous (re)construction, albeit perhaps in a particularly dramatic manner. In other words, Korea is an exemplary case of so-called compressed modernity, as Chang Kyung-Sup has conceptualized, passing through colonization, liberation, civil war, developmental dictatorship, and finally and quite exceptionally, succeeding in becoming an economically developed, democratic country in only a century.[6] Adopting a *longue durée* approach, this book analyzes how, in the process of this dynamic, drastic, and dizzying century of nation building, prostitutes or sex workers were marginalized but simultaneously mobilized by the state to devote themselves to the needs of the nation.

However, it is noteworthy that women in the sex industry were not passive beings who always responded to the state's orders. Usually independently, but sometimes either supported or opposed by middle-class feminists, they often avoided and directly protested governmental controls and even made use of state apparatuses to get recognition as citizens. The aforementioned extraordinary lawsuit is one such example, representing the vital character of Korean contemporary democracy, which was achieved only after a long, arduous struggle against successive postcolonial authoritarian governments. *The State's Sexuality* entirely rewrites this dynamic modern history of Korea from a gender perspective, through the ways in which the work and lives of prostitutes or sex workers, who have long been considered the most abased beings in Korean society, have been deeply and strategically intertwined with the lofty purpose of building the nation-state.

THE WOMEN WHO HAD MANY NAMES

Park Yeongja was born into an impoverished family on Jeju Island in 1955, two years after the Korean War ended and at the onset of the national baby boom. She had eleven siblings, of whom five died as children because of poverty and disease. At the age of seven, she was sent to an orphanage by her parents. This traumatic experience made her extremely introverted and even afraid of making eye contact with adults. In 1969, when she was fourteen years old, she left for Seoul to seek employment, following her elder sister. Her fate after this was as she testified: she was trafficked by an employment agency to a red-light district for Koreans and then to a camp-town for American servicemen.[7] According to official statistics, in the early 1970s, when Park was first forced to engage in prostitution, the number of "fallen women" (*yullak yŏsŏng*, i.e., prostitutes) registered and monitored by the government was nearly seventeen thousand. More than half of them (about 50–57 percent) served U.S. military personnel, and the rest catered for Koreans and foreign tourists, most of whom were Japanese.[8] Considering the number of unregistered prostitutes, the total number of women working in the national sex industry must have been much larger.

Yullak had been the government's official term to refer to prostitution under the Yullak Haengwi Prevention Act (1961–2004; hereafter the Yullak Prevention Act). The literal meaning of yullak is to fall and tumble (into a pit), while *haengwi* simply signifies any form of action or behavior. Today, *The Standard Korean Language Dictionary* defines yullak as (1) wandering to other towns because of a decline in power or family fortune or (2) for women to fall into a situation to sell their bodies because of their depravity.[9] *The Korean Dictionary* (1938) and *The Great Dictionary of Korean* (1957) defined it as "wandering to places away from home because of being ruined," both lacking the second meaning found in contemporary dictionaries.[10] Therefore, one could suppose that the second meaning seems to derive from the first, which implies that female prostitution was initially considered a gender-specific form of vagrancy. The women in prostitution were called *yullak haengwija, yullak yŏsŏng,* or *yullangnyŏ.* Similar to the English word prostitution, yullak indicates only the women's activity to sell sexual services, not the men's activity to buy such services. In this book, I therefore use prostitution and prostitutes as the closest translation of yullak and yullak haengwija, despite their derogatory connotations.

The Yullak Prevention Act also categorized prostitutes as "women needing protection" (*yoboho yŏja*), together with "those liable to engage in prostitution considering their circumstance, character, or behavior." However, the list of official nomenclature for women like Park Yeongja did not end there. Another notorious term was "comfort women" (*wianbu*). In general, comfort women refers to the sexual slaves drafted by the Japanese imperial army from 1932 to 1945. The Korean government inherited this term as a label for the prostitutes who served American military personnel, under the Infectious Disease Prevention Act and its regulations promulgated in 1957. The term comfort women was replaced by "special entertainers" (*t'ŭksu ŏpt'aebu,* literally, women working in a special business) in 1978, with the revisions of the regulations of the Infectious Disease Prevention Act. In addition, comfort women were categorized as "employees hired in the entertainment business" (*yuhŭng yŏngŏp chongsaja*) by the 1962 Food Sanitation Act.

As such, the women catering to the U.S. troops were labeled in several ways according to the official state categories constituted by a series of laws. They were punished by fines as prostitutes, incarcerated in female reformatories as women needing protection, registered with local governments as employees hired in the entertainment business, and finally, subject to regular, mandatory STI tests in public health clinics as well as forceful quarantine and treatment in STI detention centers as comfort women or special entertainers. Prostitutes for Korean men or foreign tourists were also subject to similar but less severe control. Ironically, by being such legal subjects, in other words, becoming subject to these complicated, meticulous laws and regulations, prostitutes were excluded from ordinary citizenship, and their basic rights were infringed. In Georgio Agamben's terms, they were held captive by a form of "inclusive exclusion," which could be considered as a parallel, analogous concept to Stoler's interior frontier.[11]

By way of contrast, there had historically been no specific legal or commonly used term to refer to the men who buy sex. While the Yullak Prevention Act categorized them as "the counterparts of prostitution" (*yullak haengwi ŭi sangdaeja*), the phrase was not commonly used, and instead, they were merely called "clients" (*kaek* or *sonnim*) in general. As various Korean dictionaries define the term, yullak is female vagrancy and its cause is "women's depravity," so state control was concentrated on female prostitutes rather than on their clients or procurers. Relying on diverse measures, the state attempted to surveil and suppress women's excessive, recalcitrant, and even subversive mobility. This was because such women were popularly believed to spread disease, disorder, and decadence, transgressing the boundaries between the public and the private, labor and sexuality, and visibility and invisibility. And while there was also a minority of male sex workers and female clients, they rarely garnered the state's attention. In this way, Korea's prostitution policies and the language of law and regulation have been exclusively framed in heterosexual and sexist terms. Thus, this book only addresses the politics and context of prostitution in the understanding that sex workers are women and clients are men, notwithstanding that male prostitution and queer sex work in Korea remain as crucial research tasks that demand greater attention within academia.[12]

Another peculiar feature of Korea's historical governmental approach to prostitution is the coexistence of prohibition and regulation. The Yullak Prevention Act was a typical prohibitionist approach to prostitution, since it criminalized, in principle at least, all the activities regarding prostitution, such as selling, buying, and procuring. In contrast, the Infectious Disease Prevention Act; the Food Sanitation Act; and their related decrees, rules, and local ordinances were regulatory approaches, functioning to register, test, and forcefully quarantine and treat prostitutes. Why, then, did the Korean state adopt not only prohibition but also regulation, and how was it capable of registering, testing, and treating prostitutes while punishing them simultaneously? What enabled the legal inclusive exclusion of prostitutes, and what was the effect of this paradoxical legal structure? This book attempts to solve these conundrums in relation to the historical processes of nation-state building.

At the same time, it is noteworthy that the policies were not simply conjured up by the Korean state but created out of a patchwork of various administrative approaches that had already been experimented with across other nations, empires, and colonies. Hence, to properly understand the significance of this case study, it is necessary to first examine when, where, and under what conditions such different institutional solutions to prostitution, which were ultimately confluent in Korea, emerged.

PROSTITUTION AND BIOPOLITICAL
STATES/EMPIRES

As several pioneering studies have noted, the first modern, "rational" solution to prostitution emerged in late eighteenth-century France after the French Revolution. Regulation (*réglementation*) (known as the French system) was epochally significant in that it approached prostitution not only as a moral issue—namely, illegitimate, debased sexual encounters—but also as a public health concern and a source of venereal disease (VD), which was the medical term used historically to refer to what is commonly termed STI today. VD had a special status compared to other contagious diseases. Since VD was transmitted through sex in general, it was regarded as a wage of sin, and sufferers were subject to severe social stigma. Even though VD was less lethal than other illnesses such as cholera and smallpox, it was considered more insidious, because of the long-term intergenerational consequences of diseases such as syphilis. Moreover, VD was often surreptitious, protracted, and thus difficult to identify. As a result, regulation targeted a specific group, an occupation, rather than the public in general, and prostitutes were viewed as the primary transmitters, like rats for plague and mosquitos for yellow fever.[13] To curb the public health threat posed by prostitutes, regulation was composed of four elements: toleration, registration, inspection, and incarceration. First, the police tolerated prostitution as a necessary evil and permitted brothels, even though prostitution was technically illegal. Second, the women who chose prostitution as their profession had to register themselves with the police and then work at brothels or on their own with official cards issued by the police, who in turn apprehended clandestine prostitutes and forced them to register. Third, registered prostitutes had to submit to regular vaginal examinations by doctors in venereal dispensaries, and if they avoided this requirement they were apprehended and punished by the police. Finally, prostitutes found infected with VD were forcibly incarcerated and treated in special hospitals designed specifically for such sex workers.[14]

The toleration of prostitution was not a new phenomenon, but the combination of toleration with other techniques of systematic disease control was "a genuinely innovative manner of handling prostitution."[15] Philip Howell distinguishes modern regulatory approaches as diverging from historical precedents relative to three factors: the development of the modern state, the authority of medical and social science, and the role of war and empire. First, the emergence of regulation coincided with "the birth of the modern, reformed and enlightened state."[16] Regulation was implemented through the moral police (*police des moeurs*), who registered, supervised, and apprehended prostitutes; venereal dispensaries, which carried out periodic medical checkups; prisons, which incarcerated the apprehended prostitutes; and hospitals, which quarantined infected ones. These state apparatuses of public order and health, in turn, were established and expanded due to regulation. Second, such regulation was combined with modern "scientific" knowledge about subjects such as medicine, social research, and statistics. The career of Alexandre Parent-Duchâtlet (1790–1836) exemplifies this tendency. As a medical doctor who had established his reputation in public hygiene by researching sewers, cemeteries, dissecting rooms, and garbage dumps, he "scientifically" legitimized regulation by publishing *On Prostitution in the City of Paris* (1836), which is considered the first systematic social and anthropological report on prostitutes.[17] Finally, this form of regulation was established and consolidated to protect French citizen armies from VD, as they fought in the series of wars that followed the French Revolution. Consequently, the practice of regulation as a project to protect the safety of soldiers and male citizens was globally adopted in the imperial era.[18]

However, regulation soon encountered the criticisms and protests of feminists and social reformers. British feminists took the lead from the late 1860s, when a series of regulatory policies was introduced in a few military areas of the United Kingdom under the Contagious Diseases Acts. The feminists complained that regulation was not effective in preventing VD. Worse still, they argued, was that the state violated prostitutes' personal integrity and civil liberty with compulsory examination and incarceration while tolerating men's sexual depravity. The campaign to abolish regulation soon spread to other countries, forming a wave of concern within the incipient international feminist movement. As a result, regulation was largely abandoned in the late 1880s within the United Kingdom, and other nations, such as the Netherlands, Russia, and Sweden, followed suit in the early twentieth century.[19] In the United Kingdom, a policy called abolition replaced regulation, punishing not prostitutes or clients but third-party procurers such as brothel owners and pimps. Abolition soon became a "global standard," since all the international treaties on prostitution and human trafficking in the first half of the twentieth century accepted this approach.[20]

Prostitution policy evolved in parallel to prohibition in the United States, as a more interventionist policy than abolition in that it criminalized not only procurers but also prostitutes and their clients. During and after the Civil War (1861–1865), a few cities adopted or attempted to adopt regulation to safeguard soldiers, but feminists and social reformers soon succeeded in abandoning regulation in those cities.[21] Encouraged by these early victories, the focus of their campaign moved from the abolition of regulation to the abolition of prostitution itself by the turn of the century. Their efforts came to fruition with the enactment of a federal law in 1910, the White-Slave Traffic Act, also known as the Mann Act, which prohibited the transporting of women across state lines for "immoral purposes," that is, prostitution.[22] Some feminists, doctors, and social reformers, who were not fully satisfied with the Mann Act, established the American Social Hygiene Association in 1913, and they drafted model laws to prohibit prostitution within a state boundary by punishing all the parties related to it and to build female reformatories to rehabilitate prostitutes and delinquent girls. They lobbied state governments to adopt their bills and succeeded in many cases. By 1920, ten states had adopted the model law to criminalize all the parties to prostitution. In addition, from 1910 to 1920, twenty-three new female reformatories opened, and older facilities were expanded, where the female internees were subject to "reformative treatment" to be reborn as "safe citizens of the state."[23]

Therefore, from the late eighteenth to the early twentieth centuries, prostitution policies in the West could be differentiated into three main forms: regulation, abolition, and prohibition. However, all these policies shared a common feature, in that all reflected a governmental imperative to intervene in sexuality in a new and direct way. In other words, with prostitution policies, the governments of nation-states were now attempting to control women's most intimate sphere: their sexual organs, activities, and morality. In this sense, modern prostitution policies signaled the establishment of what Étienne Balibar has referred to as the "national-social-state": nation-states began to intervene "in the formation of individuals, in family structures, the structures of public health and, more generally, in the whole space of 'private life.'"[24] At the same time, despite their different approaches, all the policies were conceived to protect society from VD and immorality and therefore to enhance the quality, strength, and well-being of the general population. In this regard, prostitution policies have historically represented a form of what Michel Foucault has called "biopower" or "power over life," targeting both the "discipline of the body," in this case, the prostitute's body, and the wider "regulation of populations."[25]

Seen from a Foucauldian perspective, modern prostitution policies can therefore be considered a symptom of the emergence of the "biopolitical state" in the West. This biopolitical state was also the leading component of a wider biopolitical "empire," in which "the discursive management of the sexual practices of colonizer and colonized was fundamental to the colonial order of things."[26] In this context, VD was framed not only in terms of the harm it caused to individuals but also as a threat to the entire white race, deleterious to the foundations of Western civilization and its associated imperial projects.[27] As in the imperial metropolis, the female body in the colonies was considered "the most intimate colony, as well as the most unruly" and became a special focus of governmental intervention.[28] However, prostitution policies in the colonies were different from those in the metropolis. In the British Empire, for instance, regulation in the colonies was even more intrusive and severe than the domestic version. While the Contagious Diseases Acts were implemented only in military areas in Britain, colonial laws were often widely applied to the colonized beyond the cantonments. In addition, the main targets of regulation in Britain were streetwalkers, but colonial governments preferred to tolerate brothels, which could be more easily policed than prostitutes working in public spaces. Moreover, regulation was experimented with in the colonies earlier than in Britain itself, and its oppressive elements survived in the colonies even after the Contagious Diseases Acts were abolished in Britain.[29]

Japan as an empire also vehemently adopted regulation. In the latter half of the nineteenth century, Japan was forced to open its ports to Western powers such as the United States, United Kingdom, Russia, and the Netherlands, and Western military officials demanded that the Japanese government implement VD inspections of the prostitutes serving them in the treaty port cities. In the early 1870s, when Japan rushed to build a modern state's apparatuses, the Japanese police imported regulation in earnest from France, which they considered to be a modern, civilized policy.[30] The Japanese model of regulation was more systematic and stricter than its European counterparts in several ways. First, while regulation in Europe was conducted on a local basis, the central government in Japan implemented regulation nationally based on a unified legal framework. Second, the Japanese police more successfully circumscribed prostitution in brothels than their counterparts in Europe by only permitting prostitutes to be hired by brothel owners. Third, the control of licensed prostitutes in Japan was more severe than in Europe. For instance, prostitutes were allowed to go out of red-light districts only when they obtained permission from the police.[31] This Japanese version of regulation was transplanted onto the Korean peninsula with just a few revisions during the colonial period. Thus, after the Second World War, a liberated Korea was faced with the task of how to address the colonial legacy of the Japanese prostitution policy. And this is the starting point of this book.

POSTCOLONIAL NATION BUILDING
BASED ON FEMALE SEXUALITY

Whereas the existing research cited earlier has mainly focused on the imperial period, *The State's Sexuality* analyzes prostitution policies and the making of a biopolitical state in a postcolonial setting. Several other significant studies have examined prostitution policies within newly established, postcolonial states. For instance, Tiffany A. Sippial has verified that in the process of Cuba's transition from colony to republic, the debates and reforms regarding prostitution were at the heart of constructing a new, modern state and forging a national identity.[32] In the context of East Asia, Gail Hershatter's study on prostitution in Shanghai in the early twentieth century is also groundbreaking. Hershatter has elucidated that prostitution was a critical issue relative to "urgent public discussions about what kind of sex and gender relationships could help to constitute a modern nation in a threatening semicolonial situation."[33] Focusing on a similar period, Elizabeth J. Remick has compared three municipalities in China, Hangzhou, Guangzhou, and Kunming, and investigated how different ways of regulating prostitution resulted in different types of local governments.[34] Wan-Chen Yen has examined the relationship between prostitution and postcolonial nation building in Taiwan in terms of four aspects: rescue, abolition and rehabilitation, medicalization, and policing.[35]

Prostitution was a crucial agenda not only in these semi- or postcolonial states but also in postwar Japan, which had been an empire but became a defeated nation forcefully reconstructed by the U.S. military in the aftermath of the Second World War. Sarah Kovner has explored how the changes in prostitution policies from regulation to deregulation to criminalization were involved in the changing nature of Japanese politics from the period of U.S. military occupation until the 1950s.[36] Mire Koikari has focused on both American and Japanese feminists' roles in reconstructing Japan after the

Second World War and has argued that their prostitution reforms resulted in the convergence of feminism and nationalism as well as the marginalization of prostitutes.[37] Robert Kramm has discussed how what he called "sanitizing sex," that is, governmental control over VD and prostitutes, contributed to the reproduction of hegemonic masculinity and heteronormativity, for both the occupiers and the occupied.[38] In a similar vein, pioneering research on prostitution in Korea has mainly dealt with interactions between the U.S. military and Korea. For instance, Katharine H. S. Moon has analyzed how the diplomatic politics between the U.S. military and the Korean government influenced intimate relations between Korean sex workers and U.S. servicemen, and vice versa, focusing on the period of the early 1970s.[39] In turn, Seungsook Moon has examined the cooperation of the U.S. military and Korean male elites regarding prostitution for the U.S. military, expanding the scope of her research from the commencement of the Cold War to the early 1970s, and Na Young Lee has investigated the formation and transformation of camptowns from Korea's liberation to the early 2000s.[40]

While inheriting the critical legacy offered by these preceding studies, *The State's Sexuality* is distinct from them, in that it investigates the relationship between prostitution and the nation not merely at the incipient stage of the nascent state but also relative to the long-term, ongoing process of nation building, covering more than seven decades, from 1945 to the present. By so doing, this book illuminates how and why the meaning of prostitution was not fixed but flexibly shifted according to historical upheavals in Korea. In addition, it explores how prostitution has provided a site on which the state's biopower has been exerted and how diverse actors' interactions surrounding related policies have contributed immensely to the making of the nation-state. Following these concerns, this book focuses on three aspects.

First, *The State's Sexuality* examines the way in which the contradiction between the Korean people's nationalist enthusiasm for entire decolonization and the postcolonial reality that precluded it was reflected in prostitution policies. On the one hand, the Korean people endeavored to sweep away the colonial legacy and "unsuitable participants in the body politic" or "internal enemies," who were perceived to have contaminated their cultural purity and pride.[41] The so-called public prostitution—that is, the state-regulated prostitution initiated by the Japanese colonial government—and its female proxies—that is, public prostitutes—exemplified such imperialist remnants. Nevertheless, the governing class of the newly independent Korea lacked the material, intellectual, and imaginative resources to implement its ambitious plan. The only easy, possible option was to adopt a prohibitionist policy. Whether such a policy was feasible or effective to stamp out prostitution was not that important. What was more crucial was that prohibition represented the most radical rupture from the shameful Japanese approach, which brazenly authorized prostitution.

On the other hand, while Koreans were ashamed of the Japanese legacy of the overt legalization of prostitution, they were not as critical of another legacy, "colonial medicine," which was still regarded as "an expression of the very project of modernity."[42] In this respect, many Koreans continued to believe it necessary to register prostitutes and examine them regularly in order to safeguard the new nation's public health, a concern that precluded the casting of any doubt on this colonial-period approach to sanitary administration. This ambivalent, schizophrenic attitude that Koreans showed toward the structures of the colonial regime resulted in the paradoxical combination of colonial regulation and postcolonial prohibition. This book therefore confronts the utter hybridity of postcolonial Korea's prostitution policy, which cannot be reduced to regulation, abolition, and prohibition, conceptually capturing it with a new concept of a "toleration-regulation regime." As chapter 1 will show in detail, this regime of prostitution control originated within the colonial era, then morphed into this new guise after the liberation.

Second, *The State's Sexuality* investigates how this toleration-regulation regime contributed to the constitution of the Korean nation-state. As existing studies have clarified, prostitution policies provided an impetus for the emergence of modern, biopolitical states accompanied by a sophisticated police system, public health administration, and disciplinary institutions. Similarly, Korea's nascent state grew with the administrative machinery of the toleration-regulation regime, such as the police, public health clinics, VD detention centers, and female reformatories, augmenting its power and expanding its radius of intervention to cover the most intimate lives of its citizens. These institutions of the toleration-regulation regime were established in the name of disciplining prostitutes' minds and bodies, as well as guaranteeing the public good, that is, the purity, health, and strength of the whole population. Moreover, diverse experts from fields such as medicine and social science, as well as social reformers and feminist activists, heavily participated in the making and undertaking of the toleration-regulation regime. In this sense, as Colin Gordon has pointed out relative to modern governmentality, the boundary between the state and civil society can be seen to have become blurred.[43]

Prostitution in Korea even functioned as an essential resource for national security and national development. The Korean state, heavily dependent on the United States for its military and economic aid, mobilized its female citizens to gratify American troops, raise their morale, and bring in U.S. dollars, and to some extent it achieved all these goals. As the many official documents that I analyze in chapter 2 attest, both the U.S. Armed Forces in Korea and the Korean government regarded the stable management of prostitution between GIs and Korean women and the control of STIs as an important, perhaps essential, part of their military alliance. In addition, as chapter 3 illustrates, the considerable amount of foreign currency that the women who sexually served the U.S. military and Japanese tourists earned was invested in Korea's industrial development as a form of seed money. In this regard, besides the well-being of the nation, another, perhaps even more important, goal of the toleration-regulation regime was to protect the health of U.S. military personnel and Japanese tourists from STIs. This acquiescence to such unequal, humiliating relationships was justified in the name of national security and development. It was possible mainly because many of the senior and elderly Korean elites and public servants had been educated and trained in colonial-era institutions and therefore internalized the colonial racist policy to prioritize the regnant overlords' safety over their own female compatriots' rights. The former president and military dictator Park Chung Hee (Pak Chŏng-Hŭi) was perhaps the quintessential case of this, as an ardent collaborator within the Japanese imperial system who successfully transformed himself into the founding father of the newborn nation thanks to U.S. military, economic, and political assistance.

In addition, the toleration-regulation regime also contributed to the production of the gender/sexual hierarchy within the national body politic, which assigned people to their proper subject-positions. The toleration-regulation regime consistently identified, classified, and controlled prostitutes as the main target, relegating them to a specific, visible, and stigmatized category. By contrast, men were left free from discipline or punishment and able to enjoy patronizing prostitutes as part of their "natural" sexual rights. In particular, chapter 4 demonstrates how the toleration-regulation regime functioned in terms of what Carol Smart has conceptualized as "a gendering strategy," strengthening the distinction between prostitutes and other women, as well as between women and men.[44] In other words, instead of attending to whether such policies succeeded in suppressing prostitution and its related problems, this book focuses on what the policies actually produced in subjective terms, that is, prostitutes, other ("morally upright") women, and men, all as designated national subjects or "state categories."[45]

Finally, *The State's Sexuality* considers women engaged in prostitution not simply as the main target or passive victims of the toleration-regulation regime but also as active agents who challenged and protested their oppression. Their struggles were desperate and usually failed. Yet occasionally they won victories, which even more occasionally resulted in the transformation of the regime. This book attempts to trace and connect their dispersed resistance, which cannot be compiled into a seamless narrative or chronology, throughout all its chapters. In parallel, however, sex workers also conformed to, compromised with, or sometimes made use of state apparatuses. Therefore, following Anne McClintock, I also attend to "a more diverse politics of agency, involving the dense web of relations between coercion, negotiation, complicity, refusal, dissembling, mimicry, compromise, affiliation and revolt."[46] Nevertheless, even the boldest and most noteworthy examples of the agency of sex workers failed to elicit the sympathy of the Korean people in general or potential allies within the female elites. Only in the 1980s, with Korea's transition to democracy, did newly emerged progressive feminists start to pay attention to these subaltern women and support their rights. However, as chapter 5 and the epilogue demonstrate, there remains a lingering tension between mainstream Korean feminists who regard prostitution as sexual violence per se and some women in prostitution who consider themselves prosaically as sex workers. As such, my study focuses on not only the moments of solidarity between middle-class feminists and women engaged in prostitution, but also the ongoing tensions and conflicts between the groups, produced and exacerbated by their different positions in the class and gender hierarchy.

Simultaneously, however, the process of nation building based on the commercialization of female sexuality was not an experience unique to Korea, as many other former colonial states were subjected to similar paths toward decolonization, featuring dictatorship and developmentalism. From the mid-nineteenth century, the United Kingdom, the Netherlands, and Spain all transplanted regulation onto their colonies in the region, such as Hong Kong, Malaysia, Indonesia, and the Philippines.[47] The Japanese empire also introduced regulation into its incorporated territories, not only in Korea but also in Okinawa and Taiwan.[48] After the Second World War, most of these former colonies were liberated and scrambled to reconstruct themselves as modern nation-states in earnest. In some countries, however, military occupation continued, with the U.S. military simply replacing former imperial forces, for instance, in Korea, Taiwan, and the Philippines. In all cases, prostitution for American servicemen proliferated alongside the sex industry to cater to national citizens.[49]

Developmentalism exacerbated the situation. Stimulated by the desire for economic growth, Taiwan, the Philippines, and Thailand, as well as Korea, aggressively promoted prostitution tourism as a kind of export industry.[50] This prostitution tourism was not simply an economic concern but a political and military one. The U.S. government was afraid that poverty and underdevelopment in the region could provide fertile soil for communism, and to contain this threat the U.S. government, along with the United Nations, World Bank, and World Tourism Organization, prescribed tourism as a development strategy.[51] The U.S. military's full-fledged intervention in the Vietnam War from 1964 also played a crucial role in expanding prostitution tourism in this region. For example, the Thai government licensed numerous hotels, bars, and clubs for U.S. troops' rest and recreation (R&R) facilities, which also accommodated foreign male tourists, especially after the Vietnam War.[52]

METHODOLOGY AND SOURCE MATERIAL

Therefore, while *The State's Sexuality* offers a historical analysis of Korea's case, it takes a transnational perspective, examining Korea's nation-state not as a closed system but as a contested site through/on which diverse forces have penetrated, encountered, and collided with one another, such as colonialism, decolonization, the Cold War, developmentalism, and globalization. In such terms, this book repositions Korea's experience on a broader horizon of postcolonial modernity and presents it as a reference point for understanding other postcolonial states. Moreover, since this study explores the long, continuous process of nation building through prostitution policies and the dynamic interactions between Korea's state machinery, the U.S. military, feminists, experts from civil society, and sex workers, it can be considered as occupying a confluent point of interdisciplinary approaches: historical sociology, political sociology, sociology of law and policy, gender and sexuality studies, and subaltern studies.

The State's Sexuality is based on an expansive range of archival research within the historical records of the Japanese Government General of Korea, the Korean government, the U.S. government, and the U.S. Forces in Korea. The breadth of sources researched includes laws, regulations, local ordinances, gazettes, government reports, minutes and letters, army orders and circulars, and statistics. These materials have been collected within Korea from a variety of sites, including the National Law Information Center; the National Archives of Korea; the National Assembly Library; the Diplomatic Archives of the Ministry of Foreign Affairs; the National Library of Korea; the National Institute of Korean History; Seoul Metropolitan Archives; Gyeonggi-do Multimedia Archives; Chungnam Institute of History and Culture; and various libraries of universities including Seoul National University, Yonsei University, and Korea University. In addition, substantial archival research in the United States was undertaken at the Library of Congress, the National Archives and Records Administration at College Park, and the Wilson Center.

Korea's prostitution policies were not formed and carried out exclusively by government officials, as various medical professionals, social workers, and scholars, as well as feminists, also took part in the establishment, implementation, and transformation of these directives. To understand the roles that this range of agents within civil society played, this book draws on research articles from across the fields of preventive medicine, sociology, criminology, theology, public administration, psychology, social welfare, and women's studies, as well as documents such as brochures, pamphlets, reports, sourcebooks, and periodicals produced by feminist and social reform organizations. *The State's Sexuality* also investigates how public opinion accepted, evaluated, and criticized government policies by examining media such as newspapers and magazines. These materials have been gathered from the Korea Education and Research Information Service; Korea Democracy Foundation; Korean Newspaper Archives; Naver News Library; Big Kinds; Ewha Womans University Library; and several feminist organizations such as the Durebang (My Sisters' Place), the Hansorihoe (United Voice to Eradicate Sex Trafficking), and the Magdalena Community.

Within this book, I analyze these documents as discourses, understanding them to be not objective descriptions or transparent reflections of reality but specific interpretations, representations, and constructions of the social world. Joan Wallach Scott has argued that statistical reports, for instance, are "neither totally neutral collections of fact nor simply ideological impositions. Rather they are ways of establishing the authority of certain visions of social order, of organizing perceptions of "experience."[53] Inspired by such insights, I have endeavored to read these archival materials both along and against the grain, paying attention to not only what they reveal but also what they conceal or assume tacitly or self-evidently, and consequently, how they served to produce knowledge and a sense of order in relation to objects that concern this work.

The critical limitation of archival research is the difficulty, if not impossibility, of listening to the voices of subalterns. Most materials I have collected were produced by privileged members of Korean society, such as government officials, doctors, social scientists, and middle-class feminists. Women engaged in prostitution have long been an object of elite discussion but have historically lacked the opportunity or authority to record their experiences from their own perspective. As a result, the written discourses on prostitutes often disclose more about the authors' own anxieties, fears, and desires about them, rather than explicating who such women really were.[54] At the same time, however, as Gail Hershatter has pointed out, "the subject positions occupied by subalterns in historical records were not simply assigned by the elites who kept those records but were shaped to some degree by the interventions of subalterns themselves."[55]

Korean sex workers, like their counterparts elsewhere, therefore could be said to have participated in "their representation, if not under circumstances of their own choosing," occasionally even leaving "a trace" of their own voices.[56] For instance, they occasionally succeeded in raising their voices to contribute their own opinions at the lectures designed to "enlighten" and "edify" them, and also often organized demonstrations against injustices or lavish funerals for their deceased fellows. In relation to the legal context, many also escaped from the state institutions designed to segregate and discipline them, such as VD detention centers or female reformatories, and a few even testified at the courts or filed lawsuits for their rights. While this wide range of agency was often denigrated and simply recorded as a disturbance or fuss, such events were often referenced within documents such as news articles, court records, medical papers, official statistics, and social surveys. I have applied myself to find such traces left by sex workers within the dominant discourses and to critically interpret them against the grain.

To complement my archival research, I have also conducted in-depth interviews with four women who were engaged in the sex industry, including Park Yeongja, whose testimony I cited at the beginning of this introduction, and Kim Yeon-Ja (Kim Yŏn-Ja), who had been a camptown woman in the 1960–1970s and became a Christian missionary in 1991. I give the other two women pseudonyms, Han Min-Ju and Yang Hye-Sun, to protect their anonymity. Lee Ock-jeong (Yi Ok-Chŏng), since 1985 a director of the Magdalena Community (a shelter for women in the red-light district of Yongsan, Seoul), also granted an interview. Thanks to the collaboration of all these people, I have been able to approach, and hopefully convey, their own narratives of their experiences in ways that are not present within the archival documents.

THE STRUCTURE OF THIS BOOK

Chapter 1 begins at the start of the process of nation building in postcolonial Korea, with liberation from the Japanese Empire after the Second World War and the U.S. military occupation that followed (1945–1948). During this period, prostitution, or more clearly, what colonial power had labeled as public prostitution (*kongch'angje*), surfaced as a focal point for sexual/gender politics against the background of the struggle for eradicating the Japanese imperial legacy and molding a new national identity. I maintain that the discourses on prostitution served as a forum for competing visions of a new republic: socialism versus nationalism and women's liberation versus national purification. In this contest the winner was nationalism, and paradoxically, the nationalist feminists' campaign to abolish kongch'angje, or authorization-regulation, resulted in retaining another legacy of toleration-regulation. I conceptualize the postcolonial prostitution policy, characterized by its combination of colonial toleration-regulation and newly introduced American prohibition, as a toleration-regulation regime, which continues to exist today. I also examine the conflicts between the feminists who dreamed of a new nation free of prostitution and the prostitutes who desperately adhered to the legal status that the colonial prostitution regime granted.

The next three chapters address the ways in which prostitution policies were implemented and augmented for the sake of the *nation*, in terms of *national security, national development,* and *national community.* Chapter 2 analyzes how the nascent Korean government and U.S. Forces in Korea (USFK) collaborated to control the spread of VD and reframe comfort women as patriots and crucial agents who devoted themselves to supporting the defense of Korea and the military alliance between the two countries.

During the Korean War (1950–1953), the Korean government established "comfort stations" for its military and UN troops to boost soldiers' morale and prevent VD and rapes, following the practice established by the Japanese imperial army. After the Korean War, while comfort women as a legal category remained, comfort stations gave way to clubs, bars, and dance halls in the camptowns for the U.S. bases. I explain under what conditions and how the USFK was able to control comfort women beyond its jurisdiction and gradually expand its interventions to include women's psyches as well as their bodies while guaranteeing servicemen's safety from STIs. Borrowing from Georgio Agamben, I illuminate that comfort women were not only *homo sacer* subject to the "state of exception," but also active agents who desperately struggled against the injustices inflicted on them.[57]

Chapter 3 investigates the processes by which the Korean government promoted sex tourism and endeavored to position prostitutes as contributors to economic growth. The government provided American servicemen R&R facilities, and sex and alcohol provided the twin lures to encourage GIs' frequent sojourns and substantial spending. The normalization of diplomatic relations between Korea and Japan in 1965 shifted the focus of Korea's sex tourism policy from GIs to Japanese tourists. To attract more such visitors, the Park Chung Hee regime deployed "*kisaeng* tourism," namely, prostitution tourism, according to a regional development strategy encouraged by the U.S. government. I demonstrate that both comfort women and kisaeng (originally a name to refer to traditional female entertainers but during this era simply a euphemism for prostitutes for Japanese tourists) contributed to the achievement of Korea's economic miracle. The kisaeng tourism triggered the protest of feminists, who considered themselves mothers working to criticize it as "sexual imperialism" and save the nation's "fallen daughters" (kisaeng) from the "immoral father" (the military dictatorship). I analyze the characteristics and contradictions of this nationalist, maternal feminist discourse and the tension between middle-class feminists and their disenfranchised sisters. I also show that dramatic economic development in the 1980s contributed to the expansion of the sex industry for Korean men, which rendered the decade an era of pleasure and panic, with the sex trade being massively expanded to cater to the domestic market and simultaneously sensationalized in the national media.

Chapter 4 examines the sexual/gender hierarchy that the toleration-regulation regime constituted in the national community. It starts with an exegesis of the reformatories designed for prostitutes and other women deemed as needing protection (*yoboho yŏja*), based on both interviews and documents. While these reformatories for women were built specifically to protect, socially rehabilitate, and offer education and training to prostitutes, I argue that in fact they functioned to protect the whole society from the threat that such women were perceived to pose. These facilities were not only a space exemplary of the state of exception riddled with violence and abuse, but also sites that produced knowledge on prostitutes, alongside VD clinics, VD detention centers, and designated red-light districts. In such arenas, women were held subject to the gaze of government surveillance, and experts from diverse disciplines from medicine to social science observed, surveyed, and analyzed prostitutes in an attempt to demystify them and therefore to control their alleged danger. I elucidate how the state institution of knowledge on prostitution and the toleration-regulation regime together contributed to the making of an idealized gender/sexual hierarchy in the national body politic, consisting of "prostitutes, ladies, and gentlemen."

Chapter 5 traces the processes by which the toleration-regulation regime was retrenched as feminist anti-prostitution campaigns resumed and, as a result, prohibition came to the fore. In the early 1990s, Korea witnessed both a campaign to come to terms with the Japanese military comfort women system and a campaign to root out crimes committed by American servicemen. These campaigns paved the way for radical feminist critique of prostitution, which equated prostitution with sexual violence. Apart from the activism of middle-class feminists, a few women incarcerated in the female reformatories voluntarily filed lawsuits against the state. Their legal struggles finally resulted in the closure of such facilities, which were one of the main institutions of the toleration-regulation regime. The decline of the regime became more evident in the twentieth century. The massive influx of female "entertainers" from the former Soviet Union and the Philippines that had occurred in Korea in the late 1990s directly exposed the government's inability to curb illegal human trafficking and forced prostitution. In addition, tragic fires occurred in 2000 and 2002, claiming the lives of nineteen women who were locked in brothels. I investigate how feminists' campaigning to protect prostituted women's human rights led to the enactment of more stringent laws prohibiting prostitution in 2004, sharpening the contradiction between regulation and prohibition, which had been latently set in the toleration-regulation regime for over half a century. I also examine the paradox that the new prohibitionist laws initiated by feminists were faced with the protests of numerous women, who identified themselves as sex workers and called for the entire legalization or decriminalization of the sex industry.

The epilogue sketches a few scenes after the 2004 prohibitionist laws. Due to the laws, several old-fashioned red-light districts, the most notorious, visible, and therefore vulnerable sector of the sex industry, were systematically shut down by the government. Yet in their place covert sites such as room salons, massage parlors, and internet prostitution services have survived and increased. Additionally, the sexual/gender hierarchy between female sex workers and male clients has largely remained unchanged, betraying the expectations of feminists who led the campaign to pass the 2004 laws. As such, how to address prostitution or sex work remains a difficult and divisive issue among Korean feminists. By way of contrast, the recent legal victory of former comfort women for the U.S. military against their government was made possible by a coalition between the plaintiffs, feminist activists, lawyers, and scholars. It also represents the transformation of Korea from an authoritarian client state to a democratic, autonomous one.

In conceptualizing the status of women engaged in prostitution across the history of South Korea, for me the image that persists is that of a refugee, severed from both her family and any position within the "normal" labor market.[58] I conclude *The State's Sexuality* by recording my hope that one day we might construct a nation for and by such refugees. I must admit that I do not know exactly how to reach this vision. Nonetheless, I believe that it will only be possible with both egalitarian, universal welfare policies that help women not to rely on the sex industry *and* effective labor policies that guarantee sex workers the ability to work safely and enjoy the complete rights of citizenship, that is, "a status bestowed on those who are full members of a community."[59]

ONE

The Struggle for a New Nationhood

THE LIBERATION, ABOLITION CAMPAIGN, AND POSTCOLONIALITY

ON FEBRUARY 14, 1948, the Abolishment of the Public Prostitution Law took effect, two and a half years after Korea's liberation from Japan and the result of numerous long debates. With prostitution now criminalized, all licensed vice areas would be closed, at least in principle. *Ladies' Newspaper* (*Puin sinbo*) reported the following about the scenes that day at Mukjeong-dong, a notorious red-light district in Seoul:

> Although public prostitution was abolished yesterday, the City of Seoul failed to implement any necessary measures in Mukjeong-dong (Shinmachi [in Japanese]). Brothel keepers gathered at their union office and criticized that the abolition was enforced without any government measures to protect them. Some public prostitutes [formerly licensed prostitutes] were still soliciting clients, while others were meeting to lament the abolition of their livelihood, drink alcohol, and play changgu [Korean traditional drums]. I [the reporter] searched for the City's Women's Section staff to ask about their plans to enforce the law but was informed that they had visited the scene to assess the situation for a short time in the morning and returned without doing anything. In the afternoon, five or six staffers from the Women's Bureau of the government ventured out again to Mukjeong-dong but quickly returned without conducting a substantive survey of the situation, trembling with a fear of being attacked.[1]

The eradication of authorized prostitution had long been yearned for by Korean feminists and social reformers, ever since the system had been transplanted by Japanese officials during the early colonial period. After Korea was liberated from Japan, not only activists but many Koreans in general considered the system a humiliating legacy of colonization, a point of national shame, and evidence of the weak status of their country. By and large, the public agreed to abolish licensed prostitution within the process of building a new, independent nation, entirely free of colonial vestiges. However, as the quoted excerpt shows, the situation after the abolition of prostitution was very different from their expectations, and it barely improved afterward. What, then, was the problem with properly enacting and enforcing the new law?

Joel S. Migdal has pointed out that the leaders of new postcolonial nations tend to be overconfident of their ability to mold a new society, captivated by a "can-do" spirit that their governments can easily achieve the broad goals of human dignity, prosperity, and equity. However, often this optimism soon fades, and many such states ultimately fail to bring about any significant changes to their people's behavior.[2] This could be explained by the fact that such leaders, many of whom have been anticolonial crusaders, have underestimated the ingrained influence of colonial rule. This complacency often contributes to the perpetuation of colonial-period social practices.[3] In this case, Korean feminists' efforts to abolish the colonial public prostitution regime were not an exception.

This chapter describes how the issue of prostitution surfaced as a focal point for debates on gender/sexual politics in relation to state construction and national identity formation in liberated Korea. It analyzes how elite women from within the political class attempted to totally prohibit prostitution to create a morally decent new nation, only to be compromised by the persistence of colonial conditions and unexpected neocolonial demands brought about by U.S. military occupation. It also reveals that antiprostitution discourses constituted the public presence of prostitutes as both a lamentable remnant of colonization and an enemy within the incipient nation. Finally, it illustrates that although prostitutes protested the discursive status assigned to them by openly agitating for the right to work and pursue a livelihood, they were in time subordinated within the legal system of the toleration-regulation regime, which was forged during the period of U.S. military occupation and would be gradually augmented afterward.

"AUTHORIZATION-REGULATION" AND "TOLERATION-REGULATION": THE TWO-TIER COLONIAL REGIME OF PROSTITUTION

To analyze the transformation of prostitution policies after liberation, it is first necessary to understand the colonial regulation of prostitution. The history of licensed prostitution in Korea dates to the late nineteenth century. The Chosŏn dynasty (1392–1897) prohibited prostitution, but this ban was not always successfully enforced. Prostitution flourished as the dynasty declined at the turn of the century, encouraged by a series of wars, the opening of ports, an influx of foreigners, and the expansion of capitalist relations.[4] Japanese settlers—the majority of whom were male soldiers, government officials, businessmen, and merchants—played a crucial role in spreading prostitution. Japanese prostitutes, geisha, and barmaids soon followed, and brothels and bars mushroomed around Japanese communities.[5] To control these women and safeguard their customers from venereal diseases, Japanese consulates in Korea started to implement the regulation of prostitution in 1881, an approach they had imported from France and deployed in their own country from the early 1870s.[6] With local variations, the system shared numerous common elements: zoning, registration, and the regular venereal disease inspection of women engaged in the sex industry.[7]

Some Korean intellectuals advocated that this system of regulation was modern and rational. For instance, Chi Sŏk-Yŏng, who made a considerable contribution to the Korean public health system by introducing the widespread practice of vaccination, emphasized the necessity to regulate prostitutes in a 1902 newspaper article:

> Even though it is said that an enticing prostitute is infected with syphilis, if she doesn't show any apparent symptoms, men tend to indulge in her ... as a mad butterfly indulges in flowers, without any concern about the disease. That is the reason why prostitutes transmit syphilis more than ordinary country women. ... If [the government] registers [prostitutes], inspects [them] every day, and stamps out [the disease] in its initial stages, mirroring the regulations already enacted in various other countries, we can eliminate this problem.[8]

The Great Han Empire (1897–1910), which replaced the Chosŏn dynasty and quickly fell under substantial Japanese influence, therefore accepted the Japanese practice of legal regulation. The empire adopted a "sanitary police" system and started to conduct health examinations of prostitutes in 1906, then enacted rules to license, register, and inspect prostitutes (ch'anggi) and kisaeng in 1908.[9] During the Chosŏn dynasty, kisaeng were women who entered government servitude, usually from low-status families. They were trained as female attendants to high-class men, subject to the control of the imperial court and its local bureaucracies. They entertained and served male aristocrats with singing, dancing, and the playing of musical instruments and often became their lovers and concubines. To this end, some of them had a classical education, which often served to render them ambiguous figures, popularly considered somewhere between artists, intellectuals, and courtesans.[10] With the demise of the Chosŏn dynasty, kisaeng were liberated from strict government control but found their skills subject to the demands of the capitalist marketplace. They were organized into guilds (kwŏnbŏn), dispatched to high-class restaurants, and paid by the hour. By the turn of the century, the boundary between kisaeng and professional prostitutes had become increasingly opaque, and the empire decided to subject them both to routine examinations for VD.[11]

Japan officially annexed Korea in 1910, and six years later when the Japanese imperial military started to become stationed permanently in Korea, the Japanese Government-General of Korea standardized prostitution policies nationwide by enforcing the Regulation of Brothel Owners and Prostitutes.[12] This policy legalized prostitution by licensing, registering, and subjecting prostitutes to regular sexual health examinations. Licensed prostitutes (ch'anggi) were also called "public prostitutes" (kongch'ang), and the regulation was generally referred to as "public prostitution" (kongch'angje), which meant licensed or legalized prostitution. The primary goal of this regulation was to facilitate Japanese troops in their use of prostitutes and protect them from VD. Licensing a woman as a public prostitute necessarily produced the opposite category of an unlicensed or "clandestine prostitute" (sach'ang, literally "private prostitutes"). The colonial police were therefore now directed to break into the residences of suspected clandestine prostitutes without their permission. If a woman was proven to have engaged in prostitution, the police punished her and imposed a mandatory VD examination.[13]

At the same time, the police set up a third category to address those women who worked in a realm between public and private prostitution. These women were not public prostitutes but served and entertained male clients in venues such as restaurants and bars in the tradition of kisaeng and were therefore suspected of prostitution. To surveil and control them along with overt public prostitutes, the police enacted the Regulation of Geisha, Barmaids, and Geisha Houses.[14] This regulation included in the category of geisha not only Japanese geisha but Korean kisaeng. While both professions entertained male clients at high-class restaurants and provided traditional performances, barmaids (chakpu) were not trained as traditional entertainers and usually worked at less exclusive establishments. These female service workers were not licensed prostitutes, so in principle, any engagement in prostitution by them was prohibited. Nevertheless, the colonial government also required them to register and submit to VD checkups. This suggests that the colonial government considered geisha, kisaeng, and barmaids as de facto prostitutes, regardless of the fact that they did not uniformly render sexual services.[15]

On the surface, this regulatory system seemed to guarantee women's voluntary possibility to work in prostitution or other similar occupations. However, many, if not all, were trafficked into the profession by their family members, since women did not have the right to make a contract for themselves at this time.[16] In addition, they were not allowed to work alone and were only licensed on the condition that they were hired by the owners of brothels, guilds, or bars. Once registered, not only did they have to submit to regular VD inspection, but their personal liberty was severely curtailed also. For instance, the police were able to limit the residential districts open to geisha and barmaids to live in, and geisha and barmaids had to report to the police when they traveled for more than one night.[17] Public prostitutes were even prohibited from leaving red-light districts without the police's permission.[18] Such restrictions imply that the colonial government regarded them as dangerous beings who might disturb and contaminate wider society. This legal segregation did not merely render the women indentured workers and "social outcasts"; it also empowered their employers to exploit and use violence to subjugate and control them.[19] The Japanese colonial government introduced this system following its establishment within its own metropoles. However, this colonial regulation had a few differences from the domestic version. For instance, the minimum age of public prostitutes was eighteen in Japan, but it was seventeen in Korea. Moreover, while public prostitutes in Japan were able to quit the occupation by oral declaration or in writing by mail to the police, their Korean counterparts had to submit related documents to the police.[20] In short, this meant that women in Korea entered prostitution at a younger age and had more difficulty leaving the profession than their counterparts in Japan.

Official statistics show that from 1921 to 1942 the number of licensed geisha (including kisaeng) increased threefold, from 2,003 to 6,286, while the number of public prostitutes fluctuated between 2,321 and 3,934, and the number of barmaids remained around 2,000.[21] This illustrates that geisha and kisaeng became more popular than other categories over the entire period of Japanese occupation. During the same period, the proportion of Koreans working among these groups increased dramatically, comprising the vast majority of the workforce by the end of colonial rule.[22] On average, public prostitutes and barmaids had VD examinations once a week, while geisha and kisaeng were examined once a month.[23] Nevertheless, some high-status geisha and kisaeng refused to submit to inspection, arguing that they were entertainers, not prostitutes. They often succeeded in evading inspection thanks to their powerful employers and clients, some of whom were influential Japanese capitalists and bureaucrats. In this way, the regulation of geisha and kisaeng was not enforced homogenously but concentrated on its lower social and professional strata.[24] With the increase of cafés in the 1920s emerged the role of "waitresses" (yŏgŭp), whom the colonial government suspected of also being clandestine prostitutes. In 1934 the police enacted the Standard Rules to Regulate Café Business directive, adding waitresses to the list of occupations for which registration and regular VD examinations were required.[25] Through this systematic regulation, the capitalist sex industry prospered in colonial Korea, and Korean women and men were incorporated into it as service providers and consumers alongside their Japanese counterparts.

To summarize, the prostitution regime in colonial Korea rested on two pillars: the policy toward public prostitutes and the policy for geisha, kisaeng, barmaids, and waitresses (see table 1). While the former was called public prostitution, there was no specific term to refer to the latter. To grasp the characteristics of and differences between these two approaches, I offer the analytical terms "authorization-regulation" and "toleration-regulation." Toleration or tolerance as a form of prostitution policy originated in nineteenth-century France. According to Jill Harsin, "*Tolérance* was itself hard to define, a nether region between legality and illegality. Prostitution was 'tolerated,' which meant that it was not authorized or protected or prosecuted."[26] Before the French Revolution, prostitution had been criminalized by various royal ordinances. In contrast, the French legislative assembly after the Revolution did not pass any laws to update the old ordinances on prostitution. In this legal vacuum, regulation was implemented through arbitrary "administrative decisions" made by the police, even though prostitution was technically illegal.[27] Inspired by Harsin, I call the policy for geisha, kisaeng, barmaids, and waitresses in colonial Korea toleration-regulation, to clarify that their prostitution was not only tolerated but officially regulated, in other words, positioned in a gray area between legality and illegality and overseen. Additionally, in colonial Korea, unlike in nineteenth-century France, prostitution was fully legalized in relation to the work of ch'anggi, a system of oversight I refer to as authorization-regulation.

TABLE I Colonial Two-Tier Regime of Prostitution

Analytic Concept	Authorization-Regulation	Toleration-Regulation
Historic term	Public prostitution (*Kongch'angje*)	No specific word
Related rules	Regulation of brothel owners and prostitutes	Regulation of geishas, barmaids, and geisha houses; standard rules to regulate café business
Targets	Licensed prostitutes (*Ch'anggi*), also called public prostitutes	Geishas, *Kisaeng*, and barmaids (*Chakpu*); waitresses (*Yŏgŭp*)
Policy	Licensing prostitution; registration and periodic examinations	Criminalizing prostitution; registration and periodic examinations

The colonial government's attempts to control the spread of VD were consequently entirely focused on the supervision of prostitutes and other female service workers considered liable to engage in sex work. While these working women were identified, registered, and subject to differentiated control according to the sophisticated classification system, men buying services from them were just called clients, an abstract and anonymous category, which remained entirely outside the frame of regulation. This sexist governmental approach was reflected in the common Korean name for VD, *hwaryupyŏng*, a figurative term that meant the "diseases of prostitutes." *Hwaryu* was an acronym of *noryu changhwa*, "willows by the roadside and flowers on the walls," which referred to prostitutes as those who could be owned and "deflowered" by anyone. The Japanese historically shared a common term for sexually transmitted infection as the illness *of* prostitutes, and so it was natural that the colonial government focused on regulating them as the source of this health issue, not their male clients.

Besides authorization-regulation, another key difference between colonial Korea's regulation and the French system was that Korea lacked any facilities to quarantine and treat infected prostitutes comparable to the Saint-Lazare prison in Paris. Infected public prostitutes and other regulated categories of women were merely prohibited from working until cured, and the responsibility for obtaining curative treatment was left to patients.[28] In fact, it was impossible to fully treat many of the most common and debilitating conditions. For instance, in the case of syphilis, there was no effective medicine before Salvarsan was produced in the early 1910s. Even after Salvarsan was introduced to Korea, many doctors did not entirely trust the medicine, since it was ineffective in treating hereditary or terminal syphilis and often caused severe side effects. As a result, syphilis continued to be an intractable illness until the end of the colonial period.[29] Instead, the colonial sanitary police poured its energy into hunting down infected prostitutes through regular examination and withdrawing them from the circuit of transmission. This mandatory inspection was humiliating and painful. When it was first conducted in 1906, a newspaper article reported the scene: "Following Japanese directions [a doctor] inspected [prostitutes'] vaginas with an instrument [i.e., speculum]. . . . The girls were startled and fainted due to this unexpected and shocking experience, and many of them burst out crying."[30]

This inhumane regime of inspection, coupled with the perceived immorality of legalized prostitution, triggered a campaign to eradicate the public prostitution system. Christians influenced by foreign missionaries initiated the campaign as part of a temperance movement in the early 1920s. They criticized kongch'angje for encouraging sexual degradation and failing to suppress the spread of VD. The Friends of the Roses of Sharon (Kŭnuhoe), founded in 1927, was the first nationwide women's organization to unite socialists and Christian nationalists, and it advocated for the abolition of public prostitution as part of a wider feminist, anti-feudal, anti-imperialist agenda. The term "nationalist" in colonial Korea was used in various ways. In principle, a wide variety of socialists were nationalists in that they shared the doctrine of national self-determination and struggled for national liberation. More generally, however, the nationalist refers to nonsocialist nationalist movements.[31] In the women's movement, such nonsocialist, therefore nationalist, groups consisted mainly of Christians. Kŭnuhoe, a coalition of socialist and nationalist women, was a massive organization with around six thousand members nationwide. The colonial government dismissed their demands, arguing that the kongch'angje was desirable for both public order and health. Kŭnuhoe was paralyzed in 1931 by internal ideological divisions between socialists and nationalists, and the clamor for abolition died out in the mid-1930s, particularly after the second Sino-Japanese conflict in 1937 and the brutal mobilization of Korea that attended the imperial war effort.[32]

Imperial Japan's regulation of prostitution became increasingly violent and coercive following the Japanese invasion of Shanghai in 1932. From this moment the Japanese military mobilized women and girls from across East Asia, including Korea, to serve its troops as sexual slaves, usually by misrepresentation and force. The estimated number of individuals in servitude as "comfort women" varies according to scholars from twenty thousand to over two hundred thousand, and the forms of "comfort stations" across the Pacific area were diverse, ranging from locally operated brothels to prisoner-of-war rape camps. In most cases, the Japanese military either established comfort stations directly or permitted local civilians to establish such facilities for its servicemen following its regulations. Such military regulations on comfort stations were meticulous, specifying almost everything ranging from rates to service hours to terms of employment of comfort women. In this respect, the Japanese comfort stations were de facto military facilities. The Japanese imperial government also intervened in the recruitment and transfer of women to battlefields.[33] In this regard, the comfort station system can be considered as an extreme form of the authorization-regulation regime.

The comfort stations disappeared with Japan's defeat in the Second World War, but numerous comfort women were injured, killed, or abandoned by the army. Some women managed to return to their countries, but many could not go back to their homes or families because of shame. These horrible war crimes were largely ignored within the war crimes tribunals, except for two cases in Batavia and Guam, which were in relation to the abduction of Dutch and U.S. citizens.[34] The other cases, most of which were committed against Asian women from Japan's colonies and occupied territories, were ignored within mainstream Western-centric global discourses on the Second World War. This was even the case in Korea until one survivor, Kim Hak-Sun, powerfully testified in 1991 about her past as a comfort woman (see chapter 4). Through the statements of survivors and the efforts of feminist campaigners, the comfort women issue was finally highlighted as an atrocious example of wartime sexual slavery half a century after it vanished. However, there remains another, less well-known, fact concerning the comfort station system, namely that it was revived to facilitate both Korean and UN servicemen during the Korean War between 1950 and 1953. This largely forgotten history, part of a largely "forgotten war," I address in chapter 2.

U.S. MILITARY OCCUPATION AND THE INTERLUDE OF CONFUSION

On August 15, 1945, Korea was finally liberated from Japan with the end of the Second World War. Korean historian Im Myŏng-Bang, a middle school student at the time, recalls his memories of that day in the following passage:

On August 14, a rumor spread that tomorrow the Japanese emperor would declare surrender in a special broadcast. However, it didn't get much attention because only a very few people owned radios, and it felt impossible to dream of the end of the war. . . . At noon [the next day], the Japanese emperor broadcast a statement, but since the radio didn't work properly, nobody could understand what he had said, making us more confused. . . . Then what a surprise! Around 6 p.m., I ran out of my house, attracted by the loud clamor of people in the street . . . , and encountered a truly amazing scene. Hundreds of people occupied the boulevard in front of *Aegwan kŭkchang* [a theater], with a banner saying, "Hurray for the Independence of Korea!" Shouting the same slogan, they marched to the Japanese settlers' town. . . . In this wave of people, I first glimpsed *T'aegŭkki* [the national flag of Korea] which my uncle once told me about. . . . For the first time, I realized that the eternal flame of patriotism was still alive in the spirit of all the Koreans who had for so long endured Japanese colonial rule silently like fools. . . . I could not sleep for several days [I was] so filled with excitement.[35]

However, despite this excitement, just a few weeks later the Korean people would be faced with another unexpected situation following the division of the peninsula and a new foreign military occupation. On September 7, 1945, General Douglas MacArthur issued Proclamation No. 1 from Yokohama, Japan, addressed to "the people of Korea." In this statement, MacArthur said that his command would occupy and establish military control over Korea south of the 38th parallel, to enforce the surrender of the Empire of Japan, ensure a "free and independent" Korea, and protect its people "in their personal and religious rights."[36] To this end, the 24th Corps led by Lieutenant General John R. Hodge occupied Seoul as the U.S. Army Forces in Korea (USAFIK), and the U.S. Army Military Government in Korea (USAMGIK) under Hodge's command took over from the Japanese Government-General of Korea on September 9, 1945. By the end of October, the U.S. forces in South Korea consisted of 77,643 troops.[37] Meanwhile, Korea north of the 38th parallel was occupied by the Soviet Union.

In the autumn of that year, Colonel Crawford F. Sams visited Korea as an adviser for health and welfare to the USAFIK. In his autobiography, entitled *Medic*, Sams recalls his first impressions of the Korean people:

Korean women as a matter of national pride apparently had refrained from social and sexual contacts with their occupiers during the forty years of Japanese occupation. When the American soldiers moved into Korea in the fall of 1945, the Korean girls would have nothing to do with them. In fact, the first girls who were seen in the company of American soldiers were stoned by the Korean people, who had protected their women from sexual contact with the Japanese for so many years.[38]

It seems that the Korean people's hostility toward the women associating with foreign soldiers greatly astonished Sams, who as a chief of the Public Health and Welfare Section, Supreme Commander for the Allied Powers (SCAP), witnessed different scenes in Japan. There, allied servicemen encountered groups of polite Japanese hostesses apparently willing to attend to their needs, rather than disobedient people full of hostility.[39] As a matter of fact, the open welcome was entirely deliberate and not simply a matter of national character. On August 18, 1945, only three days after the surrender ending the Second World War, the Japanese Home Ministry set up "special comfort facilities" for occupation forces across Japan. Accordingly, the Recreation and Amusement Association (RAA) was established with the full cooperation of relevant governmental bureaus and representatives from the nightlife industry. Its declared purpose was to act as "a breakwater to hold back the raging waves and defend and nurture the purity of our race." To this end, approximately fifty-five to seventy thousand young women were employed as full- or part-time prostitutes exclusively serving the occupation troops.[40] To mobilize such a huge number of women, the Japanese police devised a wide range of methods: advertising recruitment in the newspapers; enticing women with daily necessities; individually approaching former prostitutes using information from police databases; and relying on private labor brokers, who had long been suspected of deceiving and trafficking women. Even right-wing politicians and fascist groups cooperated with the police in recruiting young women to comfort the foreign military occupiers.[41]

In contrast to Japan, liberated Korea did not create a massive state-organized brothel system for the U.S. military. The Japanese Government-General of Korea passed on to the U.S. military only a few dance halls and resorts.[42] There was, after all, no way the deposed, outgoing Japanese colonial officials would be able to rapidly mobilize Koreans to placate American soldiers during the period of regime handover. Seemingly unaware of the wider geopolitical circumstances, Colonel Sams simplistically interpreted the Koreans' negative attitude toward fraternization and the comparative lack of "facilities" for his servicemen as reflecting the nation's inherent sexual conservatism. What Sams also failed to realize was that the Korean nation had largely failed to protect its women from sexual contact with the Japanese. As previously noted, even before official colonial annexation, in the late nineteenth century Japanese settlers successfully transplanted public prostitution to the Korean peninsula, facilitating the inception of traffic in disenfranchised women and girls to red-light districts to serve both Japanese and Korean men. However, Sams was vaguely aware that a new chapter in the history of Korean women's sexual encounters with foreigners was about to begin. As he noted:

> Time passed. With the usual gifts of candy and other things, the initial resistance of Korean women to association with foreign soldiers was broken down. A comparatively small segment of the Korean population then became highly infected, as far as venereal disease is concerned, by the American soldiers and, in turn, passed the infection on to other soldiers. It does not take long.[43]

As Sams described, VD resulting from fraternization between American troops and Korean women almost immediately posed a serious public health problem in the new postcolonial nation. Although Sams did not mention the word explicitly, the women associating with American servicemen were uniformly deemed to be prostitutes by both the U.S. military and the Korean people. To curb both prostitution and the spread of VD, the USAFIK introduced policies that it had implemented during both world wars.

In the twentieth century, the U.S. military had adopted a totally different approach to procurement, prostitution, and sexual health from that deployed by the Japanese empire in civilian or military contexts. Starting in the First World War, U.S. forces attempted to present themselves as "the cleanest army" in the world by prohibiting prostitution entirely and emphasizing abstinence or continence to the soldiers.[44] With the outbreak of the Second World War, the U.S. government reinforced this policy by enacting in 1941 the May Act, a federal law that prohibited prostitution around military and naval establishments.[45] During the Second World War, however, there were "changes in the basic philosophy" regarding the control of VD. This ended the system of punishment for infected servicemen and increased the emphasis on sexual hygiene education. An extensive contact tracing program was instigated alongside the quarantine and forceful treatment of infected civilians at medical facilities called "rapid treatment centers."[46] These changes had gender-discriminatory effects. On the one hand, the U.S. military permitted male soldiers the freedom to engage in sexual activity as long as they did not contract illness, providing them with free condoms and other prophylactics. On the other hand, civilian women who had sex with servicemen found infected with VD were located; examined; and if proven to be infected, forcibly quarantined until cured.[47]

The USAFIK deployed these policies in its battle against VD and prostitution. At first it was confident of victory. The 1945 annual report from the Office of Surgeon said, "Due to placing all brothels 'Off Limits,' excellent MP [military police] work, and an extensive and thorough educational program, we had had a commendable venereal disease rate."[48] In addition to these measures, prophylactic devices were also distributed widely, sometimes even forcibly.[49] However, this initial optimism soon faded as the rate of infection among the 24th Corps rose almost fivefold in 1946, from 22 per 1,000 troops to 102.[50] The military authorities variously attempted to analyze this rapid increase, but all their explanations could ultimately be reduced to one reason: the difficulty of controlling both their servicemen and Korean prostitutes. In a letter to his subordinate commanders, John R. Hodge, the commanding general of USAFIK, openly deplored his soldiers' conduct:

> I have talked to several soldiers on the subject of venereal disease and drunkenness which are closely allied. Some of the answers are startling. Too many of them take the line why should I make any effort to keep myself clean and holy. . . . They sleepwalk through the day so they can get drunk again at night. They associate loosely with Korean women or any others they can get their hands on.[51]

Military standards deteriorated, off-limits regulations were disregarded, and the patronizing of prostitutes was prevalent. In another letter, Hodge said his soldiers "act as though Koreans were a conquered nation rather than a liberated people."[52] In this respect, Seungsook Moon concludes that the actions of American soldiers in Korea during the early occupation were similar to those of Europeans in their colonies, in that both of them regarded sexual access to colored women as their natural entitlement.[53] In other words, to its military occupiers, Korea was a kind of "giant brothel" to show off its "racial virility," just as the former Asian and African colonies had been to the European colonizers.[54]

The U.S. military did not succeed in controlling local Korean women either. The military authorities thought that the women who consorted with soldiers were mostly, if not all, prostitutes, since "unmarried Korean women from respectable families are not to be seen in public with men of any race, including their own."[55] The USAFIK for a period continued the U.S. federal government's policy of attempting to shut down the sex trade by breaking up or declaring brothels off-limits and rounding up prostitutes with the help of Korean police officers. The surgeon's office admitted that this practice was "worthwhile" but was simultaneously cautious about it, arguing "it rendered more difficult the problem of following up contacts."[56] Even when Korean contacts were located, it was difficult to treat them properly due to a lack of adequate facilities, and apprehended prostitutes were usually "given inadequate treatment by prison physicians rather than being referred to the Public Health Clinics."[57] To overcome these problems, in May 1946 the U.S. military government enacted an ordinance to punish Korean women "suffering from a venereal disease in an infectious stage" who engaged in or solicited "sexual intercourse with any member of the occupying forces."[58] Under this order, even if an infected woman merely solicited but did not actually provide sexual services, she could still be arrested. In contrast, American soldiers who passed infections on to Korean women went unpunished. This ordinance enabled the police to exert arbitrary power to control Korean women. Some women and girls were apprehended and forced to submit to VD examinations for the reason that they were simply "suspected" of prostitution or had merely "loitered on the evening streets."[59]

At the same time, the military government continued regular examinations of licensed "entertainment girls," which had now become an accepted euphemism referring to actual and perceived prostitutes, utilizing the preexisting colonial regulations.[60] The military government's decision to retain the colonial practice of regulation is intriguing, considering the history of prostitution policy in the United States. As noted, in 1941 the federal government enacted the May Act to prohibit prostitution near military establishments. Moreover, by 1942 all U.S. states had criminalized at least some of the key participants in the sex industry, such as prostitutes, clients, and/or third parties.[61] By contrast, the U.S. military government in Korea preferred regulation to prohibition. Edward G. Meade, a U.S. military officer in Korea, pointed out the contradictory nature of this policy that criminalized those who spread VD rather than those engaged in prostitution itself:

> In a sense the attitude of military government toward this profession [prostitution] had an amusing facet. No attempt was made to illegalize [criminalize] the practice, and a Korean prostitute was not disobeying the law unless she engaged in sexual intercourse with any member of the occupying forces while "suffering from a venereal disease in an infectious stage."[62]

This policy obviously deviated from that of domestic prohibition as practiced in the United States, but the choice of the USAFIK here was not exceptional in the wider history of the U.S. military in occupied areas or "frontier" zones. For instance, when the United States occupied Cuba and established a military government there (1898–1902), it dissolved the regulation that the Spanish Empire had transplanted in 1898, only to revive it a month later. In this case, U.S. officials considered colonial regulation not as urgent an issue as political and economic reconstruction, and syphilis a domestic disease that had less immediate impact on the U.S. citizenry.[63] Then, during the Second World War, police and military officials in Hawaii bluntly ignored the May Act, thinking that regulated prostitution for servicemen and plantation workers was inevitable, even though Hawaii was (and is) an official U.S. territory.[64] In this respect, it is clear that the U.S. military applied a double standard toward prostitution, one of adhering to prohibition on the mainland while maintaining or leaving regulation intact elsewhere. Therefore, it probably seemed rather natural that the military governor decided to keep the established system of regulation in a temporarily occupied country located in the "Far" East.

Control over American troops was also reinforced. According to Circular No. 26, dated February 21, 1947, all major echelons of the USAFIK established VD control councils to discuss effective policies monthly.[65] In December 1947, indoctrination teams started to operate to inculcate their soldiers with the topics of sexual hygiene and continence.[66] On November 4, 1947, a VD Rehabilitation Training Center was established in Chinhae in southeastern Korea, to segregate and treat infected soldiers for at least thirty days, during which time they were subject to sexual health education. It accommodated 200–225 soldiers, many of whom felt that they were "being punished."[67]

Despite these efforts, the U.S. military failed to suppress the spread of VD. The rate of infection dropped slightly to 83 per 1,000 in 1947 but again rose to 185 in September 1948, ranking the highest in the Far East Command.[68] Commanding General Hodge attributed this "too high" rate to his soldiers' overly promiscuous "woman hunting" as well as the individual unit commanders' indifference to such misconduct.[69] Moreover, according to the VD council of one division, troops tended to consider even syphilis "no worse than [a] 'Bad Cold,' because penicillin will cure it in a short period of time."[70] In short, the instruction to soldiers to practice self-restraint had proved ineffective. To improve this situation, Hodge attempted to reintroduce punishment. He asked the Department of the Army to regard hospitalization due to VD as "not in duty"—that is, pay and veteran's benefits would be forfeited for the period of absence. However, the Army Department did not accept his suggestion, since it was precluded by federal law.[71]

In sum, the U.S. military in Korea in the period immediately after occupation combined two divergent approaches in attempting to control the spread of VD: The Japanese system of registration and the regular inspection of entertainment girls was coupled with American techniques of control such as the demarcation of hotspots as off-limits, contact tracing, free clinics, and treatment. However, there were major difficulties in transplanting American measures onto Korean soil. The off-limits strictures were often disregarded by servicemen, contact tracing was carried out on a very limited scale, and clinics were inadequate even for treating apprehended prostitutes. Another element of the military government control, that is, the continued practice of colonial regulation, was also challenged, by Korean feminists who strongly called for its abolition.

WOMEN'S LIBERATION OR NATIONAL PURIFICATION? THE ABOLITION CAMPAIGN AS A STRUGGLE FOR A NEW NATIONHOOD

The abolition campaign was revived as soon as Korea was liberated from Japan. On August 17, 1945, only two days after liberation, female activists, both nationalists and socialists, organized the Women's Alliance for Establishing the Nation (Kŏn'guk punyŏ tongmaeng). It proclaimed eight goals, one of which was "to abolish both public and private prostitution and trafficking in persons." In this way, they thought it necessary to repeal not only public prostitution but all types of prostitution. However, the organization was divided from the outset due to ideological conflicts between the socialist and nationalist factions, and the latter soon left to establish their own organizations. In December 1945 the remaining socialist members of the Women's Alliance organized the Korean Women's Federation (Chosŏn punyŏ ch'ongdongmaeng), declaring its goals to be the abolition of the vestiges of Japanese imperialism and the liberation of Korean women politically, economically, and socially.[72] During the colonial period, the socialist groups had acquitted themselves more uncompromisingly against

Japanese occupation than the nationalists, so they were better positioned to seize hegemony in the initial stage of national reconstruction immediately after liberation.[73] And the abolition campaign was no exception in this regard.

Japan's situation provided further stimulus to the abolition campaign, as on January 21, 1946, the SCAP in Japan ordered an official directive titled the Abolition of Licensed Prostitution.[74] Encouraged by this, on March 6, 1946, the Women's Federation submitted to the U.S. military administration the "Resolution for Abolishing Public and Private Prostitution," which stated: "Permitting public and private prostitution and trafficking in persons . . . in a democratic state is insulting women and impeding women's liberation."[75] Ultimately, the socialist Women's Federation believed that women's liberation, including the abolition of the kongch'angje, could only be achieved by the transformation of the whole society through revolution. Simultaneously, however, just waiting for a revolution without doing anything to address the pressing issue of abolition would be to abandon their responsibility as feminists. At a conference held on June 23, 1946, Yu Yŏng-Jun, the leader of the Women's Federation and the moderator of the conference, responded thus to a male intellectual who argued that abolishing kongch'angje would be very difficult, at least before solving basic economic and social problems:

> Of course, you are right! It might be impossible to abolish [kongch'ange] completely until women achieve entire economic independence. In that sense, we desperately yearn for building a democratic state. However, now that the issue of abolishing human trafficking has surfaced, the Women's Federation cannot do nothing. We are endeavoring [to grapple with that issue] as far as we can at this stage.[76]

Socialist feminists regarded prostitutes as oppressed women, just like female workers and peasants, all of whom deserved liberation in the new "democratic," that is, socialist, state of Korea. Their vision for gender equality was resonant with the perspective of the North Korean People's Committee, which passed the Gender Equality Law on July 30, 1946, specifying that "licensed prostitution, private prostitution, and the kisaeng system—kisaeng licenses and schools—are prohibited."[77] However, unlike the North Korean People's Committee, which had the autonomy to pass laws and carry out the radical transformation of its society, socialist feminists in South Korea were unclear on how to achieve this ideal under U.S. occupation. One possible (but unrealistic) option was to petition the military government to abolish public prostitution.

In contrast, the women's right-wing nationalist movement played a passive role in the struggle to abolish the remnants of the colonial system, including public prostitution. This was no coincidence since many of these women had directly collaborated with the Japanese Empire in the last days of colonial rule.[78] No organization representing the nationalist perspective included the abolition of kongch'angje in its platform. Only a few nationalist female leaders demanded abolition, but their rhetoric was noticeably different from that of the socialists. For instance, Im Yŏng-Sin, the leader of the Korean Women's National Party (Chosŏn yŏja kungmindang), asserted:

> Women, as well as [people across] general society, are responsible for establishing kongch'angje, due to their lack of self-awakening. Thus, I urge women to reflect on themselves. . . . Public prostitution doesn't have any merits, it is only harmful, because it contaminates society with diseases, destroys families, and exerts a bad influence on children's education.[79]

This quote indicates that Im opposed prostitution for the sake of the purity of society and family stability, rather than women's liberation. She also blamed the persistence of kongch'angje on women themselves, that is, prostitutes, rather than attempting to deconstruct the structural inequality that had rendered prostitutes in the first place. Her argument reflected the dominant perspective held by nationalist women at the time. Most were Christians and therefore privileged notions of female chastity and morality. Their main goal was to transform common women into "wise mothers and good wives" (hyŏnmo yangch'ŏ) who could contribute to the nation.[80] Thus, nationalist women had an ambivalent attitude toward prostitutes, whose lifestyle was entirely removed from their ideal of feminine behavior. On the one hand, they framed them as pitiful objects in need of salvation. On the other hand, they thought that unrepentant prostitutes would pose a threat to not only the institution of the family but also the nation.

Despite their differences, the socialist and nationalist women formed a joint organization, the Alliance for Redeeming Former Public Prostitutes (P'yeŏp kongch'ang kuje yŏnmaeng) in August 1946. This alliance was only possible because antipathy toward the kongch'angje was the only issue that united socialist and nationalist women, who were fiercely divided on other agendas.[81] Women leaders within prominent nationalist groups, who had initially not been as active as the socialists in campaigning for abolition, could no longer neglect the issue and finally cooperated with their political adversaries. This alliance across the political divide attests to the symbolic significance given to the issue of prostitution in postcolonial Korea. For many Koreans, the continuation of public prostitution was a shameful reminder of their colonial past. Mainstream newspapers described it as a "remnant of Japanese imperialism," the "vice of the century," and the "biggest shame for liberated Korean women, which simply needs to be abolished so that we can build a democratic nation."[82]

One might ask why public prostitution emerged as the most important agenda in postcolonial gender politics. It was, after all, just one of many serious gender-related issues such as concubinage, child marriage, and extreme sexual discrimination in education and the workplace. However, while these other issues could be attributed to the deep-rooted sexism prevalent in Korean society, the kongch'angje was very obviously rooted in Japanese imperialism. Therefore the abolition of this system was easily represented as symbolic of a progressive return to an imagined state of pristine Korean nationhood, reversing the damage of savage imperialism. Consequently, many Koreans believed that to restore national pride and help (re)construct a civilized nation-state free of colonial vestiges, the kongch'angje had to be repealed.

Whereas socialist feminists initially led the abolition campaign, the situation started to change in late 1946. As tensions with the Soviet Union mounted, the U.S. military government in Korea quickly started to suppress socialists to restrict their growing influence and defend the security of the "Free World." Accordingly, socialist women were forced to engage primarily in clandestine political activities against the military government and lost their leadership in the movement for abolition. Additionally, nationalist women, who were also uncoincidentally pro-American in their beliefs, gained hegemony over the mainstream political field, and the discourse surrounding abolition became more conservative. For instance, *Ladies' Newspaper (Puin sinbo)*, published by a nationalist women's organization, condemned public prostitutes as "women who indulged in vice because of their vanity . . . degrading Korean women's beautiful chastity and customs."[83] The paper even went so far as to condemn public prostitutes as "the biggest cancer threatening the women's movement."[84] The National Confederation of Women's Organizations (Chŏn'guk yŏsŏng tanch'e ch'ongyŏnmaeng), an umbrella organization of nationalist women, also labeled public prostitutes the "destroyers of families and [our] new nation."[85]

As such, women campaigners within the nationalist movement tended to regard prostitutes as internal enemies who posed a moral menace to the nation, neither victims of colonialism and women's oppression nor fellow citizens. They also believed that prostitutes harmed the entire nation's public health through propagating VD. Therefore, to protect the nation's morality and health from the dangers that prostitutes posed, nationalists advocated not only the abolition of the kongch'angje but also the implementation of a stricter regime of health examinations for all those perceived to be prostitutes. As a newspaper article from 1947 stated:

> If you asked anyone in Seoul whether kisaeng are chaste, who dare answer yes? All the housewives would curse them, calling them "bitches." . . . Despite this, on September 10, [a representative group of] kisaeng visited the Commissioner of Health and Hygiene [of Seoul] to submit a petition. In this petition, they strongly opposed the need for a second round of venereal disease examinations, arguing they had been already examined. . . . In response to this, the city authorities suggested a compromise that would permit kisaeng to get examinations at hospitals of their choosing rather than places designated by the city. . . . Public opinion strongly criticized this compromise, pointing out that it would never be effective in preventing the spread of venereal disease.[86]

This quote describing the kisaeng's response to new government rules for increased testing was written from the perspective of a generic housewife. Although in truth kisaeng played a quite ambiguous role in the sex trade, with each individual working in an unfixed manner ranging from traditional female entertainment to outright prostitution, this article simply equated them all with prostitutes and demanded more rigorous VD testing for all. The rhetoric used here by nationalist women in postcolonial Korea contrasted starkly with the approach deployed by British abolitionists in the nineteenth century, who called for the abolition of forced VD inspection by arguing that it was against the civil liberties of prostitutes. The Korean nationalist women's perspective was more similar to that of British imperialists, who viewed colonized women avoiding regulation "not as protesters, but as fettered by ignorance and incognizant of its benefits."[87] In this way, although both licensed prostitution and mandatory inspection imposed on prostitutes were measures of control jointly implanted by Japanese colonialists, the nationalist women considered only the former a savage legacy of colonization, while advocating for a continuation of the latter as a rational measure to safeguard the nation's health.

In summary, the abolition campaign became a forum for two competing visions of nation building. With the ascension of the nationalist women over the socialists, a rhetoric of national purification came to overwhelm that of women's liberation. Nationalists constituted prostitutes as social enemies within the state and prioritized the morality and health of the nation over women's rights. Therefore, they demanded to only remove the authorization component of the colonial prostitution regime while leaving the regulation measures intact. Ironically, this position assumed by nationalists was strongly reminiscent of the colonial toleration-regulation, in that they did not sanction prostitution of geisha, barmaids, and waitresses but supported regular examination of them considering them de facto prostitutes. Ultimately, the success of the abolition campaign led by women from within the nationalist movement explains why the colonial biopolitical administration persisted after liberation.

THE POSTCOLONIAL (RE-)INVENTION OF THE "TOLERATION-REGULATION REGIME"

Under American governance, Korea found itself in a postcolonial dilemma. The colonial overlords were gone but had been replaced by new foreign troops. While Korean citizens were able to enjoy more civil rights than under colonial rule, they could do so only within the boundaries that the U.S. military government established. In December 1946, the U.S. military government created the South Korean Interim Legislative Assembly with a view toward creating an independent liberal democratic government. However, the assembly had limited powers because it needed the American military governor's ratification to enact laws. In contrast, the military governor did not need the assembly's approval to promulgate any ordinances he deemed necessary.[88] As a result, although Korean politicians enthusiastically suggested a variety of reforms for their new state, most political and executive decisions, including those on prostitution, were made by the commanders of the American forces. Thus, there were two ways for female activists to seek a repeal of kongch'angje, by direct appeal to the governor or via the assembly.

At first they appealed to the governor. As mentioned earlier, in March 1946 before the military government suppressed socialism, the socialist Korean Women's Federation submitted to the military government a resolution demanding the abolition of public and private prostitution. Two months later, the governor responded with the Sale or Contracts for Sale of Female Prohibited (Ordinance No. 70), which prohibited trafficking in women and nullified all related contracts.[89] Leaders from both the socialist and nationalist women's movements welcomed this decision, considering it equal to the effective abolition of kongch'angje. However, the military governor, Archer L. Lerch, emphasized that the ordinance neither repealed the kongch'angje nor prohibited voluntary prostitution but merely criminalized human trafficking.[90] The main reason the military government hesitated to abolish kongch'angje was, as previously noted, to safeguard the sexual health of the occupying forces through the continued registering and testing of prostitutes. As such, the military government directly prioritized its troops' safety over the progressive transformation of Korean society.

After failing to persuade the military governor to abolish kongch'angje, female activists approached the interim assembly. This time, nationalist women took the lead, as socialist women were now totally excluded from the official political system, including the assembly. Among ninety members of the assembly, only four were women, and all were right-wing Christian nationalist politicians. In March 1947, Pak Hyŏn-Suk, one of these members of the assembly, submitted a bill entitled the Abolishment of the Public Prostitution Law. The bill was passed by the assembly in August 1947 with only one dissenting vote.[91] The law was very simple and composed of just four articles. Its intent was clearly framed by its opening statement of purpose: "In accordance with a democratic point of view this law is created for the purpose of abolishing and prohibiting public prostitution—a malicious custom which was established under the Japanese regime and tended to infect Korean morality."[92] The law specified not only the abolition of the Regulation of Brothel Owners and Prostitutes but also the intent to punish brothel owners, prostitutes, procurers, clients, and "any person who has tainted another with a venereal disease."[93] As such, the law only specified its purpose and the punishment of related people but lacked any measures to support the women who had quit prostitution. This represents how optimistic, naïve, and unprepared the assembly members were toward the problematic task of actually enforcing abolition.

In this way, prohibition was established as the new standard for a new nation, free of the traces of colonial rule. What is interesting is that this new Korean law was more stringent than that enacted in Japan, which was a significant point of precedence for Korean feminists. They requested that the

USAMGIK abolish not only human trafficking but also prostitution itself, arguing that it had already been abolished in Japan by the SCAP. However, the SCAP's 1946 directive Abolition of Licensed Prostitution only criminalized trafficking and binding contracts, leaving prostitution legally intact. Therefore, the Japanese directive was in fact much closer to the Sale or Contracts for Sale of Female Prohibited promulgated by the military governor in 1946 than the Abolishment of the Public Prostitution Law passed by the interim assembly in 1947. It should also be mentioned that many Japanese politicians were also unsatisfied with their own limited directive and submitted to the Japanese Diet a prohibitionist measure in 1948, titled the Bill for Punishment of Prostitution and Related Activities. While many female members of the Diet voted for this, most other members opposed it, arguing that the law would be ineffective or unfairly victimize prostitutes. As a result, the bill failed.[94]

Why then was a prohibitionist act enacted in Korea and not in Japan, and supported by not only women politicians but virtually the whole legislature? If we consider the argument that many members of the Japanese Diet opposed the prohibitionist bill on the grounds that it would be ineffective and merely introduce the possibility to further oppress prostitutes, the Korean Interim Assembly members were perhaps more optimistic about the law and/or less sensitive to prostitutes' human rights. As previously noted, prominent women within the nationalist bloc held that prostitution per se was a legacy of the colonial period and threatened the moral constitution of the new nation. Moreover, since all female members of the assembly, including Pak Hyŏn-Suk, who drafted the bill, were devout Christians, their personal moral attitude was best represented by a policy of outright prohibition. However, I would also argue that the most important force driving prohibition was the nationalist passion to eradicate the kongch'angje as a remnant of the colonial period. Many Koreans believed that Japanese imperialists had implanted in Korea not only this particular form of licensed prostitution but even the very practice of prostitution itself. Thus, to eradicate what was popularly considered a colonial vice, prostitution in its entirety had to be legally stamped out, using the full power of the new state. In this respect, even though some assembly members were possibly skeptical about the bill, they could not have spoken out against this populist act of apparent decolonization.

Faced with pressure from the assembly, the military governor eventually ratified the bill in October, two months after it passed. In fact, the governor ratified only three of eight bills that the assembly passed, and the abolition law was one of them.[95] This shows that abolition was such a powerfully symbolic issue that the military government could not help but comply. However, the governor did request that the assembly revise the bill. First, he demanded the removal of the third article of the bill, which stipulated punishment for "any person who has tainted another with a venereal disease." The governor directly argued that "it could be abused for intimidation by the lawless."[96] Second, he asked the assembly to postpone the enforcement date of the act, which was scheduled for three months after the date of its passing. He maintained that this period was too short to prepare any measures to help rehabilitate public prostitutes.[97] In response, the assembly accepted the first request but rejected the second, as the majority of members agreed it was urgent to enforce the act immediately.[98]

The new law was promulgated on November 14, 1947, and it took effect three months later, on February 14, 1948. While this new law abolished kongch'ange, that is, the colonial Regulation of Brothel Owners and Prostitutes, and criminalized all participants engaged in the sex trade, it was not extensive enough to erase all the measures to control prostitution established during the colonial era, since it left intact the Regulation of Geisha, Barmaids, and Geisha Houses and the Standard Rules to Regulate Café Business. Moreover, two weeks before the new law took effect, the military government enacted a further regulation titled: the Established Rule on the Business of Hospitality Women.[99] This recategorized kisaeng, barmaids, and waitresses as "hospitality women" (chŏpkaekpu), who were also called entertainment girls, preserving the continuation of the colonial-era practices of registration and testing for this group.

Consequently, while authorization-regulation gave way to prohibition, toleration-regulation, which had coexisted with authorization-regulation, survived liberation and became the general rule. I refer to this combination of colonial-era regulation and newly enacted prohibition as the "toleration-regulation regime." Perhaps surprisingly, women from within the nationalist coalition did not challenge this regime, even though it retained an obvious colonial legacy. Rather, they supported it, and in proposing the prohibitionist bill, they demanded not only the criminalization of prostitution but also a more rigorous approach to the VD testing of "clandestine prostitutes."[100] This concern was in sync with major newspapers such as *Tonga ilbo* and *Kyŏnghyang sinmun,* which editorially supported the regular examination of hospitality women for VD.[101]

Leela Gandhi has argued that the liberated people of former colonies tend to be overoptimistic at the moment of political independence, often believing that a new world can magically emerge out of the ruins of colonialism. This belief is problematic due to the persistence of colonialism across a wide range of social and cultural spheres. Even more problematically, such utopianism is often based on the repression of painful colonial history. This false amnesia then makes it difficult to confront and engage the most persistent and pernicious legacies of colonialism. As a result, the colonial vestiges cannot be transcended, and are often ultimately repeated.[102] Postcolonial Korea's toleration-regulation regime is just such an example of a long lingering "colonial legacy" tacitly engendered by triumphant utopianism and selective amnesia. Simultaneously, this was a "postcolonial reinvention" that enabled a compromise between the U.S. military government and Korean elites, not least women from within the politically dominant nationalist coalition in the assembly and the mainstream media. These Americans and Koreans both shared a common primary interest in combating the spread of VD to ensure the health of their servicemen and their new nation, respectively.

FROM COLONIAL REMNANTS TO INTERNAL ENEMIES

With the abolition of authorization-regulation, ch'anggi lost their legal status as public, licensed prostitutes and became subject to punishment if they refused to quit their work. The new law also criminalized the purchase of sex. Nevertheless, there was no reported case in which male clients were actually punished. Due to the toleration-regulation regime, the registration and testing of kisaeng, barmaids, and waitresses continued, but prostitution among these groups was also punishable by law. In this respect, the abolitionist movement largely failed to eradicate the colonial legacy, and the privilege of men to patronize prostitutes remained unconstrained. Moreover, the postcolonial prostitution policy sparked widespread protests from the subject of its strictures: kisaeng and ch'anggi.

Kisaeng collectively resisted the continuation of colonial regulation, and particularly continued mandatory VD inspection. In March 1946, after the government announced its plan to conduct monthly examinations, eight hundred kisaeng staged a strike.[103] After that, kisaeng's protest repeated itself against the government, which attempted to increase the frequency of

VD tests. In December 1946, a kisaeng association visited the Seoul City government to complain about VD inspection, and its leader made the following statement: "Kisaeng, both in the past and the present, are professional singers and dancers. Thus, it is insulting that the government examines us on the premise that we are serving [i.e., rendering sexual services to] clients."[104] As illustrated in the passage, kisaeng attempted to avoid being stigmatized as private prostitutes and refused to submit to VD examinations, citing their status as traditional entertainers. The government compromised by reducing the frequency of examinations from once a month to once a year. However, in September 1947, due to increased VD rates among American servicemen, the government decided to raise the frequency of checkups to twice a year. Kisaeng once again organized a strike, but their campaign failed this time due to the government's firm stance.[105]

While kisaeng opposed regulation in part by attempting to distinguish themselves from ch'anggi, the ch'anggi, who had worked as licensed prostitutes previously, simply rejected the newly introduced prohibition that nullified their legal status and criminalized them. On December 4, 1947, about twenty days after the new prohibitionist act was promulgated, a lecture was held by the Seoul city authorities to explain the reasons for the abolition to five hundred ch'anggi; included were speakers from the Department of Health and Welfare, the Women's Bureau, and the Alliance for Redeeming Former Public Prostitutes. At the lecture, the mayor of Seoul maintained that the new law was to "rescue you from an anti-civilized and inhumane chain and enable you to live a normal life." He admitted that they would be faced with numerous obstacles in starting a "new life" and emphasized that they would have to overcome such hurdles themselves. Kim Mal-Bong, a Christian feminist and the leader of the Alliance, in turn encouraged ch'anggi to free themselves from their "humiliating circumstances" and promised to shelter them. After the lectures by government officials and elite female activists ended, the audience stirred as many ch'anggi demanded to also present their perspective. Some were given the chance to speak, and what follows is a selection of their remarks.

Ch'oe Ch'un-Ja hired at Changch'ullu [name of a brothel]: Of course, we wish to get out of this humiliating life. However, because we are socially handicapped, we need strong measures to help rehabilitate us. Only enacting a new law without such measures is not far from [maintaining] the kongch'ang[je].

Ae-Ran hired at Ch'unhyangnu: The vast majority of us are refugees [who returned to Korea after liberation]. It is too harsh to abolish kongch'ang[je] in February. We have debts and families to support. I demand you postpone the enforcement date to at least April or May.

Chŏng-Suk hired at T'aep'yŏngnu: I don't think we should pretend to be like other civilized states, considering the level of our country. Nevertheless, if you really want to do this, liquidate our debts, and guarantee us a livelihood by law![106]

As such, ch'anggi understood that the abolition of kongch'angje was motivated by the Korean elites' passion to mimic other more "civilized states." However, they argued that merely abolishing it without measures to support their livelihoods could cause their situation to deteriorate and therefore attempted to persuade the government officials to provide welfare policies or postpone the enforcement of the law. These desperate requests were totally ignored. The abolition law took effect as scheduled, and the government neither invalidated ch'anggi's debts to brothel owners nor offered alternative jobs or training.[107] On February 16, two days after the enforcement of abolition, three representatives of a ch'anggi association visited the Seoul City government to request welfare policies to support them. A newspaper reported that these representatives fiercely protested, "swearing at the mayor with unspeakably foul language."[108] Another news article described "drunken ch'anggi" who were protesting out of frustration as "devils incarnate."[109] In this way, ch'anggi, who had been a symbol of colonial shame, now became enemies within the new nation. In both cases, they were not considered fellow citizens with access to civil rights. They had to simply be saved or suppressed.

In an interview to further explain her provocative essay "Can the Subaltern Speak?," Gayatri C. Spivak elaborated that she did not mean to imply that the subalterns, the people excluded from the hierarchy of power in (post-) colonial societies, is literally unable to speak. Rather, her notion was that the subaltern's particular lack of agency means that she is not able to be "heard" within the collective social discourse, "even when she makes an effort to death to speak."[110] In this respect, ch'anggi can be considered a "subaltern" group. Their demands for help were ignored and their protests, if even recognized, were simply ridiculed and condemned. Perhaps most damningly, female elites completely disregarded the demands of ch'anggi. Rather, they condemned ch'anggi's protests as an attack on both the U.S. military government and their own "feminist" movement. For instance, *Puin sinbo* criticized the ch'anggi who refused to leave the red-light district: "They [ch'anggi] are rotten to the core, they do nothing but reproach the authorities and female activists for the failure to provide any welfare support. They only demand 'Give us jobs!' 'Guarantee our livelihood!' 'Support our families!' 'We would rather become private prostitutes!'"[111]

In such terms, which could be directly identified with the perspective of "the authorities," elite women within the nationalist movement publicly scolded their disenfranchised sisters and demanded that they should address their own problems without relying on the military government for help. Some such women even acted as vigilantes, who took it upon themselves to control the attitudes and actions of women in the real world. For instance, Pak Sŭng-Ho, a member of the assembly, proudly reported her organization's activity at a roundtable entitled "To Discuss Current Women's Morality":

> [As leader of Patriot Women Calling for Independence (Tongnip ch'oksŏng aeguk puinhoe)] my organization engages in outreach on the streets to persuade women with grotesque makeup [to take it off]. We explain how such [thick] makeup looks ugly and vulgar, and it debases Korean women and encourage foreigners to cajole us.... Some women admit their faults, but others protest and argue that "it is not your business!" I even slapped one such woman's face.[112]

As this excerpt shows, the nationalist approach was to attribute American soldiers' sexual misconduct to Korean women's "grotesque" demeanor. Their aim in response to the continuation of prostitution was to attempt to control all women's public behavior in addition to the abolition of the kongch'ange. In this way, they established themselves as those who would anchor the construction of a new nation-state on the basis of female chastity. In contrast, they did not problematize the foreign occupiers' right "to cajole" and sexually harass Korean women in general. U.S. troops' male and racial superiority in relation to Korean women was deemed just and unchallengeable.

The effort of the nationalists to purify the nation was largely unsuccessful. Numerous ch'anggi refused to leave the red-light districts until the police came to forcefully disperse them. One news article reported that it was unknown where most of the expelled ch'anggi went.[113] In addition, the colonial legacy of toleration-regulation was neither confronted nor expunged, merely concealed.

TWO

Hot War, Cold War, and Patriotic Prostitutes

PROSTITUTION FOR NATIONAL SECURITY

MAC E. WOODS was seventeen years old when he volunteered to serve in the U.S. military in May 1959. After finishing basic training in Missouri and Virginia, he was finally dispatched to Camp Casey, Dongducheon, Korea. When he arrived in the war-torn country, he found that it was "nothing like Japan," which he had applied for and visited en route to Camp Casey. He lamented: "Korea was very poor, and also a very depressing place." Nonetheless, one thing did not disappoint him: the availability of Korean prostitutes. "The normal cost for sex could be as low as a pack of cigarettes," and "everybody in the Headquarter's Company appeared to be involved in one big continuous party."[1] His sexual adventures on his tour of duty motivated him to write a booklet entitled *Korea: Hills, Rice Patties, and Whores*, which starts with the following preface:

> This story basically tells about, how much United States Military Property that was given away by U.S. Army Personnel, for the payment of prostitution. This activity took place during their 13 month tour of duty in Korea.... At least 80% of the men, who were stationed in Country of South Korea, they were involved in some type of solicitation of illegal prostitution, with stolen property. All of these incidents took place after August 12, 1954, when the Korean War ended.[2]

As the typo in the title ("rice patties") and the wrong historical fact in the preface (Korean hostilities concluded with the signing of an armistice on July 27, 1953) indicate, the author published this fourteen-page booklet without having it edited. It is unclear exactly when this booklet, which represented Korea as an uncivilized land full of hills, rice paddies, and prostitutes, was published, how many copies were circulated, and how it was finally received by the Library of Congress. However, one thing is clear: it reveals sexual encounters between American soldiers and Korean prostitutes amazingly frankly from the perspective of the ranks without any censorship.

This chapter examines how policies of both the Korean government and the U.S. Forces in Korea created a sexual playground for many American servicemen from the 1950s to the 1970s: the Korean War, postwar rebuilding, the U.S. military's long-term presence, and the sudden mass reduction in forces triggered by détente. It traces the process by which such policies, in the form of the toleration-regulation regime, contributed immensely to the formation of the Korean state, with female sexuality continuously utilized as a resource essential for both the Korean War and postwar national security, augmenting government apparatuses and enlarging intervention into the bodies and psyches of "comfort women." It also analyzes the peculiar legal structure of the regime and the paradoxes of Korean state sovereignty that enabled and justified it. Finally, it examines how comfort women conformed to, utilized, and/or protested state control.

PRODUCING PATRIOTIC PROSTITUTES
FOR THE KOREA-U.S. ALLIANCE

"To Promote the Efforts of UN Forces":
Comfort Stations and VD Control during the Korean War

In chapter 1 I explored how commercial sex between the U.S. servicemen and Korean women surfaced as a critical agenda for both the U.S. military government and the governing Korean elites. This historical circumstance could have concluded as a short, extraordinary episode, since with the establishment of the Korean government in 1948 the U.S. military withdrew from Korea, leaving only five hundred military advisers in 1949. At the time of the Korean War, however, foreign troops returned, including Americans. During the Korean War, the total strength of the UN Command (UNC) was about two million, about 90 percent of which were Americans (1,789,000).[3] This reflected the fact that the U.S. military in essence led the UNC, as demonstrated by the appointment of General Douglas MacArthur as commander in chief. Moreover, on July 14, 1950, soon after the outbreak of the war, Korean president Rhee Syngman (Yi Sŭng-Man) transferred wartime operational control of Korea's armed forces to the U.S. military to conduct the war more efficiently. As a result, the national security of Korea during the Korean War was entirely subject to U.S. oversight. Since the war has never officially ended, this operational control remains in place.

As John Parascandola colorfully states, "Venus always accompanies Mars"; that is, "venereal disease and war are inextricably linked."[4] Due to the Korean War, prostitution between Korean women and Korean and foreign troops resumed, and VD became more widespread. For instance, the VD rate among American troops rose to 231 per 1,000 in May 1952.[5] *The Medics' War*, an official history of the U.S. Army's medical activities during the Korean War, cites a division surgeon's comment that VD is "an occupational disease of soldiers," showing how serious the situation was.[6] This demonstrates that the spread of VD was a constant problem that was never successfully contained during the conflict. *The Medics' War* further points out that the Korean government and the Eighth U.S. Army in Korea (EUSA) had difficulty reaching a consensus regarding how to suppress VD:

> Korean authorities followed traditional practice by informally licensing brothels and inspecting their inmates; the U.S. Army's policy of either breaking up houses of prostitution or putting them off limits, Koreans pointed out, merely drove women into the streets and put a premium on uncontrolled streetwalking. The Americans countered that actual Korean practice was extremely haphazard, with insufficient treatment of diseased women and poor contact tracing.[7]

It is noteworthy that the author here refers to the women in licensed brothels as "inmates," whereas they were usually called "prostitutes" or "entertainment girls" in the documents produced by the U.S. military during the occupation period (1945–1948). It is impossible to know the detailed situation of those inmates, because the book does not provide any more information on them. Still, the term implies that, in the author's view, prostitutes in such "informally" licensed brothels were essentially prisoners. In Korean government documents, licensed brothels and their workers limited to the exclusive use of the military were referred to as *wianso* and *wianbu* respectively, which can be literally translated as "comfort station" and "comfort woman." During the Korean War, the Korean Army organized "special comfort troops" for its soldiers, and the Korean Ministry of Health permitted civilians to establish comfort stations for UN troops.

A History of the Korean War from behind the Lines, an officially sanctioned history of the Korean Army published in 1956, depicts the special comfort troops in detail. It reveals that the Korean Army established them "to boost morale, and to prevent harmful effects accompanied by battles and . . . psychological disorders including depression caused by physiological problems due to longing for the opposite sex," even though such a program "contradicts the state policy."[8] The Korean military understood such a measure violated the existing law that prohibited prostitution, but it justified comfort stations as a necessary accommodation to win the war. Three special comfort troops units were established in Seoul and one in Gangneung, together containing eighty-nine "comfort women." *A History of the Korean War from Behind the Lines* states that the women "comforted" 204,560 soldiers in 1952. This means that a comfort woman sexually served about 6.3 Korean soldiers a day on average. Comfort women were subject to twice-weekly strict VD examinations by army surgeons. Sometimes they were dispatched to remote areas at the request of frontline units.[9] A retired Korean officer recalled in his memoir that "six comfort women were assigned to my unit for eight hours" as "the fifth supplies." Officially, there were only four types of military supplies.[10]

While the Korean Army directly organized prostitution for its soldiers, for the UN troops, the Korean Ministry of Health took charge. On October 10, 1951, the Ministry of Health instructed its officials to license comfort stations for UN forces.[11] The purpose of such facilities was to protect "ordinary residents' safety." The service was exclusively offered to UN forces, and Korean males were not allowed to use it. The Ministry of Health also stipulated details on the registration and VD testing of "comfort women, dancers, and waitresses." It defined comfort women as those "who comfort and entertain foreign troops at comfort stations." The frequency of VD examinations ranged from once every two weeks for waitresses, to once a week for dancers, to twice a week for comfort women. All these women had to carry ID cards, that is, health certificates to prove that they were registered and regularly examined. The Ministry of Health also ordered business associations of those facilities to transmit personal information about their employees to it.

The truth about comfort women during the Korean War remains hidden, since the two documents mentioned here are the only official records uncovered so far. Perhaps the main issue preventing further mainstream historical interest is that unlike comfort women for the Japanese imperial military, no survivors have stepped forward to testify about their past. What is clear, however, is that the Korean government followed what *The Medics' War* called "traditional practices." It inherited from the Japanese military not only the terms comfort stations and comfort women but also the idea that it was necessary to organize military prostitution to boost soldiers' morale, prevent VD, and protect "ordinary" women from soldiers' sexual assault. It is not surprising that the Korean government emulated the Japanese imperial military's comfort station program, given that most Korean military officers and bureaucrats were educated and trained under colonial rule, and some participated in the Second World War as Japanese troops.[12]

In this sense, the Korean War was a "total war," in which the state mobilized not only men's military power but also women's sexuality as a medium to get men ready to fight. In other words, to make young men into soldiers, the state made some women into comfort women. Surprisingly, although this mobilization was similar to that undertaken by the Japanese colonizers, it proceeded without any resistance from within civil society. Perhaps this was because Korea so overwhelmingly depended on the United States for military and economic aid, and therefore it was not compelled to negotiate with society to extract the resources requisite to conduct the war. Not to mention that the Korean government often violently abused its military power to suppress dissent within, which contributed to its monopoly on physical force within its territory.[13]

What role then did the UNC play in operating comfort stations? According to the quote from *The Medics' War*, it appears that the U.S. military that led the UNC obviously opposed the Korean government's idea of licensing brothels. However, the aforementioned document from Korea's Ministry of Health demonstrates a different picture. According to it, comfort stations were licensed "only when the UN forces demand[ed] them," and the military police of UN forces, together with the Korean national police, checked the health certificates of "comfort women, dancers and waitresses." In addition, an English translation was attached to that document, with a scribbled memo on its cover: "English copy should be presented to CACK."[14] Here, CACK refers to UNCACK, the United Nations Civil Assistance Command in Korea. It belonged to EUSA and was responsible for various civil affairs, including preventive medicine. In fact, this English copy was transferred to UNCACK the very next day, October 11, 1951. The cover letter emphasized: "The local authorities [i.e., the Korean government] are responsible for the program. We are advisors, only."[15] However, it does not seem that they were just advisers. Already in July 1951, UNCACK planned VD testing of prostitutes, dancers, and waitresses and stipulated that "if necessary the American Military Police will help the ROK Police in conducting this operation."[16]

Based on this series of documents, it is possible to draw some conclusions. First, the UN forces, or at least some individual commanders, demanded that the Korean government establish military brothels for their soldiers. Second, the Korean government accordingly licensed comfort stations for the UN forces. Third, UNCACK conceived a VD control program for Korean prostitutes including comfort women and jointly enforced it with the Korean government. Fourth, although comfort stations for the UN forces were a collaboration between the Korean government and the UNC, UNCACK evaded any direct responsibility by attributing the program to the Korean government. In this regard, the U.S. military that led UNCACK attempted to distinguish itself from its former enemy imperial Japan, which had blatantly established and operated comfort stations. Here, U.S. military command calculated that being directly involved in military brothels, following the imperial army's precedent, was antithetical to its role as the guardian of the free world and liberal democracy.

Photos taken by the U.S. Signal Corps in May 1952 illustrate "houses of ill repute" in the Pacific Area Command (PAC) area in Busan (Pusan), which are assumed to be the comfort stations for UN troops (see figures 1 and 2). The brothels (which according to the original photo captions "will be removed") were of flimsy construction and bordered with barbed-wire fencing like an army barracks. In front of these facilities stood men in military uniform and women in Korean traditional clothes. Inside a house, an English sign saying "Entertainment House Lucky Gwan, No. 9 Sumun Association" was hung (see figure 3), and another sign said "Certified as a Member of Sŏmyŏn Special Café Business Association" in a mixture of Korean letters and Chinese characters. Therefore, Sumun Association was the same as Sŏmyŏn Special Café Business Association, special cafés were brothels built in Sŏmyŏn where UN forces were stationed, and Lucky Gwan [i.e., Club] was the ninth brothel approved by the association. The brothel pictured was equipped with a waiting room (see figure 4) and several bedrooms with numbered doors from No. 2 to No. 6 (see figure 5). Figure 6 illustrates a Korean doctor examining prostitutes at an American military medical facility.

It is not known when these brothels were established and why they were being removed. However, they seemed to be the government-licensed comfort stations for UN forces, as they were located in the PAC area, their signs were written in English, and they were certified by a business association. Since the highest-numbered brothel was 20 in these photos, it seems that at least twenty comfort stations were established in Sŏmyŏn. Assuming that six

FIGURE 1. "Houses of ill repute," indigenous structures in the Pacific Area Command area, Pusan, May 17, 1952. *Source:* Signal Corps Photo, #11-885-18/FEC-52-15024 (Nadolny), RG 319, entry CE, box 40, National Archives and Records Administration, College Park, MD.

women were at each brothel on average (e.g., house no. 20 seemed to have six rooms since the hightest-numbered room was six; see figure 5), there were approximately one hundred twenty comfort women in this area.

Figure 6 was taken six days earlier than figures 1 through 5, and its photographer was different from the one who took the other images. In the photo a Korean male doctor examines with a stethoscope a woman baring her upper body, who is a prostitute according to the caption, and a female nurse seems to assist him. The other women are waiting for their turn, lowering their heads or averting their eyes as if they are reluctant to look at the woman being examined or the camera. While it is unclear whether the doctor examining prostitutes in the photo belonged to the Korean government or the U.S. military, it seems clear that the examination of the women was involuntary, since the caption says that they were "brought to the station." Unlike the other photos, figure 6 appears to be carefully staged. Not only are the doctor and nurse located exactly in the center of the image, but their faces

FIGURE 2. "Houses of ill repute" (closer view), indigenous structures in the Pacific Area Command area, Pusan, May 17, 1952. *Source:* Signal Corps Photo, #11-885-12/FEC-52-15018 (Nadolny), " RG 319, entry CE, box 40; National Archives and Records Administration, College Park, MD.

and gowns are shining brightly, making a stark contrast with the dim backdrop. Although the clinic is very simple, it is decorated with a big bundle of flowers in a vase. Moreover, considering that health checkups for prostitutes mainly consisted of vaginal examinations, the photo could be propaganda to highlight the beneficence of the U.S. military's public health administration, deliberately hiding the violent and humiliating aspects of its VD control.

As it had done during the occupation period, the U.S. military often made brothels off-limits during the Korean War. Nonetheless, as noted, it seems that some commanders of the UNC also requested that the Korean government license brothels for their soldiers. Therefore, it appears that off-limits restrictions were generally placed on unlicensed brothels and the areas frequented by unregistered prostitutes. A letter that the Far East Command sent to its armies (including EUSA) describes precisely what the term "off-limits" meant:

FIGURE 3. Typical sign on a "house of ill repute," no. 17, an indigenous structure in the Pacific Area Command area, Pusan, May 17, 1952. *Source:* Signal Corps Photo, #11-885-16/ FEC-52-15022 (Nadolny), RG 319, entry CE, box 40; National Archives and Records Administration, College Park, MD.

   a. Experience clearly indicates that police authorities, properly approached, are highly cooperative in granting their assistance in combating prostitution, especially in conducting arresting patrols in areas or streets frequented by *street walkers, solicitors, and pimps.*
   b. *A particularly powerful weapon exists in declaring large areas, and even entire towns, off limits.* This drastic measure should be taken only in very serious cases, *but civil authorities may be induced to greater cooperation* if they are aware that such action, with *its adverse effect on the local economy*, is a possibility. [emphasis added][17]

This quote shows that the U.S. military utilized off-limits restrictions not to prevent its soldiers from patronizing prostitution, but as a "powerful weapon" to elicit civil authorities' cooperation. The main target of local government policing was streetwalkers, solicitors, and pimps. Therefore, Korean authorities could interpret this message as follows: if they failed to properly control

FIGURE 4. Waiting room in a "house of ill repute," an indigenous structure in the Pacific Area Command area, Pusan, May 17, 1952. *Source:* Signal Corps Photo, #11-885-14/ FEC-52-15020 (Nadolny), RG 319, entry CE, box 40; National Archives and Records Administration, College Park, MD.

"streetwalkers," that is, unregistered prostitutes, their local economy that incorporated registered prostitutes and licensed brothels would suffer. A month later, the EUSA released a circular that included similar content.[18]

The Korean police took this statement to heart, concentrating their energy on arresting and registering "clandestine prostitutes" while issuing health certificates for registered prostitutes, dancers, and waitresses.[19] Moreover, the chief of the Korean Police sent a letter to the EUSA, declaring that the medical examinations of Korean prostitutes would be enforced "in order to promote the efforts of the UN Forces gallantly fighting this war of aggression."[20] In this way, the Korean government, with the cooperation of the U.S. military, attempted to make prostitutes into a visible and controllable group by registering them, issuing them ID cards, and restricting them to licensed brothels. The fact that VD control increased during the war can also be verified with official statistics. The number of VD examinations of prostitutes increased

FIGURE 5. Numbered rooms inside a "house of ill repute," no. 20, indigenous structure, in the Pacific Area Command area, Pusan, May 17, 1952. *Source:* Signal Corps Photo, #11-885-15/FEC-52-15021 (Nadolny), RG 319, entry CE, box 40; National Archives and Records Administration, College Park, MD.

over sixfold, from 64,934 in 1951 to 404,179 in 1953, reaching a level comparable to the colonial period when authorization-regulation had existed.[21] In this regard, it is also noteworthy that UNCACK explained that the increase in the number of examinations was "due to more frequent and thorough examinations rather than an increase in the number of registered prostitutes."[22]

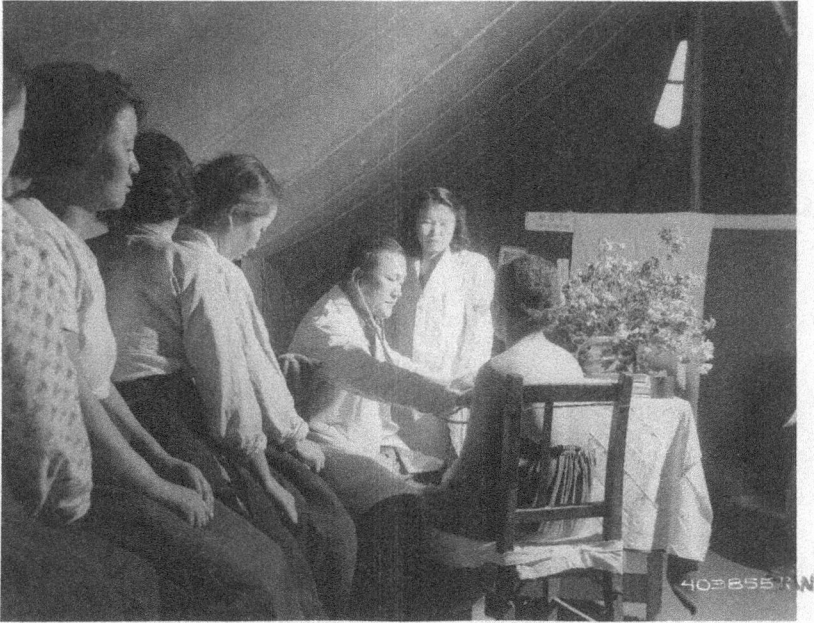

FIGURE 6. Korean doctor of the Civil Affairs Collecting Aid Station, 3rd US Infantry Division, examining prostitutes brought to the station for treatment of venereal disease, May 11, 1952. *Source:* Signal Corps Photo, #17-2755-3/FEC-52-18518 (Kryzak), RG 319, entry CE, box 40; National Archives and Records Administration, College Park, MD.

Nevertheless, the U.S. military did not seem to be fully satisfied with the Korean government's VD control program. In the view of the EUSA, there was a "glaring weakness" in the Korean government's VD policy during the war: "the failure to isolate infected individuals until non-infectious. Prostitutes return to 'work' immediately after examination."[23] As the following sections will show, it was not until a decade after the war ended that facilities to isolate and treat infected prostitutes were established.

"Sexual Promiscuity in Oriental Countries": The Postwar Formation of Camptowns

In July 1953, the armistice was signed ending hostilities in Korea. While other UN countries largely withdrew their troops from Korea around the mid-1950s, the United States, motivated by the Cold War desire to contain communism, maintained a sizable presence in Korea under the umbrella of the UNC. The number of American troops decreased from around three hundred thousand right after the war to fifty-eight thousand in 1961, and this level was maintained throughout the 1960s.[24] The United States also provided Korea with immense amounts of military aid in the form of direct finance. In 1954, for instance, the amount of military aid from the United States was US$503 million, which was five times more than Korea's own defense budget (US$100 million). As the scale of this assistance decreased gradually, the Korean government allocated more resources to defense throughout the 1950s and 1960s. However, Korea was still dependent on the United States for over half of its military expenditure by the end of the 1960s.[25] In this sense, Korea was not initially a self-reliant state but formed in the mold of what Charles Tilly has labeled a "client state," at least up until the 1960s. That is to say, its "military [was] created, trained, staffed, and supplied by other states."[26] The status of Korea as a client state was also obvious in other areas, in particular the nation's prostitution policies, in which the government endeavored to provide safe pleasure to the troops of its custodian state by regulating its own female citizenry.

With the U.S. military's long-term presence, so-called camptowns, entertainment and business districts around the U.S. military bases, started to form. Prostitution prevailed there, and VD control became more systematized. During the war, the Korean government justified licensing comfort stations in the name of the national state of emergency, even though prostitution was prohibited by law from 1948. After the ceasefire, however, the government found it difficult to justify violating the law any longer. Its solution was to license bars, clubs, and dance halls instead of comfort stations, calling them "hospitality facilities designated for UN troops."[27] In September 1955, President Rhee Syngman ordered his cabinet to "establish special zones to suppress clandestine prostitution and permit official dance halls for foreigners" in person.[28] These special hospitality facilities were de facto brothels, but by using this euphemistic term the government attempted to avoid the allegation that it was allowing prostitution. The facilities were permitted only in camptowns, and Koreans, other than those catering to the U.S. military, were not allowed to enter them. In this way, camptowns were established as special red-light districts for the exclusive benefit of American servicemen. They also functioned as buffer zones between Korean civilians and foreign troops, designed to prevent any conflicts between them including sexual violence, and therefore to safeguard wider Korean society.

While the term comfort station disappeared from official use, comfort woman survived. In February 1957, the Infectious Disease Prevention Act took effect. The act's enforcement decree specified "comfort women, dancers, and waitresses" as the subjects of forceful registration and regular VD examinations. The frequency of examinations was the same as in the war: once every two weeks for waitresses, once a week for dancers, and twice a week for comfort women. According to government statistics, there were about eight to thirteen thousand registered comfort women serving American troops annually between the end of the Korean War and the early 1980s. Considering that there were also unregistered prostitutes, the total number of prostitutes serving the U.S. troops was much larger.[29]

The control of VD rates among comfort women became more urgent to the Korean administration when the UNC moved from Tokyo to Seoul on July 1, 1957. On July 6, the ministers of health and social affairs, home affairs, and justice agreed that it was necessary to concentrate comfort women in special zones.[30] Three weeks later, vice ministers convened a conference to discuss how to control VD among comfort women and address the problem of so-called mixed children fathered by members of the UN forces. They decided to license "hospitality facilities designated for UN troops," such as bars, clubs, and dance halls in special zones; concentrate comfort women in such areas; and encourage them to use birth control.[31] These conferences demonstrate that camptown prostitution was important enough to warrant ministerial level attention, and that the Korean government had an entirely ambivalent attitude toward the comfort women. On the one hand, it believed that such women were essential to "comfort" and entertain UN troops. On the other hand, it was concerned that they could harm the soldiers of these important allies with VD. It also feared that such women could contaminate the "pure blood" of the Korean population with numerous interracial children.

With the establishment of camptowns and the cooperation of the Korean government, the U.S. Forces Korea (USFK) was able to enforce contact tracing more efficiently.[32] As mentioned in chapter 1, the contact tracing program was introduced under the U.S. military government but conducted on a very small scale. This situation did not improve during the Korean War.[33] In contrast, a document produced by the EUSA shows that contact tracing resumed in earnest at least from 1955, specifying that "if the contact lives in a nearby area appropriate Military Police authorities will be notified and they, accompanied by [the Korean] National Police, will endeavor to locate the contact and have her examined and treated."[34] The U.S. military did not merely support the Korean government's VD control program but also supervised it. A conference held at I Corps, Uijeongbu, on September 23, 1957, exemplifies how the USFK monitored Korea's VD policy. Fourteen American military officers (mainly from the EUSA and I Corps); two officials from the Office of Economic Coordinator (OEC), UNC; one official of Korea's Ministry of Health [and Social Affairs]; three Korean doctors from public VD clinics; and two Korean police officers participated in this conference.[35]

The first speaker, Dr. Lazarus, the deputy medical director of the OEC, pointed out that his office was supporting the Korean government's VD control with technical advice and assistance as well as drugs and other resources. He emphasized that the "OEC must know how these drugs and supplies are being used." Dr. Lee of the Ministry of Health and Social Affairs answered that his organization was now submitting usage reports (to the OEC). Dr. Lee also stated that "the best way to control venereal disease" was "periodic examinations of female entertainers and follow-up care of those with a venereal disease." "To accomplish this," he argued, "it is necessary to have the cooperation of the Korean National Police." Colonel Sayer, deputy surgeon of EUSA, summarized Dr. Lee's report, and a discussion of the Korean legal system on prostitution followed.[36] After that, the chief of police of Yangju (to which Dongducheon belonged) was asked to report on Korean police activity. He responded that his personnel were already "bringing prostitutes to the clinics" but confessed that they had difficulty in controlling "vagrant prostitutes." To solve this problem, he asked for the U.S. military's cooperation, suggesting the following: indoctrinating soldiers to check prostitutes' ID cards, providing information about Korean women with whom infected soldiers had sex, issuing prophylactic condoms to soldiers, and finally, instructing military police to report vagrant prostitutes to the Korean police. However, American officers did not agree with some points. Colonel Sayer expressed concern that instructing his enlisted men to check prostitutes' ID cards could send the wrong message of allowing prostitution. In response to the request to report clandestine prostitutes to the Korean police, Colonel Lancer, provost marshal of the EUSA, emphasized that "the control of Korean civilians, including prostitutes, remained the responsibility of the Korean National Police, not the U.S. Army."[37]

This conference demonstrates some salient characteristics of the VD control program in the late 1950s. First, the USFK was well informed of widespread prostitution and the resulting high incidence of VD among its soldiers.

Nevertheless, it neither officially approved prostitution nor admitted that it had failed to control its soldiers' promiscuity. Instead, it chose to suppress Korean prostitutes' VD, not its soldiers' patronization of them. Second, the OEC provided the Korean government with medical supplies for diagnosing and treating VD, but it was not sure that they were properly distributed or used. In fact, the U.S. military suspected that Korean officials misappropriated those materials, although they did not mention it explicitly. In this context, Dr. Lazarus requested that Dr. Lee provide exact information on drug usage. Other UNC officials expressed similar concerns over this period. For instance, two weeks before this conference, Stellen Wollmar, the economic coordinator of UNC, sent a letter to Son Chang Hwan (Son Ch'ang-Hwan), the Korean minister of health, criticizing the Korean government for not submitting any report, although his office had provided enough drugs to treat twenty-five thousand VD patients. Wollmar warned that he would not provide any more drugs if the ministry continued to ignore his office's repeated requests for detailed reports.[38] In a report written in August of the same year, Lieutenant General Arthur D. Trudeau of I Corps lamented also that "OEC delivers supplies directly to the ROK government but exercises very little, if any, control over subsequent distribution or the effectiveness of such aid."[39]

The third characteristic of the VD control program is that whereas the USFK did not trust the Korean government, it could not help but depend on it. Not a colonizer but an ally, the USFK was wary of directly policing Korean prostitutes, who were foreign civilians beyond its jurisdiction. This is why the USFK chose to delegate the responsibility for detecting and treating VD among Korean prostitutes to the Korean government and to surveil its policy. The Korean officials, at least apparently, declared their intention to earnestly cooperate with the USFK. A final point is that such conferences were probably periodically held in the late 1950s, given that the next conference was scheduled for a month later. This was also not the first one, considering Trudeau's report: "We have had several conferences on this problem with government officials at the province, gun [i.e., county], and local level."[40]

Due to the USFK's medical support (and probably its close surveillance of the situation), 109 VD clinics were established nationwide, and the number of VD examinations increased to about 680,000 by 1960 and more than one million by 1963.[41] More than half of the examinations were conducted on comfort women.[42] Even though the number of UN forces was about sixty thousand, less than 1 percent of the total number of Korean adult men (about six million) in the 1960s, VD control was disproportionately concentrated on the comfort women.[43] In 1960, the Ministry of Health and Social Affairs clarified that "since the prostitutes are indifferent to VD, it is forcefully taking them [to public health clinics] with the cooperation of the [Korean] police or the [U.S.] military police."[44] This shows how seriously the Korean government took VD control for the UN forces. Nevertheless, the USFK was still skeptical about the effectiveness of the Korean government's policy. In evaluating the Korean government's activities in 1959, the Medical Department of EUSA criticized the Korean government for showing "no significant reaction to the Surgeon's proposals" for creating "a sound V.D. control program."[45] The U.S. military's dissatisfaction was further expressed in a warning to its soldiers not to trust the prostitutes' health certificates that were issued by the Korean government. A pamphlet entitled *Guide to a Healthful Tour in Korea* of 1960 instructed the newcomers, using an illustration (see figure 7):

> As elsewhere in the world, prostitution exists in Korea. In a country of poor economic standards, young girls may resort to this method of earning a living. Everyone instinctively recognizes that promiscuous sexual activity is likely to spread disease and lead to trouble. However, soldiers sent overseas, separated from the moral restraint of friends and family, may succumb to temptation. All prostitutes must be considered to be infected with venereal disease regardless of how many "certificates" they carry.... Use of a rubber prophylactic (condom) is one of the best means of avoiding infection.

Based on the warning that the prostitutes' certificates did not guarantee their health, the USFK appeared to suspect that the Korean government just focused on VD testing and issuing certificates, instead of the thorough treatment of infected prostitutes. The pamphlet also reveals the U.S. military's attitude toward American soldiers and Korean prostitutes. It primarily expresses sympathy with the soldier vulnerable to being lured and harmed in a foreign country. In contrast, the illustration depicts the Korean prostitute as a bad woman dangling a cigarette, an alluring and calculating exploiter ready to take advantage of the drunken soldier. Behind the American serviceman, we can see a picture hung on a dilapidated wall, which depicts a Korean female traditional dancer against the backdrop of a traditional building, probably a Chosŏn dynasty palace. Such iconography, which feminized the notion of the Korean nation using the image of traditional kisaeng to attract foreign male tourists, was typical in tourism posters and

SEXUAL PROMISCUITY. As elsewhere in the world, prostitution exists in Korea. In a country of poor economic standards, young girls may resort to this method of earning a living. Everyone instinctively recognizes that promiscuous sexual activity is likely to spread disease and lead to trouble. However, soldiers sent overseas, separated from the moral restraint of friends and family, may succumb to temptation.

All prostitutes must be considered to be infected with venereal disease regardless of how many "certificates" they carry. Because of shortage of sanitary conveniences (running water and soap) the problem of sex hygiene and prophylaxis is much greater than in the States. While it is true that venereal disease can be cured, provided treatment is begun early and by competent medical personnel, it is also true, as with any disease, that prevention is easier and more certain than cure. Use of a rubber prophylactic (condom) is one of

FIGURE 7. Page from Eighth US Army's guide for its troops, 1960. *Source: Guide to a Healthful Tour in Korea*, August 1, 1960, 5, EUSA, Adjutant General Section, Pamphlets, 1958–63, RG 338, entry A1 269, box 21, National Archives and Records Administration, College Park, MD.

could be traced back to the colonial period.[46] In fact, as chapter 3 will show, the Korean government actually implemented a peculiar policy that framed the American servicemen as tourists and attempted to absorb U.S. dollars from them. Thus, this illustration (probably unintentionally) discloses how closely Korea's tourism policy was related to commercial sexual activity in the camptowns.

To summarize, the primary goal of the U.S. military in relation to prostitution was not to prevent its soldiers from patronizing prostitutes but to protect them from VD by encouraging the use of condoms. In this process, many racist prejudices against Korean and East Asian society came to the fore. For instance, a circular distributed in August 1958 states that "in oriental countries . . . sexual promiscuity is much more prevalent, and little stigma is attached."[47] This perspective is amazingly similar to that of the nineteenth-century British colonial officials, who maintained that "prostitution was normalized in nonwhite societies and held no stigma."[48] As such, camptown prostitution could be merely dismissed as Korean women's natural state of sexual degradation or a reflection of the inherently backward culture of Asian society. Therefore, American servicemen need not feel guilty or responsible for engaging with such women. In this frame of discussion, neither American servicemen's promiscuity nor the power imbalance between the United States and Korea was made visible.

Conception and Execution: VD Detention Centers and Mass Quarantine in the 1960s

The April Revolution of 1960 ended Rhee Syngman's twelve-year dictatorship in South Korea. The revolution was short-lived, however. On May 16, 1961, the new government was deposed by a coup d'état mounted by forty-three-year-old Major General Park Chung Hee (Pak Chŏng-Hŭi). To justify the coup, the new dictator presented his vision to fundamentally reconstruct the state. One of his goals was to establish social and moral order by "eliminating all social corruption."[49] Sexual promiscuity including prostitution was regarded as such an evil. In this context, the junta passed the Yullak Haengwi Prevention Act (hereafter the Yullak Prevention Act) only five months after the coup. As I explained in the introduction, the term *yullak haengwi* refers to the activity of engaging in prostitution as a form of female vagrancy, and the law criminalized not only prostitution but also soliciting, pimping, and patronizing.

However, not long after coming to power, the junta chose to compromise with reality instead of enforcing this prohibition strictly. In June 1962, the regime designated 104 "special zones" nationwide where prostitution was tolerated. Of these, 61 were in Gyeonggi Province, the area that hosted the most U.S. military bases.[50] In other words, the majority of special zones were camptowns, and the rest of them were for Korean men. The new government also enacted the Food Sanitation Act in the same year. The act mainly addressed food and restaurant sanitation, but it also included provisions for licensing, registering, and issuing health certificates to "employees hired in the entertainment business" (*yuhŭng yŏngŏp chongsaja*), that is, "hospitality women" (*chŏpkaekpu*). Hospitality women included comfort women, as well as entertainers and waitresses working at clubs and bars.

Not only the central government but also the local government of Gyeonggi Province played a significant role in the construction of camptowns. For instance, an official document dated September 14, 1961, from Gyeonggi argued that "establishing concentration facilities to incarcerate comfort women is urgent, in terms of controlling VD transmission, keeping morality, and comforting UN forces or enhancing their morale." It is unclear what form of "concentration facilities" the province conceived of, and they could be like Japanese military comfort stations during the Second World War. However, fortunately for the comfort women, the document admitted that it would be impracticable to carry out the plan because the cost would be enormous. Instead, it calculated how many entertainment facilities were necessary, based on the daily estimate of UN soldiers permitted to go out. According to that estimate, 7,555 soldiers would visit bars or clubs daily, and 289 such establishments were therefore necessary to accommodate them, but the existing number was just 195. In this regard, although Gyeonggi Province argued that it was urgent to "limit over-competition" among entertainment facilities, its real purpose appeared to be to permit more facilities as rapidly as possible to satisfy GIs' demand. To this end, the province requested that the Ministry of Health and Social Affairs transfer to it the authority to permit new establishments for GIs, and the ministry soon accepted this request.[51]

Gyeonggi Province also established VD detention centers (*sŏngpyŏng kwalliso*) in camptowns to quarantine infected comfort women. Five such centers were established in a short period between March and May 1965 in Yangju, Paju, Pocheon, Goyang, and Uijeongbu, and one more was established in December 1968 in Pyeongtaek.[52] At last, what the EUSA called the "glaring weakness" of the VD control program during the Korean War was overcome: "the failure to isolate infected individuals until non-infectious."[53] A series of documents produced in the early 1960s by the U.S. military and the Korean government substantiate that the former put pressure on the latter to establish VD detention centers.

In 1963 the I Corps of the USFK, concerned by the "high incidence of venereal disease in this command," conducted a study of prostitution and VD in two camptowns: Dongducheon, where the 7th Infantry Division was stationed, and Paju (Yongjugol and Taech'up'o), home to the 1st Cavalry Division. The study urged that "more emphasis be placed on treatment of prostitutes" and proposed that "two prototype medical clinics be constructed" in Dongducheon and Yongjugol.[54] The surgeon of the EUSA concurred with the I Corps's recommendations. Nonetheless, he commented that he was not sure "it is appropriate for us to ask the ROK to commit resources . . . to mask our problem of promiscuity and the failure of our men to look after themselves." He concluded: "We do not have a very good bargaining position" with the Korean government.[55] An official of the IO (International Relations Office) of the EUSA also agreed that the proposal had merit but expressed similar concern: "Our negotiating position appears to be weak, for we have no lever to force the ROKs to improve their efforts. Also, the VD problem to them is a minor one."[56] Based on this comment of the IO official, Katharine H. S. Moon has argued that "the Korean government considered kijich'on [camptown] prostitution and venereal disease primarily a US problem and offered no or little help to US military authorities."[57]

In fact, however, another document reveals that the Korean government took the I Corps's suggestion seriously. A year later, the Ministry of Health and Social Affairs drafted a plan to build an "isolation station" to quarantine and treat infected women in Dongducheon, the very place that the I Corps proposed.[58] Five more isolation stations, that is, VD detention centers, were established in other camptowns between 1965 and 1968. The reason such VD detention centers were abruptly established in 1965 was that the I Corps had conducted prior research on the issue in 1963. In short, the Americans conceived of the centers, and the Korean government executed the plan. Hence, the two EUSA officials' concern about their bargaining position vis-à-vis the Korean government proved to be groundless. Korean officials took a much more accommodating attitude toward the USFK than anticipated, without hesitating to impinge on Korean women's human rights. Since the Park administration desperately needed the U.S. government's recognition to confirm its legitimacy, it was entirely submissive to the USFK's requests.

For instance, a 1961 document from Gyeonggi Province stated that "improving the quality of entertainment establishments and providing better rest and recreation (R&R) facilities for UN forces would enhance their morale and improve their impression of Korea after the revolution." Here, the revolution referred to Park's military coup.[59] Moreover, from 1963 the Park regime was faced with massive public opposition to its efforts to normalize diplomatic relations with Japan. To overcome this nationalist antipathy, the administration sought public support from the U.S. government. In response, the United States not only endorsed the regime's diplomatic policy, but it also invited Park to the White House in May 1965 and promised to provide continuous economic aid.[60]

Thus, the establishment of VD detention centers can be interpreted as representative of further Korean fealty to the United States. This strengthened alliance resulted in an enhanced effort to bureaucratically control the bodies of comfort women. According to Gyeonggi Province statistics, there were 24,382 instances of quarantine in the VD detention centers in 1965, increasing to 45,200 in 1970. Considering the number of detainees was 4,985 in 1965 and 9,566 in 1970, each comfort woman was quarantined four to five times a year on average.[61] Thus, an era of mass quarantine began, and comfort women were a sacrifice offered on the altar of the Korea-U.S. alliance.

Controlling Body, Mind, and Conduct: The Camptown Clean-Up Campaign of the 1970s

As Katharine H. S. Moon's pioneering study clarifies, the control over comfort women by both the Korean government and the USFK increased in the early 1970s. With the Nixon doctrine to reduce American troops from East Asia in 1969, the number of U.S. troops in Korea decreased from sixty-nine thousand in 1969 to forty-three thousand in 1971.[62] In response to this, not only the Korean government but ordinary Koreans were seized with panic that the U.S. military might abandon them. In particular, many residents of the camptowns who had depended on U.S. troops for their living felt frustrated and betrayed. In addition, racial tensions inside the U.S. military escalated, influenced by the civil rights movement in the United States. The anxiety and tension were often manifested by conflict between white and African American servicemen or between American servicemen and camptown residents, particularly in the summer of 1971.[63] For instance, on July 9, 1971, about fifty African American soldiers destroyed five clubs in

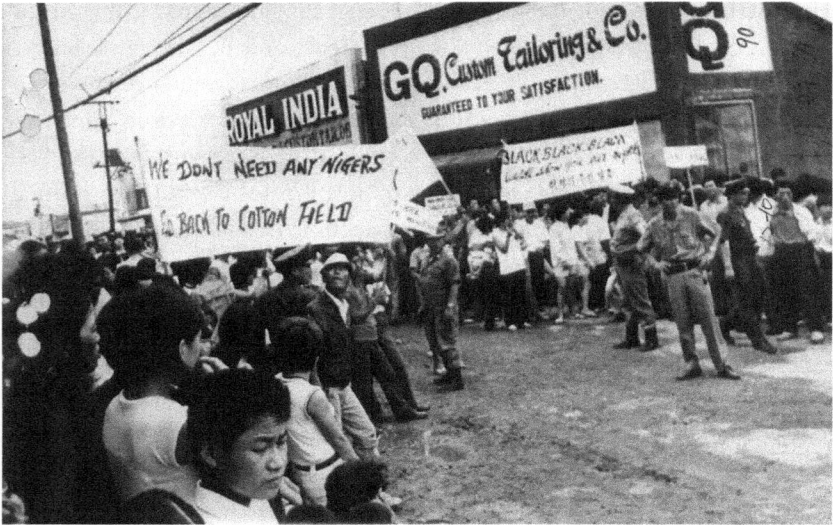

FIGURE 8. Anjeong-ri residents demonstrating against a racial riot by Black GIs, 1971. *Source:* National Police Agency, "A Report on the Plan to Prevent Collisions between Koreans and Americans," September 25, 1971, National Archives of Korea, BA0165772.

Anjeong-ri, Pyeongtaek, to protest racial discrimination by club owners and employees.[64] This racial riot in turn infuriated Korean residents, who waged a demonstration against the rioters the next day, holding racist banners (see figure 8).

To solve these racial problems, along with many long-festering issues in camptowns, in September 1971 the U.S.-ROK Status of Forces Agreement (SOFA) Joint Committee decided to organize the Ad Hoc Subcommittee on Civil-Military Relations. In December of the same year, the Korean government established the Base Community Clean-Up Committee, to support and implement the recommendations of the Ad Hoc Subcommittee. VD was the main issue discussed in those committees, with the Korean government contributing considerable money and energy to stamp out VD in camptowns.[65] In her examination of this period, Katharine H. S. Moon concluded: "In 1971, for the first time in history, the USFK succeeded in pressuring the Korean government to regulate systematically and strictly the bodies/health of camptown prostitutes through regular and effective VD examinations and treatment."[66]

However, as we have explored here, such measures, along with issuing health certificates, contact tracing, and zoning, had been gradually intro-

duced and systematized from the colonial period to the U.S. military occupation and the Korean War into the 1960s. Without this historical precedent,
it is unlikely that the Camptown Clean-Up Campaign could have been
mounted. In her work, Moon further argues that the "Nixon Doctrine and
the reduction of U.S. troops in Korea allowed the USFK to place the burden
of official responsibility and accountability for camptown prostitution fully
on the Korean government."[67] Yet this argument too should be reconsidered
in light of the history of VD policy. As this chapter has shown, the Korean
government always tried to control VD among comfort women, although
these efforts did not always succeed in fully satisfying the U.S. military.

Arguably the most important change in the early 1970s was in the U.S.
military's attitude. As noted, in the 1950s the USFK was wary of policing
comfort women beyond its jurisdiction, delegating the responsibility for
VD control to an ineffective Korean government. In contrast, in the early
1970s it was able to exert more direct control over the Korean government,
with the Nixon doctrine and the massive military withdrawal that followed putting the USFK in a superior bargaining position. The Camptown
Clean-Up Campaign was therefore a combinative outcome of the long history of VD control and the new pressures of the Nixon doctrine. During
the campaign, the Ad Hoc Subcommittee visited almost every camptown,
interviewed a considerable number of club owners and chiefs of women's
organizations, and investigated how the Korean government operated VD
clinics and detention centers. Based on this field research, the U.S. military
suggested various methods to improve diagnosis and treatment, put pressure
on the Korean police to increase efforts in the registration and rounding up
of comfort women, and requested that Korean health officials renovate and
increase the number of VD clinics and detention centers.[68] In addition, both
the Korean government and the U.S. military intensified contact tracing. In
this process, new techniques, such as sharing women's personal information
and the so-called tag system, were introduced.

At the eleventh conference of the Ad Hoc Subcommittee on July 31,
1972, the Korean government reported that it "provided copies of the ROK
Government Health Certificate required to be carried by each special entertainer and requested US cooperation in its effective use."[69] This policy
was also discussed at the fifth Korean-American Civil Affairs Conference,
held on March 2, 1973. According to its minutes, "Some units have developed photo files at clinics to assist infected military personnel in identifying
contacts." It specified another related tactic called the tag system: "Contact

slips, name tags, and business cards are also being tried to assist in the contact identification effort."[70] One of the participants, Colonel J. H. Allison of the 51st Air Base Wing, Osan, explained how the tag system was utilized in the camptown near his unit:

> Osan has qualified health personnel assigned to interview VD patients to obtain information on sex contacts. To enable patients to report these sex contacts, a registration and identification system is used in all off-base entertainer establishments. This involves assigning each girl a numbered badge to wear, the issue by the doorman of a contact slip bearing her registration number to the male escort, and maintaining photo files at the base hospital to confirm identification. This contact information is then forwarded to local Korean health officials.[71]

In this way, the Camptown Clean-Up Campaign not only enhanced the cooperation between the Korean government and the USFK but also functioned as an arena through which U.S. military units could exchange ideas on VD control to improve their policies. In a documentary produced by the Munhwa Broadcasting Corporation in 2003, Kim Yeon-Ja, who worked as a comfort woman in the clubs in the 1970s, recalled that this practice was very humiliating, saying it was as if comfort women were treated "like dogs with ID tags."[72]

Thanks to this process, the USFK was able to enormously expand a measure of control over the issue of camptown prostitution. It did not merely research the VD policies that the Korean government was implementing but even obtained personal information on the individual comfort women serving the encampments. Consequently, the control of comfort women infected with VD greatly increased. More systematic contact tracing and more VD detention centers meant that more comfort women were apprehended and quarantined. Infected women were deprived of freedom until fully cured, and forced treatment was painful, in some cases causing death due to penicillin shock. Hence, comfort women regarded VD detention centers as places of terror and hostility.[73] Sometimes they were detained longer than was necessary. For instance, Major James Hathaway, a chief of the Preventive Medicine Division, reported that a VD detention center at Waegwan, the camptown local to Camp Carroll, quarantined gonorrhea patients for a week on average in 1974. A medical officer of Camp Carroll stated that "this period is probably excessive for medical care but felt to have other psychological advantages."[74] The officer did not explain what the "psychological advantages" were, but this seemed to imply that the patients would be more careful of VD in order to avoid such a long period of incarceration in the future. As such, VD control over comfort women was implemented in a very harsh, even sadistic way, and their human rights were simply neglected for the sake of effective policy.

The Korean government even prioritized the efficiency of VD control over the lives of comfort women. In a letter sent to the minister of justice on February 8, 1978, the minister of health and social affairs noted that "some doctors are avoiding administering penicillin [to their patients] because of penicillin allergy shock." He noted that this posed "an enormous obstacle to the enforcement of the state's VD control policy."[75] Thus, he requested that the justice minister "grant immunity to the doctors," when such accidents occurred, "if they had conducted an anaphylactic reaction test in advance." One month later, the minister of justice concordantly replied that the doctors would not be punished if they took necessary emergency measures.[76] In this way, even though penicillin allergy shock could trigger life-threatening anaphylaxis, the Korean government encouraged doctors to use it, on the pretext of the importance of the state's VD control. In contrast to this directive, Dr. Antal of the World Health Organization, whom the Ministry of Health and Social Affairs consulted on the anaphylactic reaction test, was skeptical of the test's benefits. According to him, "most public health administrators do not think that the anaphylactic reaction test is practical," since it not only failed to screen all who might show an allergic reaction but also the reaction test itself could trigger an allergic shock.[77] Despite this warning, the Korean government adhered to using penicillin because of its superior effects than any other antibiotics in eradicating VD. This had a devastating impact on comfort women as the main target of the government's control measures. In their autobiographies, both Kim Yeon-Ja and Kim Chŏng-Ja, former comfort women, recalled that they witnessed a few women die of penicillin shock.[78] I also met a lady at the Sunlit Sister's Center on June 10, 2022, who told me that her friend was killed because of penicillin-related anaphylaxis while she was working as a comfort woman in the 1970s at a camptown in Jincheon, Chungbuk Province.

Moreover, the USFK attempted to control the women's minds and conduct as well as their bodies. As mentioned, the primary cause that initiated the Camptown Clean-Up Campaign was racial conflict. In its first report, the Panel on Race Relations and Equality of Treatment, one of seven panels of the Ad Hoc Subcommittee, analyzed that racial tensions arose from

African American soldiers' concern that they were discriminated against by both white servicemen and Korean service personnel at clubs. To solve this problem, the panel offered several recommendations, one of which was for hostesses to refrain from engaging in discriminatory practices in the performance of "entertainment functions such as dancing or conversing with patrons."[79] In this way, by subjecting the women's "entertainment functions" to its surveillance and control, the USFK endeavored to guarantee its soldiers' unprejudiced access to their sexual services and thus achieve interracial fraternity. When comfort women did not conform to this policy, they were criticized as unpatriotic, even treasonous, as the following case demonstrates. On June 8, 1971, at Yongsan camptown where the UNC was stationed, a racial conflict between white and African American soldiers occurred, and off-limits restrictions were placed on the area for five days.[80] Upon the lifting of the off-limits curfew, the Korean Police Yongsan Station and Headquarters U.S. Army Garrison Yongsan jointly issued a flyer stating the following:

> Your area will be again on limits for U.S. military personnel Monday, 14 June 1971. . . . This action by U.S. military authorities was necessary to prevent any further deterioration of the situation. . . . We believe that you are doing your best to provide good service for U.S. personnel. However, *your attitude or actions may have sometimes offended some of your customers.* Let's think about and correct these (Negative attitude or actions) of the past! *It is also important to know that the enemy of your country takes advantage of such undesirable incidents. In this respect, you should also realize that you are unconsciously helping your enemy, while weakening the internal security of your nation.* Remember U.S. personnel are here to help you to defend the Republic of Korea from North Korean invasion and subversion. . . . You are urged to treat all U.S. customers equally. [emphasis added][81]

This case demonstrates that both the Korean government and the USFK considered the sexual services provided by comfort women an essential element of Korea's national security and the U.S.-Korea alliance. This was the reason that they sought to control not only their bodies but also their conduct and minds. As such, although comfort women were regarded as outcasts within Korean society, they played a key function in maintaining smooth ground-level relations between the United States and Korea during the Cold War. Katharine H. S. Moon has adroitly pointed out that they were expected or forced to act as "personal ambassadors" by the two countries.[82] Comfort women were also an essential element of the "social" security of the

Korean population. Just as Korea was a seawall to defend the "free world" from communism, comfort women were a seawall to defend Korean society, and specifically "ordinary" women, from the nation's most important ally.

THE STATES OF EXCEPTION AND THE PARADOXES OF SOVEREIGNTY

Through this long process, policies to control comfort women were completed by the early 1970s, furnished by the oppressive elements of both Japanese colonial regulation and American prohibition. Chapter 1 conceptualized this combination of colonial regulation and American prohibition as the toleration-regulation regime. By the early 1970s, the toleration-regulation regime became more sophisticated as American tactics such as contact tracing and quarantine were fully incorporated and numerous public health facilities to test and treat comfort women were newly established (see table 2).

At the same time, however, it is noteworthy that there were also several differences in contact tracing and quarantine between the U.S. and Korean methodologies. First, in the U.S. case, at least in principle, suspected contacts were to be persuaded before being examined and quarantined. A manual for contact investigation published by the Office of Surgeon General in 1945 emphasized that "the persuasive approach is the most effective," and only when a suspect "refuses to report for examination, legal quarantine may have to be resorted to in a small number of uncooperative cases."[83] However, this principle was never applied to Koreans. No comfort woman has testified that she was ever persuaded to get examinations. Whenever American soldiers identified them as contacts, they were just apprehended and examined forcefully without opportunity to consent or refute.

Second, as discussed in chapter 1, rapid treatment centers to quarantine VD patients were established nationwide in the United States during the Second World War, but they were closed by 1953. John Parascandola has analyzed that the main reason was the introduction of penicillin, which enabled the treatment of VD more quickly, efficiently, and most importantly, on an outpatient basis.[84] In contrast, VD detention centers in Korea were established in the mid-1960s, more than ten years after the last rapid treatment center was closed in the United States. Both the Korean government and the USFK considered comfort women not as autonomous beings who would

	Colonial Regulation	American Prohibition	Postcolonial Toleration-Regulation
Zoning	Designated red-light districts		Designated red-light districts
Registration	Public prostitutes & perceived prostitutes		Comfort women & other hospitality women
VD testing	Registered prostitutes	Apprehended prostitutes & identified contacts	Registered prostitutes & apprehended prostitutes & identified contacts
Contact tracing		Persuasion before examining and quarantining female contacts	No persuasion before examining and quarantining female contacts
Quarantine		Rapid treatment centers	VD detention centers
Punishment	Unregistered prostitutes	All prostitutes	All prostitutes

voluntarily seek treatment. Quarantine was a much more certain and efficient way to address the problem than outpatient treatment, and women's human rights were never a concern.

Finally, the Korean government issued health certificates, and Korean police officers, public health officials, and American MPs inspected them randomly, which was never done on the mainland of the United States. Those who were not issued the certificates or not stamped regularly were taken to police stations, punished with fines or imprisonment, or locked up in VD detention centers. This process of checking health certificates was called *t'oböl* in Korean, which means "subjugating (enemies)."[85] In the early 1970s, comfort women were even forced to wear tags that inscribed their numbers, and their photos or certificates were maintained by the U.S. military. By way of contrast, such policies were never implemented in the United States. In this way, the U.S. military was able to subject Korean comfort women to more severe and harsher VD control than that practiced on American women, and the Korean government actively cooperated in this endeavor with its most important military ally. All in all, the U.S. military's VD policy was a reflection of the racist and sexist disregard it had for Korean women and the significant power imbalance that existed between the two countries.

Here a question rises. How was it possible for the Korean government to regularly examine comfort women and issue health certificates to them even though it had criminalized prostitution? Some scholars have attempted to answer that question by arguing that the Yullak Prevention Act was never enforced in reality. According to them, the act hardly took effect and even lacked an enforcement decree to implement it.[86] In fact, however, three months after the act was established, its enforcement decree was promulgated.[87] Moreover, the fact that the act was not enforced consistently does not necessarily mean that it was totally ineffective.[88] Kim Yeon-Ja describes her experience of being arrested for a breach of the act while she was a comfort woman:

> At that time, I didn't know that the Korean government prohibited *yullak haengwi* [prostitution activity]. I was so shocked to know the fact after a few years passed [since I was engaged in prostitution]. Isn't it contradictory that the government forcefully examined women and stopped those with VD from engaging in yullak haengwi, while simultaneously prohibiting it? . . . "I'm terribly unfortunate! I thought that my vagina belonged to me, but it belongs to the state!" I have also been arrested and incarcerated at a police station after a summary trial.[89]

In fact, Korea's toleration-regulation regime had a peculiar legal structure. While prohibition was based on national law, regulation was implemented through decrees, rules, and local ordinances. Prohibitory law explicitly declared the criminalization of prostitution in its title, purpose, and terms, such as the Abolishment of the Public Prostitution Law and the Yullak Prevention Act. In contrast, regulatory decrees, rules, and ordinances were surreptitiously implemented under laws such as the Infectious Disease Prevention Act and the Food Sanitation Act. These acts addressed a wide variety of issues regarding health and sanitation, without mentioning a word about prostitution in their articles. As a result, and on the surface at least, the two series of laws of prohibition and regulation did not collide with each other, which enabled their coexistence. In this regime, regulation not only circumvented prohibition but also suspended basic rights guaranteed by the Constitution. Although the Korean Constitution specified that the restriction of personal freedom should be based on law, comfort women were incarcerated in VD detention centers merely based on decrees, rules, and local ordinances. Under this system, suspected contacts could even be confined without doctors' diagnoses that they had contracted VD.

This legal structure accords to what Georgio Agamben has conceptualized as "a state of exception," in that it represents the undercutting of laws and constitution by executive action. The executive's powers were, in this case, extended to the legislative sphere through the issuance of decrees and measures. As a result, legislative power was eroded, and the fundamental hierarchy of law and regulation was disturbed.[90] In such a situation, "it is impossible to distinguish the transgression of the law from execution of the law, such that what violates a rule and what conforms to it coincide without any remainder."[91] In other words, the activity of registering, examining, and incarcerating comfort women to regulate their prostitution served to enforce the Food Sanitation Act and Infectious Disease Prevention Act, but simultaneously violated the Yullak Prevention Act and the Constitution. Agamben has referred to human beings existing in such a state of exception as *homo sacer*, "the object of a pure de facto rule" and free of "judicial oversight."[92] In this context, comfort women can certainly be considered as *homo sacer*, since they were subject to executive action and control while being simultaneously excluded from constitutional rights. This condition of *homo sacer* was further perpetuated by the actions of the U.S. military, which conceived, recommended, and participated in this draconian program of VD control, despite the women's status as foreign citizens outside U.S. jurisdiction.

In contrast, the USFK did not expend much energy controlling the sexual behavior of its servicemen. It merely emphasized abstinence as the best way to prevent VD, while imposing no discipline against infected soldiers "unless they failed to report it."[93] Mac E. Woods, the author of the booklet quoted in the introduction of this chapter, shows how this message was received by soldiers:

> The Army Chaplain would give us Sex Moral Classes twice a month. It was a total waste of time. The main reason was, because all the soldiers new [sic] that our do-good Chaplain, was paying for the housing of two prostitutes in the local village.... Some of the soldiers followed him to the same Village, as soon as the Class was over.... The U.S. Government was very generous to the soldiers, they gave us free condoms. A large box of condoms were [sic] always located at the door of the barrack where you would sign out for your Off-Duty Pass. The Duty Officer would always advise the soldiers to put a handful of the condoms in their pocket, just in case.[94]

To summarize, the Korean government and the USFK controlled VD in camptowns in a very discriminatory way. Even though both men and women were equally able to transmit VD to their partners, only comfort women were subject to a wide variety of oppressive measures, while GIs remained entirely free of any punishment or discipline. This VD policy therefore exacerbated existing power imbalances between comfort women and GIs, as women and men, the sellers and the buyers of sex, and Koreans and Americans. While comfort women became *homo sacer*, subject to harsh control by both the Korean government and the USFK, GIs were bureaucratically and practically enabled to enjoy this particularly exploitative form of sexual activity in a foreign country. Unsurprisingly, the huge disparity of power this situation represented sometimes found expression in acts of extreme violence, as numerous comfort women were badly battered, assaulted, and violently killed by GIs.[95]

The Korean government had no jurisdiction over the crimes committed by U.S. personnel before the Status of Forces Agreement was signed in 1967, and even after the SOFA took effect, the Korean government could not exercise its jurisdictive power properly because of the many individual articles that limited its reach.[96] This shows the paradox of Korea's sovereign power being extremely strong in controlling the women's bodies but amazingly weak in protecting their lives. Paradoxically, the Korean state was able to exert control over comfort women, making them "live and let die" at the hands of GIs, since it was subject to the U.S. military.[97] In addition, the Korean government granted immunity to the doctors even when comfort women died because of penicillin anaphylaxis. Comfort women were, therefore, *homo sacer* in the original sense of archaic Roman law, as someone who killed such a woman would not and could not be condemned for homicide.[98] They were the living body that seemed "no longer to belong to the world of the living," and thanks to their "consecration" in the service of the Korea-U.S. alliance, "the entire community was able to be spared" from the violence of the U.S. military.[99]

THE FURY OF THE "CONSECRATED": THE COMFORT WOMEN'S PROTESTS

Camptowns were riddled with a variety of violent conflicts, and there were even fights among comfort women. Kim Yeon-Ja remembered that the registered women working at clubs often fought with the unregistered streetwalkers like "cats and dogs." The former considered themselves "professionals" issued with health certificates and had complete disdain for the latter, while the latter were proud of their freedom and fought back against the registered.[100] In this way, comfort women accepted and even actively internalized the state classification system to distinguish themselves from other women and even other prostitutes. Perhaps unsurprisingly, some women participated in this control over their colleagues and enhanced their own position. For instance, the staffers of the councils of comfort women usually cooperated with government officials in cracking down on unregistered prostitutes and mobilizing the women to attend lectures designed to indoctrinate them with a patriotic attitude.[101] According to Kim Chŏng-Ja's autobiography, the head of the women's council in Uijeongbu not only got a salary from the Uijeongbu City government but also even won a prize from the president for her efforts to mobilize and control the women on behalf of the government.[102] Just as Tiffany A. Sippial has remarked in her study on Cuban prostitutes at the turn of the twentieth century, the "lines of domination and resistance were drawn not only between state officials and prostitutes but also among prostitutes themselves."[103]

Sometimes, however, comfort women united to struggle against the injustices inflicted on them, even despite the conditions of strict military dictatorship. One of the main issues they grappled with was VD control, such as contact tracing and quarantine. Kim Yeon-Ja depicts a demonstration in Dongducheon one day in the 1960s:

> At that time, we gathered in front of the 7th Division gate, blocked a road, and lay on it [as a protest]. If a GI contracted VD, he identified his contact. However, most GIs tended to indicate more than one woman who looked similar. Then, medics on a military jeep picked up all the women who were pointed out and sent them to the Monkey House [VD detention center]. In fact, it was almost impossible for GIs to identify the exact contact, because even in one night they often slept with several women, for instance, with Sun-Ja of Arirang Club after Yŏng-Ja of Paradise Club. One day, a woman scratched a GI's face who had falsely indicated her as a contact. As a result, she was sent to prison, and this sparked the protest. We flocked [to the protest] one by one, and it was not only the women who had been incarcerated on false charges but also many other women working at the clubs.[104]

Comfort women also protested against corruption on the part of the Korean health personnel. For instance, some VD clinic doctors inflated the number of the infected to receive more treatment fees.[105] Many health workers also took bribes from comfort women in order to exempt them from examinations, and the women who refused to give bribes were often falsely diagnosed as positive.[106] The following newspaper article reports one such demonstration against a VD clinic doctor:

> From 1 pm on [July] 3, about three hundred comfort women serving GIs in Paju-ri and Yeonpung-ri staged an eccentric "demonstration" against Pak Tong-Il, the chief of Paju [Public] Clinic (the 2nd VD clinic in Paju). They requested that he resign since he did not examine them thoroughly and reported to the American MPs an exaggerated number of patients, which resulted [in their camptown being put] off-limits and therefore threatened their livelihood. This "demonstration" continued for three hours.[107]

Another main issue of protest was violence, particularly the murders committed by American servicemen. By organizing demonstrations, comfort women publicly mourned their colleagues and demanded punishment for the perpetrators. Sometimes they even brought the deceased's coffin to the demonstration to express their anger and sorrow. At one demonstration, the lavishly decorated coffin, surrounded by a mass of comfort women all wearing Korean traditional white mourning dresses and hats, created a spectacular contrast to the American MPs safeguarding their garrison. The details of the scene are described in the following national newspaper report:

> In the afternoon, on November 7 [1967], five hundred comfort women in white mourning dress waged a demonstration at the garrison of the 7th Division of the U.S. Army, carrying their colleague Kim Ch'un-Ja's coffin, who was strangled by African American Private Taylor of the 7th Division. On the day, five hundred comfort women, who belonged to Northern Posan-ri [an area of Dongducheon] branch of the comfort women's council, participated in her funeral. When they arrived at the gate of the 7th Division on the way to the cemetery carrying her coffin, they together tried to enter the garrison. As they were blocked by around fifty MPs, they finally set down her coffin ten meters inside the garrison and staged a sit-in for about an hour, chanting "Make a polite apology for the deceased, Commander!"[108]

No matter how desperate their demonstrations were, it was very difficult, if not impossible, for these women to succeed in challenging such overt injustice. As subaltern social outcasts, their struggles were easily ignored by both the USFK and the Korean government. This circumstance notwithstanding, one exceptional case of a soldier being brought to justice can be seen in the following episode from the late 1970s. Between June and July 1977, at the so-called America Town in Gunsan, a midsize city in Jeonbuk Province, two comfort women were brutally murdered: one was strangled and burned and another was stabbed. The first victim indicated a particular GI as her attacker to her neighboring women before she died, and the same GI was then witnessed coming out of the second victim's house. Infuriated by this double murder, hundreds of comfort women staged a demonstration demanding that the government investigate the cases thoroughly and punish the perpetrator. The victims' friends and neighbors also testified about what they had witnessed and heard the victims say at the trial. In this way, the deceased victims' voices were recovered through the vital testimony of their fellow comfort women. The court saw fit to trust this emotive evidence and imposed a sentence of life imprisonment on the accused man in 1979. This GI became the first American to be sentenced to life imprisonment in Korea.[109]

Korean society under the military dictatorship did not pay much attention to this case. I found that only three newspaper articles reported it. Given public indifference, the prisoner's sentence was commuted to twenty years in 1980, and he returned to the United States in 1983, three years later.[110] Both the tragedy of these murders and the short-lived victory of the successful prosecution were lost from public memory until Kim Yeon-Ja published her autobiography in 2005.[111] To gain widespread attention for their suffering and win another landmark legal victory, the comfort women in camptowns would have to wait for over another decade, an issue we return to in chapter 5.

THREE

"Pivotal Workers to Obtain Foreign Currency"

PROSTITUTION FOR NATIONAL DEVELOPMENT

MANY FORMER "comfort women" for U.S. servicemen testified that they were periodically forced to attend lectures designed to inculcate patriotism and the spirit of service. Kim Yeon-Ja described the lectures that she attended in the early 1970s in Pyeongtaek, where the Osan Air Base was located:

> The lecturers were community leaders and the county's welfare department officials. Speaking into the microphone, all of them regurgitated the same verbiage. "Ahem . . . You are patriots. Please have courage and pride! You should not forget that you are contributing to obtaining dollars. I appreciate unsung patriots like you. American soldiers came here to help our country. So, please be decently dressed for them and do not use vulgar slang. Today we invited a famous English teacher. Please study hard!"[1]

In this way, camptown women were interpellated as "patriots," a process further examined in chapter 2. What is intriguing in this speech is that the women's sexual labor was considered essential not only for national security in boosting the morale of American soldiers who "came here to help our country," but also for national development in that they were "contributing to obtaining dollars." In fact, Korea was heavily dependent on the U.S. military for its economic trickle-down assistance as well as its military power. Korea, devastated by the civil war and still extremely underdeveloped, did not have the access to foreign currency necessary to import raw materials, machinery, and skilled technicians. In relation to this deficit, not only did the U.S. government provide Korea with a huge amount of military aid, but its troops also spent a considerable amount of dollars on entertainment and prostitution in camptowns. In other words, one of the essential nexuses of the flow of dollars into Korea was through the women catering to American servicemen. The Korean government aimed to invest these individually expended GI dollars to develop its industry, by encouraging comfort women to fully gratify U.S. soldiers and extract as much money from them as possible.

In the late 1960s, another group of patrons garnered the government's attention: Japanese tourists. Sex workers who catered to the Japanese were called kisaeng or more specifically, tourist kisaeng (*kwan'gwang kisaeng*). As mentioned in chapter 1, the category of kisaeng transitioned from female servants for male aristocrats in the Chosŏn dynasty to figures with a more ambiguous role in the colonial period, whose work ranged somewhere between entertainment and prostitution. In the late 1960s the term evolved once again into a euphemism to refer to sex workers who served foreign tourists, in particular Japanese men. The Korean government willingly facilitated kisaeng tourism with a variety of measures, to obtain another major currency, the Japanese yen. However, the idea for this policy of sex tourism did not originate in Korea but was a developmental strategy tacitly suggested by the U.S. government. This chapter raises and answers the following questions. How did the Korean government deploy prostitution for national development as another goal of nation building? Why did the U.S. government prescribe (sex) tourism for Korea as a way of economic growth? What contribution did the sex tourism make to Korean economy, and what reactions did it trigger within Korean society? And finally, what impact did that national development have on the domestic sex industry?

CAMPTOWNS AND "PRIMITIVE ACCUMULATION" IN THE TOURIST INDUSTRY

The first tourism policy of the Korean government was initiated in the late 1950s. The Rhee Syngman administration established the Tourism Section under the Ministry of Traffic in 1955. However, Korea did not have enough money, infrastructure, or know-how to properly promote tourism. For instance, in 1960 there were only seventeen hotels nationwide, which could accommodate 1,060 guests.[2] The biggest issue was that Korea was not an attractive tourist spot because of the mass destruction caused by the war and the lingering military tension even after the ceasefire. Given this situation, the government decided that "the easiest tourist targets are UN troops."[3] In fact, the Rhee administration was entirely dependent on the United States for its economic resources, since Korea enjoyed little export income because it refused to normalize its diplomatic relationship with Japan.[4] Thus it desperately attempted to get more money from not only the U.S. government but also its servicemen in Korea. It endeavored to invite them as "tourists" by introducing tourist sites for furloughed troops and even holding lectures for "hospitality women serving foreigners" to improve their service for these soldiers.[5] Despite these efforts, the plan failed to attract foreign soldiers. The USFK refused to establish or designate R&R facilities in Korea for both reasons of military security and the lack of decent amenities. As a result, most American servicemen headed to Japan or Hong Kong for their leave.[6]

Only in 1960 when the U.S. military permitted its soldiers to use R&R facilities in Korea did the government designate three state-operated hotels for R&R and specifically license a few clubs and bars for American troops.[7] Still, this limited range of facilities was not able to absorb enough GI dollars effectively, as the following news article lamented in March 1961:

> There are a couple of special entertainment facilities to serve only foreigners in Seoul. The UN troops stationed in Korea and other foreigners staying in Korea are heading to as far as Japan for their leave, wasting a considerable amount of foreign currency there, and coming back to Korea empty-handed. The purpose of these facilities is to make them spend money by satisfying their taste. . . . The most salient feature of these places might be breathtaking strip dances performed by foreign girls with blond hair and blue eyes. . . . To absorb as much foreign currency as possible, it would be ideal to substitute all consumables for domestic products. To my sorrow, however, the reality here tells a different story: both the alcohol and girls are imports.[8]

The journalist argues that an effective way of "satisfying their [i.e., foreign tourists'] taste," and therefore obtaining dollars from them, is "alcohol and girls," and it calls for the tourist facilities to replace these "imports" with "domestic products" to make more profit. The new military government that seized power in a coup two months later shared the same idea. The military junta led by Park Chung Hee passed the Tourism Promotion Act in August 1961, established the International Tourism Organization in April 1962, and licensed a far greater number of tourist facilities. Still, in the early 1960s the focus of tourism policy remained on American servicemen. In 1963 the number of tourist recreation facilities, that is, bars and clubs for foreign tourists, was 241, accounting for 77.7 percent of all tourist facilities (310) registered by the government. Of these, 204 bars and clubs, that is, 84.6 percent of all tourist recreation facilities, were concentrated in Gyeonggi Province, the

FIGURE 9. Inside a club in a camptown, 1965. *Source:* Kuwabara Shisei, *Naega parabon kyŏktong ŭi han'guk: Kuwabara Shisei han'guk sajin chŏnjip* (Seoul: Nunbit, 2008), 145.

primary area that hosted the U.S. military.[9] This meant that the main guests for this tourist entertainment were American troops, and the government was successful in replacing foreign dancers with Korean entertainers, who were called comfort women (see figure 9). On top of that, the government exempted tax on the beer sold in those places starting in 1964, and it estimated that this new policy resulted in a huge increase in tourism income by more than $1 million a year.[10]

In this way, the military government took advantage of "alcohol and girls" to lure foreign tourists, that is, American troops, into spending more money. This bizarre policy that regarded GIs as tourists and camptowns as tourist sites was a desperate option for Korea, which did not possess any other resources for tourism or developed industry. Despite the unconventional nature of this policy, it worked. In 1964, American servicemen spent over US$12 million on entertainment, which constituted 80 percent of the national income from international tourism and equaled 10 percent of Korea's total amount of exported goods (US$120 million).[11] In other words, military prostitution in camptowns was a significant export industry, that is, a source to obtain foreign currency, and therefore comfort women were pivotal agents of national industry. A news article evaluated the contribution made by so-called Western princesses, that is, prostitutes for American servicemen, to the Korean economy:

> These Western princesses have magnificent power. Although they are like flowers that have bloomed in the shade [i.e., within the socially marginalized camptowns], ironically they have become pivotal workers in obtaining foreign currency, which is the top priority of our nation. The dollars they earn dominate black markets, becoming an informal source of foreign currency in the nation. If each of the 16,000 western princesses earns at least 50 dollars a month, the total revenue amounts to about one million dollars [a month]. . . . They also get paid with goods such as cigarettes, liquor, gum, and clothes, which many Koreans badly want. . . . As a result, these Western princesses are a formidable economic resource for our nation.[12]

This conception of comfort women as "pivotal workers" recognized their importance as a crucial national workforce that played a tremendous role in obtaining dollars in the early 1960s, when Korea's tourism industry was not developed enough to attract any actual foreign tourists.

Karl Marx has referred to the sixteenth-century Europe from which nascent capitalism originated as existing in a state of "so-called primitive accumulation."[13] Silvia Federici reinterprets primitive accumulation and the transition from feudalism to capitalism in early modern Europe from a feminist perspective. Women were excluded from many areas of production, and therefore prostitution proliferated across Europe. As Federici states, "Once women's activities were defined as non-work, women's labor began to appear as a natural resource, available to all, no less than the air we breathe or the water we drink."[14] In a somewhat parallel manner, the Korean state under the Park regime utilized this "natural resource" of women's sexuality as a means of accumulation for economic development. As Marx said, such crudely acquired capital "comes dripping from head to toe, from every pore, with blood and dirt."[15] Following this gritty perspective, we might consider Korea's tourism industry was born dripping from head to toe in beer and sperm.

KISAENG TOURISM AS A JOINT ENTERPRISE BETWEEN KOREA AND THE UNITED STATES

A new phase of tourism started during the latter half of the 1960s. With the normalization of diplomatic relations between Korea and Japan in 1965, the Japanese, Korea's nearest and richest neighbors in Asia as well as its recently deposed colonizers, resumed visiting Korea, now as tourists. The number of Japanese tourists skyrocketed from 5,110 in 1965 to 363,879 in 1975, a seventyfold increase in just ten years. As a result, the proportion of the Japanese among foreign tourists increased from 15.3 to 57.5 percent during the same period. Thanks to this massive influx of Japanese tourists, over one million foreign tourists visited Korea in 1978 for the first time in its history, and 61.8 percent of them were Japanese. Accordingly, tourism revenue soared almost twentyfold in thirteen years, from US$21 million in 1965 to US$408 million in 1978.[16]

There are several factors that gave rise to this explosive increase in Japanese tourists from the late 1960s. The first, of course, was the political reconciliation between Korea and Japan in 1965. Park Chung Hee attempted to normalize diplomatic relations with Japan immediately following his election as president in 1963. The U.S. government persuaded him to push ahead with this policy, arguing that Japanese economic aid to Korea and Korea's access to Japanese markets after reconciliation would be essential for the rapid economic growth of Korea. Despite a series of massive nationalist demonstrations against normalization, the government finally reached the Treaty on Basic Relations with Japan in June 1965, which was ratified by the National Assembly in August of the same year.[17] In response, Japan offered Korea economic aid amounting to US$300 million along with a US$200 million loan at low interest as a reparation for its colonial rule. This fund was spent on raw materials for the textile, fertilizer, and chemical industries among other investments, and to build economic infrastructure for steel and manufacturing production, along with dams, railways, and highways. As expected, this aid made a huge contribution to accelerating Korea's economic development. Trade between the two countries also expanded dramatically, but this was a double-edged sword. Although Korea's exports to Japan increased steadily, these were always far exceeded by Japanese imports. As a result, Korea suffered from chronic trade deficits vis-à-vis Japan. In this situation, tourism emerged as a very useful solution to overcome the trade imbalance. For instance, the Korean government officially recognized tourism as "the only industry to make a surplus, and thus to reduce the trade deficit," incorporating it in the third five-year economic development plan (1972–1976) as one of the state's strategic industries.[18]

The second factor is Korea's kisaeng tourism as a continuum of the alcohol and girls strategy of the early 1960s. In the early days of the Republic of Korea, the socially elite high-ranking officials and businessmen were enthusiastic about the staging of banquets served by kisaeng. Even during the height of the violence and chaos of the Korean War, kisaeng houses (*yojŏng*) were filled with corrupt bureaucrats, high-ranking military officers, and politicians, a fact that infuriated the Korean people.[19] Park Chung Hee, who ironically had declared it his mission to root out all forms of old corruption and decadence through military order, had himself become highly enamored of kisaeng parties. Not only professional kisaeng but famous actresses and singers were called to the parties to sexually serve the VIPs, and a lot of important political decisions were made within yojŏng.[20] Given the pervasiveness of this practice, it is perhaps unsurprising that government officials came up with the idea to entice overseas tourists by transforming their own recreational culture into a form of tourist attraction. In 1968 the Park administration officially announced "a new plan to develop Korea's traditional kisaeng houses and kisaeng into tourist programs."[21] An Tong-Jun, the newly inaugurated president of Korea's International Tourism Organization in 1971, officially recognized Korea's traditional "clothes, food, alcohol, and women," that is, kisaeng, as an excellent means of promoting tourism.[22] This program was carried out immediately. On June 4, 1973, the popular American periodical *Time* described a kisaeng party in an article entitled "South Korea: The Seoul of Hospitality":

> [A] typical party begins when the kisaeng, each bearing a numbered tag, flutter into a banquet room filled with an equal number of Japanese males. Matching their numbers to those borne by the guests, the giggling girls kneel and begin serving food and drinks. A band plays, but the guests never quite enter into the party spirit. Instead, after an hour or so of eating and nervous fidgeting by the guests, the kisaeng leave, change swiftly into bell-bottoms or miniskirts, then lead their partners to a line of cabs and off to a hotel.[23]

The final factor is Japanese masculine culture. Like their Korean counterparts, Japanese male elites historically used geisha houses not only to discuss military, political, and business agendas but also to establish fraternal bonds and trust. With rapid economic growth in the 1950s and 1960s, this tradition was transformed into "corporate entertaining" at various venues including hostess bars, geisha restaurants, and cabaret clubs and spread to ordinary middle-class men.[24] In addition, as overseas travel was liberalized in 1964, this corporate entertainment was expanded to neighboring countries such as Korea and Taiwan. Throughout the 1970s, over 90 percent of Japanese tourists to Korea were men. Some Japanese companies even offered workers overseas trips as a bonus. The most popular type of trip was the all-inclusive package tour, which incorporated not only flights, sightseeing, and hotels, but also prostitution.[25]

Therefore, while kisaeng tourism must have appealed to almost all foreign male tourists in general, the primary participants were Japanese men. According to a survey conducted by the Ministry of Traffic in the early 1970s, Japanese tourists' favorite destination was kisaeng houses, followed by palaces and temples, whereas Westerners preferred markets, rural villages, and Panmunjom in the Demilitarized Zone.[26] Travel agencies in Japan promoted trips to Korea under banners such as "complete kisaeng service, a man's paradise" or "the charm of a South Korean kisaeng party."[27] In fact, this kisaeng culture had been heavily consumed by Japanese male travelers or elites in Korea during the colonial period.[28] As a result, this reinvention of postcolonial kisaeng tourism satisfied not only Japanese men's exotic sexual fantasies about Korean women but also aroused nostalgic sentiments about the lost colony and memories of the past empire. Matsui Yayori, a Japanese feminist journalist, interviewed a Japanese sex tourist who said, "In South Korea the spirit of rendering oneself completely to a man still exists among the women, and their exhaustive service is irresistible." What he found in the "man's paradise" was akin to the dream of colonial female subjects ready to submit to their master's desires. In the Japanese male tourist's imagination, the docile and backward Korean women stood in contrast to self-interested, modern Japanese women. Another of Matsui's interviewees lamented: "You can't find a decent geisha in Japan, even at a hot springs resort. They're not very friendly and a rip-off, too. South Korea's much better."[29]

To meet the demand of Japanese tourists, the number of kisaeng increased in famous tourist spots such as Seoul, Busan, Gyeongju, and Jeju. There are no official statistics that show exactly how many kisaeng operated in the late 1960s and 1970s, but news articles estimated that around five to eight thousand women worked as kisaeng.[30] The number of hotels to accommodate tourists also skyrocketed: from 37 with 1,837 rooms in 1965 to 130 with 15,327 rooms in 1978.[31] The surplus of international tourism amounted to over US$200 million in 1978.[32] Considering the trade deficit was US$1,937 million in the same year, tourism made a considerable contribution to reducing the imbalance in international payments.[33] In this regard, kisaeng, along with camptown women, were hidden but essential contributors to Korea's economic growth.

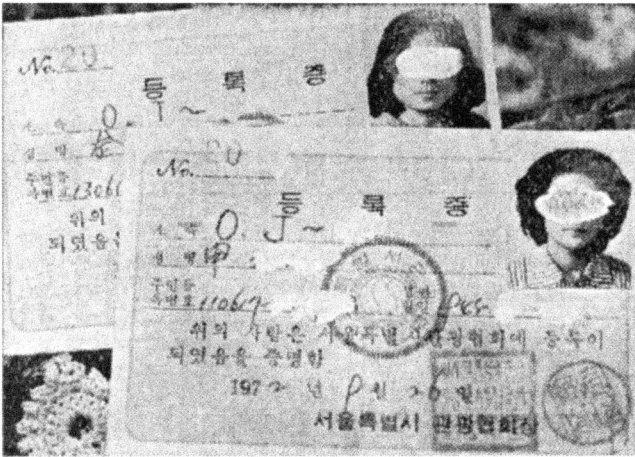

FIGURE 10. ID cards issued to kisaeng working in Seoul, 1972. *Source: Kyŏngyang sinmun,* October 5, 1972.

To extract more profit from tourism, the government set a target number of tourists annually and put pressure on travel agencies to achieve these goals. For instance, a target was set of 1,050,000 tourists in 1978, and the actual number of tourists was 1,070,0000, surpassing the goal. If the travel agencies failed to achieve their allocated targets, the government stopped offering a variety of benefits to them and sometimes even confiscated their licenses. As a result, these commercial agencies did almost everything to entice overseas tourists, and kisaeng tourism was a certain and convenient means to do so.[34] To encourage tourists' consumption, the government also exempted taxes on entertainment, food, and drink for foreigners intermittently from 1964.[35] In 1972 it also pressured the Korea Tourism Association to register kisaeng and issue them certificates, that is, ID cards, allowing only women carrying these cards to serve at kisaeng houses and visit hotels with their clients (see figure 10). This measure was implemented on the pretext of guaranteeing the high quality of their service, but the ID cards were criticized as being essentially nothing more than prostitutes' licenses.[36]

Moreover, the government attempted to make the kisaeng a safe and submissive workforce operating smoothly in the service of the nation, and the registered kisaeng were subject to sexually transmitted infection testing once a week.[37] In 1969, the government reinforced the compulsory STI testing of sex workers including kisaeng, by enacting the Regulation on Sexually Transmitted Disease Checkups, a regulation that introduced punishment of prostitutes who evaded registration and periodical examinations. The government and the Tourism Promotion Association also held regular lectures for kisaeng. Speaking in the early 1970s, Ms. Kim, the owner of a kisaeng house and former chief of Kisaeng House Section, a Seoul branch of the Tourism Promotion Association, explained the themes of the lectures:

> We frequently invite related experts as lecturers to improve the quality of hostesses' service. We thoroughly train them to be cultivated and well-mannered. We are also striving to make them submit to regular health checkups, prevent them from demanding excessive tips, and instill in them a firm resolution to devote themselves to the nation and sacrifice themselves for it.[38]

These "patriotic" *hanbok*-clad kisaeng were unique to Korea. However, kisaeng tourism was not entirely an original invention of Korea but related to the wider range of developmental strategies that the U.S. government prescribed for "Third World" countries during the Cold War. As Thanh-dam Truong has clarified, the U.S. government from the late 1950s, and in particular the U.S. Departments of Commerce and State, anticipated that international tourism would contribute to leveling the international balance of payments by helping developing countries absorb surplus income and capital from the West and therefore aid the full integration of such countries into the global capitalist system. The first manifestation of this vision was *The Future of Tourism in the Pacific and Far East* of 1961, commissioned and published by the Department of Commerce.[39] In the foreword to the report, Luther H. Hodges, the secretary of commerce, argued that "tourists bring wealth into a country—wealth in the form of good will and understanding; wealth in the form of foreign exchange, vitally needed for international trade," and emphasized the policy of the U.S. government as being "to assist free nations . . . in order that they remain economically viable and politically free."[40] This argument shows that international tourism was not only an economic means to develop Asian and Pacific countries but also a political project to contain the influence of communism in the region and to help it remain "politically free."

The Future of Tourism suggested diverse ideas and strategies to promote tourism in Korea. One of the tips was that

> the development of things to do and see at night, particularly in the Seoul area, will be an important part of Korea's tourism development program if tourists are to be held for an average stay of 2 to 3 days. Wherever possible, such entertainment should be included as part of a package tour of Korea.[41]

Although the report did not mention what night entertainment would be, it is not difficult to imagine that Korean government officials came up with their focus on kisaeng tourism following this advice.

In 1965 the U.S. Agency of International Development sponsored a travel expert named Morton D. Kauffman to conduct more specific research on tourism in Korea. His report, *Tourism to Korea*, was published by the United States Operations Mission to Korea in 1966. This report suggested the development of the kisaeng house dinner experience into a tourist program, a focus offered in a more explicit tone than that of *The Future of Tourism*:

> I think it most desirable that a film be made of a kesaeng [*sic*] house dinner, from beginning to end. The men entering, then the bow at the door as the girls come in, the serving of the food, the exchange of cups, the girls helping and feeding the men, the games, the dance music, the singers and drum players would make a film ideal for showing abroad. This is one of the most potentially influential tourism subjects available for distribution abroad.[42]

The scene Kauffman described is akin to that previously cited from the *Time* article of 1973. It testifies to the fact that the formula of the kisaeng party was established in the mid-1960s at the latest and repeated across numerous kisaeng houses with few modifications. In the preface, Kauffman noted that he had offered recommendations to the Korean people since his arrival, and many of his suggestions were already reflected in tourism policies even before the report was published. He also showed satisfaction that the president and the prime minister paid attention to his suggestions, praising Koreans' "shoulder-to-the-wheel attitude."[43] Of course, Americans did not devise kisaeng tourism. What Americans did was to give Koreans the confidence and motivation to push ahead with this "most potentially influential tourism subject." In this regard, kisaeng tourism can be considered a joint enterprise supported by the two governments of Korea and the United States.

THE SEOUL OLYMPIC GAMES
AS THE APOGEE OF SEX TOURISM

The increase in overseas tourists slowed down at the end of the 1970s and early 1980s owing to a series of political disruptions and ongoing economic turmoil, such as the second oil crisis, the assassination of President Park, the subsequent military coup staged by Major General Chun Doo-hwan (Chŏn

Tu-Hwan), and the resulting Gwangju Uprising and massacre in 1980. The number of tourists rebounded in the mid-1980s, partly because of the Seoul Asian Games in 1986, and more importantly, the Seoul Olympic Games in 1988. Consequent to these events the number of foreign tourists doubled, from one million in 1978 to two million in 1988. The income from tourism also increased eightfold, from US$408 million in 1978 to $US3.26 billion in 1988.[44]

Still in the 1980s, over half of the tourists in Korea were Japanese, and over 80 percent of them were men, while about 60 percent of tourists of other nationalities were men. For instance, in 1988 Japanese male tourists numbered about nine hundred thousand, 43 percent of all overseas tourists. The Korean government continued to depend on kisaeng tourism as a means to appeal not only to Japanese men but to all male tourists. For instance, the *Sporting News*, a global sports magazine, issued a special supplement regarding the Seoul Olympics in October 1985. It introduced its readers to Korean food with a photo of a hotel dinner, at which women in hanbok served and fed Western tourists, mostly men. It was reported that the Korean government assisted the journal to cover the story and take photos. The exact reason the government did so is unknown, but at the time it was widely blamed within Korea for attempting to take advantage of the kisaeng image to entice overseas tourists for the Olympics.[45]

As mentioned, kisaeng tourism was already known in the West, as the *Time* news article of 1973 shows. The Seoul Olympic Games provided momentum to further propagate it to Westerners. In October 1988, when the Olympics were held, the *Hustler*, a pornographic magazine, published an article entitled "Hustler's Olympic Goer's Guide to Korean Sex," which started with a colorful image of four naked women in the flaming Olympic Torch. The article was written as a rough guide for sex tourists, covering the prostitution venues in Seoul such as Itaewon and Hyehwadong, a well-known camptown and a kisaeng tourism area respectively, and thus was full of vulgar and abhorrent descriptions of Korean women grounded in misogyny and orientalism. Nevertheless, it contained some acute and pithy observations that are difficult to immediately dismiss. For instance, the writer argued that "centuries of foreign domination have produced a society where prostitution is an ingrained institution."[46] While there was some element of truth in this perspective, recent authoritarian administrations, alongside a thoroughly modern history of foreign domination, had in fact served to render prostitution an essential contemporary institution, encouraged in support of both national security and development. In this regard, the article also keenly noted the undeniable fact that "the Korean tradition of the kisaeng, or geisha, was effectively updated to modern times[, and Korean women are] available to all comers, black and white, foreign and domestic."[47]

To provide safe sex to this visiting international array of "all comers," the administration of President Chun Doo-hwan made substantial preparations. For example, it enacted the Rule on Health Checkups of Employees in Sanitary Field in 1984. Belying this vague gender-neutral title, this legally stipulated rule was in fact a prostitution policy, which expanded over twofold the scope of female service workers subject to regular STI testing, from 68,793 in 1984 to 145,802 in 1985. The targets included not only existing categories such as "special entertainers," which had replaced comfort women in 1978, and hospitality women, but also new groups such as "those working in a motel or inn," "those working in a ginseng tearoom or [just] a tearoom," and "helpers in a Turkish bath [steam bath]." In the late 1980s the government conducted over two million STI examinations on such women annually to "prepare for large-scale international events."[48] This means that registered female service workers were tested about sixteen to eighteen times annually on average. In this regard, the Seoul Olympic Games can be considered as offering the climax for sex tourism in Korea, with the tradition continuing to linger by 1994 when the newly elected civilian government officially put an end to kisaeng tourism.[49]

THE CRITIQUE OF SEXUAL IMPERIALISM AND THE SILENCES OF THE KISAENG

As we have seen, from 1965, just two decades after Korea was liberated from Japan, Japanese men had again returned to Korea, albeit this time as sex tourists rather than as colonizers. In this period, successive Korean military governments encouraged female citizens to sexually gratify these visitors in the name of national development. The obvious fact of this situation aroused feelings of national shame and insult to many Koreans, many of whom had experienced and vividly remembered the injustices of Japanese colonial rule. In response, progressive feminists took action to stop the kisaeng tourism policy. Contrary to *Hustler*'s diagnosis that "prostitution is an ingrained institution" in Korea, they argued that not only kisaeng tourism but also prostitution itself were completely antithetical to Koreanness, that is, the essence of Korea's national identity. Why then did kisaeng tourism prevail to the degree that it did? Their answer was clear: the twin influences of Japanese imperialism and the immoral Korean military government were the culprits.

This anti-kisaeng tourism campaign emerged in July 1973 and was spearheaded by the Korea Church Women United (KCWU). This moment was one of the darkest chapters in South Korea's democratic history because of the October Yusin (October Restoration) of 1972, Park Chung Hee's second coup d'état that enabled his lifelong presidency. Many intellectuals and college students protested, and the government responded severely, with imprisonment, torture, and even execution and assassination. One of the leaders of the dissent was Yi U-Jŏng, the president of the KCWU. She had been a feminist professor of theology but was expelled from her college in 1970 for publicly rebuking the dictatorship. After being dismissed she committed herself to the anti-government movement more earnestly, and one of her activities was the anti-kisaeng tourism campaign. In July 1973 she and her colleagues proposed to place kisaeng tourism on their activist agenda at the first joint conference held by Christian leaders in Korea and Japan since Korea's liberation.[50] This conference provided the momentum to help forge feminist solidarity between Korean and Japanese Christian women against kisaeng tourism. They cooperated to conduct field research into kisaeng tourism, hold a series of conferences to fully expose the practice, spread press releases to denounce it, and staged demonstrations to criticize Japanese tourists at airports. Their activism had wide repercussions in both Korea and Japan, and a wide spectrum of women's organizations joined the movement. For instance, on February 26, 1974, a conference on kisaeng tourism was held at the YWCA hall in Seoul, which over five hundred participants from ten women's organizations attended.[51]

However, the campaign was short-lived due to the government's severe suppression of protesters. After the large conference on February 26, Yi U-Jŏng suffered from constant police surveillance and threatening phone calls telling her to stop the campaign. Then in April 1974, there was a period of sweeping political persecution, during which around two hundred dissidents were imprisoned and eight were ultimately unjustly executed. This massive roundup and persecution of dissenters was enforced under the Yusin Constitution, which was enacted in 1972 to enable Park Chung Hee's lifelong dictatorship. It guaranteed the president the ability to declare so-called emergency measures (*kin'gŭp choch'i*) to suspend citizen's basic rights without the consent of the National Assembly. In particular, Emergency Measure

No. 4 was enforced on April 3, 1974, with the specific purpose of arresting and punishing anti-government students and related dissidents.[52] This horrific oppression was justified on the pretext of protecting the security of the state and the constitution. With memories of the Korean War still lingering, the military dictatorship was able to falsely portray these dissenters as national enemies who desired to overturn the Republic of Korea and benefit North Korea.

In this crackdown, Yi U-Jŏng was also taken by the police, on charges of allegedly passing political funds to college students who conspired to create a rebellion. She was interrogated by government officials and tortured with sleep deprivation for a week to find out about her activities, including the anti-kisaeng tourism campaign.[53] Even though she was ultimately freed, the campaign to oppose kisaeng tourism was completely disrupted and only revived in the early 1980s, when the Chun administration temporarily loosened its suppression of political dissent. In 1983 the KCWU published its report on kisaeng tourism in four famous tourist spots, Seoul, Gyeongju, Busan, and Jeju. When a photo of a kisaeng party was publicized in the *Sporting News* in 1985, the KCWU sent a letter of protest to the government, which responded perfunctorily with a promise not to repeat such a case.[54] To expand public opposition against kisaeng tourism and therefore to prevent the military regime from promoting it in relation to the Asian Games and the Olympics, it organized two large-scale conferences on kisaeng tourism: Prostitution Issue and Women's Movement in 1986 and Women and Tourism Culture in 1988.[55]

Despite this feminist campaign, the government did not give up utilizing kisaeng as a tourist attraction until after the Olympic Games. However, these feminist activists did succeed in damaging the moral legitimacy of successive military administrations, which ultimately yielded positive effects. In 1993 Kim Young-sam (Kim Yŏng-Sam), a leading dissenter against the dictatorship, was inaugurated as the first civilian president, following thirty-two years of military rule. The Kim administration attempted to root out the legacies of the military regime, one of which was the kisaeng tourism policy. In 1994 the government proclaimed the end of kisaeng tourism, arguing that it had damaged Korea's global reputation.[56] The unprecedented economic boom in the late 1980s and early 1990s also contributed to the termination of the policy. The GDP of Korea skyrocketed, from US$3 billion in 1965 to US$100 billionin 1985 to US$464 billion in 1994.[57] This immense economic expansion must have given the government confidence to concentrate on its global reputation as a developed, "normal" nation not dependent on sex tourism for economic growth. In this way, although the anti-kisaeng tourism campaign officially ended in 1988, it ultimately came to fruition in 1994.

The anti-kisaeng tourism campaign was also of historical significance for other reasons. First, it shows how feminist activism against prostitution had been revived in a quarter of a century since the abolition campaign in the mid-1940s. As analyzed in chapter 1, while socialist women took the lead in the abolition campaign that was instituted under the U.S. military rule of Korea, they were finally defeated by nationalist women, who had a conservative attitude toward prostitutes and blamed them as internal enemies of the nascent nation. Many of these nationalist female leaders then collaborated with authoritarian administrations afterward and were hesitant to criticize any government policies. In contrast, the anti-kisaeng tourism campaigners in the 1970s and 1980s publicly opposed the oppressive dictatorship and its sexist, immoral policies. They conducted research on kisaeng houses and hotels, the venues that forbade or strongly discouraged "chaste women" from visiting.[58] Based on this research, they attempted to reconceptualize kisaeng tourism and prostitution from a feminist perspective. For instance, at the anti-kisaeng tourism conference in 1986, Yi Mi-Gyŏng, a feminist activist who would become a member of the National Assembly in the late 1990s, defined prostitution as "the most severe form of discrimination, oppression, and exploitation against women."[59] Son Tŏk-Su, a feminist professor of social welfare and another lecturer at the conference, referred to kisaeng tourism as "sexual imperialism."[60] After this conference, similar conceptualizations of kisaeng tourism, such as it being an "imperialist sexual invasion" or "sexual colonization," were widely circulated.[61] In this regard, the anti-kisaeng tourism campaign can be considered one primary starting point of the progressive women's movement in Korea, which was positioned between liberal and radical feminism.

Second, the campaigners addressed kisaeng tourism not as a single issue but as part of the long history of sexual oppression suffered by Korean women at the hands of the Japanese, which they traced back to the Japanese military comfort women system. In the report of 1983, the KCWU called kisaeng tourism "a new version of Women's Volunteer Labor Corps (yŏja chŏngsindae)."[62] Termed chŏngsindae (teishintai in Japanese), this idea literally refers to the people decidedly devoting or sacrificing themselves to their mission for the sake of the Japanese emperor and the empire. Japan holistically mobilized its subjects, both at home and in the colonies, in the name of chŏngsindae during the Second World War, which resulted in Korean girls and women being taken to munitions factories both in Korea and Japan. However, some girls and women were deceived into joining the yŏja chŏngsindae but instead abducted or trafficked to military "comfort stations" for battlefields. As a result, many Koreans equated this notion of chŏngsindae with the forced mobilization of girls and women and thus the historical crime of Japanese military comfort women. Therefore, kisaeng tourism reminded the KCWU women of the painful colonial history of comfort women, and they considered kisaeng to also be the victims of Japanese sexual imperialism. In addition, at the KCWU conference in 1988, Yun Chŏng-Ok, a feminist activist and professor of English literature, reported on her field research on tracing Korean comfort women in Japan. As a contemporary witness during the 1940s to the existence of Japanese military comfort women, Yun's desperate search for survivors and their historical traces stunned the audience, and this moment can be considered as providing a major impetus to the contemporary Korean campaign for justice for Japanese military comfort women.[63]

The participants at the KCWU conferences also discussed the issue of prostitution for American servicemen and Korean men. For instance, Yu Pong-Nim, a feminist activist working in support of camptown women, lectured about the history of camptowns for the U.S. military at the conference in 1986. A woman who had worked in a red-light district for Korean men was also invited as a speaker at the conference in 1988, to give voice to her past experiences and her new activities in attempting to make a haven for her former fellows. In this regard, the anti-kisaeng tourism campaign functioned as an incubator to form feminist solidarity among the diverse range of activists attempting to combat sexual oppression in Korea, as well as helping to encourage and generate a new trend of activism. It also contributed to building international feminist solidarity. The 1988 conference invited about 120 feminist activists from nine countries, making kisaeng tourism a global feminist issue.[64] The anti-kisaeng tourism campaign itself was born from the feminist coalition between Korean and Japanese Christian women, which would provide fertile ground for the development of international activism in support of comfort women enslaved by the Japanese military from the early 1990s.

Despite these contributions, the anti-kisaeng tourism campaign had several limitations. First, the campaigners attempted to conjure up or reinvent female chastity as a national tradition. In denouncing the damage that kisaeng tourism inflicted, they in turn emphasized how pure both their nation and women had been before this Japanese sexual invasion. This rhetoric is clearly shown within the following invitation letter for a conference, which was held by the KCWU and several other women's associations on December 28, 1973:

> The tradition of Korean women's pure chastity is helplessly collapsing. Our pride, the purity of our nation, has been degenerated into a topic of disgraceful gossip. The heartbreaking scandal that Korea is a den of whores is spreading. We lament about the reality of defiling our daughters' chastity under the pretext of obtaining foreign currency. We organized a conference to protect the chastity of our nation and the chastity of our daughters. Please attend it and work together![65]

In this way, the campaigners played into the conservative discourse that not only privileged female chastity but also equated it with ideas of national purity. The statement also suggests the campaigners' ambivalent feelings toward kisaeng. On the one hand, they viewed kisaeng as the victims of Japanese sexual imperialism. On the other hand, they considered that kisaeng were defying national tradition and pride by abandoning their chastity and submitting to former colonizers. Interestingly, in the cited excerpt, the campaigners contrasted victims with collaborators, referring to them with different names: "our daughters" and "whores." Such rhetoric was then successively repeated. For instance, the KCWU's 1983 report on kisaeng tourism referred to the kisaeng as "daughters" in depicting their suffering: "The daughters of our land are being sold at a ridiculously low price and faced with harsh ordeals."[66] In contrast, it described them as pathologically flawed beings due to their endeavors to gratify the Japanese: "How many are the kisaeng girls who are frantically following Japanese tourists at night?"[67] One poem in a pamphlet on the topic, which a liberal Christian organization published to denounce kisaeng tourism in 1983, even called kisaeng "the toadstools of the night, soullessly and blindly pursuing greed for money."[68] Such examples illustrate the irony that this activism for the sake of the kisaeng also regularly engaged in demonizing the women who did not fit the ideal victim stereotype.

Second, the campaigners regarded themselves as mothers acting to save their fallen daughters, the kisaeng. The preface from the booklet produced to accompany the KCWU's 1986 conference illustrates their conception of this familial hierarchy:

Kisaeng tourism which rapes the daughters of our land in the name of obtaining foreign currency is officially included in the package tour programs of travel agencies. As a human being, and as a mother who raises children, we cannot disregard our daughters' crisis, which would be exacerbated with the massive influx of tourists [owing to the Olympic Games] in 1988.[69]

In his historical analysis of the British abolitionist campaign in the late nineteenth century, Alan Hunt argues that abolitionist feminists were preoccupied with their moral obligation to exercise the "maternal authority of middle-class ladies over unruly working-class girls." He calls this tendency "maternal feminism."[70] Similar to their predecessors in the nineteenth-century United Kingdom, Korean middle-aged feminists from the middle-class also wanted to rescue impoverished young girls from the sex industry. In rendering themselves and the kisaeng as "mothers" and "daughters" respectively, they imagined the nation as an enlarged family. In this imaginary purview, the military government was conceived as the "bad father (*mon-nan abi*)" forcing his daughters to engage in prostitution with the former colonizers.[71]

Finally, this imaginary familial hierarchy both denied the agency of kisaeng and worked to maintain their silence. On the one hand, as the victims of sexual imperialism and the daughters of the nation, kisaeng were considered to lack agency, just waiting to be rescued, while being represented by their feminist mothers. Therefore, they either could not speak for themselves or there was no need for them to speak since these feminists always spoke on their behalf. On the other hand, as collaborators in the practice of sex tourism, kisaeng were conceived to have excessive agency relative to their "irresponsibly trafficking in" Japanese tourists' "fantasies and commodification."[72] Thus, in respect to both their helplessness and malevolence, the kisaeng's qualifications for national membership were problematized, and their right to speak was limited or negated. In fact, during these conferences the campaigners invited not a single kisaeng to contribute their own narrative or voice to the proceedings. These women did not and/or could not speak.

In this sense, the 1988 conference was exceptional. One of the speakers was a woman who had worked in a red-light district for Korean men. She criticized the hypocrisy that underlay the divisive conception of chaste women and prostitutes, arguing that in patriarchal Korean society the latter simply prostituted themselves to many men while the former prostituted themselves to just one man, their husbands. Her speech deeply moved the audience, making them feel sisterhood with the women engaged in prostitution, whom they had thought of as fallen women and totally different from them.[73] As a result, the familial hierarchy between mothers and daughters was replaced with a more egalitarian relationship between sisters. Still, the speaker was not a kisaeng as such. She had engaged in the sex industry that catered specifically to domestic men, but more importantly, she had left prostitution to become a feminist activist herself, which was probably the main reason she was invited to the conference. At the same conference, a questionnaire survey on kisaeng in Jeju was presented. It was based on demographic questions about the kisaeng such as their age and birthplace, medical history, and grievances about the profession, without asking their opinion on kisaeng tourism itself or the anti-kisaeng campaign.[74] As such, kisaeng were again not entitled to speak for themselves, even within the feminist discourse.

Cynthia Enloe maintains that "nationalism typically has sprung from masculinized memory, masculinized humiliation, and masculinized hope."[75] In a similar vein, most Korean feminist critiques of Korean nationalism usually target its male-oriented fantasies and practices.[76] However, the case of the anti-kisaeng tourism campaign shows that a feminist discourse is not inherently immune to nationalism. In this nationalist discourse, female chastity functioned as a synecdoche of the purity and pride of the beloved nation. What is interesting is that the campaigners not only accepted the family model of nationalism but also reconstructed it to suit their own agenda. While the nation is often imagined as an enlarged family dominated by the patriarch, these feminists positioned themselves as heroic mothers working to protect their daughters from the evil father. However, in this new version of Korean nationalism, the kisaeng as defiled and/or fallen daughters had to remain silent.

However, this does not mean that kisaeng were entirely without voice. Like other subaltern groups they spoke, but elites largely did not, or could not, listen. On May 31, 1973, a Korean newspaper reported on kisaeng tourism, translating the 1973 *Time* article I cited previously:

> Correspondent Chang asked a kisaeng who earns two hundred thousand won per month what she thought about the Japanese, she replied. "There are some whom I can endure. However, we must work not only for ourselves and our families but also for our country's future. Our country needs a lot of foreign currency for its economic development."[77]

In this way, most Koreans were only able to listen to this kisaeng's voice in double translation, first from Korean into English and then from English to Korean. We cannot know what she felt when she said, "we must work," whether it was frustration, lamentation, resolution, or something else. Nor can we know whether her comment "our country needs a lot of foreign currency" was her genuine opinion or the result of self-censorship due to the unexpected situation in which she had to speak to a journalist on behalf of the kisaeng community. In another news article eight years later, another kisaeng had a rare chance to speak with more clarity: "Miss L (21-year-old) from S kisaeng house emphasized: 'There are about five thousand girls in our situation in Seoul. We are working here mostly because of our poor family backgrounds. Despite this, our minds are not corrupt, not Japanized.'"[78]

Here we can notice the gap between the feminist representation of kisaeng and this speaker's voice. Whereas feminists depicted kisaeng as the persecuted daughters of the nation or pathological collaborators with Japanese exploiters, this speaker considered herself to be a worker who could not help but cater to Japanese tourists because of her poverty, but who also tried to keep her self-dignity as a Korean. In this way, her language was quite different from that of the feminists who believed themselves to be struggling for her sake.

According to Yang Yun-Se, a former economic secretary in the Presidential Secretariat in 1973, some kisaeng even attempted to organize a nude demonstration against the anti-kisaeng tourism campaign. He recalled that the kisaeng were outraged by the feminists, who they thought could not understand their situation, since they "grew up sheltered by well-off parents." Afraid of a global scandal if the kisaeng had really waged a nude demonstration, he, as a representative of the government, not only persuaded them against such an action earnestly but also mobilized the police to prevent their protest.[79] This unknown episode shows that the feminists' anti-kisaeng tourism discourses triggered the outright antipathy of at least some kisaeng. And even though their attempt failed, kisaeng's naked bodies were, in this example, their powerfully chosen language to confront feminists' rhetoric. The class gap among women, which never appeared in the feminist discourse as an issue for critical self-reflection, was at the heart of the kisaeng's resentment. Ironically, how to bridge this gap remains a crucial issue in Korean feminism today, as chapter 5 and the epilogue will show.

In the late 1980s, Korea witnessed a period of dramatic economic development, a moment of substantive national expansion that was often referred to in Korea as "the biggest growth since *Tan'gun*," the mythical progenitor of the Korean nation five millennia ago. Per capita income increased more than three times over the decade, from US$1,715 in 1980 to US$5,817 in 1989, a growth that ushered in a new era of mass consumption.[80] The economic policies of the Chun administration also greatly encouraged people's consumption. In stark contrast to the previous regime of Park Chung Hee, which forced Koreans to practice austerity and saving to accumulate the domestic capital necessary for industrial development, the Chun government shifted from extreme retrenchment in the late 1970s and early 1980s to economic stimulus from 1983, which paved the way for the mass expansion of private consumption.[81] The triple favorable conditions within the Korean economy (low interest rates, low oil prices, and the weakness of the Korean won) caused an unprecedented economic growth rate of over 10 percent from 1986, and huge trade surpluses for the first time in Korean history. Consequently, in the 1980s Korean people started to buy more consumer durables (such as televisions, washing machines, refrigerators, and cars), based on their increased income.[82] The service economy to satisfy consumer demands also underwent unprecedented expansion by 9.7 percent on average throughout the 1980s.[83] All these economic conditions opened a new phase in the history of prostitution, based on the explosive growth of the adult entertainment industry for Korean men.

As examined in chapter 1, prostitution for Korean men was prevalent in Korea from the late nineteenth century onward and was legalized with the introduction of authorization-regulation policy in the colonial period. Despite the abolition of the authorization-regulation system and introduction of prohibition in 1948, prostitution not only for foreigners but also for Koreans continued to expand due to extreme poverty, gender disparity, and social confusion in the aftermath of the Korean War. While elite Korean men satisfied their sexual appetites and established political and economic networks at kisaeng houses, low-class men visited brothels for brief sexual encounters or overnight stays or frequented cheap bars served by barmaids or inns to use call-girl services. These establishments were clustered within the red-light districts that formed around train stations and downtown back streets, areas that were entirely distinct from the camptowns that served the U.S. military and the high-end kisaeng-staffed restaurants that catered to Korean elites or

Japanese tourists. In Seoul, Jongno sam-ga and the areas around main transport hubs, such as the Seoul, Yongsan, and Cheongnyangni train stations, were some of the notorious red-light districts frequented by relatively low-class Koreans. The prostitutes catering to Koreans were often called *ch'angnyŏ*, a term that differentiated them from the *wianbu* who served American troops and the kisaeng who were oriented toward Japanese tourists. According to the statistics of the Supreme Prosecutors' Office, the number of ch'angnyŏ under government surveillance in 1963 totaled 7,199, while the number of wianbu was 13,947.[84] This shows that the primary focus of government control was on comfort women for the U.S. military, as the nation's most important ally and state guest. Considering that many low-status prostitutes presumably evaded government supervision, the total number of ch'angnyŏ for Koreans must have been much larger than the official statistics.

From the late 1960s, a new form of prostitution emerged bridging the gap between high-class kisaeng houses and cheap brothels. These sex workers were associated with a new space for meeting their clients called "salons" or "room salons."[85] Equipped with Western-styled interior decoration and female service workers called *hostis*, that is, "hostesses," the room salons appealed to newly emerged middle-class men in the cities. The hostesses, in a similar way to kisaeng, provided sexual services at hotels after serving their prospective clients at the salons.[86] In addition, female dancers at cabarets and nightclubs also increasingly engaged or were forced to engage in prostitution during the late 1960s. The official category that the government used to refer to room salons, cabarets, and nightclubs was "entertainment restaurants." The government classified a salon or cabaret as an entertainment restaurant if it employed "female entertainers" or hospitality women.[87] In other words, the term entertainment restaurant was a euphemism for the new forms of adult entertainment venues that stood apart from the old-fashioned brothels. The number of entertainment restaurants was about two thousand in the 1960s, a number that grew to three thousand in the 1970s.[88]

However, the number of such venues started to skyrocket in the mid-1980s, from 5,147 in 1984 to 18,550 in 1990. The number of tearooms (*tabang*) also took off during the same period, from 30,822 to 40,874.[89] Tearooms were a type of cafe in which the customers were served by young waitresses. Being faced with this new form of fierce competition, as well as mimicking the new style of room salons, some tearooms started to provide sexual services to male guests in the mid-1980s.[90] Many hotels, inns, saunas, and even barber shops also took part in this wave.[91] The epicenter of this explosion in prostitution was Gangnam, a newly developed area south of Seoul. Here, starting in the early 1980s young and beautiful hostesses, waitresses, and other so-called hospitality women provided sexual services to men within the expanding middle and upper classes. These services were supplied in the luxurious room salons, bars, nightclubs, saunas, massage parlors, and hotels that characterized the newly developed area.[92] This new trend of night-time culture soon spread to other cities and even rural areas across Korea. For example, "ticket tearooms," instead of room salons, functioned as the main venue for prostitution in the countryside. Here, a ticket referred to a pass to take a waitress out of the tearoom and have sex with her, and of course this service was one a male guest had to pay for.[93]

This sector of the sex industry for domestic men was also under the toleration-regulation regime but enforced at a weaker register than within the camptowns until the mid-1980s. The government designated the red-light districts for Korean men as special zones along with the camptowns, tolerated prostitution there, and registered prostitutes, even though prostitution was prohibited by law.[94] It also conducted STI examinations of prostitutes in some districts, but not as extensively as in the camptowns.[95] Moreover, no records have been found so far to show that the forceful incarceration of prostitutes in VD detention centers, contact tracing, or culture lectures to improve their service were carried out in red-light districts for Korean men. In fact, VD detention centers were established only in camptowns. Nevertheless, this policy of control relative to the domestic sex market can still be labeled as part of the toleration-regulation regime, since sex workers in the urban red-light districts were subject to both prohibition, that is, sporadic crackdowns and punishment, and regulation, in the form of registration and STI testing.

However, from the mid-1980s the focus of the prostitution policies started to shift from the camptowns to the red-light districts that served Koreans. As noted earlier, the government promulgated the Rule on Health Checkups of Employees in Sanitary Field in 1984 to prepare for the Asian Games and the Olympics, with its primary purpose being to provide safe commercial sex for foreign tourists. Another purpose of this measure was to protect domestic men from STIs by subjecting to periodic testing the whole spectrum of sex workers that had emerged within the rapidly expanding domestic market in the 1980s. The categories of "tearoom waitresses" and hospitality women were the top two groups recorded, with 61,563 and 60,152 respectively in 1985, and most of their clients were Korean men. In contrast, the number of registered special entertainers for the U.S. military, who had been labeled comfort women in the past, was only 11,456.[96]

In this way Korea, once notorious as a sexual paradise for American soldiers and Japanese tourists, now became a nation of pleasure for its own men, regardless of where they lived and what class they belonged to. The Chun administration, which gained power by brutally suppressing the people's demand for democracy, was in turn extraordinarily generous in satisfying male sexual desire. In August 1980, three months after the Gwangju Uprising, the government repealed measures to limit the number of entertainment restaurants within any given urban area and the minimum distance between such venues.[97] In January 1982 the evening curfew was lifted, thirty-six years after it had first been implemented under U.S. military rule. Many critics have argued that the corrupt military dictatorship deliberately implemented the so-called three S policy that boosted the sex, screen, and sports industries to turn people's attention away from politics.[98] Although it is difficult to prove what the intention behind the policy was, its immediate and predictable outcome was clear, in that it resulted in the nationwide expansion of the sex industry. Even small cities and rural areas, which had been comparatively untouched by the commercial sexual activity that prevailed in major cities in the 1960s and 1970s, now fiercely followed the trend of expansion. In this respect, the increase in entertainment restaurants and tearooms in small cities and rural areas was much greater than that within major cities.[99]

Who then served these men? According to surveys carried out in the 1960s and 1970s, the vast majority of women working in brothels had received only elementary education or less, and they had often worked as maids or factory workers before entering the sex industry. In contrast, by the 1980s, 30–50 percent of hospitality women had graduated from high schools, many of whom were from "middle-class" backgrounds. However, these two generations of women shared the same motivation: to earn money.[100] Serious gender discrimination in the labor market therefore also played a major role in pushing many young women into the sex industry, along with the fact that women in Korea on average worked longer and earned much less than men. In 1985, for instance, female employees worked 229.3 hours per month and earned 189,845 KRW on average, while male employees worked 223.5 hours and earned 397,265 KRW.[101] In contrast, the average monthly income of brothel prostitutes was 300,000 KRW, and that of hostesses was 340,000 KRW.[102] According to a study, about 40 percent of the hospitality women started in the profession via their friends' mediation or introduction, and more than

30 percent entered independently into it.[103] In response to this situation, a female official of the Ministry of Health and Social Affairs lamented: "How can we guide those who voluntarily chose prostitution to earn more?"[104]

In this way, the national development that all Koreans so ardently yearned for was coupled with a highly gender-specific effect: guaranteeing most male citizens the freedom to enjoy commercial sex, while rendering many female citizens sex workers in the service of their compatriots. However, not every woman "chose" to work in the adult entertainment industry. Some were forced or trafficked. From 1988 to 1991, major newspapers were filled with horrible stories detailing how gangs had abducted girls and women using violence and drugs, before trafficking them to red-light districts.[105] The mass media, scholars, and social reformers all concurred that this new phenomenon of trafficking was caused by the sudden expansion of the adult entertainment industry. In other words, trafficking emerged as a means of forcibly recruiting women, they argued, since the supply of voluntary sex workers failed to meet male demand.[106] As such, the production of a nation of pleasure came to arouse a state of nationwide moral panic in the newly democratized nation.

In response, social reformers took rapid action to curb not only trafficking but also the entire sex industry. This time, progressive Christian men took the lead and feminists followed. In October 1988, the YMCA held a conference to criticize the adult entertainment industry and started self-salvation campaigns in an attempt to limit the widespread male desire for prostitution.[107] Then, in December 1988 the Korean Women's Associations United (KWAU), an umbrella organization that had coordinated progressive feminist groups since 1987, announced a proclamation to demand that the government thoroughly crack down on trafficking in women.[108] Feminists also waged huge anti-trafficking demonstrations, held conferences to discuss how to suppress trafficking, and opened an emergency call center for victims or witnesses of trafficking to report the crimes.[109] All this activism represented a turning point in the history of Korean feminism. Whereas the abolition campaign criticized public prostitution as a legacy of Japanese colonialism, and the anti-kisaeng tourism campaign denounced the continuation of sexual imperialism by Japanese tourists, this new activism in the late 1980s highlighted the sexual deviance, criminal activity, and the widespread exploitative female oppression that was being carried out primarily by Korean men:

In the early 1970s, we, as a nation, were infuriated by kisaeng tourism of the Japanese who came to Korea to buy Korean women's sexual services. We criticized them as "sex animals," a Japanese neo-colonial invasion, and [their activity as] the imperialist sexual plunder of Korean women. Ten years later, we now take seriously not only the sexual plunder committed by Japanese tourists or American soldiers but also the terrible violation of the human rights of Korean women committed under the hoof of Korean men.[110]

As such, the issue of prostitution and human trafficking committed by Korean men inside Korea, which had been sidelined within anti-prostitution activism for a long time, now emerged as a major national concern. In relation to the powerful idea of a wholistic Korean national family, feminists also focused not only on the idea of the immoral "father" who forced his "daughters" to have sex with foreigners but also the notion of his "sons" who sexually violated their "sisters." They viewed prostitution as an entirely masculinized form of violence and crime and directly equated the practice with paid rape.[111] As chapter 5 will show, this radical feminist perspective would dominate the mainstream approach of Korean feminism in the 2000s.

The 1980s in Korean history have been remembered as an era of development and progress. During the decade, Korea achieved an economic miracle as well as the establishment of a political democracy, putting an end to the military dictatorship that had lasted for twenty-six years.[112] This chapter has shown that it was also an era of pleasure and panic caused by the rapid expansion of the sex industry for Korean men. Equally, however, it is notable that the fear and anxiety that haunted the period were often dramatized or exaggerated. For instance, in 1989 the YMCA conducted research to ascertain the true scale of the sex industry, concluding that over one million women, a fifth of all young Korean women aged from fifteen to twenty-nine, were engaged in this sector. This staggering estimate, however, was considerably exaggerated and based on unscientific research methods. The YMCA deduced this number as follows: there were over four hundred thousand adult entertainment venues in 1988, and assuming each facility hired three hospitality women on average, the total number of hospitality women would amount to 1.2 million. However, they included in the category of adult entertainment venues not only entertainment restaurants but ordinary restaurants, condominiums, swimming pools, bakeries, and even beauty shops.[113] In addition, the YMCA did not present any logical reason why it assumed that the average number of women hired at each facility was three. Despite such issues with the report, many activists repeatedly cited the idea that a fifth of young Korean women worked in the sex trade and came to consider this extreme estimate a kind of self-evident fact.[114] Arguably, they did so in good faith to help denounce the tremendous scale of the sex industry and to call for urgent action to suppress it. Nonetheless, such an exaggeration helped to deepen the moral panic. It caused many Koreans to shudder at the idea that their neighbors and acquaintances, who looked so innocent, or even perhaps their own daughters, could be working in this clandestine and dangerous industry.

In this regard, the discourse on human trafficking was also considerably sensationalized. According to a survey conducted by the Korean Institution of Criminology, the vast majority of trafficking events in the late 1980s and early 1990s were committed by individual men who lured victims by lying about possible employment or first establishing romantic relationships with their victims.[115] In contrast, the mass media mainly focused on the much less common cases of abduction that involved organized gangs, even going as far as to report unsubstantiated rumors or disappearances as suspected trafficking events.[116] This melodramatic approach helped to establish a populist media narrative of diabolical criminals and innocent victims and doubtless was used to satisfy the voyeuristic desire of the readers. Social reformers also seemed to have paid more substantial attention to the rare extreme cases in which gangs battered, drugged, and raped victims to make them work as prostitutes.[117] In this diatribe, the structural forces that pushed most women into the sex industry, such as gender discrimination in the labor market and gender-specific economic development, disappeared as objects of critique. Meanwhile, the more widespread injustices faced by sex workers who were not exactly the innocent victims of trafficking but chose their profession because of hard economic reasons did not garner widespread national attention.

In response to the moral panic, the government finally declared a "war on crimes" in October 1991, with increased specialist police officers, and strengthened crackdowns on trafficking and illegal activities within entertainment restaurants.[118] Simultaneously, the moral panic that reached a climax in 1989 started to diminish in the early 1990s, and the issue was apparently gradually forgotten by the mid-1990s. It is not clear exactly what put an end to the panic, whether the government "war" on illegal activity was effective or media sensationalism just withered away. However, one thing is clear: the adult entertainment industry that motivated this fear did not decrease at all afterward. As a result, the embers of public fear and outrage were never entirely extinguished, and further outbreaks of moral panic and feminist outrage were to be repeated in different guises in the following years, as chapter 5 will examine.

FOUR

Ladies and Gentlemen (and Prostitutes)

THE MAKING OF A NATIONAL COMMUNITY
AND GENDERED CITIZENRY

FROM 1958 TO 1994 the government instructed all cinemas in Korea to screen *Korea News* (*Daehan News*) before starting every feature film presentation. Produced weekly by the government, this ten-minute newsreel provided an efficient means to propagate state policies and "enlighten" the people. An episode from October 12, 1963, "News from My Town," reported on a mass wedding ceremony:

> A joint wedding ceremony for 125 couples was held at the plaza of Korea Adolescent Pioneers located in Mowol-ri, Seosan-gun, Chungcheongnam-do. The grooms were former vagrants who had lost their families and had helplessly turned their back on the bright world. The brides were disadvantaged women who had fallen into the trap of prostitution. They [have come to] settle in this area while the government has provided help for them to support themselves.[1]

What the newsreel did not mention was that the brides had been internees of the Seoul Municipal Reformatory to Protect and Guide Women (Seoul sirip punyŏ poho chidoso; hereafter the Seoul Reformatory). This institution had arranged for its inmates to marry the members of the Korea Adolescent Pioneers (Taehan ch'ŏngsonyŏn kaech'ŏktan), a parallel institution for young men who had been (perceived as) vagrants, ragpickers, gang members, and homeless.[2] Immediately after the coup, the military junta carried out a massive crackdown on the people who were considered to pose a menace to the national body politic or simply those who represented "social evils," such as gangs, vagrants, prostitutes, corrupt public servants, and even those who went to dance halls. In addition, the new government established camps and reformatories to detain and rehabilitate some "deviants" or "non-productive" groups.[3] The Korea Adolescent Pioneers and the Seoul Reformatory were such institutions. All this arbitrary persecution and incarceration without due process was implemented in the name of national reconstruction. Starting with the Seoul Reformatory in 1961, similar institutions were established nationwide after the military coup d'état and continued to exist for more than three decades until the first half of the 1990s. Given the long-standing nature of the reformatory system, this chapter asks the following questions. What sort of institutions were the female reformatories? What tasks did they carry out, and why did they set up this marriage program? How were these women incarcerated at the reformatories, what experiences did they have there, and why did they "choose" to marry members of the Korea Adolescent Pioneers?

The era of female reformatories was also that in which prostitution studies emerged in Korea. In fact, the female reformatories functioned as one of the primary sites that facilitated the production of knowledge about prostitutes. Scholars from a wide variety of social sciences, from sociology to social work to public health, conducted research at the reformatories, as well as within other state-fostered spaces directly related to prostitution, such as the VD clinics and detention centers that examined and treated prostitutes, and the "special zones" that openly tolerated prostitution. They mobilized diverse "scientific methods," including questionnaires, interviews, participatory observation, and statistical analysis, to clarify who the prostitutes were and why they had become "debased." For what purpose and with what will, desire, or obsession did such experts occupy themselves with prostitution studies? What facts did they find and fail to find? Do their investigations share similar themes and methods, despite the differences in the researchers' disciplinary backgrounds? In other words, was their work dominated by a certain "spirit of the era" or not? And if so, were there any studies that went against the dominant trend?

To answer these two sets of questions, this chapter explores both the female reformatories and the history of social research on prostitution. It examines not only what happened inside the reformatories and what contents the studies included, but also how a negative notion of prostitutes was constituted through both the facilities and the research, as well as the impact of this on gender relations in Korean society. In other words, this chapter investigates these two apparatuses as modes of power that functioned to produce gendered subjects and a national community composed of such, in the form of gentlemen, ladies, and prostitutes.

THE TAMING OF THE SHREW?
INSIDE FEMALE REFORMATORIES

Prison or Welfare Facility?

In his memoir *The State, Revolution, and Me* (1963), Park Chung Hee asserted that urgent and powerful administrative measures were necessary to address the issue of prostitution, since "wherever prostitutes go, they accompany evil, violence, and other forms of social anxieties."[4] In this context, the Seoul Reformatory was established in June 1961, only one month after the coup. In a similar mode, its twin institution to incarcerate alleged male vagrants, ragpickers, and gang members, the Korea Adolescent Pioneers, was established five months later in November 1961. Through the female reformatory, debased women would now be subject to not only punishment but also rehabilitation. The Yullak Prevention Act, which was enacted in November of the same year, also specified that the state would establish reformatories across the nation. The purpose of such institutions was "to guide and protect women needing protection," that is, "those who habitually engage in morally degrading behavior [*yullak haengwi*] and those liable to do so considering their circumstance, character, or behavior" (Article 7). The reformatories had to conduct a wide range of tasks, including counseling, inquiry into the cause of prostitution, incarceration, job placement, the entrustment of inmates to families, and so on. Nonetheless, the top priority of the reformatories was incarceration. The Yullak Prevention Act also required that "the state establish vocational training facilities and conduct vocational training to foster the spirit and capability of the women needing protection to support and rehabilitate themselves" (Article 8). Although the act differentiated between reformatories and vocational training facilities, in reality the former also functioned as the latter from the outset of their establishment. For this reason, numerous reformatories had titles such as the Female Job Training Institute or the Female Technical Institute.

What then was a female reformatory? Was it a prison or a welfare facility? The Yullak Prevention Act specified the purpose of female reformatories as "guidance and protection," and the Social Welfare Service Act of 1970 also classified female reformatories as a "social welfare service" (Article 2). Simultaneously, however, the Yullak Prevention Act defined guidance and protection as a security measure to replace punishment.[5] The act therefore exempted first-offender prostitutes from punishment when they showed repentance for their crimes and allowed them instead to be "guided" at reformatories or vocational training facilities (Article 13). Nevertheless, the act and its enforcement decree did not specify the processes and terms of incarceration. As a result, the "women needing protection" were confined to the reformatories without trial or definite terms of internment. Considering the general punishment for prostitution was a monetary fine, this approach of imprisonment as a mode of guidance or a security measure was far harsher than the general penalty. Such acts of incarceration therefore constituted a punishment beyond punishment or a state-sanctioned reprimand that was in a sense illegitimate, in that it violated the basic principles of the Constitution and the Penal Code such as due process, void-for-vagueness, and a ban on indeterminate imprisonment.

Another loophole within the Yullak Prevention Act was that its enforcement decree allowed nonprofit foundations to establish and operate female reformatories (Article 1). This enabled religious and private social welfare organizations to conduct this institutional security measure, which in principle should have been carried out exclusively by the state. The female reformatories run by nonprofit foundations, like private prisons, needed to maintain a certain number of inmates to receive subsidies from the government continuously. In other words, the facilities had to continuously "produce" women needing protection for the sake of their own existence. This necessity resulted in a highly aggressive approach to the acquisition of internees. Moreover, the category of women needing protection itself was incredibly vague and inclusive. As discussed earlier, the Yullak Prevention Act defined them as "those who habitually engage in morally degrading behavior and those liable to do so considering their circumstance, character, or behavior." However, the aspects of "circumstance, character, or behavior" that would determine whether a girl or woman would be "liable to" engage in prostitution were left undefined and entirely open to interpretation. Because of this ambiguity, not only those who committed the crime of prostitution but simply those whom the police or other public officials arbitrarily considered liable to be prostitutes, even vagrant women or women with mental disorders, were indiscriminately apprehended and incarcerated.[6]

Despite such vagaries and discrepancies, one thing remained clear: all the inmates were females since the Yullak Prevention Act specified that only women should be protected at reformatories. In addition, even though the act stated that their male clients should be punished equally, they were barely ever apprehended.[7] Despite this tremendous violation of human rights and gender disparity, the Yullak Prevention Act continued without revision until the mid-1990s. Therefore, for over thirty years this massive incarceration of women continued systematically in the name of state protection. During this period, around thirty female reformatories were established in cities and camptowns, and the cumulative number of inmates reached over two hundred thousand by the mid-1990s.[8]

In the few reports that circulated in the 1960s, it was stated that the reformatories were surrounded by "high walls like a prison," and that the gates were "locked firmly even in the daytime."[9] But little exists in the historical record of independent reports or testimony as to what happened behind the walls of the reformatories. Therefore, to understand the experiences of the inmates, I interviewed four former "comfort women" for American servicemen who had been incarcerated at the reformatories. One of them was Kim Yeon-Ja, whose autobiography I cite in chapters 2 and 3. In May 2018 I had a chance to introduce myself to her at a conference that specifically focused on the lawsuit filed by former comfort women. At this initial meeting, Kim explained that she already knew that I had testified at the court as an expert witness for the plaintiffs. About four months later, I was able to interview Kim at her home in Cheonan, thanks to arrangements made by filmmaker Lee Ko Woon, who had been documenting her life story as part of a project on comfort women who served the U.S. military.[10] The two-hour-long interview started with her giving me an extensive description of Seoul in the early 1960s, from the city's upscale theaters performing Shakespeare's plays, to lively music halls, to the hustle and bustle of department stores. It ended with her detailing her disappointment with and future hope for feminist activists and scholars. In this chapter, I focus on her experience at the Seoul Reformatory.

I also interviewed Park Yeongja, whose testimony I cited in the introduction to this book. Like Kim Yeon-Ja, Park consented to the disclosure of her name in this book. To protect the anonymity of another two of my interviewees I have given them pseudonyms, Han Min-Ju and Yang Hye-Sun. I was introduced to these three women through You Youngnim (Yu Yŏng-Nim), the former director of the Durebang (My Sisters' Place), a counseling center for camptown women established in 1986 (see chapter 5). Since You had established trust with the women for almost twenty years and she introduced me to them as a scholar who "helped to win the [aforementioned] lawsuit," the women willingly granted my request for interviews. Han Min-Ju had been a representative of the internees at a reformatory in Incheon and stayed there for more than a year, so she remembered a lot of details about the institution. In contrast, Park Yeongja and Yang Hye-Sun were incarcerated for about five months, but their experiences at the reformatories had a great influence on their lives. I interviewed Han twice and the other women once. All three women were incarcerated at reformatories against their will, so they considered it no more than their conscientious mission to testify about the injustices they had experienced there.

These four interviewees testified to largely similar experiences, even though they were locked up at different institutions across three different decades: Kim Yeon-Ja at the Seoul Reformatory in 1963, Han Min-Ju at the Hyŏpsŏng Female Technical Institute (Incheon) in 1975, Yang Hye-Sun at the Dongducheon City Female Technical Institute in 1981, and Park Yeongja at the Uijeongbu Female Welfare Reformatory in 1982. The last interviewee was Lee Ock-jeong (Yi Ok-Chŏng). As the director of the Magdalena House (now the Magdalena Community) at Yongsan red-light district in Seoul since 1985, she personally witnessed numerous police crackdowns on prostitutes and their subsequent incarceration at female reformatories (see chapter 5). The interviews were conducted from July to October 2018.

Confinement

Kim Yeon-Ja entered the Seoul Reformatory in 1963 when she was twenty years old. At that time she left her hometown of Yeosu, a southern city in Jeonnam Province, for Seoul, to live with her father, who had abandoned her mother to start a new family. After failing to obtain the support of her father, she lived precariously through daily work such as shoe shining. One day, a neighborhood woman recommended that she go and get job training at the Seoul Reformatory if she did not want to continue her insecure existence and potentially fall into prostitution. Scared by this warning, Kim voluntarily went to the facility. Her autobiography depicts the moment when she was admitted: "When I rang a doorbell, a guard came out. 'What's up?' He asked. 'I came here because I was told this facility offers job training.' 'How strange! Did you come alone?' 'Yes, alone.' 'Really?' He looked strangely at me and brought me to the office."[11]

It is not surprising that the guard considered Kim to be extraordinary, given most internees were forcefully detained in police crackdowns. A news article describes the normal process of detention: "Every morning, C and D police stations in Seoul, which are conducting massive crackdowns, are filled with the cries of women who are being transferred to reformatories." The article went on to state that "most prostitutes hate to go to reformatories

FIGURE 11. Admission ceremony at the Seoul Reformatory, October 23, 1961. *Source:* Seoul Metropolitan Archives, October 23, 1961, IT4595.

more than prisons," since they were deprived of their freedom for six months and barred from going out and having visitors.[12] Figure 11 shows an official ceremony at the Seoul Reformatory in 1961 to admit new arrivals, two years earlier than Kim's admission. As can be seen here, all the new internees in uniform were compelled to lower their heads like prisoners.

Two of my interviewees offered examples of this circumstance drawn from their personal experience. Han Min-Ju, born in 1957, worked in factories throughout her teens to support her impoverished family. She eventually ran away to escape her painful life as a factory girl when she was around seventeen years old. She served Japanese tourists as a kisaeng for one year starting in 1974, and then moved on to working in a low-class bar for Korean men, believing that she could earn easy money there. However, there she suffered from abuse and forced prostitution and eventually fled the bar with a friend. A few days after her escape in February 1975, she met the same friend at a bar recreationally and was caught up in a sudden police crackdown. She and her friend were apprehended since they were mistaken for prostitutes and did not carry health certificates. They were ultimately confined to a reformatory in Incheon, because "nobody could help us be released since we didn't have pimps" to negotiate with or bribe the reformatory employees. While interned at the reformatory for over a year, Han found out that the massive police crackdowns were concentrated in January–February and July–August, when internees "graduated from" the reformatory. Han herself assumed that the facility must have conspired with the police to find the required number of inmates and therefore obtain a continuous subsidy from the government. Yang Hye-Sun was also forcibly locked up in a reformatory in Dongducheon in the summer of 1981 when she was a high school senior. As she recounted, while dancing at a club with her friend she was falsely identified as a prostitute by the police: "I was a student then, a student! But it was no use [stating this fact]."

In this way, these three interviewees were admitted to the reformatories according to two different paths: voluntary admission or forceful incarceration. Despite this difference, they shared several commonalities. First, none were engaged in prostitution when admitted, as both Kim Yeon-Ja and Yang Hye-Sun had no experience of prostitution, and Han Min-Ju had stopped, at least temporarily. Instead, all these women had merely deviated from gender norms. Kim and Han ran away from home, and Han and Yang were at a bar and a club respectively, places that "good" Korean girls would not frequent. Such deviations provided sufficient conditions to determine their status as women needing protection liable to be prostitutes and made possible their incarceration at the reformatories.

By contrast, Park Yeongja was a twenty-seven-year-old comfort woman when she was placed in a reformatory in Uijeongbu in 1982. She attempted suicide after a quarrel with the brothel owners over money. Fortunately, she failed in this but was then transferred to the reformatory by the owners:

> It was winter. I hated the brothel owners. [Do] you know a briquet stove? I added two more briquets on the stove, such black briquets [as a way to commit suicide through carbon monoxide poisoning]. I thought either outcome was OK, to die or not. . . . Unexpectedly, the next morning, around 7 a.m., the brothel owners opened the door of my room. They had never done so before. They were startled to see the two additional briquets on the stove and sent me to the reformatory.

While Han Min-Ju and Yang Hye-Sun passionately emphasized their wrongful arrest, Park Yeongja just plainly stated that "they sent me to the reformatory." Her attitude here reflected her dire state of self-abandonment at the time, due to the brothel owners' extreme control over her life, as evidenced by her suicide attempt. Park's case here demonstrates that reformatory incarceration was abused by pimps and brothel keepers as a convenient means to discipline or take revenge on prostitutes. And in this respect, Lee Ock-jeong also testified that a woman in Yongsan in the 1980s was committed to a reformatory by her brothel keeper after she informed the police about his criminal activities. Through such examples, it is made clear that the process of confinement was based on extremely arbitrary circumstances. The one consistent element in all cases of internment was that no internee was either tried for or convicted of prostitution. This open-ended detention without trial was possible because reformatory incarceration was not considered a form of "legal" punishment but designed as a mode of "social protection" and a "security measure."

Violence, Hunger, and Death

After being admitted to the reformatories and allocated to their cells, the first experience that the internees were subject to was violence at the hands of the staffers and bullying inmates. Every interviewee testified that this physical cruelty was routine in the institutions. For instance, Park Yeongja remembered that each newcomer was stripped naked and beaten by her roommates. Han Min-Ju considered that such violence was a form of ritual to "demoralize" new internees. However, this abuse did not end with their arrival, as it was repeated every day:

> We had to wake up and put on our clothes when a bell loudly chimed in the early morning. Then, even in the cold winter, everybody had to go out and stay in the front-leaning rest position.... We were forced to crawl, singing, such a song like "Have I Come to Cry?" Then, girls started to cry singing the song in such cold weather. [The staffers] hit the girls with sticks because they cried.

Yang Hye-Sun testified that she was also forced to wake up at 5:30 a.m. and run around a track in the yard every morning, and once she seriously injured her ankle due to excessive running but was left untreated for many days. Unlike the other interviewees, she was born into a wealthy family and did not run away from home. Although she pleaded with the staffers to permit her to call home, they refused since she did not have money to bribe them. She remembered that there were a few women who were not prostitutes like her but "wrongfully" incarcerated, and some were even apparently the wives of members of the social elite, such as a university professor and a member of the National Assembly. However, such women were often immediately released because they bribed the employees with finger rings or necklaces.

Another constant source of distress for the interviewees was hunger. They vividly and painfully recalled how meager the meals were, as the usual diet for inmates was composed of soup with corn dough, which Kim Yeon-Ja was told was made of U.S. aid corn flour, or barley rice, and pickled radish. As a result, the internees suffered from malnutrition, and Yang Hye-Sun, for instance, recounted suffering psoriasis on her face and losing considerable weight, going down to around 43 kilograms. On the rare occasions when the quality of diet improved, it was usually when special guests visited the facilities. Han testified that Park Geun-Hye (Pak Kŭn-Hye), the first daughter (who would later become president in 2012 and was impeached in 2017), visited her reformatory in 1975. I found several photos of this visit at the National Archives of Korea, and in figure 12 one can see the striking contrast between Park Geun-Hye's broad smile and the inmates' stiff expressions. Han remembered that on this day the reformatory provided the inmates with a special soup made of pork bones, which ironically made some of them sick because their bodies were not used to digesting this relatively large amount of protein and fat.

I also found photos of the visits or inspections made by other high-ranking public officials.[13] For instance, figure 13 shows the governor of Gyeonggi Province's visit to the Yangju Female Technical Institute in 1979, which changed its name to the Dongducheon City Female Technical Institute and two years later incarcerated my interviewee Yang Hye-Sun. Such regular visits by political grandees were probably made because the reformatories were eager to garner government recognition that they were being operated properly. In turn, the guests were able to portray themselves as the benevolent guardians of disenfranchised women. However, for the inmates these visits engendered no substantial changes in the conditions of their captivity. After taking photos for the press and providing special meals to the internees, the routine of harsh violence and poor diet resumed. And because these important and influential guests had no interest in the actual conditions of the facilities, the fact of the uniformly harsh environment of the reformatories was never publicly disclosed.

Nevertheless, there are a few clues that the government noticed the miserable conditions of these institutions. In its yearbooks, the Ministry of

FIGURE 12. First Daughter Park Geun-Hye's visit to the Hyŏpsŏng Female Technical Institute, Incheon, September 17, 1975. *Source:* National Archives of Korea, Seoul, September 17, 1975, CET0024329.

Health and Social Affairs included the statistics of deaths that occurred in the reformatories. The number fluctuated from two in 1963 to seventy-seven in 1970.[14] The reason for each death was left unspecified, and such statistics disappeared from the yearbooks entirely from 1974. Yang Hye-Sun testified that at least one death occurred while she was locked up:

> I didn't witness it with my own eyes because I was sleeping. But [I heard] the head inmate of my cell say to a roommate "I came back after dealing with it." A roommate asked, "Dealing with what? Did somebody die?" [The head inmate] replied someone was dead in cell no. 7. We belonged to cell no. 9. So, it was two doors away. I didn't ask why because I was too young. But the others kept asking. "Why did she die?" "What? Did she die from tuberculosis?" [The head inmate replied,] "She was battered to death. I dealt with it."

FIGURE 13. Gyeonggi governor Son Chae-Sik's visit to the Yangju Female Technical Institute, December 18, 1979. *Source:* Gyeonggi-do Multimedia Archives, https://exciting .gg.go.kr/board/inqire.do?bbsId=BBSMSTR_000000000221&nttId=37876&bbsTyCode =&bbsAttrbCode=BBSA01&authFlag=Y&pageIndex=1&menu_id=3, December 18, 1979.

Yang was left uncertain if the head inmate in her cell was involved in the murder from her ambiguous response, but she seemed affirmatively involved in dealing with the aftermath of the killing. Across the thirty-five-year history of the reformatories, it is impossible to know how many women died from such formal and arbitrary institutionalized violence or maltreatment, or how their bodies were disposed of, and it remains a horrific irony that any such forlorn, forgotten deaths could so easily occur in facilities that were established by the state to "protect" women.

To Be Servants or Brides

As mentioned previously, the female reformatories provided job training to "rehabilitate" their inmates. However, my interviewees held the consensus that such training was of no use in the outside world. This was mainly because the skills they learned were in outmoded "feminine" labor practices such as embroidery, knitting, hairdressing, and dressmaking. In considering

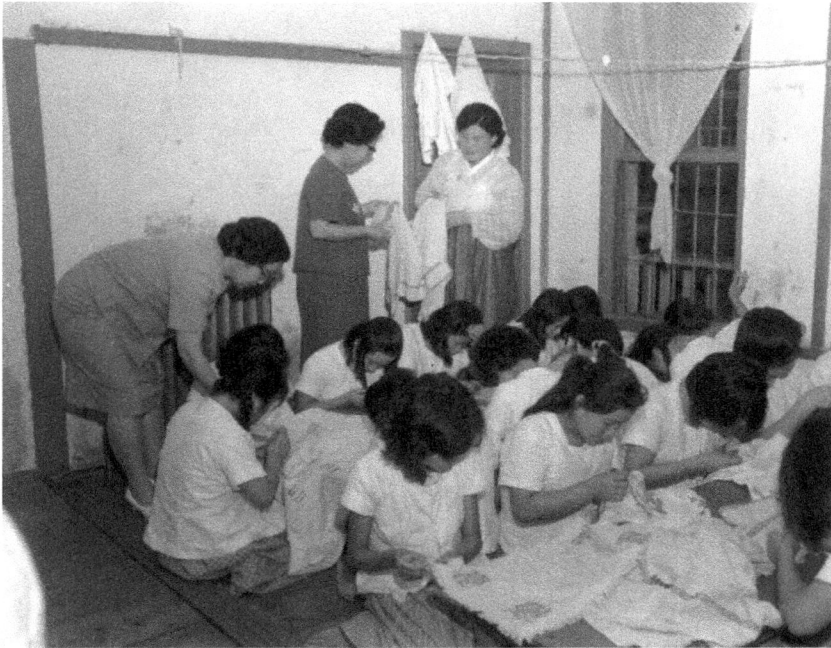

FIGURE 14. Embroidery class at the Seoul Reformatory, September 10, 1963. *Source:* Seoul Metropolitan Archives, September 10, 1963, IT4595.

why the Seoul Reformatory taught, for instance, embroidery (perhaps the most impractical skill on this list), Kim Yeon-Ja guessed it was, if nothing else, a repetitive practice intended to teach the inmates "control over their minds, [so that they might] live ordinary lives in society, without engaging in prostitution." Figure 14 shows an embroidery class at the Seoul Reformatory in 1963, during the period when Kim was interned.

Han Min-Ju learned to cut hair after mastering knitting at her reformatory. However, when she was hired at a barber shop after being released, she found that her skills were completely impractical. She complained that the job training at the reformatory had just made the internees into *sida*, a term that originates from the Japanese word *sita* and refers to a subordinate or servile worker. In a similar vein, Kim said that only a few pretty inmates succeeded in gaining employment at barbershops after learning to cut hair, and she was told that they did not even cut hair but provided massages and sexual services to male clients. According to the statistics of the Ministry of Health and Social Affairs, from the 1960s to 1980s, the employment rate

FIGURE 15. Mass wedding ceremony held at the plaza of the Korea Adolescent Pioneers, Seosan, Chungnam Province, September 26, 1963. *Source:* Chungnam Institute of History and Culture, September 26, 1963, 400536-001.

for discharged female reformatory inmates was under 30 percent, and more than half were just transferred to their guardians.[15] Given this situation, a reformatory run by a Christian foundation even introduced its inmates to Christian families as housemaids (*singmo*).[16] Unfortunately, a considerable number of prostitutes had actually been housemaids before entering the sex industry, so obviously this profession was unlikely to provide newly released inmates with any long-term stability.[17]

The final way to rehabilitate inmates was through arranged marriages. The Seoul Reformatory, in this regard, married off 125 inmates in 1963, 225 in 1964, and 390 in 1966.[18] The grooms were members of the Korea Adolescent Pioneers, the same group who participated in the mass wedding ceremony mentioned at the outset of the chapter (see figures 15 and 16). In terms of the typical background of such grooms, the military government often conducted massive roundups of alleged vagrants, gangs, ragpickers, and the homeless, then resettled them in remote areas and subjected them to backbreaking labor such as tideland reclamation. The government doubtless

FIGURE 16. Mass wedding ceremony held at the Seoul Citizens Hall, November 24, 1964.
Source: Seoul Metropolitan Archives, November 24, 1964, IT4130.

considered that these young, forced internal migrants needed housewives to make families and settle successfully. In parallel, the organizers of the Seoul Reformatory also thought that such marriage would be an efficient way of preventing their inmates from engaging in prostitution.[19] The procedure of choosing partners was highly restrictive and rapid. In an interview conducted by feminist scholar Won Mi Hye, an inmate of the Seoul Reformatory in the 1960s testified that they were able to refuse the candidates introduced to them through group meetings "only twice." She recalled that many inmates "chose" marriages as a means of escaping the reformatory, and she herself got married to a candidate only to run away from him three months later.[20]

Han Min-Ju witnessed arranged marriages while she was interned in 1975, although on a much smaller scale. According to her, the institution she was placed in was established by a Christian foundation, and it introduced its inmates to male Christians of "low intelligence." Some women got married to them to be released from the reformatory, even though they did not like their partners. While mass weddings were not regularly arranged at every reformatory, those staged by the Seoul Reformatory in the early 1960s were mimicked by another institution in 1975.

Escape, Release, and the Aftermath of Incarceration

As mentioned previously, the Yullak Prevention Act did not specify the terms and procedures of reformatory internment. Consequently, the periods of detention varied according to institutions, from three months to two years. As Yang Hye-Sun said, a few women were released earlier because they bribed the staffers. Yang herself also managed to get discharged after five months, one month early, because she somehow contacted her mother, who then offered substantial money to the reformatory employees. Yang's family background was doubtless also helpful for her release since her uncle had been a member of the National Assembly.

The last resort other than bribery or arranged marriage was escape. Park Yeongja succeeded in breaking out of the reformatory after five months. She was fortunate since her attempt succeeded. At the same time, however, it was possible in part because her institution had a poorer surveillance system than others because it was newly established and run on a small scale for roughly fifteen inmates. It was much more difficult to escape larger reformatories. Kim Yeon-Ja witnessed an escape that several internees attempted at the Seoul Reformatory, in which they successfully cut through iron bars and then climbed over "incredibly high walls topped with barbed wire." Ultimately, however, most of the escapees were arrested and returned to the institution.

Han Min-Ju and Yang Hye-Sun said that many escapees were arrested by the police because the residents near the institutions acted as informers and received money or goods such as rice or wheat flour from the institutions in return. In other words, neighbors were paid off and colluded to further surveil the internees on behalf of the institutions. Lee Ock-jeong told me of one episode in which she helped a woman to escape in the 1980s by personally paying more money to residents than the reformatory would and asking them to hide her. These obstacles did not prevent inmates from escaping on an increasingly substantive scale. According to the statistics of the Ministry of Health and Social Affairs, the number of escapees fluctuated from 41 to 609 during the period from 1962 to 1973. Although the ministry did not make public the statistics from 1974, breakouts continued to occur even in the 1980s, as evidenced here by Park herself escaping, Han and Yang witnessing an attempt, and Lee assisting her friend.

What happened to the interviewees after escaping or being discharged? Park resumed working as a comfort woman at another camptown in Uijeongbu. Han also started to work as a comfort woman in Uijeongbu, through introduction by an acquaintance at the reformatory. Ironically, Kim voluntarily entered the Seoul Reformatory to avoid "falling" into a life of prostitution, only to become dragged into it after her release. Similarly, Yang had no prior experience of sex work, but soon after leaving she also became engaged as a comfort woman. All the women noted that the social networks they formed at the reformatory were essential for them to gain entry to the underworld of the sex trade. Yang summarized her experience of detention in the following simple terms: "Our state sent me to the reformatory, which means that it made me into a *yanggalbo* [Western whore, i.e., comfort woman for the U.S. military]."

While it may be too much to assume that all female reformatory inmates followed a similar path as my interviewees, these four were certainly not exceptions. In principle, there were three ways that the reformatories saw fit to "return" their inmates to society: if they gained employment, went back home to their families, or got married. All these measures were intended to limit or remove the potential physical mobility of the women, who were believed to spread disorder and decadence across society, by subjecting them to the close surveillance of male employers, supervisors, or family patriarchs. However, the state overwhelmingly failed to achieve its goals. As mentioned, the employment rates were low, and even an employee of the reformatory in the 1960s and 1970s admitted the job training they provided was "obsolete."[21] Although a few women succeeded in getting new jobs, they were often forced to continue sex work as a sideline or were tempted to resume it because of the extremely low-income work they were confined to and the stigma that they had been prostitutes or inmates of the reformatories.[22] The vast majority of inmates were merely handed over to familial guardians. In many cases, this was not a solution at all, since many inmates had run away from home before detention to escape poverty, neglect, or domestic violence. According to Lee Ock-jeong, a few women at Yongsan even fabricated familial relations with their procurers to get released. The approach to rehabilitating the inmates as housewives was also deeply flawed. This was not only because these arranged marriages were based on highly fragile superficial relations, but also because the new husbands were in most cases former vagrants or handicapped and therefore it was difficult, if not impossible, for them to be family breadwinners. Thus, prostitution remained always one of the very few options that these women had for survival.

DEMYSTIFYING THE "DAUGHTERS OF DARKNESS"

Prostitution Studies as Power-Knowledge

In 1966, Kim Yong-A earned her PhD from the graduate school of public administration, Seoul National University, the third such female graduate in the school's history.[23] One year earlier she had published an article titled "A Factual Report on Prostitutes: Focusing on the Inmates of the Seoul Municipal Reformatory to Protect and Guide Women."[24] In fact, she was the director of the reformatory from 1961 to 1972, which enabled her to access the personal information of six hundred inmates. However, she did not monopolize the opportunity to study her inmates and opened the doors of her institution to other researchers. The case of Kim Yong-A and the Seoul Reformatory was not unusual. Several directors of reformatories and VD clinics either studied women needing protection themselves or helped other researchers to do so.[25] Some scholars also visited the special zones, within which the government tolerated prostitution, police stations, and VD detention centers, to conduct field research.[26]

While the researchers came from a wide variety of disciplines, from venereology and public health to sociology, social welfare, public administration, law, education, psychology, and theology, their work shared several characteristics. The most remarkable feature was that they exclusively focused on prostitutes, rather than on clients or third-party procurers. Another commonality is that the vast majority of researchers used what were considered the cutting-edge scientific methods of social science research. These prostitution studies can be considered an attempt to uncover the secrets of prostitutes, who belonged to an urban underclass novelist Yi Ch'ŏl-Yong called "The Children of Darkness."[27] It wasn't until the late 1980s that this trend was gradually superseded by a new stream of research that focused on the political, economic, and social factors of prostitution, influenced by progressive social movements including feminism (see chapter 5).

Inspired by Michel Foucault, I consider the development of the discourse of prostitution studies in Korea as a form of "power-knowledge." Foucault argued that power does not simply function in a prohibitional or repressive manner but serves to produce knowledge on its objects (in this case people), and that such knowledge is not just a tool of power but itself a field of power, domination, and struggle.[28] In formulating this idea, Foucault paid particular attention to the relationship between the production of new forms of knowledge and modern penal reform. According to him, "veridiction" came to occupy a new central position within penal practice in the nineteenth century and replaced the old question of "jurisdiction"—that is, "What have you done?"—with a brand-new question: "Who are you?" In other words, rather than the actual violations of an actual law, the potential of a criminal or a delinquent to commit a crime became a more important concern. Following this transformation, the judiciary lost its monopoly control over the penal system, and other modern disciplines such as psychology, psychiatry, criminology, and pedagogy gradually expanded their influence within this arena. The newly expanded role of these modern professional specialties followed the notion that using such knowledge might help governments preemptively identify and suppress dangerous criminals or delinquents.[29]

Prostitution studies in the second half of the twentieth century in Korea followed a similar concern with veridiction. These studies undertaken within diverse disciplines attempted to reveal the identities and lifestyles common to prostitutes and find out the methods through which the state would be able to control their possible dangerousness, complementing the judicial concern with punishment. Following the Foucauldian notion of the mutually constructive dynamic between power and knowledge, in this chapter I examine the social contexts in which prostitution studies emerged and the power effects that these studies exerted. From the early 1960s to the late 1980s, over one hundred research articles and theses on prostitution were produced, and here I have examined eighty-eight of these, excluding those with a narrow focus on venereology.[30]

The Coalition of the State and Social Science

The first question I would like to address is: Why did prostitution studies begin in the 1960s? One of the answers is not difficult to find: modern social research itself began in the late 1950s. The modern American academic system was imported into Korea after the Second World War. For instance, in 1947 the U.S. military government succeeded in integrating the colonial-era Keijō Imperial University and other colleges and transforming them into Seoul National University following American standards of organization and teaching.[31] However, Korean universities were still dominated by professors who had been educated and trained under the Japanese imperial system. Therefore, after the Korean War the United States embarked on a program of "educational aid" to reeducate young Korean professors at American universities. After taking courses and earning degrees, they returned home equipped with American ways of studying and teaching.[32] One such skill they learned was "scientific" social research methodology, including sampling, questionnaires, interviews, case studies, ethnography, content analysis, and statistics.[33] Thus in Korea the period from 1958 to 1963 was termed "the era of social research," when social scientists passionately introduced social research methods from America.[34]

Why then were many social scientists attracted to the subject of prostitution? Their stated research interests may give a clue to help answer this question. Two trends of interest primarily appeared in their academic papers. The first was on STIs from the perspective of public health. Many scholars from medicine, nursing, and public health considered prostitutes "a reservoir of STIs" and conducted research "to identify the basic facts for STI control."[35] This framework resonated with both colonial regulations that considered STIs the "diseases of prostitutes" and the postcolonial toleration-regulation that similarly succeeded the colonial approach in a new guise.

The second trend characterized prostitution as a moral threat or social evil, and the authors emphasized the destructive impact it had on the nation. For instance, as Kim Yong-A argued in her aforementioned article: "Prostitution fosters every element to degenerate people, decay the society, and eventually destroy the state."[36] Many authors reached a similar consensus on the devastating menace of prostitution, arguing that it was "the biggest social problem related to women" and a "hotbed of social evil and cancer of social problems."[37] As examined in chapter 1, Christian abolitionists pioneered this perspective in the colonial period, and from the 1960s, now that prostitution was criminalized, this became the dominant scholarly opinion. In such studies, academics articulated their desire to reveal the causes of prostitution and devote themselves to its elimination. What is interesting, however, is that they did not substantiate why prostitution was so fatal, particularly to the hyperbolic extent that it might "eventually destroy the state." The malignancy of prostitution was simply self-evidently assumed.

To summarize, while the interest in STIs as prostitutes' diseases was already prevalent in the colonial period, the interest in prostitution as a social evil became more prevalent after the state prohibited the practice, stimulating many researchers to study it. Besides, the state actually took the lead in the prostitution studies. From 1955, immediately after the armistice, the Ministry of Health and Social Affairs started to investigate the demographic features of "hospitality women" (*chŏptaebu*)—one of the official euphemisms to refer to prostitutes registered by the government—such as their age, education, and regional distribution, as well as the number of VD examinations and infection rates among them.[38] The Yullak Prevention Act facilitated this research further. Article 7 specified that the female reformatories should "investigate the character, family, and environments of the women needing protection."

By contrast, Japanese colonial power (as manifested through its bureaucratic and intellectual surrogates) never demonstrated any desire to know about prostitutes in detail. This was mainly because under Japanese rule, Korean women became prostitutes by contract, and the specific propensities of prostitutes in individual and collective terms were not considered. To be permitted to work as a public prostitute, a woman had to submit to the police a copy of the contract that her guardian made with the brothel owner, along with other documents.[39] On this legal basis of practice, it was not important to know what sort of women became prostitutes, since in principle any woman could be a prostitute if she was equipped with legitimate documents. Only minors under seventeen years old, femes covert, those with infectious diseases, and those without their guardians' permission were not allowed to be public prostitutes.[40]

In short, a colonial-period prostitute was an abstracted legal subject bound by contract, regardless of how unequal the contract was, and therefore the discursive manifestations of knowledge under colonial power neither raised nor answered the question of who the prostitutes really were. Instead, the colonial power's curious gaze was only concentrated on prostitutes' individual bodies. To identify whether prostitutes were infected with VD or not, the colonial police instructed doctors to regularly examine parts of their bodies "under the navel," such as "umbilical region, thighs, . . . the groin region, external genital, anus, . . . and vagina."[41] From this perspective, it is clear why the Japanese Government-General of Korea only recorded the physical condition of prostitutes, namely, the number of VD examinations and infection rates, as well as their legal status, such as occupation (*ch'anggi, yegi,* and *chakpu*) and nationality/ethnicity (Japanese, Koreans, and foreigners). "The character, family, and environment" specific to prostitutes remained of no interest to the colonial power.

The will to know about prostitutes more concretely, therefore, emerged after prostitution was criminalized. Thus, it was no coincidence that prostitution studies suddenly increased from the early 1960s, when the Yullak Prevention Act was enforced. Not only government officials like Kim Yong-A, who held a PhD in public administration, but other researchers asked and attempted to answer questions such as: "What kinds of women become prostitutes?"; "Why do they engage in prostitution, which is no longer a legitimate occupation but a crime?"; and "How can the state and society rescue them from prostitution?" The state also demarcated places to conduct research, such as reformatories, VD clinics, VD detention centers, and special zones. In other words, the places to concentrate, confine, and control the prostitutes were also those that served to produce knowledge about them. Simultaneously, this knowledge was deemed to be essential for the effective operation of power, as it was thought to be impossible "to present solutions [to prostitution] without empirical research on the actual problems."[42] As such, the governance of prostitutes and the search for knowledge about them combined. It was truth working on behalf of the government, and "the government in the name of truth."[43]

Statistics as a Moral Science

Among a diverse range of social research methods, the most generally used was statistics; in the eighty-eight articles I reviewed, only twelve (13.6 percent) did not use statistical analysis at all. Forty-seven, the vast majority (53.4 percent), were based on both questionnaires and statistics. Most surveys confined the object of the inquiry to prostitutes, who were recruited from red-light districts, police stations, VD clinics or detention centers, and reformatories. Only a few papers investigated other people as comparison groups: six compared prostitutes with men, two with the national average, and one with so-called normal women.[44] The number of samples ranged from fifty to over one thousand. Ian Hacking has identified that the study of statistics was termed a "moral science" in nineteenth-century France. This label reflected the discipline's early development as an empirical science through which it was possible to study immoral activities such as deviance, crime, suicide, divorce, and prostitution, with Émile Durkheim's sociological work *The Suicide* being an exemplary case.[45] Statistics functioned in a similar way in Korea under the military dictatorship, where the method of statistical analysis was believed to offer a modern and effective scientific tool to find out the causes of prostitution and offer consequential solutions.

The lists of questions varied according to studies, but almost every questionnaire included age, level of education, marital status, original family relations, birthplace, religion, previous occupation, reasons for starting prostitution, and monthly income. Numerous papers also asked about parents' occupation and education, the number of siblings and children, the age of the first menstruation and intercourse, the age prostitution started, the duration of working as a prostitute, the reason for continuing prostitution, the experience of abortion and STIs, knowledge on STIs, monthly living expenses, the number of family members to support, anxieties, and hopes. A few studies investigated intelligence quotient (IQ), character, the first partner of intercourse, the number of daily male clients, the amount of debt and savings, the amount of money sent to families, drinking and smoking, hobbies, and even the weekly frequency of going to movies or blood types. Surprisingly, almost every new work in the field failed to review the existing studies before raising its own research questions. In other words, each new contribution failed to explain its precise research rationale against the extensive existing number of studies in the field.[46] As a result, a range of immensely similar surveys with similar questions were repeatedly carried out for thirty years, with only a few variations in facets such as the place of research and the number of questions and samples.

How successful was this repetitive and tenacious raft of studies? Did these surveys on prostitutes comprehensively reveal the intimate details of their lives? Ultimately, many such studies were riddled with methodological defects and biases, and their findings provided little information that was not already common knowledge. For instance, as regards their age and marital status, every study found that the vast majority of prostitutes were unmarried and in their twenties, a commonsense fact fully predictable without the need for a survey. The researchers also noted that prostitutes' educational level was low. According to the studies produced in the 1960s and the 1970s, about 50–60 percent of prostitutes were only educated to the level of elementary school (roughly six years of education) or less.[47] Considering that the censuses showed that across Korean society 54.7 percent of adult women in their early twenties (twenty to twenty-four years old) had this level of education in 1970 and 42.3 percent did in 1975, it is certain that the educational level of prostitutes was a bit lower than average.[48] However, based on this simple fact, many researchers then concluded that "the level of intelligence of prostitutes is destined to be low," and that less-educated women fell into the abyss of prostitution due to their lack of "the ability to think, reason, and judge."[49] Similarly, two researchers who investigated the prostitutes' IQ reached an agreement that the vast majority of them were "feebleminded," which was the main reason for their falling into vice.[50] These findings strengthened the widely accepted notion of the period that uneducated women easily became prostitutes and therefore most prostitutes were intellectually deficient.

This flawed perspective ignored the fact that poverty and gender inequality were endemic in the 1960s and the 1970s, and therefore the low educational level was a general condition of impoverished women and not specific to prostitutes. Notwithstanding this fact, researchers neither investigated the educational background of other disenfranchised women such as housemaids and factory girls nor compared them with prostitutes. As a result, a lack of education was emptily presented as the main reason for prostitution, and prostitution was signified as a wrong choice made by "feebleminded" women. The two studies on prostitutes' IQ were also unreliably conceived because the IQ tests were conducted in a red-light district and a reformatory respectively, places in which it was very difficult to concentrate on the tests. In addition, the respondents did not have any motive to concentrate on the tests. In this regard, Yi Mun-Ja, a researcher who tested IQ and was a staffer at the Seoul Reformatory, conceded that her inmates were not cooperative in taking the tests.[51]

Most studies found that the number one reason for starting or staying in prostitution was financial, though the rate varied according to the study from about 20 to 60 percent.[52] Nevertheless, a few researchers understated the frequency of this answer or even openly distrusted it. For instance, Yi Mun-Ja insisted on the following in a booklet entitled "A Survey Report on Immoral Women," published by the Seoul Reformatory in 1966:

> When their clients, or other people they don't have any rapport with, ask them about their reasons for engaging in prostitution, they generally reply with economic difficulties. One reason they do so appears to be that they want to justify their shameful, immoral life with the excuse of economic difficulties. Another reason is that they are scheming to get paid more based on their clients' sympathy toward them.[53]

Although Yi admitted that "the poverty of their families" was one of the reasons for entering prostitution, she still emphasized that conflict between family members, emotional instability, and ignorance were more important factors.[54] Based on the same survey, Kim Yong-A also stressed that "prostitution does not have an absolute correlation with economic difficulties."[55]

While it is certainly true that not every poor woman engages in prostitution, it is also obvious that prostitution has been one of a few options that women in financial need are often forced to choose. Why then did these researchers underrate the compelling nature of economic hardship, even though their respondents overwhelmingly replied that this was the factor driving their engagement in prostitution?[56] This perspective is likely to be related, at least in part, to the fact that both Yi Mun-Ja and Kim Yong-A were staffers of the reformatory. Given their position, it would have been clear to them that their institutions had failed to improve their inmates' economic conditions upon their release, as not merely did they provide training only for low-income feminine jobs, but also the employment rates were low. However, in contrast to their clear inability to help their former inmates gain decent work, the reformatory staffers seemed to believe that they could do something to improve their internees' moral conditions. For instance, Kim Yong-A stressed that the reformatory was basically "a correctional institution to perfectly rescue [prostitutes] from immoral lives."[57] Thus, these reformatory staffers might have wanted to insist that not money but morality was the source of the problem of prostitution in order to justify their institution, and accordingly their activities in it. In this respect, it begins to make sense that the Seoul Reformatory's booklet of 1966 did not include any articles on job training and only addressed the history of women's welfare policies, the institution's management, the survey report on the inmates, STIs, moral guidance textbooks, and mass weddings.

A few researchers included questions on respondents' sexual experiences before prostitution in their questionnaires and found out that the vast majority had experienced it to varying degrees.[58] Mun Su-Yŏng, with a theology master's degree, interpreted such premarital sexual activities as a reason for prostitution, arguing that "those who lost their virginity are destined to give themselves up and live on impulse without any plans."[59] In her MA thesis in social work, Yu Song-Ja argued that prostitutes' premarital sexual experiences originated from an unconscious desire to compensate for their unsatisfactory relations with their parents. Similarly, using the jargon of Freudian psychoanalysis, she attributed the women's character flaws such as depression, anxiety, disorder, and aggression to "the distortion of the relationship with their mothers in the oral stage," and "repression in the anal stage."[60] As such, these researchers implied that the probability of prostitution was from the outset a latent risk for such immoral individuals and unhealthy families. However, again, the researchers did not compare prostitutes and other groups of women, so it remained entirely unclear if this premarital sexual behavior was unique to prostitutes. Moreover, even if someone might have considered undertaking such a comparative study, they could not have carried out this kind of project, since prostitutes were probably the only group of women in conservative Korean society that researchers could so bluntly ask about their premarital sexual experiences.

The researchers also endeavored to find out about the circumstances of "character, family, and environment" common to prostitutes, as the Yullak Prevention Act stipulated, but the results were completely contradictory according to the samples, and it was impossible to extract specific patterns and regularities. For instance, some studies suggested that only a limited number of prostitutes had lived with both biological parents before running away, while others argued that the majority had.[61] Some revealed that prostitutes mainly came from cities, while others pointed out that they were mainly from rural areas.[62] Some discovered that the majority maintained religious beliefs, while others found that the majority did not.[63] Given this diverse range of characterizations, the only possible conclusion anyone reading this range of studies could come to was that women engaged in prostitution were not a homogenous group with shared characteristics but a diverse collection of individuals from varied environments. In other words, any woman in financial need could become a prostitute, regardless of whether she had both biological parents or not, came from cities or rural areas, and practiced religion or not.

Guidelines for "Protection and Guidance"

In an article published in 1981, Choi Jai-Seuk, a sociology professor at Korea University, reviewed twelve prostitution studies produced in the 1960s and the 1970s. He criticized several methodological faults in them, and one of his comments was that "simply enumerating statistics results does not qualify as research."[64] Choi's frustration doubtless came from the fact that numerous authors of prostitution studies during this period just presented statistical tables and described the results without any analysis. One reason for this seemed to be that they had difficulty explaining their results, given that their primary aim was often to define the common characteristics of a prostitute. In this sense, prostitution studies failed to answer the key question of what specific kinds of women became prostitutes. However, the flawed nature of prostitution studies as a form of academic research does not necessarily mean that the researchers involved were without power themselves. On the contrary, they had considerable influence in justifying existing policies and suggesting new ones.

As noted, several researchers pointed out not only prostitutes' personal flaws but also their "unhealthy" family backgrounds, which failed to provide them with proper socialization. For instance, Kim Yong-A argued that "the relations with parents and other family members in childhood" were a more important factor in fomenting prostitution than social disorder, poverty, and a lack of education.[65] This rhetoric tacitly supported the reason for the existence of female reformatories as an alternative apparatus to resocialize the women. Sŏ Yŏn-Sun anticipated that the reformatories could alleviate "the irregular and pathological influences of their parents."[66] Yu Song-Ja maintained that 80 percent of her respondents expressed "infantile characteristics" and lacked "ordinary home training for basic living and a minimum standard of etiquette." In this vein, she advocated for the creation of a private reformatory program to educate these women about things like how to cook, do laundry, make tea, and receive guests, "to prepare them to be a mother keeping a family."[67]

Some researchers also justified the job training that the reformatories provided based on their research. Yi Mun-Ja emphasized that "generally the inmates are less intelligent than average, [suffering from] strong suggestibility and emotional insecurity," so the reformatory should provide "simple but interesting job training not needing a high level of concentration."[68] Mun Sŏn-Hwa asked the inmates of a private reformatory about their future hopes for employment, and they responded that they hoped to become hairdressers, knitters, seamstresses, retailers, and so on. She interpreted that these responses attested to the "possibility [for them] to become assistants for men."[69] One survey even contributed to the initiation of a program of mass weddings, as in the 1966 booklet from the Seoul Reformatory, Kim Nak-Chung, the vice president of the Seoul City Committee to Guide Prostitutes, recalled that he proceeded with this endeavor after finding out that many inmates were concerned that they could not marry.[70]

A few researchers expressed the concern that comfort women with their low educational level could misrepresent Korea to their American allies. For instance, Yi Ŭng-In argued that "prostitutes' low intelligence, in other words, their bad personal quality, is the greatest obstacle to giving a good impression [of Korea] to the U.S. servicemen." He even attributed the prostitutes' "misfortune with the servicemen," namely, the violence of the U.S.

soldiers, to their inability to communicate in English.[71] This opinion resonated with the government policy to implement so-called cultural classes
to enhance the women's English proficiency, which I cited in Kim Yeon-Ja's
autobiography in the introduction of chapter 3.

Similarly, researchers from medicine or public health advocated for more
systematic STI control. After investigating the inmates of the Seoul Reformatory in 1966, Yang Chae-Bok called for the government to quarantine and
treat the prostitutes infected with STIs, or at least syphilis.[72] In 1975 Nam
T'aek-Sŭng found out that the comfort women in Yongsan district, Seoul,
were examined for STIs three or four times a month on average, while the enforcement decree of the Infectious Disease Prevention Act specified they were
to be examined twice a week. He anticipated that the infection rates would decrease if the government conducted more coercive and stricter examinations.[73]

These examples demonstrate that most researchers in prostitution studies
operated within the magnetic field of the state power, in that the state provided researchers with the cause and venues to study prostitution, and the
researchers contributed to justifying, systematizing, and augmenting state policy. However, there were a few researchers who went against this trend. For
instance, in her MA thesis in 1968, Hong Jin Ok claimed that prostitution
originated from gender inequality in the labor market and criticized the sexist
double standard that blamed only prostitutes, not their clients.[74] Then, from
the late 1970s onward, several researchers in geography and sociology started
to explore the social environments common to prostitutes, rather than their
individual characteristics.[75] As the mid-1980s progressed, a few studies even
went so far as to approach prostitution as an extension of the service economy,
which had been expanded through the tacit encouragement of the late capitalist state, rather than a lifestyle that emerged due to the immoral behavior
and character of degenerate women.[76] Finally, in the late 1980s several feminist studies, which analyzed prostitution as a manifestation of the wider gender disparity across the nation, started to emerge.[77] It is the transformation of
knowledge triggered by these feminist studies that I examine in chapter 5.

MAKING GENDERED CITIZENS
AND THEIR NATIONAL COMMUNITY

In the previous chapters I demonstrated how schizophrenic the toleration-
regulation regime was. On the one hand, the nascent Korean state intro-

duced prohibition to expunge its shameful colonial past and identify itself as a moral nation. On the other hand, it retained the colonial legacy of the regulatory system of prostitution in a new form, on the pretext of national security, national development, and public health. This contradictory alignment between prohibition and regulation was sealed as the latter overwhelmed the former, creating a new postcolonial toleration-regulation regime. In this chapter I have revealed that prohibition itself also represented another schizophrenic aspect of the state. The Yullak Prevention Act was unique in that it included both elements of criminal law and social welfare law. On the one hand, prostitutes were regarded as wicked offenders and a threat to society, so they had to be punished. On the other hand, they were considered poor daughters and sisters abandoned by their families and exploited by brothel owners, so they had to be protected and rehabilitated. This contradiction resolved itself in the fact that state protection was a de facto harsher punishment or a form of punishment beyond punishment, which complemented the legal criminal punishment for prostitution such as fines. Therefore, although the Yullak Prevention Act stipulated that the state should protect prostitutes, the state instead sought to protect society from these dangerous women by incarcerating them.

To illuminate another contradiction demonstrated by the state "protection" of prostitutes, it is helpful to compare the category of women needing protection with other groups that the state defined as "needing protection." The Child Welfare Act, which followed immediately after the Yullak Prevention Act in 1961, defined "children needing protection" (*yoboho adong*) as "those missing, abandoned by, or ran away from their guardians, or those whose guardians are inappropriate or unable to raise them." The Livelihood Protection Act, enacted together with the first act, defined "people needing protection" (*yobohoja*) as "those who cannot sustain a personal livelihood, due to old age, disease or other loss of the ability to work." Women needing protection were similar to children needing protection, in that both were considered abandoned by their protectors. Therefore, the government as a pseudo-guardian opted to protect such women as pseudo-children within reformatories that functioned as pseudo-homes. Children needing protection shared a commonality with people needing protection, in that both were perceived to lack the ability to make a living for themselves. However, this was a critical difference between them and the women needing protection, because as numerous prostitution studies revealed, considerable numbers of prostitutes supported not only themselves but also their families.[78]

What is interesting is that a series of regulation policies already recognized the status of prostitutes as de facto workers, whereas the prohibition act negated such recognition. For instance, the enforcement rule of the Food Sanitation Act of 1962 specified the need to license, register, and issue health certificates to "employees" or hospitality women hired in the entertainment business. The Rule on Sexually Transmitted Disease Checkups, which was enacted as an enforcement rule of the Infectious Disease Prevention Act in 1978, simply replaced the existing term comfort women with special entertainers (t'ŭksu ŏpt'aebu). The enforcement rule of the Tourism Promotion Act of 1973 referred to comfort women and tourist kisaeng as "hospitality personnel" (chŏpkaek yowŏn). All these examples show that the government ostensibly regarded prostitutes as service sector workers. However, these definitions did not guarantee prostitutes' status as legitimate workers since they were still also de jure criminals due to the Yullak Prevention Act.

As examined, there were three paths by which the female reformatories served to protect and rehabilitate these women needing protection: job training, returning them to their homes and families, and arranged marriage. Even though all the programs were not successful, they possessed significant ideological power. The category of women needing protection itself had considerable gender-specific implications across society, as adult women were framed as always in need of guardians to protect them. Since prostitutes did not have their own proper guardians, the state had to step in as a pseudo-guardian. Thus, the subject-position of women needing protection contributed to producing other gendered positions: so-called ordinary women as "wards," that is, women already protected by their male "guardians," that is, their fathers or husbands.

Additionally, these guardians were also endowed with the privilege to pursue their own desire for sexual gratification outside of their married family life. The Yullak Prevention Act effectively constituted prostitution as a crime committed by women and a sexual right for men, by only punishing prostitutes and not their clients. In this vein, celebrated urbanist Son Chŏng-Mok asked, "Who dares to declare that 'they have never been to Jongno sam-ga [a notorious red-light district]' among the men who lived in or traveled to Seoul in the 1950s [and] 1960s?"[79] Even the 1962 enforcement decree of the Food Sanitation Act specified that "[female] employees hired in the entertainment business" should "always serve the [male] guests kindly" (Article 18).

In this way, the Korean national community was composed of not only ladies and gentlemen but also prostitutes; in other words, women needing protection, women already protected, and men as protectors. Prostitutes, the most despised women in the nation, were pivotal not only for national security and development but also for the construction of the national, iniquitous gender hierarchy since they provided a foundational substratum to bolster and subdivide it. Positioned above them were the legitimate, righteous so-called ordinary women, and superior to all women were Korean men. In this regard, Korea's prostitution policy can be considered exemplary of what Carol Smart has defined as a "gendering strategy," as it formally established differences not only between so-called normal and abnormal women but also between women and men.[80]

However, not every man was qualified as a protector. In this context, it is of profound significance that the organization of alleged vagrants was named the Korea Adolescent Pioneers, even though they were of marriageable age. This terminology was used because the state regarded men who were not independent breadwinners not as men, but as "adolescents." Following this logic, the meaning of the mass wedding ceremony described in the introduction of this chapter becomes clear as a symbolic ritual to turn adolescents into "true" male adults, namely, guardians, by making women needing protection into their wards. In this light, the nationwide publicizing of the mass wedding ceremony through media outlets such as *Korea News* can be seen as an attempt by the state to inculcate the whole population with this hierarchical gender ideology of the nation.

FIVE

Feminist Attempts to Reconstruct a Moral Nation

ON SEPTEMBER 24, 2004, all major national newspapers reported massive police crackdowns on red-light districts the previous day, when the Act on the Punishment of Arrangement of Commercial Sex Acts and the Act on the Prevention of Commercial Sex Acts and the Protection of Victims took effect. One of these reports offered the following details:

> At the start of 23, on the first day of the enforcement of the laws against commercial sex acts, red-light districts and entertainment establishments across the country lapsed into silence. There were few visitors, and those who were seeking to sell sex were not seen. . . . The brothel owners and prostitutes of "Miari Texas" [a red-light district in Seoul] waged a demonstration against police crackdowns at dawn. . . . Nevertheless, the police adopted a policy to continue the roundups until the acts are consolidated. On that day, 3,082 police officers arrested 138 perpetrators. In particular, the clients of prostitution, who had been released in the past, were now "unconditionally" charged. 48 brothel owners and 21 voluntary prostitutes were also apprehended.[1]

This scene was a repeat of what happened on February 14, 1948, echoing the moment when the colonial legacy of public prostitution was abolished and prostitution itself was criminalized under the U.S. military occupation, as discussed in chapter 1. Like the abolitionist act of 1948, these new acts of 2004 were also enacted under the leadership of feminists, and police crackdowns were concentrated on red-light districts.

At the same time, however, the new acts were unlike the act of a half century earlier. The most remarkable difference is that the police now started to apprehend all the involved parties under the new laws, while their previous roundups had mainly concentrated on prostitutes. In 2005, for instance, of the 18,508 people apprehended for violating the new laws, male clients constituted 62.0 percent (11,474), third parties 22.0 percent (4,071), and female sellers 16.0 percent (2,963).[2] In this regard, the new acts redressed the element of severe gender inequality that defined the implementation of the previous prohibitionist acts, at least immediately after their implementation.

The second divergence was that while the act of 1948 resulted in the creation of the toleration-regulation regime, the new stricter acts of 2004 sharpened the contradictions of the regime. As discussed in chapter 1, female nationalist campaigners after liberation openly supported regulation to "purify" the nation and compromised with the U.S. military government, which hesitated to completely abolish the colonial legacy of "public prostitution." In contrast, the twenty-first-century feminists who took the lead in enacting these new laws directly confronted the state's toleration of prostitution, and this brought about the decline of the toleration-regulation regime.

The final difference was that the new acts triggered a series of mass demonstrations by sex workers. The 1948 act also witnessed the protest of former "public prostitutes," but it was spontaneous, temporary, and on a small scale. By contrast, the 2004 protest was nationwide, lasted several years, and gave birth to the new identity of "sex worker." This process was abrupt, unexpected, and particularly paradoxical, because the current anti-prostitution campaigners, unlike the 1940s abolitionists who had often been hostile toward prostitutes, wholeheartedly hoped to protect their disenfranchised sisters and believed it necessary to enact the new laws on their behalf.

Despite such differences, both the 1948 act and the 2004 acts represented variant forms of nation building led by women, who yearned to create a decent, morally upright nation free of prostitution, or at least superficially intolerant of it. This chapter explores the process by which the issue of prostitution gradually moved from the margin to the core of Korean feminist concerns, across a period that ranged from the late 1980s to the early 2000s, and how this increased interest resulted in the achievement of stricter prohibitionist laws and therefore a weakening of the toleration-regulation regime.

CREATING THE FIRST FRACTURES

Shelters and Counseling Centers for Sisters

As we have seen in previous chapters, prostitutes were often framed as social pariahs, confined in diverse "states of exception" or "heterotopias," limited to places and institutions that the state had specifically created to house them, such as red-light districts, VD clinics and detention centers, and female reformatories or vocational training centers.[3] These places were considered to be so tainted by vice and violence that "ordinary" women should not approach them, lest they become contaminated. However, in the mid-1980s a few "extraordinary" women dared to visit red-light districts, and some even opened shelters and counseling centers to share the suffering of their abased sisters and give them rest. The first feminist shelter was the Magdalena House (Maktallena ŭi chip) established in 1985. Lee Ock-jeong, a devout Catholic activist whose interview I cited in chapter 4, embarked on a mission to counsel the women in the Yongsan red-light district in 1984. The next year, Jean Maloney, an American nun whose Korean name is Mun Ae-Hyŏn, joined Lee, and the official history of the Magdalena House began. Living together with women who had abandoned or escaped prostitution, Lee and Mun took care of the ill, held funeral services for the deceased, and prepared weddings for brides-to-be. They also negotiated with brothel keepers to liquidate the women's debt, rescued women incarcerated at reformatories, and waged an antidrug campaign devoted to red-light district residents.[4]

The second feminist organization, this time a counseling center for camptown women, was established in 1986 by Harriet Faye Pinchbeck, whose Korean name is Mun Hye-Rim. She participated in anti-dictatorship movements in the 1970s with her husband, a Korean progressive pastor named Mun Tong-Hwan. While working as a social worker at a U.S. military base, she witnessed the pain of the women in the local camptown. Supported by the American Presbyterian Church, she opened the Durebang (My Sister's Place) in Uijeongbu with Yu Pong-Nim, a young Korean female missionary, to support those who worked as "comfort women" for the U.S. military. *Dure* (*ture*) means Korean traditional communities in which people cooperate with each other, and *bang* (*pang*) refers to a room or place. In her autobiography (written with her daughter), Mun explained that she started the Durebang for camptown women, because "nobody listened to their stories." To help the women in the camptown the Durebang started English classes, held wedding ceremonies, served meals, and protested the U.S. military's injustice against them such as contact tracing. The staffers also taught the women to make bread to provide alternative employment for them, and they ran childcare facilities for the young mothers.[5]

There were also extraordinary women inside the camptowns. For instance, in the late 1970s Kim Yeon-Ja was a comfort woman in a camptown called America Town, Gunsan. After witnessing numerous murders and suicides suffered by camptown women (including the serial killings examined in chapter 2), Kim was completely devastated and started to attend a Christian church. She raised funding and finally succeeded in establishing a small church for camptown women in 1979, but she and her friends left the church due to the conflicts with the minister and other believers, who disregarded the inclusion of local prostitutes. In 1986 Kim again built a church with her friends, this time using a makeshift tent as a base. Under its nylon roof, her congregation gathered, prayed, and lamented; a few women even lived there, since they did not have any other place to go. In managing this community, Kim stopped engaging in prostitution and entered a seminary in 1988, when she was forty-five years old. In the early 1990s, as a missionary, she opened the Christian House at a camptown in Songtan, which was renamed Mission for Real Love (Ch'amsarang Sŏn'gyowŏn) in 1992. Under a sign that stated "God Loves Amerasian Children," the mission functioned as a church and day-care center for camptown women and their children for three years, before it closed due to various difficulties.[6]

Despite differences in the background of their founding members, the Magdalena House, the Durebang, and Kim Yeon-Ja's mission shared a key feature: they were autonomous organizations created by women for women. Kim recalled of her tent sanctuary, "It did not have a minister, a missionary, a cross, or a platform, but it was the most beautiful church I have ever seen."[7] The female subalterns of the camptowns, whose words no one would listen to, could frequent these places at their own choice and share in their suffering and joy. Although the organizations were all based on Christianity, they did not enforce Catholic or Protestant religious doctrines or sermons and simply "accepted the women as they were," as Lee Ock-jeong emphasized.[8] They assisted the women in finding ways to leave the sex industry but did not persuade them to get out of it. Instead, they paid attention to the women's concrete needs and focused on empowering them. These activists recognized that the women engaged in prostitution not as passive victims waiting for rescue and redemption, but as fellow citizens deserving of social acceptance. Mun Hye-Rim, the establisher of the Durebang concluded, "I intended to help the camptown women, but I have learned more from them. . . . I met a female Jesus at the camptown. . . . A camptown woman, uneducated and poor, was practicing Jesus's love every day."[9]

In March 1987, the Magdalena House and the Durebang took the lead in organizing the Hansorihoe, an umbrella organization of shelters and counseling centers for women in prostitution. Hansori represented two meanings: "one voice" and a "voice from deep sorrow."[10] The Magdalena House, the Durebang, and the Hansorihoe effectively fractured the previously unchallenged face of the toleration-regulation regime, since they provided alternative models to the oppressive incarceration of "women needing protection." However, they still remained at the margin of feminist movements and were unable to properly challenge the power of the state.

Grappling with Post/Coloniality and the Overwriting of the National Memory

On August 14, 1991, a woman in her late sixties started to speak out at a press conference. Her speech was sometimes interrupted by tears. However, her voice was clear, her gaze was straightforward, and her attitude was commanding.[11] Moreover, what she said was so formidable that not only her immediate audience but also the whole country and people in neighboring Japan were completely astonished.[12] The person in question was Kim Hak-Sun (1924–1997), a former comfort woman for the Japanese military. Her speech offered evidence of one of the most atrocious war crimes in modern Korean history with the most obvious proof: the direct testimony of a survivor.

As a matter of fact, the issue was far from unknown within Korea prior to Kim's statement. Although the actual term comfort woman was not widely circulated in Korean society, since it was jargon or a euphemism used by Japanese imperial officials, the Korean government had recently "recycled" the appellation to officially refer to the women catering to the U.S. military, as examined chapters 2 and 3. In addition, the memories of the "drafting virgins" (ch' ŏnyŏ kongch'ul) and "women's volunteer corps" (yŏja chŏngsindae) during the Pacific War were vividly alive in the minds of many senior citizens who experienced colonial rule.[13] Additionally, in the popular media from as early as 1941 several history novels depicted the women drafted or trafficked to battlefields, and between 1961 and 1991 at least four popular films on women's volunteer corps were produced. Finally, in the late 1970s real survivors started to appear: in 1979 Pae Pong-Gi, who had been abandoned in Okinawa; in 1984 No Su-Bok, who had been abandoned in Thailand; and Pae Ok-Su, who lived in Seoul. In general, these novels, films, and reports were just ephemerally consumed and ignored within the realm of popular culture, often serving to titillate voyeuristic male fantasy.[14]

The issue surfaced as a political matter only with the inception of democratization in the late 1980s, a moment when numerous crimes and injustices committed and concealed by previous authoritarian governments were revealed in the public domain, such as the Gwangju massacre in 1980. The Korean Church Women United (KCWU), which had waged anti-kisaeng tourism campaigns in the 1970s and 1980s, located the comfort women system to highlight the historical basis of kisaeng tourism and the origin of Japanese "sexual imperialism." In February 1988 the KCWU dispatched two members to Japan to investigate the historical records of comfort women with Yun Chŏng-Ok, a professor at Ewha Womans University.[15] Yun reported on their joint research at the international conference Women and Tourism Culture, a moment that became the start of the campaign to come to terms with colonial-period Japanese military sexual slavery.[16] Yet these feminist activists had not located any survivors to come forward and speak out about their own experiences. Then Kim Hak-Sun, a long-awaited "living" survivor, finally publicly emerged in 1991.[17] Her testimony was followed by that of other survivors, and 240 such women were registered with the Korean government.[18] The massive effect of the survivors' testimony sent ripples toward North Korea and other countries, such as China, the Philippines, Indonesia, the Netherlands, and Australia.[19] Following this mass emergence of survivors, Japanese military sexual slavery was constituted as a global topical issue of women's human rights, not just a historical crime.

About one year after Kim Hak-Sun's testimony, another event, related to another type of comfort woman, shocked Korean society once again. This occurred on October 28, 1992, when Yun Kŭm-I, a twenty-six-year-old comfort woman for the U.S. military, was cruelly murdered by Private Kenneth Markle of the USFK 2nd Division in Dongducheon.[20] As examined in chapter 2, numerous camptown women had been battered, assaulted, and murdered by American servicemen. While the wider local community of camptown women often fiercely struggled on behalf of the victims, in most cases the government was not able to, or did not want to, exercise its jurisdictional power over the American perpetrators. Korean society also paid no attention to the victims because they were considered social outcasts responsible for their own victimization. However, this dismissive perspective was turned upside down in 1992, as more than fifty progressive nongovernmental organizations (NGOs) and three political parties participated in a joint committee for Yun Kŭm-I. Then, on November 7, ten days after the murder, a demonstration with more than two thousand participants was held in

Dongducheon to demand the Korean government thoroughly investigate the crime and properly punish the offender, and large-scale demonstrations spread to other major cities, including Seoul.[21]

What triggered this unprecedented wave of mass protests regarding the murder of Yun Kŭm-I, in contrast to other cases of such crimes committed by U.S. troops? One of the reasons was the brutality of the murder. When Yun was found dead her body had been severely brutalized, detergent was poured over her naked body, her mouth was filled with matches, and her vagina and anus were penetrated with bottles and an umbrella. The photo of her body outraged people across the whole society, many of whom participated in the petition and/or demonstrations.[22] Another more crucial reason was that the newly democratized Korean civil society no longer tolerated not only the crimes of American servicemen but the Korean government's submissive attitude toward its most crucial ally. Radical college students and activists branded the USFK an incarnation of America's neo-imperialism and demanded U.S. forces leave Korea, and these students took the lead in demonstrating for justice for Yun. Both the Korean government and the U.S. military were embarrassed by this unexpected, nationwide protest and took it seriously as an expression of anti-Americanism and a threat to their alliance. In order not to exacerbate the situation, the U.S. military transferred the suspect Kenneth Markle to the Korean government, and he was sentenced to life in prison at first, ultimately to fifteen years, by the Korean courts and incarcerated at a Korean prison.[23]

Both Kim Hak-Sun's testimony and the protests regarding Yun Kŭm-I's death challenged the legacies of the colonial and postcolonial military regimes, which had given birth to the toleration-regulation regime. As we have seen in previous chapters, the Korean government inherited and perpetuated several elements of the colonial regulation of prostitution, and even the "comfort station" system, to provide a hygienic and regulated service to U.S. troops. Now Korean society started to publicly call into question the past and present crimes committed by the Japanese and the American military against Korean women. Yet the campaigns related to Kim and Yun had several differences as well.

The most striking difference was represented by the fact that Kim was a surviving grandmother and Yun was a murdered young woman. For a long time, the Japanese military comfort women had been considered unfortunate, miserable, and even somewhat eroticized "others" within society, and therefore were forced to keep their silence. Given the context of the sexist, conservative Korean perspective that valorized women's chastity even over their lives, the survivors had been compelled to hide their past as "violated" women. This silence was broken by Kim Hak-Sun, who refuted the Japanese government's denial of the existence of comfort women with her being. When she was only sixteen years old, her stepfather tried to traffic her into the entertainment industry as a kisaeng, and Japanese soldiers abducted, raped, and forced her to be a comfort woman.[24] This narrative of pure victimization committed against an innocent girl had the effect of rendering Kim's personal history a reflection of the tragedy of the whole nation, since countless poor girls under colonial rule could have easily suffered her fate. Her old age also contributed to neutralizing the erotic implications historically attached to comfort women. After her testimony, the comfort women issue was newly illuminated as one of the most brutal crimes of the Japanese Empire, particularly in relation to Korea. As a nation that had recently achieved both economic development and political democracy, the Korean people decided to finally confront the need to come to terms with their national history of colonial persecution, a task that had been postponed for over half a century.

In contrast, Yun was found dead, and her naked body was horrifically defiled. Her miserable situation epitomized her country's ongoing military and sexual subjection to the whims of U.S. troops, and her mutilated body allegorically functioned to reflect the wider suffering of the national community under U.S. hegemony.[25] While Kim Hak-Sun's age and her story of extreme violence effectively removed the stigma of promiscuity imposed on Japanese military comfort women, Yun's status as a contemporary, young, and above all "voluntary" prostitute failed to do so. Even in the brief biography published by an NGO's task force team for Yun, she was described as having "been naturally drawn to the world of pleasure with no place to go," after quitting her work at a factory.[26] As a result, Yun's peers in the camptowns still had to keep their silence, just as Japanese military comfort women survivors had done in the past. Nonetheless, there was now one way for them to find a voice, which was ironically through being killed. Only after her death could Yun be revived as "a daughter and a sister of the nation," a figure whose tragedy exposed the circumstances of contemporary Korea's compromised sovereignty and provided a trigger for mass protests to redress the issue. In this respect, Chŏng Hŭi-Jin criticized the nationalist rhetoric of the campaign regarding Yun, recognizing her as a "woman who could become alive only when she is dead."[27]

In other words, only after Yun died was she able to "speak out" about her victimization, through the medium of her "silent," defiled body. By contrast, the still living camptown women were not given any right to speak for themselves. Instead, campaigners spoke on their behalf, and their strategy to emphasize the brutality of Yun's case had the unexpected effect of trivializing the less cruel, more mundane violence, oppression, and discrimination that camptown women suffered daily. Like the tourism kisaeng, they were markedly not invited to campaign on their own behalf as witnesses to the injustice inflicted on them by American servicemen, the Korean government, and other Korean people. Kim Yeon-Ja criticized this situation:

> I suspected that none of them [the campaigners] would have had any interest in her, if Yun Kŭm-I had not been murdered and was just an ordinary camptown woman drugged and drunken. I worked in camptowns for 25 years. We were the forgotten people, or rather those who had to be forgotten and invisible. . . . They said that Yun's case was the first life sentence [in the Korean courts] given for a crime committed by Americans. In fact, however, the American Town women [in Gunsan] achieved it for the first time after Yi Pok-Sun and Yi Yŏng-Sun were murdered in 1977 [see chapter 2]. To the extent that nobody knows about it, the suffering of camptown women has never been known.[28]

Another significant difference between Kim Hak-Sun and Yun Kŭm-I is that unlike the former, the latter was not publicly labeled as a comfort woman. As we have seen, since the Korean War, comfort woman functioned as a legal term used by the Korean government to refer to the women who sexually served American troops. The fact that it had originated in the practice of Japanese military sexual slavery had faded into oblivion together with its victims. For instance, from 1951 to 1989, 720 news articles in four major newspapers contained reports on comfort women, 91.5 percent (659) of which were referring to the sex workers in U.S. camptowns.[29] In contrast, by the early 1990s, the term had begun to refer to Japanese military comfort women exclusively. In 1990, only three articles reported on camptown women, while another thirty articles were reports on Japanese military comfort women. From 1990 to 1999, news on the latter group skyrocketed to over three thousand articles, so by this point the fact that it was an official term used to refer to camptown sex workers was forgotten.

This continual "overwriting" of the national memory rendered the continuity that existed between the two types of comfort women invisible. Or rather, a form of selective amnesia had to operate to erase any knowledge of the continuum. For the Korean government, as an independent state, to encourage the procurement of Korean women for the U.S. military and then mobilize them as "patriots" in the name of national security, it had to be concealed that such policies had been adopted from the practices of the nation's former colonial rulers. In contrast, over four decades after Korean independence, for the Japanese military comfort women to be positioned as the pure victims of Japanese imperialism and therefore a symbol of the historically persecuted Korean nation, they had to be protected from any form of confusion with the "voluntary" sex workers catering to the U.S. military, even though some survivors could, presumably, have been both.[30] Thus, the term could be used as a label for only one group at a time, and as such, the overwriting of public memory was not a coincidence but a necessity. The suppressed history of American military comfort women could be revived publicly only after another two decades had passed, when some of them would unite to file a lawsuit against the Korean government in 2014, as mentioned in the introduction.

Female Reformatory Inmates' Struggle for Justice

In the early 1990s, another monumental crack was occurring in the toleration-regulation regime. However, unlike Kim Hak-Sun's testimony and the murder of Yun Kŭm-I, this was a discrete, almost imperceptible process, initially unknown even to feminists. On September 1, 1991, a woman was arrested by the police at a hotel in Seoul for violation of the Yullak Prevention Act, ending up with her incarceration at the Seoul Reformatory. This kind of crackdown and subsequent detention was usual, as I discussed in chapter 4, but the apprehended woman was unusual in her desire to fight back against the system. On October 10, after being incarcerated for over a month, she filed a lawsuit against the Korean government at the Constitutional Court.[31]

The plaintiff's complaint maintained that "the protection accompanying incarceration is unconstitutional in that it violates her basic rights guaranteed by the Constitution." It enumerated the legal bases to prove the unconstitutionality of the detention: a violation of principles of void-for-vagueness, a ban on indefinite imprisonment, due process, and the limitation of delegated legislation. The woman also filed an administrative appeal against the mayor of Seoul City, who was in charge of the institution. Thanks to these lawsuits, she was finally released on November 4, two months after being incarcerated. This woman's pioneering struggle was followed by several inmates' legal struggles. In total, fifteen lawsuits were filed against the mayor of Seoul City, and the plaintiffs were hurriedly released from the reformatory even before the courts reviewed the cases.[32] Such legal struggles by the reformatory inmates themselves confronted one of the most vicious aspects of the toleration-regulation regime: the arbitrary, violent, and indefinite detention of the women needing protection. In response to this series of lawsuits and the ensuing public interest, *PD Note*, a famous television investigative news program, reported on female reformatories on February 22, 1994. In that program, the chair of the Seoul Reformatory said that her institution functioned as not only "a warning to prostitutes and those who want to engage in prostitution" but also "a bastion of a moral life for women."[33]

In 1988, a few years before these legal challenges were successfully realized, feminist activists attempted to revise the Yullak Prevention Act but failed, since they could not reach a consensus about whether to decriminalize the sex industry or reinforce prohibition by punishing both clients and prostitutes equally.[34] Meanwhile, not only the act but also the unconstitutional incarceration of women continued without challenge. For instance, in 1991 when the first plaintiff filed her constitutional appeal, 3,039 women were incarcerated at female reformatories.[35] In a direct challenge to this situation, the reformatory inmates' lawsuits, in particular the constitutional appeal, put direct pressure on the government to revise the act. The Ministry of Health and Social Affairs, which was responsible for supervising the female reformatories, immediately embarked on this revision, promising "to do its best to closely cooperate with the Ministry of Justice and the City of Seoul so as to win the [constitutional] appeal."[36] It even sent an official document to the president of the Constitutional Court to ask him to delay the decision until it revised the act.[37]

On January 25, 1996, around four years after it was filed, the Constitutional Court finally decided to dismiss the appeal. It specified that the appeal had no benefit to protect the rights of anyone including the plaintiff, since "the related articles of the act were already abolished."[38] In fact, this disingenuous statement masked the fact that the Yullak Prevention Act had been revised to remove the forcible detention of women at reformatories and enforced on January 6, 1996, just nineteen days before the Constitutional Court's decision. In other words, the constitutional appeal, a direct action undertaken by a sex worker, effectively ended this practice of unconstitutional incarceration and contributed to rectifying the act for the first time, thirty-four years after it was initially enforced. Political democracy, achieved in the late 1980s, also played a significant role in this legal struggle, since the Constitutional Court was born in 1988 as a product of the revised Constitution in the wake of democratization. Through her challenge, the anonymous sex worker therefore proved that she was a legitimate citizen by using this democratic institution and finally winning a highly significant legal victory, something feminist activists had notably failed to achieve.

Under the Yullak Prevention Act, the cumulative number of women incarcerated at female reformatories reached 224,221.[39] While a few women might have entered the institutions voluntarily, like Kim Yeon-Ja, Won Mi Hye's research, based on interviews with women who had engaged in prostitution at the Yongsan red-light district in Seoul, conveys that some of her interviewees were forcibly detained at the reformatories more than once.[40] By way of contrast, my interviewees featured in chapter 4 had all been incarcerated just once. Given this difference, it is impossible to accurately estimate the total number of women confined against their will. Even roughly assuming that every inmate was detained twice, more than one hundred thousand women experienced the brutal conditions of reformatories under the pretext of "protection."

Perhaps even more tragically, the revision of this act did not occur soon enough. On August 21, 1995, just five months before the revised act was first enforced, a huge fire occurred at the Gyeonggi Female Technical Training Institute, a site operated by the Presbyterian Church of Korea and commissioned by Gyeonggi Province. Like most reformatories, it provided impractical job training and severely disciplined its inmates, locking every entrance to prevent escape. Consequently, the inmates, most of whom were in their late teens, were outraged by the reformatory's mistreatment of them. On the evening of August 21, some of these inmates set fire to the building in an attempt to escape, expecting the administrators would open the locked entrances upon seeing the fire. However, the doors to the building were opened too late, and forty inmates were killed.[41] If the Yullak Prevention Act had taken effect just a few months earlier, this tragedy would not have happened. For the young women who lost their lives on that horrific evening, the revision was too late, just as the human rights of all the women deemed needing protection had been entirely neglected for thirty-four years.

From the mid-1990s, the process began of shutting down VD detention centers, another draconian form of institution designed to control prostitutes. For instance, both Dongducheon and Paju enacted local ordinances to close their notorious VD detention centers in 1996, followed by

Uijeongbu in 2001.[42] While it is evident that the female reformatories were shut down due to inmates' lawsuits, it is not clear why the VD detention centers were closed. It seems to have been related to the general democratization of society from the late 1980s onward, the decline of camptowns, and the subsequent decrease in comfort women. As we have seen, the female reformatories and VD detention centers had oppressed women in the name of the discipline, correction, and treatment of these so-called depraved individuals and the protection of Korean society. Only in the mid-1990s, these two pillars of the toleration-regulation regime were finally phased out more than three decades since their establishment.

The Transformation of Knowledge

Fractures occurred in academia as well as in social movements and state policies, after feminist studies on prostitution started to appear in the late 1980s. The center for feminist research on prostitution was Ewha Womans University, which had established a women's studies graduate school in 1982. The most notable feminist study in the late 1980s was conducted by Kang Young Su, a master's sociology student at Ewha in 1989. She criticized the methodological approaches used in the extant range of prostitution studies for focusing on individual women engaged in prostitution and producing a superficial range of knowledge based on simplistic questionnaires. To overcome such limitations, she conducted participatory observation and in-depth interviews with eighteen women involved in prostitution, one procurer, and one brothel keeper in the Yongsan red-light district, all of which were possible due to the student's volunteer work teaching children at the Magdalena House. She also analyzed prostitution as constituting an informal economic sector engendered by the state-led rapid economic development, the discriminatory labor market against women, and insufficient programs for social welfare. Combining qualitative research and structural analysis, Kang illuminated the sex industry's basis in "economic and sexual oppression" and represented the reality of the women engaged in the sex industry as impoverished women suffering from brothel owners' exploitation, arbitrary police crackdowns, and reformatory incarceration.[43] As chapter 4 showed, the state apparatuses of toleration-regulation regime had functioned as the loci of knowledge production to control prostitutes from the 1960s to the 1980s. Similarly, the Magdalena House, a shelter run by feminist activists, became an incubator to engender alternative feminist knowledge.

Another pioneering study was produced in 1997 by Won Mi Hye, who was also a master's student in women's studies at Ewha. While previous prostitution studies focused on why some women became prostitutes, Won asked why some women were not able to leave the sex industry. To answer this question, she conducted in-depth interviews with the women engaged in prostitution, their male clients, feminist activists, police officers, and the members of municipal councils. She found out that such women were isolated individuals, largely blocked from other social relations, and suffered from economic exploitation, social stigma, and sexist legal controls. Borrowing from the American radical feminist Kathleen Barry, she concluded that prostitution was a form of paid rape, in that both prostitution and rape represented the male dominance of women and caused severe harm to the victims.[44]

Won was also active in a prostitution research group organized by the women's studies graduate school at Ewha, and some of her colleagues there produced several meaningful feminist studies on prostitution. For instance, Lee Hyo-Hee wrote a master's thesis on adolescent prostitution in 1998; Back Jae Hee completed research on Filipina migrant entertainers working at camptowns in 2000; and Chŏng Kŭm-Na and Kim Ŭn-Jŏng translated Kathleen Barry's book, *The Prostitution of Sexuality* (1995), into Korean in 2002.[45] As such, Ewha Womans University functioned not only as a supportive feminist environment to produce alternative empirical studies on prostitution but also as a window to introduce Western feminist theories, in particular the ideas of radical feminism, which would become the mainstream ideology driving Korean women's movements in the 2000s.

PROHIBITION, AN OLD BUT NEW PROJECT FOR A MORAL NATION

Economic Crisis and Anxieties over "Sexual/Sacred" Boundaries

The diverse range of struggles waged by women against the state from the 1980s onward challenged the toleration-regulation regime, but each moment of activism and challenge was carried out in isolation. For instance, the shelters and counseling centers were separate from the campaign to come to terms with Japanese military sexual slavery, and the lawsuits by the reformatory inmates were filed without any support or assistance from feminist organizations.[46] From the late 1990s, by contrast, feminists had formed a more widespread and cohesive movement of solidarity against prostitution, which reached its apogee with the enactment of new prohibitionist acts in 2004. Unexpected events, for instance the financial crisis in 1997 and the occurrence of several tragic fires in red-light districts, contributed to framing prostitution as a major issue within the feminist project of nation (re)building.

The economic crisis that swept East Asia in the winter of 1997 radically transformed Korean society. In return for requesting a bailout from the International Monetary Fund (IMF) on the verge of an economic breakdown, the Korean government and its people had to accept the humiliating terms of neoliberal restructuring. Korea's national credit rating plunged from AA− to B−, and major companies were bankrupt, subject to structural adjustment, or sold at a low price to overseas investors. As a result, a huge number of workers were laid off, national optimism about continuous economic growth and job security collapsed, the gap between the rich and poor expanded, and the suicide rate skyrocketed. The image of downtown Seoul Station being crowded with newly emerged homeless people came to epitomize the gloomy days of this financial depression in Korea.

Disrupting every sense of stability and order, the economic crisis also increased sexual concerns and anxiety across society. One of the terms that was symptomatic of such unrest was *wŏnjo kyoje*. This originated from the Japanese *enjo kōsai*, which can be translated literally as "dating with aid" or "subsidized dating." Wŏnjo kyoje first appeared in the newspapers in 1997, right before the economic crisis, in a report on Japanese schoolgirls engaging in prostitution with adult men in return for pocket money or gifts, such as clothes and cell phones.[47] The next year, however, the Korean news media exposed that this practice was also occurring in their country. For instance, investigative journalism program *PD Note* sensationally reported on the sex trade between schoolgirls and adult men using evidence recorded with a hidden camera on June 16, 1998.[48] In response, the Committee to Protect Youth under the Office of the Prime Minister decided to revise the Youth Protection Act to punish adults who had sex with adolescents, interpreting wŏnjo kyoje as a result of the "aftermath of the economic crisis."[49]

Unlike other issues related to prostitution, here the government rapidly took the initiative to combat wŏnjo kyoje, and the women's movement subsequently cooperated. This collaboration between the state and feminists was possible mainly because of the election as president in 1997 of Kim Dae-Jung (Kim Tae-Jung), who had been a respected dissident against authoritarian regimes and historically a supporter of progressive feminist movements. In contrast to the military dictatorship of the past, the new liberal government greeted feminists as partners in governance. As a result, feminist organizations including the KCWU, Korea Women's Hot Line, Korea Sexual Violence Relief Center, and the Womenlink participated in an advisory group for the Committee to Protect Youth in 1998, and they campaigned against wŏnjo kyoje under the banner of "protecting our sons and daughters from the adult entertainment industry."[50]

Thanks to this cordial relationship between the government and feminists, as well as public support, the Youth Protection Act was smoothly revised in 1999, adding articles to punish adults who had sex with adolescents with imprisonment of no greater than three years or fines no greater than 20 million KRW (about US$20,000). This was a much heavier punishment than that levied for commercial sex acts between adults, that is, imprisonment of no greater than one year and fines no greater than 3 million KRW (about US$3,000) according to the revised Yullak Prevention Act. In 2000, a more specific new law to protect adolescents from sexual crimes including prostitution was enacted. The Act on the Protection of Youth against Sex Offenses imposed probation on adolescents who sold sex, instead of punishment, while subjecting convicted adults to the public disclosure of their identity alongside other punishment.

In this way, Korean society right after the IMF crisis witnessed both the new phenomenon of wŏnjo kyoje and new systematic legal responses to prevent it. However, adolescent prostitution itself was not new. In the early 1990s, for example, so-called chick serving bars (yŏnggye sulchip) were prevalent, and here, in parallel to the colloquial English, the word "chick" (yŏnggye) was a sexualized term to refer to a girl.[51] On January 19, 1968, a newspaper article reported that about 40 percent of the prostitutes in the "special zones" ranged in age from eleven to nineteen.[52] Two of my interviewees in chapter 4, Park Yeongja and Han Min-Ju, also started or were forced to engage in prostitution as teenagers in the 1970s. In this regard, while adolescent prostitution did not first emerge in the late 1990s, it was newly constituted as a social problem in that period. Therefore, the wŏnjo kyoje scandal can be interpreted as a symptom of the anxiety surrounding financially motivated sexual activity caused by the economic crisis, as well as being symbolic of the many broken homes and families that were unable to protect their young daughters due to the difficulties of the time. On behalf of such parents, the liberal government was expected to protect their adolescent daughters and alleviate the widespread concerns about sexual activity in society.

Although adolescent prostitution was not new, wŏnjo kyoje in the late 1990s had a new feature. Many of the girls engaged in it not as professionals but as amateurs or even as students. This is why it was called kyoje, that is, "dating." This new generation preferred meeting male clients using the internet instead of being employed at brothels or bars.[53] As such, the boundary between what constituted "innocent schoolgirls" and "seasoned prostitutes" became blurred in the public imagination. This conceptual frame was not limited to teenagers. On August 26, 1998, a newspaper article reported on a change in the sex industry caused by the economic crisis:

> After the IMF crisis, many "ordinary women" such as housewives, career women, and college students started to make a living through prostitution. The theory that one of the social pathologies during the economic depression is women's sexual decadence is being proven in our society. . . . Sociology professor Han T'ae-Sŏn at Hanyang University said "[This phenomenon] has originated from a confusion in values among young women with overspending habits, who consider prostitution [relative to] their personal right to overcome economic poverty."[54]

Interestingly, the title of this article was "The Breakdown of the Sexual Sanctuary: An Increase in Prostitution among Women Who Cannot Forget the Bubble Era." In other words, the reporter lamented that while the sexuality of so-called ordinary women had been kept in a form of "sanctuary" in the past, that is, monogamous fidelity to their husbands, now some of them, and in particular those who suffered from the habit of overspending, violated the standard boundaries of sexual activity that had separated prostitutes and "normal" women. In this way, adult women who newly entered the sex industry after the crisis were depicted as the incarnation of consumerism, not as people in need of economic support. Thus, they did not deserve the special treatment of legal impunity, which was levied on the teenagers engaged in wŏnjo kyoje. Therefore, unlike wŏnjo kyoje, adult prostitution did not emerge as a national concern in the late 1990s, but this situation changed just a few years later.

Human Trafficking as a "National Shame"

Another noticeable change in the late 1990s sex industry was the influx of foreign women from neighboring countries, particularly those from the former Soviet Union and the Philippines. It started in 1996 in earnest, and the economic crisis in 1997 did not hinder the trend. Although Korea's status within the global economy plummeted, conditions within Russia, its satellite states, and the Philippines were even worse. Thus, women from those countries frequently migrated to Korea to find better economic opportunities, and many ended up in prostitution.

There were three paths through which foreign women entered or were forced to enter the Korean sex industry. First, the most prominent way was to get the art and entertainment visa (E-6 visa). Second, some women came to Korea with various tourist visas (B or C visa) and continued to stay illegally. Finally, a few women got the spouse visa (F-2, now F-6 visa) through sham marriages.[55] Whereas it is impossible to gauge what portion of women with tourist or spouse visas engaged in the sex industry, it is well known that many with E-6 visas worked at clubs, bars, and hotels, which were also the main venues for commercial sex. In fact, from 1996 the owners of those facilities, in particular the proprietors of camptown clubs, frequently utilized the E-6 visa to hire "foreign entertainers."[56]

Why did the camptown clubs take the lead in importing foreign women? From the late 1980s onward, the financial incentives associated with working in the camptown environment rapidly declined, and the club owners had difficulty employing Korean women. This followed Korea's economic development and the appreciation of the KRW, which left the purchasing power of American military personnel comparatively diminished.[57] Consequently, club owners' profits also decreased, and working at camptowns became a less lucrative option for Korean women. Faced with low-profit margins and labor force shortages, the club owners turned their attention to importing cheap labor from more impoverished countries. After several years, the Korea Special Tourism Association, an official organization operated by camptown club owners, succeeded in getting permission to hire foreign women, in 1996. One of the top staffers of the association testified that he personally helped persuade government officials in the Agency for National Security Planning and the Ministry of Culture and Tourism to permit the use of foreign women workers in camptowns. This meant that managing the general upkeep of the camptowns and providing women to satisfy the sexual demands of U.S. troops was still considered an essential issue of national security, to the extent that the Agency for National Security Planning was involved in facilitating their legal employment. The staffer also admitted that foreign women worked at the clubs as de facto "hospitality women," a common euphemism for prostitutes, and not as "entertainers."[58]

The number of foreign women entrants holding E-6 visas increased from 345 in 1995 to 5,578 in 2000, as much as sixteenfold in five years. From 1995 to 1998, Filipino women were the main group, being about 40 percent of E-6 visa holders, but from 1999, Russian women outnumbered Filipinas, making up over 50 percent of the total.[59] While both Filipinas and Russians were hired at camptowns to cater to American troops, a considerable number of Russians also served Korean men at nightclubs, bars, and room salons, satisfying their sexual desire for white women.[60] According to a survey commissioned by the Ministry of Gender Equality in 2003, about five to ten thousand migrant women were estimated to be engaged in the Korean sex industry, and many of them were subject to poor conditions, such as long working hours without regular holidays, income exploitation, arbitrary penalties, violence, and forced prostitution. Based on these facts, the survey concluded that most foreign female entertainers were the victims of human trafficking.[61]

Feminist activists of the KCWU, the Durebang, and the Saeumtŏ (another shelter for camptown women established in 1996) criticized the government for overlooking the fact of human trafficking associated with the E-6 visa.[62] The issue of trafficking in women, which had panicked the whole of Korean society in the late 1980s, was now reignited over ten years later, only this time it was the lives of foreign women at stake. Yet a few feminist scholars were critical of the tendency to regard all foreign female entertainment visa holders as the victims of human trafficking. According to their research, while some migrant women chose to return to their countries due to the exploitative conditions, others wanted to stay in Korea to work and fight for decent pay and legitimate rights. A few even reentered Korea after going back to their countries of origin to get another economic opportunity. Therefore, these scholars warned that if feminists merely reductively regarded such women as the victims of human trafficking, they ran the risk of erasing any recognition of the wider spectrum of a migrant woman's potential agency as a "desiring subject," borrowing from feminist anthropologist Sealing Cheng.[63]

Regardless of these debates inside feminism, human trafficking surfaced as an important agenda in Korea during the early 2000s. This focus was mainly due to the trafficking in persons (TIP) report released by the U.S. Department of State on July 13, 2001. It ranked Korea as a tier 3 nation, that is, one of the countries in which human trafficking occurs most seriously, denoting Korea as "a country of origin and transit for trafficking in persons." It also noted that "while South Korea is a leader in the region on human rights and democracy generally, the Government has done little to combat this relatively new and worsening problem of trafficking in persons."[64] Interestingly, the report focused on the trafficking of Korean and Chinese women to the United States and never once mentioned camptown prostitution and the related traffic in female entertainers. Ironically, here the U.S. government, which stationed its troops in Korea and therefore was also responsible for the existence of camptown prostitution, acted as a neutral judge, or even a moral guardian, and an advocate for women's human rights in Korea.

The Korean government considered this report a matter of national shame and immediately sought to rebut it. Simultaneously, however, the government acknowledged the need to combat human trafficking.[65] On August 29, 2001, the Supreme Prosecutor's Office instructed the prosecutors to intensify police attention on crimes related to human trafficking. From September, the Joint Task Force on Trafficking in Persons, consisting of prosecutors, police officers, and other related public officials, started to crack down on the diverse forms of human trafficking associated with the prostitution of both Korean and foreign women.[66] In addition, the Immigration Bureau strengthened the screening of visas and refused to issue visas for entertainers belonging to improper agencies.[67] Based on these immediate legal measures, Korea was classified as a tier 1 country in the 2002 TIP report, becoming the only country that had been elevated from tier 3 in the previous report. The report stated that "the Government of the Republic of Korea fully complies with minimum standards for the elimination of trafficking."[68] Ultimately, in just one year the Korean government was able to regain U.S. recognition of it as "a leader in the region on human rights and democracy."

Due to such policies, the number of foreign women entrants with E-6 visas decreased from 6,971 in 2000 to 2,498 in 2004, around 65 percent in four years. What is more noticeable is a change in the ratio of nationalities among them. Russian women dramatically decreased, from 3,518 to 166 in the same period, but Filipino women contrastingly increased, from 1,599 to 1,854. Consequently, the portion of Filipinas in the female entertainer visa category increased from 22.9 to 74.2 percent, while that of Russians decreased from 50.5 to 6.6 percent. It is unclear what caused this change in the nationalities of foreign female entertainers. However, one thing seems obvious: considering that the Filipinas were mainly hired at camptowns, the steady number of Filipinas holding E-6 visas shows that the camptowns were not severely impacted by the government crackdown on human trafficking. In fact, the Ministry of Culture and Tourism had strengthened the minimum standards for entertainment venues to employ foreign entertainers in 2003. However, since the owners of the camptown clubs that had already hired E-6 visa holders had protested this decision, the ministry decided not to apply those standards to their existing workforce.[69]

The appearance of foreign women in the Korean sex industry posed a significant challenge to both the Korean government and the national women's movements. The government, which had conveniently accepted the camptown club owners' request to import foreign entertainers, was now unexpectedly confronted with the embarrassing shame of being a country incapable of suppressing the trafficking of women across its borders. Korean feminists, who had mainly focused on the rights of Korean women, were now encountered with a new set of questions, most of which are still yet to be fully resolved. These include issues such as whether there is any way to protect foreign female entertainers even though the Korean prostitution laws are considered insufficient to protect Korean women. Moreover, what is the right course of action in this case? Is it to prevent this form of migration as human trafficking? Or is it to guarantee the safe migration of these women if they desire, and allow them to work within the Korean adult entertainment industry that might include prostitution? As I examine further in this chapter, such questions have not been limited in scope to only foreign entertainers and a few related feminist NGOs. In the vortex of appalling accidents involving prostitution, these questions emerged as critical issues in wider Korean society.

Tragic Fires and Feminist Anti-Prostitution Campaigns

On the morning of September 19, 2000, a fire occurred in an unlicensed three-story building in a red-light district for Korean men in Gunsan. It claimed the lives of five women who were found to be incarcerated in the building and forced to engage in prostitution behind iron bars.[70] One year and four months later, on January 29, 2002, another fire broke out at an entertainment bar, which was only one kilometer away from the site of the previous fire. This time fourteen women and one man were killed. They attempted to escape the bar but failed because the entrance was locked. It was then revealed that the female victims had been forced to engage in prostitution through violence, surveillance, and oppressive illegal contracts.[71] The fact that some women, and in particular Korean women, were still being coerced into slave-like forms of prostitution in the twenty-first century shocked Korean society.[72]

Faced with these tragedies, feminists immediately took action. A week after the first fire, the Gunsan branch of the Korea Women's Hot Line organized a task force committee with diverse local NGOs. In October, other feminist organizations such as the Korean Women's Associations United (KWAU), the Korea Women's Hot Line, the Hansorihoe, and the Saeumtŏ joined the task force committee. Instead of using stigmatized words such as prostitution and prostitutes, feminists now used rather neutral terms like "commercial sex acts" (*sŏngmaemae*, literally "selling and buying sex") and "women [engaged] in commercial sex acts" (*sŏngmaemae yŏsŏng*). They accused not only the brothel keepers but also police officers and other related public servants of being bribed by the brothel keepers and/or neglecting their duties to crack down on sŏngmaemae, supervise the safety of the building, and rescue the sŏngmaemae yŏsŏng.[73] They also filed a lawsuit against the national government, Gunsan City, and the brothel keepers to demand reparations for the victims, and they finally won. On September 23, 2004, the Supreme Court decided that the government should pay compensation of 67 million KRW (about US$67,000) in total, and the brothel keepers should pay 590 million KRW (about US$590,000) in total to the victims' families.[74] Faced with the second fire, feminist groups adopted the same strategy. They filed a lawsuit against the national government, Gunsan City, and the brothel keepers, and achieved victory with the court's decision that the government and the brothel keepers should pay 273 million KRW (about US$273,000) and 2.5 billion KRW (about US$2.5 million) to all the victims, respectively.[75]

This cluster of feminist activism sparked by the two Gunsan fires was in stark contrast to the situation in 1995 when the fire occurred at the Gyeonggi Female Technical Training Institute. The number of deaths in 1995 was forty, a much larger number of people than those who perished in the Gunsan fires. Nevertheless, only the member organizations of the Hansorihoe established a task force committee, and other feminist organizations, including the KWAU, did not take part in it. By contrast, the two fires in Gunsan provided the momentum by which the issue of prostitution was embraced by the mainstream women's movement. Not only did national organizations such as the KWAU and the Korea Women's Hot Line join the task force committees, but the KWAU chose the 2000 fire as the top news story of the women's movement that year.[76] This shift represented the fact that prostitution emerged as a central issue for Korean feminism in the early 2000s.

Simultaneously, the activists within local anti-prostitution NGOs had the opportunity to express their opinions about national policy on the national stage. For instance, Kim Hyŏn-Sŏn, the director of the Saeumtŏ for camp-town women in Gyeonggi Province, was invited as a main speaker to several conferences on prostitution policy following the 2000 Gunsan fire. She became a member of the Sexuality and Human Rights Committee in 2001 and a corepresentative of the Special Committee to Legislate the Commercial Sex Prevention Act in 2002, both of which were set up under the auspices of the KWAU.[77] In tandem with this, the subtitle of Saeumtŏ changed in 2001 from the Shelter for Camptown Women and Their Children to the Supporting Center for the Victims of Commercial Sex Acts, expanding its reach from specific local targets to nationwide prostitution.[78] Another main speaker was Jeong Mi Rye, a former secretary of the Gunsan Women's Hot Line, which played a critical role in constituting the Gunsan fires as a main issue of concern for national feminism. She became another corepresentative of the Special Committee to Legislate the Commercial Sex Prevention Act in 2002.[79]

These two activists took the lead in the campaign to legislate a new prohibitionist act. Kim Hyŏn-Sŏn, who had suggested the revision of the existing Yullak Preventing Act at a conference in October 2000, decided to advocate for a brand-new act at another conference held two months later. She defined prostitution per se as serious violence against women, and therefore the new act should decriminalize the women engaged in prostitution while punishing male clients and third parties, following the Swedish model.[80] At the same conference, Jeong Mi Rye agreed with Kim, asserting: "To solve sŏngmaemae, the will of the state is crucial. It is time for us to struggle, believing that sŏngmaemae shall be eradicated definitely if the state has a will."[81] Their arguments had a great resonance in the mainstream women's movement, and the KWAU immediately drafted a bill as early as October 2001, just one year after the first Gunsan fire.[82]

Feminists also relied on international supporters to boost their cause. For instance, the Saeumtŏ organized an international conference in October 2001. Around fifty anti-prostitution activists from the Philippines, Hong Kong, Japan, the United States, and Korea were invited to the conference, and the keynote speaker was Kathleen Barry. At the conference, Barry summarized her book *The Prostitution of Sexuality* (1995) and emphasized the necessity for countries to legislate as national law the Convention against Sexual Exploitation that she had proposed.[83] Another unexpected but also crucial ally was the U.S. Department of State. Feminists utilized its 2001 TIP report as leverage to put pressure on the Korean government. For example, during the opening address of the conference to discuss the new bill in October

2001, the KWAU blamed the Korean government for not devoting sufficient energy to suppressing the prevalence of commercial sex activity and the related occurrence of human trafficking, "to the extent that Korea was ranked as a tier 3 nation."[84] In contrast, when the 2002 TIP report elevated Korea to tier 1, Jeong Mi Rye criticized the U.S. State Department's decision, arguing that it merely believed the Korean government's official reports without properly monitoring the actual circumstances of prostitution in Korea. However, instead of requesting that the United States downgrade Korea, she called for the Korean government to legislate a new act to prevent this "national shame" and reflect the nation's "status as a tier 1 country."[85]

As such, prostitution emerged as the most impassioned agenda to unite mainstream feminists in the early 2000s. Unlike in the late 1980s, they reached a clear consensus to support the creation of a more stringent law to suppress prostitution. They also had firm confidence in the state as the most crucial and effective agent in curbing prostitution. Therefore, their legislative campaigns were based on a collective feminist project to build a moral nation free of prostitution by making use of state power. However, this approach provokes several questions. Is it even possible for the state to eradicate prostitution? Can governmental intervention effectively prevail over the powerful dynamics of both male social dominance and the capitalist economy, which in combination force many women to engage in prostitution? These questions are difficult to answer, but one thing is clear. To utilize state power, feminists must "translate" their causes and terms into the language of state governance in advance, that is, through laws and policies. During this process, however, the campaigners' ideals and causes often get transformed, compromised, and distorted. And this very thing happened in Korea during the early 2000s.

The bill that the KWAU drafted in 2001 specified its purpose as being "to punish and prevent the activities to arrange commercial sex acts or engage in commercial sex acts, and to protect the human rights of the prostituted and aid their return to society" (Article 1). It continued by defining "commercial sex acts" as being: "to buy or sell sex in return for or promising money or valuables, or other profits." "Sex acts" included not only vaginal intercourse but sexual stimulation using parts of the body such as the mouth and anus, and other tools (Article 2). To suppress such commercial sex acts, the bill proposed to increase the punishment of the mediators from a period of imprisonment no greater than five years to no less than five years (Article 13), while introducing a wide variety of welfare programs and facilities to protect the prostituted (chapter 4).[86]

As noted, the bill referred to prostitution as sŏngmaemae, which replaced the derogatory term *yullak*, that is, the morally degrading behavior of women. Another important term in the bill is "the prostituted" (*sŏngmaemae toen cha*) of Article 1. This seemed to originate from the phrase "prostituted women," which was first used by Filipino anti-prostitution activists and popularized by Australian radical feminist Sheila Jeffreys.[87] This language shows again that Korean feminists adopted a radical feminist perspective to legally frame women engaged in prostitution as those victimized by male clients and third parties, and not as the agents of sex work. Yet they neutralized the term to include reference to a few, if any, male victims. At the same time, however, the bill narrowed down the category of "the prostituted" to people with disabilities, foreign women, adolescents, and other victims of human trafficking, incarceration, rape, assault, threat, deception, debt, and drug abuse (Article 2). In addition, it introduced another category, "sellers of sex," and subjected this group to the same punishment as "buyers of sex," with imprisonment of no greater than one year or fines no greater than 3 million KRW (around US$3,000) (Article 14).

From the viewpoint of radical feminists, women cannot sell sex voluntarily. According to them, all prostitutes are de facto prostituted women, and thus sellers of sex is a sort of oxymoron. By contrast, the bill differentiated sellers of sex from the prostituted and suggested punishing the former while exempting the latter from punishment. In this regard, Korean feminists compromised their cause of radical feminism and their ideal of the Swedish model to adapt to the existing grammar of prohibition, which maintained the laws that had existed since 1948. In principle, they argued that sŏngmaemae "should not be considered a [valid] profession or a necessary evil in society, but violence against and exploitation of women."[88] In reality, however, they drafted a bill to punish sellers of sex, if they could not be admitted into the category of the prostituted.

The drafters of the bill recognized that it was a compromise but justified this by emphasizing the urgent need to enact a new law. For instance, at a public hearing at the National Assembly in July 2003, Kim Hyŏn-Sŏn responded to a lawmaker's question about whether she supported the decriminalization of all women engaged in prostitution with the following statement: "I think this should be realized in the long term, but this bill expands protection to the women, since it includes articles to support and protect not only the prostituted but also voluntary sellers of sex."[89] In fact, the bill proposed immunity or the commutation of punishment for some sellers of sex if they surrendered themselves to justice or reported third parties or traffickers (Article 17), as well as a diverse range of welfare programs for them along with the prostituted (chapter 4).[90]

In this way, Korean feminists failed to fully translate their radical language of sexual exploitation into their bill, by giving up their cause of decriminalizing all women engaged in prostitution and compromising with the state's language of prohibition. Perhaps more damningly, they were also unsuccessful in incorporating the voices and perspectives of women engaged in prostitution into their bill. Only the Saeumtŏ conducted a telephone survey to ask thirty "former" sŏngmaemae yŏsŏng participating in its self-reliance programs about their opinions of the bill in 2001.[91] All thirty interviewees unanimously opposed the punishment of voluntary sellers of sex, but the bill included this measure anyway. What is worse, the bill still faced a more difficult passage ahead, as the National Assembly was dominated by a vast majority of male lawmakers.

New Prohibitionist Acts and the Decline of the Toleration-Regulation Regime

To pass the bill into law, the KWAU had to find a sympathetic partner among the lawmakers of the National Assembly, and Cho Pae-Suk, a female member of the ruling liberal Millennium Democratic Party, played such a role. Cho revised the bill based on consultation with the Legislative Counseling Office of the National Assembly and proposed it to the assembly with seventy-four supporting members across different political parties in July 2002. However, the proper standing committee to examine the bill could not be determined, since it had elements of both penal and welfare laws. Hence, Cho divided the bill into two, a bill to punish all the parties involved in prostitution and a bill to protect both prostitution victims and the women voluntarily engaged in prostitution, to enable their review by the Legislation and Judiciary Committee and the Gender Equality Committee, respectively. She proposed the bills in September, now with the support of eighty-six members. However, their ultimate legislation was frustrated due to the opposition of many members of the judiciary committee.[92]

The inauguration of President Roh Moo-Hyun (No Mu-Hyŏn) in 2003 provided a turning point to break this deadlock. As a former human rights lawyer who worked against the military dictatorship, Roh was an important ally of mainstream feminists, succeeding his predecessor, Kim Dae-Jung.

During his presidential campaign, Roh promised to legislate a stricter prohibitionist act and build a task force team to grapple with prostitution.[93] After he took office, he unprecedentedly appointed four female ministers to his administration. In particular, Kang Kŭm-Sil, the first female minister of justice and a former feminist lawyer, and Chi Ŭn-Hŭi, the minister of gender equality and a former representative of the KWAU, played a significant role in the legislation of the bills. The minister of gender equality led the Task Force Team to Prevent Commercial Sex Acts, a public-private partnership organization established in June 2003 according to the president's promise, coordinating inclusive prostitution policies and preparing for the enactment of new laws. The Ministry of Justice, which had been skeptical about the bills in the previous administration, changed its perspective due to the appointment of a new feminist minister to advocate for the new laws. Finally, the two bills were submitted to the assembly plenary session on March 2, 2004, and it was passed into law almost unanimously, as all members except one voted in favor. It was the last plenary session of the 16th National Assembly, so all lawmakers, regardless of their political affiliation, were keen to court female voters due to the impending election.[94]

As a result, after forty-three long years, the notorious Yullak Prevention Act finally gave way to new acts, specifically titled the Act on the Punishment of Arrangement of Commercial Sex Acts and the Act on the Prevention of Commercial Sex Acts and Protection of Victims (hereafter the Sŏngmaemae Prevention Acts). On the day of the bill's ratification, the KWAU released a statement to celebrate the legislation, arguing that it "is very meaningful since the state recognizes its responsibility to protect sŏngmaemae yŏsŏng, who have been socially disregarded." Simultaneously however, the KWAU admitted that the new laws had several limitations, particularly in that feminists had failed to achieve the decriminalization of sŏngmaemae yŏsŏng "due to the opposition of members of the National Assembly."[95] These limitations were substantial, as the term the prostituted in the bill was replaced with "the victims of commercial sex acts" in the enacted law, and this new category was considerably narrower than the former, excluding foreign women and women in debt.[96] Moreover, the possibility of immunity and commutation being granted for sellers of sex was entirely jettisoned. The KWAU argued that the decriminalization of all women engaged in prostitution was frustrated by lawmakers in the assembly. However, it did not mention that in its own draft bill it had already introduced the distinction between the prostituted and sellers of sex and proposed to punish the latter.

With the enforcement of the Sŏngmaemae Prevention Acts, the number of people arrested in relation to commercial sex acts increased substantially, from 9,987 in 2003 to 18,508 in 2005. What is more dramatic is the change in the ratio of gender among those arrested. While the 2003 statistics did not split the arrested into subcategories such as third parties, clients, and prostitutes, by gender the ratio was 45.5 percent (4,546) men and 54.5 percent (5,441) women.[97] By contrast, in 2005, third parties were 22.0 percent (4,071), male buyers were 62.0 percent (11,474), and female sellers were 16.0 percent (2,963).[98] This reflects the shift in police attention from female sellers to male buyers and third parties. But beyond arrest, what judicial decisions were the arrested ultimately subject to? According to a study by the Korean Women's Development Institute in 2007, from September 2004 to May 2007, 37.6 percent of sellers, 42.6 percent of buyers, and 71.9 percent of third parties were prosecuted. Most of the prosecuted prostitutes (93.5 percent) and clients (90.8 percent) were sentenced to fines, while 66.9 percent and 24.8 percent of the prosecuted third parties were sentenced to fines and imprisonment, respectively. The average fine was 1.14 million KRW for sellers (around US$1,140), 1.30 million KRW for buyers (around US$1,300), and 2.74 million KRW (around US$2,740) for third parties.[99]

The Sŏngmaemae Prevention Acts therefore resulted in fewer female sellers being arrested, prosecuted, and punished than male buyers and third parties. However, the fact that some female sellers were still arrested, prosecuted, and punished shows that the laws contradicted not only the KWAU's radical feminist orientation but also the interests of the women in the sex industry. What was worse, the average fine for female sellers increased as much as 90 percent, from 0.60 million KRW in 2001 to 1.14 million KRW following the passage of the new laws, while the fines for male buyers and third parties increased only 4.8 percent and 10.9 percent respectively over the same period.[100] Arguably, such harsh financial penalties would make it more likely that these women would return to the sex industry instead of leaving it, to earn the money to pay the fine.

The enforcement of the Sŏngmaemae Prevention Acts also sharpened the contradiction between regulation and prohibition, which had been set in the toleration-regulation regime for over half a century. As prohibition came to the fore, regulation was retrenched. For instance, the number of female service workers registered for periodic STI testing decreased by over 30 percent, from 158,892 in 2003 to 108,403 in 2005, and the number of accumulated STI testing cases also diminished from 2.85 million to 1.95 million during the same period.[101] On July 14, 2006, a staffer of the Korea Centers for Disease Control and Prevention, which was in charge of regular STI testing under the Ministry of Health and Welfare, attributed this decrease to the Sŏngmaemae Prevention Acts, arguing that intensified crackdowns on prostitution only dispersed prostitutes from red-light districts and forced them to go underground.[102] In response to this comment, the Ministry of Gender Equality and Family immediately released a retort, emphasizing prohibition as a solution to prevent STIs. It also expressed concern that the practice of mandatory STI testing imposed on only women "could violate women's human rights." It is notable here that the Ministry of Gender Equality and Family did not assert that gender-discriminatory STI testing actually "did violate" women's human rights. Moreover, although it suggested an "improvement of the current STI control policy," it did not have enough power to push ahead with this measure.[103] As a result, with the Sŏngmaemae Prevention Acts, the toleration-regulation regime retrenched but still continued.

Unexpected Conflicts among Sisters: Sex Workers' Protests against the New Acts

When the Sŏngmaemae Prevention Acts took effect, the media, in particular conservative newspapers such as *Chosŏn ilbo* and *Chungang ilbo*, expressed skepticism that the laws would not eradicate the necessary evil of prostitution and only end up with the so-called balloon effect—that is, squeezing one part of the sex industry would lead to the dispersal of prostitution into other, more secret sectors of practice.[104] However, the most dramatic scenes that the Sŏngmaemae Prevention Acts produced were arguably the protests staged by the women engaged in prostitution. On the very day when the laws took effect, about five hundred prostitutes and brothel keepers waged a demonstration at Miari Texas, a red-light district in Northern Seoul, which spread to other major cities such as Daegu, Pyeongtaek, Incheon, and Busan. On October 7 and 19, around three thousand women in prostitution and brothel keepers gathered in front of the National Assembly and at the Cheongnyangni Plaza, Seoul, respectively (see figure 17). The demonstrators blamed anti-prostitution feminists as "female overlords" and called for the government to delay the enforcement of the laws and guarantee their right to a livelihood. On November 1, the Hantŏ Alliance of Female Employees (Hantŏ yŏsŏng chongsaja yŏnmaeng; hereafter Hanyŏyŏn), an organization of women in red-light districts, was launched. It was associated with

FIGURE 17. Sex workers' demonstration in front of the National Assembly, October 7, 2004. *Source:* Photo by Lee Jong-Ho, *Ohmynews*, October 7, 2004.

the Hantŏ National Association (Hantŏ chŏn'guk yŏnhap), an organization of brothel keepers.[105] Then, on the same day, about twenty members of the Hanyŏyŏn staged a hunger strike in front of the National Assembly, which lasted for seventy-three days. On November 6, about ten members of the the Hanyŏyŏn staged a sit-in in front of the Ministry of Gender Equality. They wore Korean traditional white mourning clothes to symbolize that they were not able to live because of the new laws.[106]

In this way, the women who had been invisible nocturnal beings confined to red-light districts abruptly occupied prominent public spaces in broad daylight. They wore face masks to hide their identities but protested loudly, with pickets and banners, with some using microphones to vocally demand a delay in the enforcement of the laws. Throughout this struggle, this group gradually started to call themselves sex workers, and the Hanyŏyŏn changed its name to the National Solidarity of Sex Workers Hanyŏyŏn on June 29, 2005.[107] At the same time, however, the organization kept Hanyŏyŏn in its name, showing its close relationship with the Hantŏ National Association, the brothel keepers. On August 27, the same year, the Democratic Solidarity of Sex Workers was organized. Based in a red-light district in Pyeongtaek, it established itself as a local labor union and reached a collective agreement with its brothel keepers ten days after its launch.[108]

The feminists, who had campaigned for legislation to protect the women in red-light districts and save them from brothel keepers, were utterly embarrassed by the unexpected and unprecedented collective activism of their disenfranchised sisters. Chi Ŭn-Hŭi, the minister of gender equality, described the demonstrators as victims of "the Stockholm syndrome," that is, psychologically traumatized hostages who sympathize with their captors (brothel owners).[109] Jeong Mi Rye, a corepresentative of the National Solidarity against Sexual Exploitation of Women, an umbrella organization of counseling centers and shelters for women in prostitution established in June 2004, criticized the demonstrations as "a prearranged strategy by brothel keepers to throw a wet blanket on the will of the government and feminist organizations to eradicate prostitution."[110] Cho Yŏng-Suk, the secretary of the KWAU, argued that witnesses to the demonstrations raised concern that "the demonstrators' claims" do not reflect the "real voices of the women in prostitution."[111]

However, a few researchers interviewed these women who identified themselves as sex workers and found that they emphasized their voluntary participation in the demonstrations and organizations and were not being mobilized by brothel keepers.[112] The interviewees expressed animosity toward feminists, who, they thought, neglected their voices considering them "liars" or passive victims enslaved and "brainwashed" by brothel keepers. They agreed that human trafficking should be punished, but they asserted that they had "chosen" their job due to desperate economic hardship. Most interviewees did not want to continue in prostitution for a long time, but they felt anger at being forced to stop with no alternatives on offer. In the process of protesting the laws, they attained a new form of identity as sex workers. They considered that this new appellation offered them a new, more positive notion of themselves and self-being in relation to their professional and social status:

> I kept participating in demonstrations. One day [at a demonstration], a sister said that we are sex workers. The moment I heard the word, I realized "I am not a dirty woman to earn money by selling sex." My heart was beating with the word sex worker, so I thought it was necessary to change the name of the organization.[113]

> When I was arrested through the police roundup, a police officer asked me "What do you want me to fill in the profession space [on the police report]?"

"Why do you ask me? [Of course] you should fill it in with a sex worker." As I said that, the police officer wrote sex worker, smiling. How can I describe the feeling, the pleasure?[114]

The initial enforcement of the new laws provoked widespread and determined protests on the part of the women engaged in prostitution. These were primarily because the government focused on crackdowns without offering economic alternatives for the women. To overcome this limitation, the KWAU and the Ministry of Gender Equality embarked on a "model project for red-light districts" on November 3, 2004, about forty days after the laws took effect. Thanks to this program, centers to provide counseling and job training were established in two red-light districts to help women abandon prostitution. The women who participated in the job training program were paid 370,000 KRW (about US$370) monthly for one year as a form of emergency benefits, which was the same as the official minimum cost of living for one person in 2004.[115] Some participants in this program were able to quit prostitution and find other jobs, and this model project spread to twelve more districts in the following two years.[116] However, the sex workers' organizations complained that the provision of a benefit amounting to the minimum cost of living was too small to allow women to support themselves, not to mention their families. They argued that only the decriminalization of the sex industry could guarantee their right to earn a livelihood.[117]

The Sŏngmaemae Prevention Acts ignited conflicts and tensions not only between feminists and sex workers but also among feminists. Witnessing the protests of sex workers, a few NGOs such as the Research Center for Women's Culture and Feminist Theories, People's Solidarity for Social Progress, Women's Solidarity for Anti-Globalization, and the Power of Working Class supported sex workers' organizations. Based on the perspectives of socialism, libertarianism, and/or intersectionality, these organizations criticized the mainstream feminists' seemingly radical but de facto moralistic approach to prostitution and advocated for the entire decriminalization of the sex industry.[118] Some feminists, who had introduced radical feminist perspectives on prostitution into the Korean discourse, reflected that their previous studies had only focused on the aspects of sexual oppression in prostitution. For instance, Won Mi Hye argued, "prostitution is an outcome of patriarchy and a 'dangerous' choice for women, yet simultaneously, it is an economic means, a sexual relation, and a form of life as well." Thus, she suggested that feminists should pay attention to the complicated and multilayered experiences of women in the sex industry and how to empower them without forcing them out of prostitution.[119] However, unlike both the anti-prostitution feminists and pro-sex work feminists, Won and her colleagues have not presented any clear legal solutions to prostitution, such as the decriminalization of only prostitutes or the entire sex industry.

As we have examined throughout this book, the state of Korea has consistently guaranteed men's privilege to seek commercial sexual pleasure while harshly controlling sex workers as archetypal fallen women and internal enemies. Then, in the twenty-first century, mainstream Korean feminists attempted to refigure a new version of the nation, free of prostitution, by calling for the state to control the arrant unregulated procurement of sex by the male population through penal law. Thanks to the new laws, they succeeded in closing several red-light districts, which constituted the most visible and therefore most juridically vulnerable sector of the sex industry. However, today a few red-light districts are still open, while less visible arenas for the procurement of sex such as room salons, cabarets, karaoke, massage parlors, and in particular the internet have become the main venues for prostitution.[120] In addition, the feminists not only failed to decriminalize the women engaged in prostitution but also encountered passionate protests by sex workers in response to their endeavors, demanding the entire decriminalization of the sex industry. Given all these issues, the following questions remain: Will it ever be possible to materialize the feminists' ideal of a nation free of prostitution? And if so, how? While no one seems to know the answer to these questions, it seems to be clear that it will remain impossible to reach this vision in Korea under the current prohibitionist laws.

Epilogue

AFTER THE SŎNGMAEMAE PREVENTION ACTS

In this book I have explored Korea's nation-building process through the lens of prostitution from 1945, when the colonial public prostitution system emerged as a critical issue in the struggle for removing colonial remnants and forging a new national identity, to 2004, when the Sŏngmaemae Prevention Acts were enacted by feminists who envisioned a new moral nation intolerant of prostitution. Through successive chapters that each examined specific themes, I have demonstrated that prostitution was no trivial or marginal phenomenon but a constitutive element of nation building.

The biopolitical state of Korea was formed, augmented, and consolidated due to the apparatuses that enforced the toleration-regulation regime, such as the police, public health clinics, VD detention centers, and female reformatories. A wide range of social science research on prostitutes complemented and justified the state's biopolitical approach. Furthermore, for the U.S. military and foreign tourists, prostitution contributed considerably to national security and national development. To maximize the utility of the women engaged in prostitution while suppressing the threat they posed to the troops of its most important military and political ally, foreign tourists, and the whole of society, the Korean state implemented harsh measures against them, such as sporadic police crackdowns, mandatory STI testing, and forceful incarceration at detention centers and reformatories. This is why women like Park Yeongja, whose testimony I cited in the introduction, could justifiably consider themselves to paradoxically be "stateless patriots." Women working in the sex trade also functioned as a substratum to support the ideological gender hierarchy of their national community. They were

FIGURE 18. Former U.S. military "comfort women" and activists celebrating their legal victory at the Supreme Court, September 29, 2022. *Source:* Photo by Lee Ko Woon, September 29, 2022.

constituted as "women needing protection," over whom were positioned other female members of society already protected by their male guardians, with men duplicitously operating as both the protectors of "ladies" and the patrons of prostitutes. The disenfranchised and persecuted women working in the Korean sex industry usually adapted to the rules or negotiated with state control, but sometimes they protested against it. While their desperate struggles often failed, they occasionally achieved their goals, eventually making significant fractures in the toleration-regulation regime.

Now that Korea has achieved full recognition as an independent nation through the attainment of economic growth and political democratization, prostitution is no longer an urgent issue relative to the process of decolonization, nor is it an essential resource relative to maintaining national security and development. As a democratic country, Korea is now faced with the need to disclose the truth about the violence and injustice suffered by the women who were engaged in prostitution under successive authoritarian regimes, address their grief and pain, and illuminate their role as hidden agents of nation building. The recent legal victory of former "comfort women" for the U.S. military against the Korean state is a meaningful step to come to terms with this past (see figure 18). This was a confluent point of the long history of the protests staged by camptown women and the efforts of those who have stood by them, such as the feminist activists, pro bono lawyers, and feminist researchers. Through this lawsuit, the history of camptown women was restored, and both the Korean government and the Korean people had to confront this dark chapter of national history. The courts not only recognized the state's culpability in infringing upon these women's human rights but also declared that there is no statute of limitations on the illegal actions committed by Korea's past authoritarian governments.

This victory of these former stateless patriots over the state can be seen as an episode that reflects the radical transformation of Korea from an authoritarian state to a democratic one. It also signifies that Korea is being shifting from being a helpless client state to becoming a functioning autonomous nation. Unlike authoritarian governments that had been severe in controlling their female citizenry but feeble in protecting them from their military benefactor, the current and hopefully future governments will not be able to sacrifice their female citizens' rights for the country's military alliance, notwithstanding its continued reliance on the United States for its national security. However, this democratic state has now outsourced the "entertainment" of U.S. military personnel resident within its borders to foreign women from more impoverished countries.

In addition, other injustices committed by past authoritarian governments still remain historically hidden and have failed to garner attention from either social activists or academic researchers. The notorious female reformatories that I investigated in chapter 4 offer such a case. Although numerous girls and women were incarcerated at those facilities without due process for more than three decades, and a few of them even lost their lives there, only in 2021 did a few victims and their families start to take action to reveal the truth. One such man, whose mother went missing in 1983 and was later found to have been incarcerated in a female reformatory before being transferred to an institution for the homeless in Seoul, requested that the Truth and Reconciliation Commission, an independent body created to uncover past state violence, investigate the case. It seems his mother was a hairdresser and was assumed to have been apprehended by the police during a crackdown on the "women needing protection" under the Chun Doo-hwan regime.[1] Similarly, a few women from the Durebang, including my interviewees Park Yeongja, Han Min-Ju, and Yang Hye-Sun, submitted a petition to the Truth and Reconciliation Commission in 2022, imploring the panel to investigate the circumstances of their mistreatment at female reformatories.

Among the issues of nation building that I have explored, the only contemporary one related to prostitution is the gender hierarchy in the national community. Nearly two decades have passed since the passage of the 2004 Sŏngmaemae Prevention Acts, which are currently enforced with some minor revisions. The feminists initially dreamed of a nation free of prostitution created through the acts, or at least they thought these laws would restrain the male population's access to commercial sex and save as many women from prostitution as possible. In other words, they attempted to utilize for women's sake the "repressive state apparatuses" of the police and the public prosecution service, which had historically been used to oppress women in this very context.[2] However, their hopes are far from being realized. For one thing, while police crackdowns on prostitution temporarily intensified in the aftermath of the acts, this resolve ultimately weakened over time. For instance, the number of people arrested reached 69,287 in 2009 but diminished to 7,311 in 2022, decreasing 89.4 percent in thirteen years. Simultaneously, the portion of women among those arrested increased from 18.6 percent to 34.5 percent during the same period.[3] These numbers suggest that the approach underlying these police crackdowns is to decrease their frequency to that of the period before the Sŏngmaemae Prevention Acts, considering that in 2003 the number of the arrested was 9,987, among whom women constituted 54.5 percent. This demonstrates that it has been extremely difficult to redirect the police to go against their original and underlying sexist bias. In this regard, it is utterly tragic that in November 2014 a woman jumped to her death from the sixth floor of a motel when she was on the verge of being arrested in a police entrapment operation. This woman was later discovered to be a single mother raising a seven-year-old daughter.[4]

While the Sŏngmaemae Prevention Acts have contributed to the closure of several old-fashioned red-light districts, it is unclear whether the laws have effectively reduced the total scale of the sex industry.[5] One of these laws, the Act on the Prevention of Commercial Sex Acts and Protection of Victims, specifies that "the Minister of Gender Equality and Family shall investigate the status of commercial sex acts domestically and overseas . . . every three years" (Article 4). According to a 2010 study commissioned by the gender minister based on this provision of the act, the estimated number of women working in old-fashioned red-light districts (in which window brothels and other establishments specialized for prostitution are concentrated) was 4,917, and that of women working at other adult entertainment establishments (at which the main functions are drinking, dancing, singing, or massage, but prostitution is frequently arranged there) was about 160,000.[6] However, Statistics Korea (the official statistical recordkeeping branch of the Korean government) did not recognize this 2010 study within the realm of state-approved statistics, judging that it lacked reliability based on its insufficient number of samples and inappropriate methodology.[7] Since this point, there has been no state-approved statistical analysis to estimate the scale of prostitution arranged in adult entertainment establishments outside of the red-light districts. Nevertheless, it is obvious that prostitution occurs not only in red-light districts but also in other adult entertainment establishments on a much larger scale.

The most well-known places to offer sexual services other than brothels are "entertainment bars" (*yuhŭng chujŏm*), which were referred to as "entertainment restaurants" until the early 1990s (see chapter 3). The current Enforcement Decree of Food Sanitation Act defines "entertainment bar business" as the "business of cooking and selling mainly alcoholic beverages, where female workers entertaining guests may be employed or entertainment facilities may be established, and customers may sing or dance" (Article 21). According to the official statistics, the number of entertainment bars in 2021 was 26,897. Sinbak Chin-Yŏng, an activist of the National Solidarity against Sexual Exploitation of Women, an anti-prostitution organization, found out that this number is larger than the number of Chinese restaurants (24,179) across Korea.[8] Generally speaking, in such entertainment bars male guests are served by gaudily dressed female workers. The guests can touch the women and watch their performances while drinking at the bar, and in general, it is possible to pay them for sexual services at a local hotel afterward.

However, the category of entertainment bars is not homogenous but highly hierarchical according to the commercial rate and "size" of the women involved, a common slang term to refer to the grade of their attractiveness. For instance, in Gangnam, Seoul, the mecca of "room salons" since the 1980s (see chapter 3), each man has to pay over 500,000 KRW (around US$500) for the full service of highly "sized" young ladies at bars and hotels lasting about two hours, while they can enjoy similar services for much cheaper prices at low-class bars in small cities. On average, the women get paid about half of the fee, and therefore some can earn a considerable income. For instance, during her research on the political economy of the sex industry, Kim Joohee interviewed fifteen women working at diverse venues of prostitution and found out that those working at room salons earn a monthly income ranging from 4,000,000 to 8,000,000 KRW. Considering that the average monthly wage of Korean women was about 2,408,000 KRW in 2020, 64.7 percent of men's average wage (3,722,000 KRW), these women earn much more than not only ordinary female workers but also male workers.[9] However, to earn such a high income, the women must endure stressful, often humiliating emotional and sexual labor as well as the trial of their "choice," the colloquial term given to the process of being picked by their clients to get an opportunity to serve them. Moreover, to be chosen more frequently, such women generally spend a substantial amount of their income on luxurious outfits, cosmetics, and hairstyling and often undergo expensive and sometimes dangerous plastic surgery. They might also have to pay high interest rates on their debts for housing, college student loans, or plastic surgery, which will be offered to them through complicated financial chains of bonds and banks. Kim Joohee labels such a woman "a Lady Credit," that is, a rational but gendered economic person who manages to balance debts and personal freedom, living their life entirely captured within contemporary financial circuits.[10]

From the late 1990s, the internet has become the main platform through which the sex trade is contracted. According to a 2019 study by the Korean Institute of Criminology, prostitution is contracted, arranged, guided, and advertised through a wide variety of random chat apps, websites, social network services, and even YouTube. The study found that no minors were hired in red-light districts, but girls can easily access the internet, and some of them are lured and sexually exploited by men through online communication. A few girls and women in need actively participate in "conditional dating" (chokŏn mannam), a euphemism for prostitution that particularly emphasizes that conditions such as rate, time, place, and type of sex are negotiated in advance.[11]

Regardless of their workplace or mode of operation, all sex workers can encounter abuse and violence from their clients during the process of their intimate, illegal labor practice, but the girls and women involved in conditional dating are generally more vulnerable than sex workers hired at brothels or entertainment establishments, since they are young and usually "amateur," and more importantly, work in isolation. According to the abovementioned study, among seventy-eight female adolescents who experienced conditional dating, forty-eight (61.5%) were victimized by their clients, who paid less than was negotiated, then insulted or threatened them, refused to use condoms, forced unwanted sexual postures on them, and so on.[12] To evade such misfortune, some girls and women choose to work under the protection of procurers, but this often leads to other forms of victimization such as exploitation and violence at the hands of their pimps.[13]

A portion of the workforce in the sex industry consists of migrant women. Not every foreign woman holding the culture and entertainment visa (E-6 visa) works at a camptown entertainment venue, but the vast majority of foreign women working in camptowns are Filipinas with the E-6 visa.[14] In 2021 Filipinas staying in Korea with the E-6 visa numbered 1,286, constituting 61.5 percent of all the foreign women holding the visa (2,090).[15] As in the past, the vast majority of women at camptowns work as waitresses and are forced or lured into providing sexual services, rather than, or in addition to, performing as dancers or singers. Migrant women from other nations, such as Russia, China, and Thailand, also come to Korea with entertainment, tourism or spouse visas, and some of them go on to work at entertainment bars or massage parlors for Korean men. Because of their status as foreigners and the language barrier, these women are generally more vulnerable to exploitation, human trafficking, and violence than are Korean sex workers.[16] Along with these migrant women, older Korean women occupy the lowest ladder in the hierarchy of the sex industry. While some women over forty years old are working in old-fashioned red-light districts, many older women have difficulty finding jobs at brothels or entertainment establishments and therefore tend to work alone in rented rooms or inns located in the backstreets of red-light districts or close to the parks in which old men gather. They get paid little because of their old age and run the risks inherent to working alone.[17]

In tandem with the huge scale and diverse forms that the sex industry assumes in contemporary Korea, the toleration-regulation regime still continues. On one level, the draconian methods of STI control, such as contact tracing, police apprehension, and forceful incarceration, disappeared along with VD detention centers in the late 1990s, with the official legal ground to quarantine and treat those infected with STIs being removed only in 2006.[18] This notwithstanding, mandatory STI testing has survived. The Enforcement Rule on Health Checkups for STI and AIDS, which succeeded the 1984 Rule on Health Checkups of Employees in Sanitary Field in 2013, specifies that "female workers entertaining guests" (*yuhŭng chŏpkaegwŏn*), masseuses, and "those working at venues in which, province governors, mayors, county governors, and the presidents of boroughs recognize, activities prone to transmit STI and AIDS to many and unspecified persons occur," that is, prostitutes, should submit to STI examinations once every three months and AIDS examinations once every six months. Waitresses working at "ticket tearooms" should also take STI and AIDS examinations every six months (Article 3). Those evading the regular examinations are not allowed to work at entertainment restaurants, massage parlors, and ticket tearooms, and if someone, that is, an employer, makes others work there without STI checkups, they are suppsoed to be punished with fines of no more than 2 million KRW (around US$2,000) (Articles 19, 45, and 81 of the current Infectious Disease Control and Prevention Act).

Due to the Sŏngmaemae Prevention Acts, the number of cumulative checkups decreased by about 90 percent, from 2.85 million in 2003 to 1.49 million in 2011 to 313,392 in 2021.[19] Nevertheless, the fact that the regular STI testing of prostitutes and female workers in the adult entertainment industry is still mandatory and conducted on such a huge scale means that regulation, and therefore the toleration-regulation regime, has not entirely been abolished but has simply been retrenched.[20] As illustrated in this book, the primary purpose of the Korean state STI control policy has evolved from the protection of U.S. troops and foreign tourists to the safeguarding of the public health of the general (male) population. Despite this change, its main target has always been prostitutes or sex workers, and the burden of mandatory STI testing is still exclusively put upon this so-called high-risk group. However, such a policy focusing on one specific group can make it difficult to cope with other paths of transmission. For instance, according to a survey conducted on 541 male patients suffering from STIs in 2010, the largest group of transmitters was the employees of entertainment bars (28.9%), the second was girlfriends (26.1%), and the third was casual sexual encounters, or one-night stands (10.1%).[21] This shows that the spread of STIs has been diversified, notwithstanding that prostitution remains the number one source. And even though sex workers have more risk of contracting STIs, the plunge in the number of them submitting to mandatory STI testing after the 2004 acts means that this approach cannot be sustainable. To achieve the goals of both protecting public health and guaranteeing the human rights of sex workers, it is therefore perhaps necessary to encourage diverse high-risk groups, not limited to sex workers, to undergo voluntary testing, while simultaneously protecting the anonymity and privacy of all examinees and patients. Through this approach, STI control could be practiced holistically as a public health issue and not merely as a prostitution policy.[22] This change would make the Korean biopolitical state far more democratic and universal in its operation.

The most significant progressive outcome produced by the Sŏngmaemae Prevention Acts was arguably the systematization of support for the victims and those wanting to leave sex work. In 2021, thirty-one counseling centers, thirty-nine support facilities, eleven group homes, and thirteen rehabilitation support centers nationwide provided the girls and women who wanted to get out of commercial sex with a diverse range of services such as psychological counseling, legal assistance, medical care, shelter, cost-of-living allowances, education, job training, joint workshops, and so on. As examples, a woman can use the services of the support facility for a maximum of two and a half years and those of a rehabilitation support center for a maximum of four years.[23] In addition, some local governments, in particular those attempting to close red-light districts, provide additional benefits to the women who were working in those areas.[24]

Considering that previous authoritarian governments incarcerated suspected prostitutes as women needing protection and violated their rights under the pretext of offering them protection, this change in government attitude is remarkable. Thanks to this state support, pioneering feminist counseling centers and shelters established in the late 1980s and 1990s, such as the Magdalena House and the Durebang, along with many newly established feminist or religious organizations, can now help the women thanks to government subsidies. The government, however, in turn puts pressure on these facilities to achieve results, in terms of the number of clients or the women who succeeded in quitting prostitution, passing qualification exams, or finding jobs, to justify the budget expenditure. As a result, feminist activists within such facilities are often caught in a dilemma between the feminist desire to empower women and the task allocation that the government demands.[25] Moreover, these programs cover only a small number of women who have experienced prostitution. In 2022 the cases of counseling reached about 90,000, but the clients of support facilities and rehabilitation support centers were 921 and 782, respectively, some of whom overlapped.[26] This verifies that government support is not yet sufficient to provide realistic alternatives for many women in prostitution.

THE FEMINIST SEX WAR: A KOREAN VERSION

As this sketch of the terrain since the implementation of the Sŏngmaemae Prevention Acts illustrates, the sex industry still prospers, and the women involved in prostitution are still discriminated against, exploited, and often violated or even trafficked by their clients, employers, and those manipulating debt chains. Above all, male buyers can exert the power of money over sex workers' bodies and minds, and the act of buying sex is still widely tolerated as reflective of men's "natural" release of their "uncontrollable" sexual appetite. According to a 2019 study by the Korean Institute of Criminology on fifteen hundred adult men, 42.1 percent of them had bought sexual services once or more during their lives, and 14.0 percent had done so over the previous year. This study also demonstrated that men with a lower sensitivity to gender equality; familial backgrounds of gender oppression or domestic violence; and histories of violent behavior, sexual violence, or sexual harassment are more prone to pay for commercial sex acts.[27] In this regard, not only is gender inequality reflected in the practice of female prostitution, but female prostitution itself is a manifestation of gender inequality.

To challenge the gender hierarchy between male buyers and female sellers, as well as between men and women in general, anti-prostitution feminists and some prostitution survivors have demanded a revision to the Sŏngmaemae Prevention Acts so that the laws punish only clients and third parties and decriminalize the women involved in prostitution, following the Nordic model.[28] A few politicians have also attempted or promised to introduce this model. For instance, feminist lawmakers Nam In-Sun and Kim Sang-Hŭi took the lead in proposing bills to decriminalize women engaged in prostitution in May and September 2013, respectively, but their proposals were not presented to the National Assembly. In July 2014 Kim Sang-Hŭi again proposed to exempt the sellers of commercial sex acts from punishment if they report third parties or human trafficking associated with prostitution, which was also rejected.[29] During the presidential campaign of 2017, the front-runner Moon Jae-In (Mun Chae-In) promised to decriminalize women in prostitution, but this pledge was not fulfilled.[30] This shows that the national consensus that something should be done to reform the sex industry, which formed in the immediate aftermath of the aforementioned two tragic fires in the early 2000s, has now largely disappeared. No candidates raised the issue of the Sŏngmaemae Prevention Acts during the 2022 presidential election, and the only mention of the subject in the media was a scandal in which the son of a powerful candidate patronized prostitutes.[31]

A few feminists and sex workers approach the Sŏngmaemae Prevention Acts from a totally different perspective from mainstream feminists. They argue that the criminalization of the sex industry only leads to the violation of sex workers' rights and call for the state to guarantee sex work as a form of legitimate service work.[32] They are also critical of the Nordic model, arguing that it marginalizes commercial sex, burdens the sex workers with the duty to protect clients from police crackdowns, and increases the vulnerability of sex workers to attacks by violent clients.[33] Right after the Sŏngmaemae Prevention Acts were enforced in the fall of 2004, this position gained ground among many sex workers, who waged demonstrations and organized labor unions, supported by a few feminist groups (see chapter 5). However, since the two labor unions of sex workers stopped their activities in the late 2000s, only a small number of feminists, such as Giant Girls (2009–2018) and Scarlet ChaCha (2018–), have advocated for this position.[34] In 2012 a sex worker filed a constitutional lawsuit against the Sŏngmaemae Prevention Acts, arguing that the criminalization of the voluntary selling of sex acts was unconstitutional. However, the Constitutional Court decided that prostitution contributed to "spreading decadent entertainment culture, and ultimately to demolishing sound sexual mores and sexual morality," and therefore the criminalization of prostitution was ruled constitutional in 2016.[35]

In this way, as in many countries, Korean feminists are divided into two camps: those who regard prostitution as sexual slavery or exploitation and demand to punish only the third parties and male clients, and those who advocate for sex workers' right to work and seek to decriminalize the sex industry. However, in Korea neither solution would be easy to realize. The anti-prostitution feminists are faced with three difficulties. First, unlike the Scandinavian countries that have a long tradition of state feminism and welfare, it is very difficult for the radical ideas of feminists to be translated into the laws of the Korean state. The historical experience of enacting the current prostitution laws in 2004 and the recent failure of politicians to decriminalize women working in prostitution demonstrate that the Korean legislature and governmental administration are very unlikely to accept the Nordic model.

The second difficulty is related to the sexist inertia inherent in repressive state apparatuses in Korea. Anti-prostitution feminists have attempted to destabilize the gender hierarchy of men, women, and "prostituted women" by suggesting the criminalizing of male clients, not the prostituted women. However, since the number of police crackdowns has returned to that of the days before the 2004 acts, even in the highly unlikely event that the Nordic model is introduced, it is doubtful that the repressive state apparatuses such as the police, prosecution, and courts would operate according to the feminists' intentions. Additionally, in Scandinavian countries such as Sweden, the Nordic model of eradication was introduced only after gender equality had been substantially achieved in many areas (at least to a greater degree than in most other countries), including in the labor market. Therefore, the Nordic model could be seen as a relatively final step within a much longer process of gender reforms.[36] In contrast, in Korea, gender inequality in the labor market remains a very serious issue. For instance, the gender wage gap was 35.0 percent in 2022, the largest among Organisation for Economic Co-operation and Development countries.[37] As a result, prostitution, however exploitative and abusive it may be, still manages to entice many women owing to the much higher income it offers in comparison to most other "feminine" jobs. In this sense, it is uncertain that the Nordic model, which is basically a penal law to punish male clients and third parties, would be the most urgent and efficient means to eradicate prostitution and destabilize the gender hierarchy.

The third and final barrier preventing campaigners from achieving the complete eradication of the sex trade is that anti-prostitution feminists view all women involved in prostitution as the victims of sexual slavery or trafficking. Such a perspective has often been a source of tension and conflict between them and some of the women engaged in the sex industry, who either do not think of themselves as victims or positively identify themselves as sex workers. In fact, some feminists regard sex workers who advocate for their right to work as irrational, pathological beings who suffer from false consciousness or have been brainwashed by their exploiters, or even as "collaborators" for their role in maintaining the social patriarchy and the subjugation of women. For this reason, some sex work advocates denounce anti-prostitution feminists as "sex workers exclusionary radical feminists (SWERF)."[38]

By contrast, pro-sex work feminists seek to decriminalize prostitution, recategorize the practice as a legitimate service industry, and dismantle the gender hierarchy by blurring and eventually removing the boundaries between sex workers and other workers. However, this strategy is again very difficult to realize, for three reasons. First, as the Constitutional Court's decision in 2016 verifies, the legal apparatus of the Korean state is rigidly sanctimonious in its characterization of prostitution as an inherently immoral activity. Therefore, to entirely decriminalize the sex industry would be as difficult as to introduce the Nordic model of total eradication.

Even if pro-sex work feminists were to achieve decriminalization, the second problem would be that the social stigma attached to prostitution would not easily disappear. In Korea, as in many developed countries, the dichotomy between the realms of public and private life is solidly maintained, and an individual's sexual activity is considered to belong strictly to the sphere of the private. In simple terms, the commonly held social belief is that money should not have any impact on a person's sexual activity, which is idealistically considered as determined by non-pecuniary emotive ideas such as love, honor, shame, and loyalty, rather than the transactional power of the market. Therefore, sexual services, unlike other forms of labor power, are not considered suitable or appropriate for market exchange.[39] In addition, due to the strong tradition of familism in Korea, both current and former sex workers are generally viewed as shameful daughters, wives, and mothers, who are often disowned by their families. Kim Joohee has found out that the most terrifying and thus most efficient threat that the creditors of women involved in prostitution use to force them to pay is: "I will let your family know that you are a prostitute."[40] As a result, the social stigma attached to prostitution is too deeply entrenched in Korean society to be simply removed, even by the entire decriminalization of sex work. Additionally, the factor of stigma is also a primary obstacle that prevents sex workers from becoming effectively organized to advocate for their rights.

Finally, considering that female sex work is a manifestation of gender inequality in society, simply decriminalizing it without addressing the wider contexts of sexism could maintain or even expand the marginalization and discrimination suffered by women. This is because clients would now be able to exert their control over sex workers, requiring them to temporarily suspend or surrender their will, a power imbalance that already occurs in many other employment contracts.[41] In addition, prostitution is normally based on a very gender-specific contract, in that most clients are men and most workers are women. Thus, in the context of the sole decriminalization of prostitution, the balance of power that conditions the practice of commercial sex work would be determined not only by iniquitous capitalist relations but also by the social context of gender inequality.

BUILDING A FUTURE NATION FOR THE "WOMEN RIDING ON THE BACKS OF WOLVES"

As in most other countries, prostitution is a dangerous undertaking in Korea. Women can experience economic exploitation by their employers, humiliation, and violence at the hands of their clients; the risk of pregnancy, STIs, and other gynecological problems; and last but not least, social stigma. In stark terms, numerous sex workers have even been murdered by their clients while working.[42] Therefore, the feminists of the Magdalena House refer to sex workers as "brave women, riding on the backs of wolves."[43] Due to the dangerous nature of the work, an anti-prostitution or radical feminist perspective has become dominant among Korean feminists. Nonetheless, however dangerous and oppressive it may be, prostitution is socially perceived as different from rape. Unlike the latter, the former is socially imagined and practiced as if it were based on "a mutual and voluntary exchange" of money for services by its participants, that is, not force but contract. As such, most sex workers themselves protest the notion that a prostitute is "publicly available to be raped."[44] Moreover, there are many disenfranchised women who find themselves making the dangerous "choice" to engage in sex work, mainly because of the low wages within feminine jobs and insufficient social welfare programs. In Korea, one old proverb states simply, "The throat is policed (*Mokkumŏng i p'odoch'ŏng*)," and this implies that the boundary between survival and legal prohibition is narrow and that many people run the risk of being arrested simply to make a living for themselves and their families. Today, sex workers could be considered such unfortunate individuals. For these women, contemporary Korean neoliberal capitalism is the "satanic mill," borrowing from Karl Polanyi, which pushes them into the sex industry.[45]

Recently, a few women who have worked in prostitution have started to speak out through oral history projects, autobiographies, social network services, and blogs.[46] The following two excerpts are small portions of their wider accounts of their lives and experiences, published in an autobiography, *Across the Road Is the Edge of the Cliff*, and in the Scarlet ChaCha's Sex Work Project.

> Clients justified their violence on the grounds that they gave me money. They seemed to think that I had to satisfy their desires since I had been paid. It was impossible to know what might happen when I was alone with a client since there was no protection. I had to follow the clients' orders obediently not to be battered, not to die. . . . I endured my clients' ugly behavior alone, thinking that this was only my personal experience. However, in sharing my stories with other women who experienced prostitution, I realized the universal nature of the violence that every woman in prostitution experiences. Based on my twenty years of experience, I believe that prostitution can decrease only by removing the clients who buy sex from women and the pimps who arrange prostitution using vulnerable women. . . . My current aim is to disclose and reveal every detail of my former clients' ugly behavior.[47]

No sex worker is unaware that they can be sexually violated at the scene of their work. Sex workers know better than others that sexual violence occurs frequently since they have experienced it in person. However, sex workers have to go there, and work there, even though they know better than others that their workplace, their work is dangerous. While you can in theory choose not to do it, this does not mean that everyone can make that choice. It is a sort of privilege not to have to sell your vulva. It can be a form of power to live without having to do sex work. This is because some cannot choose to abandon sex work. It is also a form of power to be able to quit sex work whenever you want to. This is because many cannot quit sex work even though they want to. . . . The theory of sex work is the politics of life and another name for the right to live. It offers a name for sex workers who live in the here and now. I want a safe society in which I can say that I am a prostitute.[48]

While the first voice highlights the violence inherent in prostitution and dreams of a future in which the sex trade does not exist, the second depicts the gloomy reality that some women cannot avoid the profession and advocates for the need to guarantee sex workers' right to safety. Which statement is correct? Which statement offers a useful perspective from which to continue the urgent work of feminist nation building? In my opinion, it is necessary to consider both viewpoints in unison. Relative to my own research, I have come to the conclusion that while prostitution is perniciously different from any other form of capitalist labor, it remains impossible to deny that it is also an established and widespread means for many women to earn a living.

On the one hand, prostitution is different from other forms of labor because it is related to the most private, intimate activity of sex, a social practice that many people believe should be based on interpersonal reciprocity and protected from public exposure and monetary influence. In this regard, sex workers are subject to severe social stigma because they violate this belief, and sex work is often well paid in part because of the attached stigma. It is also extremely gendered, as most clients are men and most sex workers are women. Female sex workers are subject to male clients' demands and are expected to satisfy their clients' selfish, sometimes dehumanizing, misogynistic fantasies. Therefore, in most cases female prostitution is a manifestation of gender inequality and the epitome of women's economic and sexual subjection to men. On the other hand, prostitution is reducible to a context of male domination and female subordination, which can be found in virtually every social arena, from family life to the corporate employment structure, the media and entertainment industry, and the operation and governance of the state itself. In many cases, prostitution is based on a contract, which is the essence of a capitalist relationship and the principle of wage labor and thus different in basis from the context of rape or sexual violence committed by force. Believing in the promise of a high income, some desperate women "choose" this dangerous economic option due to their lack of other options.

For this reason, ideally and/or ironically, I believe that women's right to engage in sex work *and* their right to leave or stay away from the sex trade both must be guaranteed by the state. In other words, it should be guaranteed not only that sex workers can work safely and be empowered enough to protect themselves from mistreatment, poor working conditions, and health hazards, but also that women need not be compelled to choose the profession and should be empowered to quit it when they desire, through a diverse range of supportive social policies. I concede that this position is perhaps even more unrealistic than the Nordic model of eradication or the alternative of total decriminalization. But what, then, are the other, realistic, alternatives? How can sex workers at last become recognized as citizens and full members of the national community of Korea? How can we at least reduce the exploitation and violence that occur in the sex industry, if we cannot abolish the industry right now? As always, there are no easy or immediate answers. However, one thing seems clear. As I have explored in this book, feminists and sex workers will not stop in their bold attempts to improve the current situation and challenge the oppressive national gender hierarchy, despite the numerous trials and errors committed in the past. Far from being over, the progressive project of nation building for and by the women riding on the backs of the wolves continues unceasingly into the future.

NOTES

ACKNOWLEDGMENTS

1. Parts of chapter 1 appeared in the article "Liberation or Purification? Prostitution, Women's Movement and Nation Building in South Korea under US Military Occupation, 1945–1948," *Sexualities* 22, nos. 7–8 (2019): 1053–1070. Parts of chapter 2 originated from "Kŏn'ganghan pyŏngsa (wa 'wianbu') mandŭlgi: Chuhan migun sŏngpyŏng t'ongje ŭi yŏksa, 1950–1977 nyŏn," *Sahoe wa yŏksa* 124 (2019): 265–307; and "Han'guk kijich'on sŏngmaemae chŏngch'aek ŭi yŏksa sahoehak, 1953–1995 nyŏn: Naengjŏn'gi saengmyŏng chŏngch'i, yeoe sangt'ae, kŭrigo chukwŏn ŭi yŏksŏl," *Han'guk sahoehak* 49, no. 2 (2015): 1–33, which was also included in *Singminjuŭi, Chŏnjaeng, Kun 'wianbu,'* edited by Song Yeon-ok and Kim Gwi-ok (Seoul: Sŏnin, 2017). Chapter 3 is based on "Palchŏn kwa seksŭ: Han'guk chŏngbu ŭi sŏngmaemae kwan'gwang chŏngch'aek, 1955–1988 nyŏn," *Han'guk sahoehak* 48, no. 1 (2014): 235–264; "Sŏng chegukchuŭi, minjok chŏnt'ong, kŭrigo 'kisaeng' ŭi ch'immuk: 'Kisaeng kwan'gwang' pandae undong ŭi chaehyŏn chŏngch'i, 1973–1988 nyŏn," *Sahoe wa yŏksa* 101 (2014): 405–438, which was also included in *T'ŭraensŭ naesyŏnŏl inmunhak ŭroŭi ch'odae*, edited by Kim Sang-Hyun (Seoul: Hanyang taehakkyo ch'ulp'anbu, 2017), 197–228; and "K'waerak kwa kongp'o ŭi sidae: 1980 nyŏndae han'guk ŭi 'yuhŭng hyangnak sanŏp' kwa insin maemae," *Yŏsŏnghak nonjip* 33, no. 2 (2016): 31–62. Parts of chapter 4 appeared in "Yŏja ka poho rŭl mannassŭl ttae: Yoboho yŏja sisŏl, kirok kwa chŭngŏn," *Asia yŏsŏng yŏn'gu* 60, no. 1 (2021): 45–86; and "Paradoxes of Gendering Strategy in Prostitution Policies: South Korea's 'Toleration-Regulation Regime,' 1961–1979," *Women's Studies International Forum* 37 (2013): 73–84. Finally, parts of chapters 1, 2, and 5 appeared in "It'yŏjin chadŭl ŭi t'ujaeng: Han'guk sŏng p'anmae yŏsŏngdŭl ŭi chŏhang ŭi yŏksa," *Yŏksa pip'yŏng* 118 (2016): 407–435.

1. Park Yeongja, "Kkok alligo sipta," *Han'guk nae kijich'on migun 'wianbu,'*
yŏksa wa sosong ŭi ŭimi, May 28, 2018, 27–28.

2. Venereal disease (VD), sexually transmitted disease (STD), and sexually
transmitted infection (STI) all refer to any infections transmitted from person to
person by direct sexual contact. In the past the initialism VD, which originated in
reference to Venus, the goddess of love, was widely used; it then gave way to STD
and STI in the late twentieth century. In Korea, *hwaryupyŏng*, a figurative term that
meant the "disease of prostitutes," was used in the first half of the twentieth century
and replaced with *sŏngpyŏng* (sexual disease) in the late twentieth century. In this
book I most often use STI, since not every infection develops into a disease. However, in historical contexts where VD or STD was used, I retain that form.

3. Shin Min-Jung, "S. Korean Supreme Court Rules State Must Compensate
Camptown Women Who Worked Near US Bases," *Hankyoreh*, September 30, 2022.

4. Here I depend on Stoler's reading of Balibar. Ann Laura Stoler, *Interior Fron-*
tiers: Essays on the Entrails of Inequality (Oxford: Oxford University Press, 2022),
ch. 1; and Ann Laura Stoler, *Race and the Education of Desire: Foucault's "History of*
Sexuality" and the Colonial Order of Things (Durham, NC: Duke University Press,
1995), 10–11.

5. Stoler, *Interior Frontiers*, 28.

6. Chang Kyung-Sup, *South Korea under Compressed Modernity: Familial Po-*
litical Economy in Transition (London: Routledge, 2010).

7. Park Yeongja, "Chinsulsŏ" (evidence material submitted to the Seoul Central
District Court on July 7, 2016), Supreme Court of Korea Electronic Case Filing System, accessed December 5, 2019, https://ecfse.scourt.go.kr/ecf/ecfE00/ECFE00.jsp.

8. Pogŏn sahoebu, *Pogŏn sahoe t'onggye yŏnbo* (1974): 386–387; and Yi Ok-Sun,
"Yullak yŏsŏng sŏndo," in *Yullak yŏsŏng mit mihonmo e taehan charyojip* (Seoul:
Han'guk puinhoe ch'ongbonbu, 1985), 12.

9. Kungnip kugŏ wŏn, *P'yojun kugŏ taesajŏn*, accessed December 5, 2019, https://
stdict.korean.go.kr/main/main.do.

10. Mun Se-Yŏng, *Chosŏnŏ sajŏn* (Keijō: Chosŏnŏ sajŏn kanhaeng hoe, 1938),
1104; and Han'gŭl Hak'oe, *Chosŏn mal k'ŭn sajŏn* (Seoul: Ŭryu munhwasa, 1957),
2375.

11. Georgio Agamben, *Homo Sacer: Sovereign Power and Bare Life* (Stanford,
CA: Stanford University, 1998), 21–22.

12. Todd A. Henry's recent research is pioneering in that it investigates the sex/
service work of gender nonconforming citizens and the Korean government's con-
trol over them. "'In the Shadows of Women': Male-Bodied Service Labor, the Mass
Media, and Gender Policing in Authoritarian South Korea" (presented at the 28th
Colloquium of the Research Institute for Comparative Culture and Society, Yonsei
University, February 23, 2021).

13. Peter Baldwin, *Contagion and the State in Europe, 1830-1930* (Cambridge:
Cambridge University Press, 2004), 355–357; and Phillipa Levine, *Prostitution, Race,*

and Politics: Policing Venereal Disease in the British Empire (New York: Routledge, 2003), 42–44.

14. Jill Harsin, *Policing Prostitution in Nineteenth-Century Paris* (Princeton, NJ: Princeton University Press, 1985), ch. 1; Alain Corbin, *Women for Hire: Prostitution and Sexuality in France after 1850* (Cambridge, MA: Harvard University Press, 1990), pt. 1; Alain Corbin, "Commercial Sexuality in Nineteenth-Century France: A System of Images and Regulations," in *The Making of the Modern Body: Sexuality and Society in the Nineteenth Century*, ed. Catherine Gallagher and Thomas Laquer (Berkeley: University of California Press, 1987), 209–219; and Park Jeong-Mi, "Hasudo, p'ihaeja, wihŏm (e ch'ŏ) han yŏja: 19–20 segi ch'o 'ŭiryo-todŏk chŏngch'i' wa sŏngmaemae chŏngch'aek ŭi hyŏngsŏng," *Sahoe wa yŏksa* 120 (2018): 327–330.

15. Harsin, *Policing Prostitution in Nineteenth-Century Paris*, xvi.

16. Philip Howell, *Geographies of Regulation: Policing Prostitution in Nineteenth-Century Britain and the Empire* (Cambridge: Cambridge University Press, 2009), 6.

17. Howell, *Geographies of Regulation*, 8–10; Charles Bernheimer, *Figures of Ill Repute: Representing Prostitution in Nineteenth-Century France* (Durham, NC: Duke University Press, 1997), 8–16; Harsin, *Policing Prostitution in Nineteenth-Century Paris*, ch. 3; and Corbin, *Women for Hire*, ch. 1.

18. Howell, *Geographies of Regulation*, 11–12; and Stephanie Limoncelli, *The Politics of Trafficking: The First International Movement to Combat the Sexual Exploitation of Women* (Stanford, CA: Stanford University Press, 2010), 23–27.

19. Judith R. Walkowitz, *Prostitution and Victorian Society: Women, Class, and the State* (Cambridge: Cambridge University Press, 1980), chs. 6–7; Alan Hunt, *Governing Morals: A Social History of Moral Regulation* (Cambridge: Cambridge University Press, 1999), ch. 3; Frank Mort, *Dangerous Sexualities: Medico-Moral Politics in England since 1830* (London: Routledge, 2000), pt. 3; Limoncelli, *Politics of Trafficking*, 24; and Park, "Hasudo, p'ihaeja, wihŏm (e ch'ŏ) han yŏja," 332–334.

20. Mellissa Hope Ditmore, ed. *Encyclopedia of Prostitution and Sex Work* (Westport, CT: Greenwood Press, 2006), 3–7; and Sheila Jeffreys, *The Idea of Prostitution* (North Geelong: Spinifex Press, 1997), 11–15.

21. John Parascandola, *Sex, Sin, and Science: A History of Syphilis in America* (Westport, CT: Praeger, 2008), 31–36; and Barbara Meil Hobson, *Uneasy Virtue: The Politics of Prostitution and the American Reform Tradition* (New York: Basic Books, 1987), 147–148.

22. Roth Rosen, *The Lost Sisterhood: Prostitution in America, 1900–1918* (Baltimore, MD: Johns Hopkins University Press, 1982), ch. 7; and David J. Langum, *Crossing over the Line: Legislating Morality and the Mann Act* (Chicago: University of Chicago Press, 1994).

23. American Social Hygiene Association, *Social Hygiene Legislation Manual, 1921* (New York: American Social Hygiene Association, 1921), 22–23, 51–63, 69–75; Allan M. Brandt, *No Magic Bullet: A Social History of Venereal Disease in the United States since 1880* (Oxford: Oxford University Press, 1987), ch. 1; Kristine Luker, "Sex, Social Hygiene, and the State: The Double-Edged Sword of Social Reform," *Theory*

and Society 27, no. 5 (1998): 614–617; and Park, "Hasudo, p'ihaeja, wihŏm (e ch'ŏ) han yŏja," 339–342.

24. Étienne Balibar, and Immanuel Wallerstein, *Race, Nation, Class: Ambiguous Identities* (London: Verso, 1991), 92.

25. Michel Foucault, *The History of Sexuality*, vol. 1, *An Introduction* (New York: Random House, 1978), 139–146; and Michel Foucault, *"Society Must Be Defended": Lectures at the Collége de France, 1975–76* (New York: Picador, 2003), ch. 11.

26. Stoler, *Race and the Education of Desire*, 4, 7, 35–36.

27. Levine, *Prostitution, Race, and Politics*, 2, 196.

28. Tony Ballantyne and Antoinette Burton, *Bodies in Contact: Rethinking Colonial Encounters in World History* (Durham, NC: Duke University Press, 2005), 5, 406–407.

29. Levine, *Prostitution, Race, and Politics*, 55–57; Philip Howell, "Prostitution and Racialised Sexuality: The Regulation of Prostitution in Britain and the British Empire before the Contagious Diseases Acts," *Environment and Planning D: Society and Space* 18 (2000): 321–339; Alison Bashford, *Imperial Hygiene: A Critical History of Colonialism, Nationalism and Public Health* (London: Palgrave Macmillan, 2004), ch. 7; and Stephen Legg, "Governing Prostitution in Colonial Delhi: From Cantonment Regulations to International Hygiene (1864–1939)," *Social History* 34, no. 4 (2009): 447–467.

30. Fujime Yuki, *Sŏng ŭi yŏksahak: Kŭndae kukka nŭn song ŭl ŏttŏk'e kwalli hanŭn'ga* (Seoul: Samin, 2004), 93–95; and Elizabeth J. Remick, *Regulating Prostitution in China: Gender and Local Statebuilding, 1900–1937* (Stanford, CA: Stanford University Press, 2014), 37–38.

31. Remick, *Regulating Prostitution in China*, 39–40.

32. Tiffany A. Sippial, *Prostitution, Modernity, and the Making of the Cuban Republic, 1840–1920* (Chapel Hill: University of North Carolina Press, 2013).

33. Gail Hershatter, *Dangerous Pleasure: Prostitution and Modernity in Twentieth-Century Shanghai* (Berkeley: University of California Press, 1997), 6–7.

34. Remick, *Regulating Prostitution in China*.

35. Wan-Chen Yen, *Governing Sex, Building the Nation: The Politics of Prostitution in Postcolonial Taiwan (1945–1979)* (Newcastle upon Tyne: Cambridge Scholars Publishing, 2015).

36. Sarah Kovner, *Occupying Power: Sex Workers and Servicemen in Postwar Japan* (Stanford, CA: Stanford University Press, 2012).

37. Mire Koikari, *Pedagogy of Democracy: Feminism and the Cold War in the U.S. Occupation of Japan* (Philadelphia: Temple University Press, 2008).

38. Robert Kramm, *Sanitized Sex: Regulating Prostitution, Venereal Disease, and Intimacy in Occupied Japan, 1945–1952* (Oakland: University of California Press, 2017).

39. Katharine H. S. Moon, *Sex among Allies: Military Prostitution in U.S.-Korea Relations* (New York: Columbia University Press, 1997).

40. Seungsook Moon, "Regulating Desire, Managing the Empire: U.S. Military Prostitution in South Korea, 1945–1970," in *Over There: Living with the U.S. Military Empire from World War Two to the Present*, ed. Maria Höhn and Seungsook

Moon (Durham, NC: Duke University Press, 2010); and Na Young Lee, "The Construction of U.S. Camptown Prostitution in South Korea: Trans/formation and Resistance" (PhD diss., University of Maryland, 2006).

41. Stoler, *Race and the Education of Desire*, 10, 62.

42. Levine, *Prostitution, Race, and Politics*, 9.

43. Colin Gordon, "Governmental Rationality: An Introduction," in *The Foucault Effect: Studies in Governmentality*, ed. Graham Burchell, Colin Cordon, and Peter Miller (Chicago: University of Chicago Press), 36.

44. Carol Smart, *Law, Crime and Sexuality: Essays in Feminism* (London: Sage, 1995), 192–198.

45. Tani E. Barlow, *The Question of Women in Chinese Feminism* (Durham, NC: Duke University Press, 2004), 59–63.

46. Anne McClintock, *Imperial Leather: Race, Gender and Sexuality in the Colonial Contest* (New York: Routledge, 1995), 15.

47. Howell, *Geographies of Regulation*, ch. 6; Levine, *Prostitution, Race, and Politics*; and Lin Lean Lim, ed., *The Sex Sector: The Economic and Social Bases of Prostitution in Southeast Asia* (Geneva: International Labor Office, 1998).

48. Park Jung Ae, "Ilche ŭi kongch'angje sihaeng kwa sach'ang kwalli yŏn'gu" (PhD diss., Sookmyung Women's University, 2009); Park Jeong-Mi, "Migun chŏmnyŏnggi Okinawa ŭi kiji sŏngmaemae wa yŏsŏng undong," *Sahoe wa yŏksa* 73 (2007): 226–229; Hans Tao-Ming Huang, "State Power, Prostitution and Sexual Order in Taiwan: Towards a Genealogical Critique of 'Virtuous Custom,'" *Inter-Asia Cultural Studies* 5, no. 2 (2004): 239; and Yen, *Governing Sex, Building the Nation*, 7–8.

49. Saundra Pollack Sturdevant and Brenda Stoltzfus, *Let the Good Times Roll: Prostitution and the U.S. Military in Asia* (New York: New Press, 1992).

50. Yen, *Governing Sex, Building the Nation*, 131–140; Cynthia Enloe, *Bananas, Beaches & Bases: Making Feminist Sense of International Politics* (Berkeley: University of California Press, 1990), 84–90; and Ryan Bishop and Lillian S. Robinson, *Night Market: Sexual Cultures and the Thai Economic Miracle* (New York: Routledge, 1998), 92–111. On Korea, see chapter 3 of this book.

51. Thanh-dam Truong, *Sex, Money and Morality: Prostitution and Tourism in South-East Asia* (London: Zed Books, 1990), ch. 3.

52. Truong, *Sex, Money and Morality*, ch. 5.

53. Joan Wallach Scott, *Gender and the Politics of History* (New York: Columbia University Press, 1988), 115.

54. Michael Pickering, *Stereotyping: The Politics of Representation* (London: Palgrave, 2001), 48–49, 74.

55. Hershatter, *Dangerous Pleasure*, 26.

56. Hershatter, *Dangerous Pleasure*, 194.

57. Agamben, *Homo Sacer*; and Georgio Agamben, *State of Exception* (Chicago: University of Chicago Press, 2005).

58. Jin-Kyung Lee also focuses on this metaphor of "refugee," within her analysis of Cho Sŏn-Jak's popular novel *Miss Yang's Adventure* (1975). Cho calls his heroine

Miss Yang a "refugee" subject to "a blast of wind, the so-called modernization." However, he does not depict her as a passive victim but as an agent of free will, though constrained. In a word, she is also an "adventurer" or "explorer who is stepping into the uncivilized territories." Jin-Kyung Lee, *Service Economies: Militarism, Sex Work and Migrant Labor in South Korea* (Minneapolis: University of Minnesota Press, 2010), 35, 113–115. In the following chapters I investigate these ambiguous, liminal, and confusing characteristics of prostitutes or sex workers as both abject victims and active agents or beings situated between these two poles.

59. T. H. Marshall, *Citizenship and Social Class and Other Essays* (Cambridge: Cambridge University Press, 1950), 28.

1. THE STRUGGLE FOR A NEW NATIONHOOD

1. *Puin sinbo*, February 15, 1948.

2. Joel S. Migdal, *Strong Societies and Weak States: State-Society Relations and State Capabilities in the Third World* (Princeton, NJ: Princeton University Press, 1988), 4–9.

3. Leela Gandhi, *Postcolonial Theory: A Critical Introduction* (Crows Nest: Allen & Unwin, 1998), 6–7.

4. Kang Jeong Sook, "Taehan cheguk ilche ch'ogi Seoul ŭi maech'unŏp kwa kongch'ang chedo ŭi toip," *Sŏurhak yŏn'gu* 11 (1998): 199–202.

5. Son Chŏng-Mok, "Kaehanggi han'guk kŏryu ilbonin ŭi chigŏp kwa maech'unŏp koridaegŭmŏp," *Han'guk hakpo* 6, no. 1 (1980): 98–112; Yamashita Yŏng-Ae, "Han'guk kŭndae kongch'ang chedo silsi e kwanhan yŏn'gu" (master's thesis, Ewha Womans University, 1992), 9–15; and Kim Jong-Geun, "Singmin tosi Kyŏngsŏng ŭi yugwak konggan hyŏngsŏng kwa kŭndaejŏk kwalli," *Munhwa yŏksa chiri* 23, no. 1 (2011): 115–119.

6. Fujime Yuki, *Sŏng ŭi yŏksahak: Kŭndae kukka nŭn song ŭl ŏttŏk'e kwalli hanŭn'ga* (Seoul: Samin, 2004), 93–98; Elizabeth J. Remick, *Regulating Prostitution in China: Gender and Local Statebuilding, 1900–1937* (Stanford, CA: Stanford University Press, 2014), 38; and Song Yeon-ok, "Ilche singminjihwa wa kongch'angje toip" (master's thesis, Seoul National University, 1998), 7–13.

7. Park Jung Ae, "Ilche ŭi kongch'angje sihaeng kwa sach'ang kwalli yŏn'gu" (PhD diss., Sookmyung Women's University, 2009), 36–45.

8. *Hwangsŏng sinmun*, November 17, 1902, quoted in Shin Kyu-hwan, "Kaehang, chŏnjaeng, sŏngpyŏng: Hanmal ilche ch'o ŭi sŏngpyŏng yuhaeng kwa t'ongje," *Ŭisahak yŏngu* 17, no. 2 (2008): 248.

9. Jung Keun-Sik, "Singminji wisaeng kyŏngch'al ŭi hyŏngsŏng kwa pyŏnhwa: Singminji t'ongch'isŏng ŭi sigak esŏ," *Sahoe wa yŏksa* 90 (2011): 225–226; Yamashita, "Han'guk kŭndae kongch'ang chedo silsi e kwanhan yŏn'gu," 23–29, 33–39; and Song, "Ilche singminjihwa wa kongch'angje toip," 43–48.

10. Yi Nŭng-Hwa, *Chosŏn haeŏhwa sa* (Seoul: Tongmunsŏn, 1992); and Chŏng Pyŏng-Sŏl, *Na nŭn kisaeng ida: Sosurok ilkki* (Seoul: Munhak tongne, 2007).

11. Suh Ji Young, "Singminji sidae kisaeng yŏn'gu (1): Kisaeng chiptan ŭi kŭndaejŏk chaep'yŏn yangsang ŭl chungsim ŭro," *Chŏngsin munhwa yŏn'gu* 28, no. 2 (2005): 267–294; and Yoon Hyaesin, "Ilche sidae kisaeng ŭi chŏgŭp'wa tamnon e taehan yŏn'gu" (master's thesis, Seoul National University, 2006).

12. *Chōsen sōtokufu kanbō* 1095 (1916): 445–448, National Library of Korea (NLK), Seoul; and Sin Chu-Baek, "Hanbando esŏŭi ilbon'gun yŏksa (1904–1945)," in *Kundae wa sŏngp'ongnyŏk: Hanbando ŭi 20 segi*, ed. Song Yeon-ok and Kim Yŏng (Seoul: Sŏnin, 2012), 224–227.

13. Chang Wŏn-A, "Taranago ssaunŭn yŏjadŭl ŭi yŏksa ro pon pullidoen segye," in *Pulch'ŏbŏl: Sŏngmaemae yŏsŏng ŭl ch'ŏbŏrhanŭn sahoe e tŏnjinŭn p'eminijŭm sŏnŏn*, ed. ELoom (Seoul: Hyumŏnisŭtŭ, 2022), 145.

14. *Chōsen sōtokufu kanbō* 1095 (1916): 443–445.

15. Park, "Ilche ŭi kongch'angje sihaeng kwa sach'ang kwalli yŏn'gu," 61–62, 75–76.

16. Park, "Ilche ŭi kongch'angje sihaeng kwa sach'ang kwalli yŏn'gu," 68–70.

17. Article 6 and Article 18 of the Regulation of Geisha, Barmaids, and Geisha Houses. *Chōsen sōtokufu kanbō* 1095 (1916): 443–444.

18. Article 20 of the Regulation of Brothel Owners and Prostitutes. *Chōsen sōtokufu kanbō* 1095 (1916): 446.

19. Chang, "Taranago ssaunŭn yŏjadŭl ŭi yŏksa ro pon pullidoen segye," 148–153.

20. Park, "Ilche ŭi kongch'angje sihaeng kwa sach'ang kwalli yŏn'gu," 64–65.

21. *Chōsen sōtokufu tōkei renbō* (1925–42), "kenkōshindan," "shōgi geigi oyobi shakufu kenkō shindan," National Assembly Library (NAL), Seoul.

22. From 1921 to 1942, Korean public prostitutes went from 32.7 to 53.9 percent; Korean geisha, that is, kisaeng, went from 43.7 to 71.4 percent; and Korean barmaids went from 54.4 to 85.1 percent. *Chōsen sōtokufu tōkei renbō* (1925–42).

23. *Chōsen sōtokufu tōkei renbō* (1925–42).

24. Park, "Ilche ŭi kongch'angje sihaeng kwa sach'ang kwalli yŏn'gu," 81–88.

25. Park, "Ilche ŭi kongch'angje sihaeng kwa sach'ang kwalli yŏn'gu," 77–78, 132–133.

26. Jill Harsin, *Policing Prostitution in Nineteenth-Century Paris* (Princeton, NJ: Princeton University Press, 1985), 95.

27. Harsin, *Policing Prostitution in Nineteenth-Century Paris*, 56–95.

28. Article 27 of the Regulation of Geisha, Barmaids, and Geisha Houses. *Chōsen sōtokufu kanbō* 1095 (1916): 447; and Park Jung Ae, "Chosŏn ch'ongdokpu ŭi sŏngpyŏng yebang chŏngch'aek kwa hwaryupyŏng yebangnyŏng," *Sarim* 55 (2016): 304–305.

29. Ch'oe Ŭn-Gyŏng, "Ilche kangjŏmgi sŏngpyŏng e taehan ŭiryojŏk silch'ŏn: Ch'iryo wa yebang, tamnon ŭl chungsim ŭro," in *Yŏksa sok ŭi chilbyŏng, sahoe sok ŭi chilbyŏng*, ed. Seoul taehakkyo pyŏngwŏn ŭihak yŏksa munhwawŏn (Seoul: Solbitkil, 2015), 121–130.

30. *Cheguk sinmun*, February 8, 1906, quoted in Park, "Chosŏn ch'ongdokpu ŭi sŏngpyŏng yebang chŏngch'aek kwa hwaryupyŏng yebangnyŏng," 306.

31. Pak Ch'an-Sŭng, "Purŭjua minjokchuŭi, up'a minjokchuŭi, chwap'a minjokchuŭi," *Yŏksa pip'yŏng* 75 (2006): 286–290.

32. Nam Hwa-Suk, "1920 nyŏndae yŏsŏng undong esŏŭi hyŏptong chŏnsŏnnon kwa kŭnuhoe," *Han'guksaron* 25 (1991): 201–249; Lee Na Young, "Sŏngmaemae kŭnjŏlchuŭi undong ŭi yŏksajŏk hyŏngsŏng kwa pyŏnhwa," *Han'guk yŏsŏnghak* 25, no. 1 (2009): 5–34; and Yoon Eun-soon, "1920–30 nyŏndae han'guk kidokkyo chŏlche undong yŏn'gu" (PhD diss., Sookmyung Women's University, 2001), 123–132.

33. George Hicks, *The Comfort Women: Japan's Brutal Regime of Enforced Prostitution in the Second World War* (New York: W. W. Norton, 1997); Yoshiaki Yoshimi, *Comfort Women: Sexual Slavery in the Japanese Military during World War II* (New York: Columbia University Press, 2001); Margaret Stetz, and Bonnie B. C. Oh, eds., *Legacies of the Comfort Women of World War II* (London: Routledge, 2001); Chung Chin Sung, *Ilbon'gun sŏngnoyeje: Ilbon'gun wianbu munje ŭi silsang kwa kŭ haegyŏl ŭl wihan undong* (Seoul: Seoul taehakkyo ch'ulp'anbu, 2004); Sarah Chunghee Suh, *The Comfort Women: Sexual Violence and Postcolonial Memory in Korea and Japan* (Chicago: University of Chicago Press, 2008); and Kang Jeong Sook, "Ilbon'gun 'wianbu' je ŭi singminsŏng yŏn'gu: Chosŏnin 'wianbu' rŭl chungsim ŭro" (PhD diss., Sungkyunkwan University, 2010).

34. Ilbon ŭi chŏnjaeng ch'aegim charyo sent'ŏ yŏn'gu samguk, "Tokyo chaep'an esŏ simp'an padŭn ilbon'gun wianbu chedo," in *Ilbon ŭi kun wianbu yŏn'gu*, ed. Ilbon ŭi chŏnjaeng ch'aegim charyo sent'ŏ (Seoul: Tongbuga yŏksa chaedan, 2011).

35. Im Myŏng-Bang, "Injung sijŏl kwa t'aegŭkki e taehan kiŏk," *Hwanghae munhwa* 5 (1994): 160–161.

36. "Proclamation No. 1 by General of the Army Douglas MacArthur, Yokohama, September 7, 1945," accessed December 5, 2019, https://history.state.gov/historicaldocuments/frus1945v06/d776.

37. Pak Ch'an-P'yo, *Han'guk ŭi kukka hyŏngsŏng kwa minjujuŭi: Naengjŏn chayujuŭi wa posujŏk minjujuŭi ŭi kiwŏn* (Seoul: Humanitasŭ, 2007), 48–51.

38. Crawford F. Sams, *Medic: The Mission of an American Military Doctor in Occupied Japan and Wartorn Korea* (New York: M. E. Sharp, 1998), 108.

39. Sarah Kovner, *Occupying Power: Sex Workers and Servicemen in Postwar Japan* (Stanford, CA: Stanford University Press, 2012), 18.

40. John W. Dower, *Embracing Defeat: Japan in the Wake of World War II* (New York: W. W. Norton, 2000), 124–132; Robert Kramm, *Sanitized Sex: Regulating Prostitution, Venereal Disease, and Intimacy in Occupied Japan, 1945–1952* (Oakland: University of California Press, 2017), 44–54; and Kovner, *Occupying Power*, 22–24.

41. Kramm, *Sanitized Sex*, 47–53.

42. Lee Im-Ha, "Migun ŭi tongasia chudun kwa seksyuŏliti," in *Tongasia wa kŭndae, yŏsŏng ŭi palgyŏn*, ed. Tongasia yugyo munhwakwŏn kyoyuk yŏn'gudan (Seoul: Ch'ŏngŏram, 2004), 272–274.

43. Sams, *Medic*, 108.

44. Allan M. Brandt, *No Magic Bullet: A Social History of Venereal Disease in the United States since 1880* (Oxford: Oxford University Press, 1987), 96–121; and

John Parascandola, *Sex, Sin, and Science: A History of Syphilis in America* (Westport, CT: Praeger, 2008), 47–70.

45. May Act, 18 U.S.C § 1384 (1941).

46. US Army Medical Department, *Preventive Medicine in World War II*, vol. 5, *Communicable Diseases Transmitted through Contact or by Unknown Means* (Washington, DC: Department of the Army, 1960), 139–140; and Parascandola, *Sex, Sin, and Science*, 105, 108, 119–120.

47. Parascandola, *Sex, Sin, and Science*, 121–126; and Park Jeong-Mi, "Kŭmyok esŏ yebang ŭro: 2 ch'a segye chŏnjaenggi migun ŭi sŏngppyŏng t'ongje, saengmyŏng kwŏllyŏk kwa chendŏ," *Kyŏngje wa sahoe* 113 (2017): 234–263.

48. Office of the Surgeon, Headquarters (hereafter HQ) XXIV Corps, "Annual Report," January 29, 1946, 13; 314.7 Organizational Histories (Surgeon's Files) 1945; US Army Forces in Korea (hereafter USAFIK), Adjutant General, General Correspondence (Decimal Files), 1945–1949 (hereafter AG, GC); Records of General Headquarters, Far East Command, Supreme Commander, Allied Powers, and United Nations Command, Record Group 554 (hereafter RG 554), entry A1 1378, box 70, National Archives at College Park, MD (NACP).

49. HQ USAFIK, "Venereal Disease Control Measures," August 29, 1946; 726.1 Weekly Summaries of Venereal Disease 1947–48; USAFIK, AG, GC; RG 554, entry A1 1378, box 147, NACP.

50. Office of Surgeon, HQ XXIV Corps, "Annual Report of Medical Department Activities," March 11, 1947, 31; AG 314.7 Military History XXIV Corps 1947; USAFIK, AG, GC; RG 554, entry A1 1378, box 70, NACP.

51. HQ USAFIK, "Increase in Venereal Disease," August 13, 1947, 1; AG 726.1 Venereal Disease 1947; USAFIK, AG, GC; RG 554, entry A1 1378, box 147, NACP.

52. HQ XXIV Corps, "Deterioration of Standards," May 3, 1946; Adjutant General 250 Military Discipline; USAFIK, AG, GC; RG 554, entry A1 1378, box 50, NACP. Office of the Commanding General, HQ USAFIK, "Courtesy Drive," November 6, 1946; Adjutant General 250 Military Discipline; USAFIK, AG, GC; RG 554, entry A1 1378, box 50, NACP.

53. Seungsook Moon, "Regulating Desire, Managing the Empire: U.S. Military Prostitution in South Korea, 1945–1970," in *Over There: Living with the U.S. Military Empire from World War Two to the Present*, ed. Maria Höhn and Seungsook Moon (Durham, NC: Duke University Press, 2010), 43.

54. Phillipa Levine, *Prostitution, Race, and Politics: Policing Venereal Disease in the British Empire* (New York: Routledge, 2003), 180; and Ann Laura Stoler, "Making Empire Respectable: The Politics of Race and Sexual Morality in 20th-Century Colonial Cultures," *American Ethnologist* 16, no. 4 (1989): 634.

55. Office of Surgeon, HQ XXIV Corps, "Annual Report of Medical Department Activities," 32.

56. Office of Surgeon, HQ XXIV Corps, "Annual Report of Medical Department Activities," 32.

57. HQ USAMGIK, "History of the Department of Public Health and Welfare September 1945 to May 1947," 1947, 7; Hist: Public Health & Welfare; USAFIK, XXIV Corps, G-2, Historical Section; RG 554, entry 1256, box 40, NACP.

58. Article 70 of the Offenses against the Military Government (Ordinance No. 72, May 4, 1946), in *Migunjŏng pŏmnyŏng ch'ongnam [Yŏngmunp'an]* (Seoul: Han'guk pŏpche yŏn'guhoe, 1971), 162.

59. *Puin sinbo*, June 30; *Puin sinbo*, November 11, 1947; and *P'yŏnghwa ilbo*, September 17, 1948.

60. HQ USAMGIK, "Venereal Control Program in South Korea," July 27, 1948, 1–2; AG 726.1 Venereal Disease 1948; USAFIK, AG, GC; RG 554, entry A1 1378, box 147, NACP.

61. American Social Hygiene Association, *Digest of Laws Dealing with Prostitution and Other Sex Offenses* (New York: American Social Hygiene Association, 1942), 433.

62. Edward G. Meade, *American Military Government in Korea* (New York: Kings Crown Press, 1951), 220–221; and Moon, "Regulating Desire, Managing the Empire," 45.

63. Tiffany A. Sippial, *Prostitution, Modernity, and the Making of the Cuban Republic, 1840–1920* (Chapel Hill: University of North Carolina Press, 2013), 131–139.

64. Beth Bailey and David Farber, *The First Strange Place: Race and Sex in World War II Hawaii* (Baltimore, MD: Johns Hopkins University Press, 1992), 98–100.

65. HQ 80th Medical Group, "Monthly Meeting of Venereal Disease Control Council," December 13, 1947, 1; AG 726.1 Venereal Disease 1948; USAFIK, AG, GC; RG 554, entry A1 1378, box 147, NACP. HQ 6th Infantry Division, "Meeting of Venereal Disease Council," December 11, 1947, 1; 726.1 Venereal Disease Control 1947–48; USAFIK, AG, GC; RG 554, entry A1 1378, box 147, NACP.

66. Office of the Surgeon, HQ XXIV Corps, "Annual Report of Medical Department Activities 1947," February 1, 1948, 14; 314.7 Annual Report of Medical Department Activities 1947–9, XXIV Corps Office of the Surgeon; WWII Administrative Records, 1940–1949; Records of Office of the Surgeon General (Army), Record Group 112 (hereafter RG 112), entry 54A, box 567, NACP. Office of the Surgeon, HQ USAFIK, "Annual Report of Medical Department Activities 1948," January 21, 1949, 14; WWII Administrative Records, 1940–1949; RG 112, entry 54A, box 567, NACP.

67. HQ USAFIK, "Venereal Disease Rehabilitation Training Center," October 24, 1947; AG 726.1 Venereal Disease 1947; USAFIK, AG, GC; RG 554, entry A1 1378, box 147, NACP. HQ XXIV Corps, "Visit to Venereal Disease Rehabilitation Training Center," December 15, 1947, 1–3; 726.1 Venereal Disease Control 1947–48; USAFIK, AG, GC; RG 554, entry A1 1378, box 147, NACP. Moon points out the discriminatory aspects of VD control over American troops based on rank, class, and race. For instance, infected commissioned officers, mostly white and from affluent familial backgrounds, were not sent to the Rehabilitation Center. Moon, "Regulating Desire, Managing the Empire," 48–49.

68. Office of the Surgeon, HQ XXIV Corps, "Annual Report of Medical Department Activities 1947," 13. General Headquarters Far East Command, "Health

of Far East Command Troops, November 1948," December 29, 1948; 726.1 Health Report 1948; Historical Unit Medical Detachments ("HUMEDS"); RG 112, entry 1012, box 500, NACP.

69. Office of the Commanding General, HQ XXIV Corps, "Venereal Rate and Discipline," April 14, 1948, 1; AG 726.1 Venereal Disease 1948; USAFIK, AG, GC; RG 554, entry A1 1378, box 147, NACP.

70. HQ 6th Infantry Division, "Meeting of Venereal Disease Council," March 22, 1948; AG 726.1 Venereal Disease 1948; USAFIK, AG, GC; RG 554, entry A1 1378, box 147, NACP.

71. HQ USAFIK, "Venereal Disease Cases Considered Not in Line of Duty," February 18, 1948; AG 726.1 Venereal Disease 1948; USAFIK, AG, GC; RG 554, entry A1 1378, box 147, NACP.

72. Mun Kyŏng-Nan, "Migunjŏnggi han'guk yŏsŏng undong e kwanhan yŏn'gu" (master's thesis, Ewha Womans University, 1989), 44–45.

73. Bruce Cumings, *The Origins of the Korean War*, vol. 1, *Liberation and the Emergence of Separate Regimes, 1945–1947* (Princeton, NJ: Princeton University Press, 1981).

74. Kramm, *Sanitized Sex*, 82–83.

75. *Seoul sinmun*, March 9, 1946.

76. *Hyŏndae ilbo*, June 24, 1946.

77. Suzy Kim, *Everyday Life in the North Korean Revolution, 1945–1950* (Ithaca, NY: Cornell University Press, 2016), 185–186.

78. Yang Dong Sook, "Haebang hu uik yŏsŏng danch'e ŭi chojik kwa hwaltong yŏn'gu" (PhD diss., Hanyang University, 2010), 20–24.

79. *Tonga ilbo*, June 2, 1946.

80. Yang, "Haebang hu uik yŏsŏng danch'e ŭi chojik kwa hwaltong yŏn'gu," 16.

81. Mun, "Migunjŏnggi han'guk yŏsŏng undong e kwanhan yŏn'gu," 106–110; and Yi Sŭng-Hŭi, *Han'guk hyŏndae yŏsŏng undong sa* (Seoul: Paeksan sŏdang, 1994), 154–156.

82. *Tonga ilbo*, May 27, 1946; and *Chosŏn ilbo*, Ocober. 31, 1947.

83. *Puin sinbo*, June 29, 1947.

84. *Puin sinbo*, August 20, 1947.

85. *Tonga ilbo*, January 7, 1947.

86. *Puin sinbo*, September 11, 1947.

87. Levine, *Prostitution, Race, and Politics*, 87.

88. An Chin, *Migunjŏng kwa han'guk ŭi minjujuŭi* (Seoul: Hanul ak'ademi, 2005), 229.

89. Sale or Contracts for Sale of Female Prohibited (Ordinance No. 70, May 17, 1946), in *Migunjŏng pŏmnyŏng ch'ongnam [Yŏngmunp'an]*, 154.

90. *Hansŏng ilbo*, May 29, 1946.

91. *Namjosŏn kwado ippŏp ŭiwŏn sokkirok* 130 (1947): 12, NLK.

92. The Abolishment of the Public Prostitution Law (Pub. Act No. 7, November 14, 1947), § I, in *Migunjŏng pŏmnyŏng ch'ongnam [Yŏngmunp'an]*, 44. The Korean version specified its purpose somewhat differently: "abolishing

public prostitution and prohibiting all kinds of prostitution in order to eradicate a malicious custom which was established under the Japanese regime and enhance humanism, in accordance with the equality between men and women." Korean Law Information Center (KLIC), Sejong, accessed December 6, 2019, https://law.go.kr/.

93. Abolishment of the Public Prostitution Law, in *Migunjŏng pŏmnyŏng ch'ongnam [Yŏngmunp'an]*, 44.

94. Kovner, *Occupying Power*, 104–105; and Kramm, *Sanitized Sex*, 83–84.

95. An, *Migunjŏng kwa han'guk ŭi minjujuŭi*, 230.

96. *Namjosŏn kwado ippŏp ŭiwŏn sokkirok* 167 (1947): 2.

97. *Namjosŏn kwado ippŏp ŭiwŏn sokkirok* 167 (1947): 2.

98. *Namjosŏn kwado ippŏp ŭiwŏn sokkirok* 200 (1948): 10, 21–23; 201 (1948): 16–17; 202 (1948): 6, 12–13; and Public Act Number 7 Amended (Pub. Act No. 9, February 12, 1948), in *Migunjŏng pŏmnyŏng ch'ongnam [Yŏngmunp'an]*, 47.

99. Pogŏn husaengbu, "Chŏpkaekpu (kisaeng, chakpu, yŏgŭp) hŏga e kwan-han kŏn," February 3, 1948, *Wisaeng kwangye yeguch'ŏl*, National Archives of Korea (NAK) (BA0127535), Daejeon.

100. *Kyŏnghyang sinmun*, April 27, 1947.

101. *Tonga ilbo*, December 10, 1946; May 9, 1947; June 14, 1947; November 11, 1947; and *Kyŏnghyang sinmun*, November 4, 1947; November 26, 1947; and July 8, 1948.

102. Gandhi, *Postcolonial Theory*, 6–7.

103. *Chosŏn ilbo*, March 19, 1946.

104. *Tonga ilbo*, December 10, 1946.

105. *Kyŏnghyang sinmun*, September 28, 1947; *Puin sinbo*, September 25, 1947; and October 9, 1947.

106. *Puin sinbo*, December 6, 1947.

107. *Tonga ilbo*, February 20, 1948.

108. *Chosŏn ilbo*, February 17, 1948.

109. *Puin sinbo*, February 19, 1948.

110. Gayatri C. Spivak, "Subaltern Talk: Interview with the Editors," in *The Spivak Reader*, ed. Donna Landry (London: Routledge, 1995), 292.

111. *Puin sinbo*, March 7, 1948.

112. Puinsa, "Hyŏnha yŏsŏng p'unggi rŭl marhanŭn chwadamhoe," *Puin* (April 1947): 32.

113. *Chosŏn ilbo*, March 31, 1948.

2. HOT WAR, COLD WAR, AND PATRIOTIC PROSTITUTES

1. Mac E. Woods, *Korea, Hills, Rice Patties, and Whores* (n.p.: n.p., [2001]), 3–10, Library of Congress (LOC), Washington, DC.

2. Woods, *Korea, Hills, Rice Patties, and Whores*, 1.

3. Pak Tong-Ch'an, *T'onggye ro pon 6.25 chŏnjaeng* (Seoul: Kukpangbu kunsa p'yŏnch'an yŏn'guso, 2014), 282.

4. John Parascandola, *Sex, Sin, and Science: A History of Syphilis in America* (Westport, CT: Praeger, 2008), 47.

5. Eighth United States Army (hereafter EUSA), "Annual Report, Army Medical Service Activities (RCS MED-41) 1952," 1953, annex III, 4; Army Medical Service Activities Eighth U.S. Army 1952; EUSA, Medical Section, Historical Report, 1949–53 (hereafter EUSA, MS, HR); Records of U.S. Army Operational, Tactical, and Support Organizations (World War II and Thereafter), record group 338 (hereafter RG 338), entry A1 205, box 1557, National Archives at College Park, MD (NACP).

6. Albert E. Cowdrey, *The Medics' War: United States Army in the Korean War* (Washington, DC: Center of Military History, United States Army, 1987), 183.

7. Cowdrey, *The Medics' War*, 249.

8. Yukkun ponbu, *Yugio chŏnjaeng hubang chŏnsa: Insap'yŏn* (Seoul: P'ungmunsa, 1956), 148; and Kim Gwi-ok, "Ilbon singminjuŭi ka han'guk chŏnjaenggi han'gukkun wianbu chedo e mich'in yŏnghyang kwa kwaje," *Sahoe wa yŏksa* 103 (2014): 90.

9. Yukkun ponbu, *Yugio chŏnjaeng hubang chŏnsa*, 148–150; and Kim, "Ilbon singminjuŭi ka han'guk chŏnjaenggi han'gukkun wianbu chedo e mich'in yŏnghyang kwa kwaje," 90–93.

10. Kim, "Ilbon singminjuŭi ka han'guk chŏnjaenggi han'gukkun wianbu chedo e mich'in yŏnghyang kwa kwaje," 97.

11. Pogŏnbu, "Ch'ŏngso mit chŏpkaek yŏngŏp wisaeng samu ch'wigŭp yoryŏng ch'uga chisi e kwanhan kŏn," October 10, 1951, *Wisaeng kwangye yegyuch'ŏl*, 266–284, National Archives Korea (NAK) (BA0127534), Daejeon.

12. Kim, "Ilbon singminjuŭi ka han'guk chŏnjaenggi han'gukkun wianbu chedo e mich'in yŏnghyang kwa kwaje," 94–101.

13. Gregg Brazinsky, *Nation Building in South Korea: Koreans, Americans, and the Making of a Democracy* (Chapel Hill: University of North Carolina Press, 2007), 23–31; and Moon Sangseok, "Han'guk chŏnjaeng, kŭndae kungmin kukka hyŏngsŏng ŭi ch'ulbalchŏm: Chawŏn dongwŏnnon ŭi kwanchŏm esŏ," *Sahoe wa yŏksa* 86 (2010): 96–102.

14. Pogŏnbu, "Ch'ŏngso mit chŏpkaek yŏngŏp wisaeng samu ch'wigŭp yoryŏng ch'uga chisi e kwanhan kŏn," 266, 280–281; and The Ministry of Health, "Health Preventive No. 1726," October 10, 1951, *Wisaeng kwangye yegyuch'ŏl*, 342–345.

15. HQ United Nations Civil Assistance Command Korea (hereafter HQ UNCACK), "Venereal Disease Control," October 11, 1951, 1; Command Reports September 1951 to October 1951; UNCACK, Adjutant General Section, Command Reports, 1950–53; Records of General Headquarters, Far East Command, Supreme Commander, Allied Powers, and United Nations Command, record group 554 (hereafter RG 554), entry A-1 1300, box 1, NACP.

16. HQ UNCACK, "Plan for VD Control Program in Korea," July 8, 1951, 2; 726. 1; UNCACK, Adjutant General Section, General Correspondence (Decimal Files), 1951–55; RG 554, entry A-1 1301, box 27, NACP.

17. HQ Far East Command, "Venereal Disease Control and Repression of Prostitution," July 7, 1952; 726.1; EUSA, 1944–56, Adjutant General Section, Security-Classified General Correspondence 1952 (hereafter EUSA, AGC, SCGC); RG 338, entry A1 133, box 844, NACP.

18. "Local authorities should be informed that assistance in this matter [establishment of arresting controls in areas frequented by street walkers, solicitors, and pimps] is encouraged so as to preclude placing the entire local area 'off limits.'" EUSA, "Circular No. 116. I, Venereal Disease Control and Repression of Prostitution," August 16, 1952, 2; 726.1 Backing Papers 1952; EUSA, AGC, SCGC; RG 338, entry A1 133, box 844, NACP.

19. HQ UNCACK, "Plan for VD Control Program in Korea," 2.

20. EUSA, "Annual Report, 1951," 1952, 49; Army Medical Service Activities, Eighth Army 1951; EUSA, MS, HR; RG 338, entry A1 205, box 1557, NACP.

21. Pogŏn sahoebu, *Pogŏn sahoe t'onggye yŏnbo* (1958): 132–133.

22. UNCACK, "PHW Report, December 1952," January 30, 1953, 5; Monthly Civil Affairs Activities in Korea—PH&W Reports 1952; Medical Section, Public Health & Welfare Division, Subject File 1945–53; RG 554, entry A1 137, box 6, NACP.

23. EUSA, "Annual Report, 1951," 48.

24. Nam Chŏng-Ok, *Hanmi kunsa kwan'gye sa* (Seoul: Kukpangbu kunsa p'yŏnch'an yŏn'guso, 2002), 677.

25. Han Yong-Sŏp, "Han'guk kukpang chŏngch'aek ŭi pyŏnch'ŏn kwajŏng," in *Kukpang chŏngch'aek ŭi iron kwa silche*, ed. Ch'a Yŏng-Gu and Hwang Pyŏng-Mu (Seoul: Orŭm, 2002), 81.

26. Charles Tilly, "War and the Power of Warmakers in Western Europe and Elsewhere, 1600–1980," CRSO Working Paper 287 (1983), 17–18. In fact, Tilly has classified Korea as a "clone": one that is comparatively self-sufficient in military resources while its military organization was imposed by the United States. However, Jeong Young Sin has argued that the status of Korea has changed over time: from a "client state" in the 1950s–1960s, to a "clone state" in the 1970s–1980s, to a contemporary "autonomous state." Jeong Young Sin, "Tong asia ŭi anbo punŏp kujo wa pan kiji undong e kwanhan yŏn'gu" (PhD diss., Seoul National University, 2012), 95.

27. Ch'ongmuch'ŏ, "UNgun saryŏngbu idong e subanhanŭn sŏngpyŏng kwalli munje (che 29 hoe)," July 29, 1957, *Ch'agwan hoeŭirok*, 592–593, NAK (BA0085311).

28. Ch'ongmuch'ŏ, "Che 53 hoe kungmu hoeŭirok," September 2, 1955, *Kungmu hoeŭirok (Che 18 hoe–88 hoe)*, 811, NAK (BA0085175).

29. *Gyeonggi-do kijich'on yŏsŏng saenghwal silt'ae mit chiwŏn chŏngch'aek yŏn'gu* (Suwon: Gyeonggi-do yŏsŏng kajok chaedan, 2020), 31–35.

30. The Ministry of Health merged with the Ministry of Social Affairs, becoming the Ministry of Health and Social Affairs in 1955.

31. Ch'ongmuch'ŏ, "UNgun saryŏngbu idong e subanhanŭn sŏngpyŏng kwalli munje," 592.

32. On July 1, 1957, the U.S. forces in East Asia were reorganized. Not only UNC moved from Tokyo to Seoul, but U.S. Army Forces Far East (AFFE) was

discontinued with the establishment of USFK. EUSA was consolidated with USFK and UNC with headquarters in Seoul. The Eighth Army, "History," accessed October 17, 2019, https://8tharmy.korea.army.mil/site/about/history.asp.

33. EUSA, "Annual Report, 1951"; and Cowdrey, *The Medics' War*, 249.

34. HQ EUSA, "Circular No. 49: Preventive Medicine," June 18, 1955, 7; 720; EUSA, 1944–56, Adjutant General Section, General Correspondence 1956; RG 338, entry A1 132, box 670, NACP.

35. EUSA, "Venereal Disease Control Conference," September 30, 1957, 1; 710. Diseases, Injuries, Remedies; EUSA, Medical Section, General Correspondence, 1950–60; RG 338, entry A1 206, box 1563, NACP.

36. EUSA, "Venereal Disease Control Conference," 1–2.

37. EUSA, "Venereal Disease Control Conference," 2–4.

38. Stellen C. Wollmar, "Dear Mr. Minister," September 10, 1957, *C-Ŭiyakp'um*, NAK (CTA0001857).

39. Arthur G. Trudeau, "Dear General H. Decker," August 3, 1957, 1–2; 720; EUSA, Adjutant General, General Correspondence Files, EUSA, 1957–58; RG 338, entry A1 278, box 135, NACP.

40. Trudeau, "Dear General H. Decker," 1.

41. Pogŏn sahoebu, *Sŏngpyŏng yŏnbo* (1960): 18, 26–27; and Pogŏn sahoebu, *Pogŏn sahoe t'onggye yŏnbo* (1970): 100–101.

42. The Ministry of Health and Social Affairs produced statistics on the total VD examinations of registered prostitutes, but it classified them according to locales, not women's status in the late 1950s. However, the vast majority of camptowns were concentrated in Gyeonggi Province, and Gyeonggi was a rural area where the sex industry for Korean nationals was not much developed. Therefore, the instances of examinations in Gyeonggi can be considered an approximate value of that of comfort women. In 1969, for example, the total of VD examination instances was 1,141,114, and that in Gyeonggi was 710,881 (62.3 percent). Pogŏn sahoebu, *Pogŏn sahoe t'onggye yŏnbo* (1970): 100–101; and Gyeonggi-do, *Gyeonggi t'onggye yŏnbo* (1970): 210.

43. Nam, *Hanmi kunsa kwan'gye sa*, 677; and T'onggyech'ŏng, *In'gu ch'ongjosa* (1960), accessed January 10, 2023, https://kosis.kr/statHtml/statHtml.do?orgId =101&tblId=DT_1IN6001&vw_cd=MT_ZTITLE&list_id=A11A1&scrId=& seqNo=&lang_mode=ko&obj_var_id=&itm_id=&conn_path=MT_ZTITLE& path=%252FstatisticsList%252FstatisticsListIndex.do

44. Pogŏn sahoebu, *Sŏngpyŏng yŏnbo*, 4–5.

45. EUSA, "Army Medical Service Activities Report," March 22, 1960, 13; Annual Report 1959—HQ EUSA; Office of Surgeon General (Army), Historical Division, US Army Medical Department (AMEDD) Records, 1947–61; Records of Office of the Surgeon General (Army), Record Group 112 (hereafter RG 112), entry 1001, box 198, NACP.

46. Kwŏn Hyŏk-Hŭi, *Chosŏn esŏ on sajin yŏpsŏ* (Seoul: Minŭmsa, 2005), pt. 2, ch. 7; Yi Kyŏng-Min, *Kisaeng ŭn ŏttŏk'e mandŭrŏjyŏnnŭn'ga: Kŭndae kisaeng ŭi*

t'ansaeng kwa p'yosang konggan (Seoul: Ak'aibǔ puksǔ, 2005), ch. 5; and Todd A. Henry, *Assimilating Seoul: Japanese Rule and the Politics of Public Space in Colonial Korea, 1910–1945* (Berkeley: University of California Press, 2014), 99–102.

47. EUSA, "Medical Service: Prevention and Control of Venereal Disease," Circular No. 40-15, August 11, 1958, 4; AG Library; EUSA, Adjutant General Section, Circulars, 1957–63; RG 338, entry A1 268, box 13, NACP.

48. Phillipa Levine, *Prostitution, Race, and Politics: Policing Venereal Disease in the British Empire* (New York: Routledge, 2003), 8.

49. Park Chung Hee, *Kukka wa hyǒngmyǒng kwa na* (1963; Seoul: Kip'arang, 2017), 85–88.

50. *Punyǒ haengjǒng 40 nyǒn sa* (Seoul: Pogǒn sahoebu, 1987), 112.

51. Gyeonggi-do, "UNgun kani t'ǔksu ǔmsikchǒm yǒngǒp hǒga samu ch'wigǔp sebu kijun surip," *Yegyuch'ǒl* (2-1), September 14, 1961, NAK (BA0864577); and Pogǒn sahoebu, "UNgun yong kani t'ǔksu ǔmsikchǒm yǒngǒp wisaeng haengjǒng samu ch'wigǔp yoryǒng ilbu kaejǒng," December 15, 1961, *Yegyuch'ǒl* (2-1), September 14, 1961, NAK (BA0864577).

52. Yangju-gun, "Yangju-gun sǒngpyǒng kwalliso sǒlch'i chorye," *Chorye*, March 1, 1965, NAK (BA0172135); Paju-gun, "Paju-gun sǒngpyǒng kwalliso sǒlch'i chorye," March 5, 1965, *Chorye wǒnbon*, NAK (BA0175569); Pocheon-gun, "Pocheon-gun sǒngpyǒng kwalliso sǒlch'i chorye," March 8, 1965, *Chorye kongp'o wǒnbon*, NAK (BA0175597); Goyang-gun, "Goyang-gun sǒngpyǒng kwalliso sǒlch'i chorye," March 9, *Chorye wǒnbon taejang*, NAK (BA0175583); Uijeongbu-si, "Uijeongbu-si sǒngpyǒng kwalliso sǒlch'i chorye," April 26, 1965, *Chorye wǒnbon ch'ǒl*, NAK (BA0175657); and Pyeongngtaek-gun, "Pyeongtaek-gun sǒngpyǒng kwalliso sǒlch'i chorye," *Chorye wǒnbon ch'ǒl (Pyeongtaek-gun)*, December 30, 1968, NAK (BA0049021).

53. EUSA, "Annual Report, 1951," 48.

54. I Corps (Group), "Construction of Medical Clinics," April 25, 1963, Kathy Moon Papers, Wilson Center (WC), Washington, DC.

55. Surgeon, EUSA MD, "CG I Corps Letter, 'Construction of Medical Clinics,' dated 25 April 1963," May 2, 1963, Kathy Moon Papers, WC.

56. IO, EUSA, "Construction of Medical Clinics," May 3, 1963, Kathy Moon Papers, WC.

57. Katharine H. S. Moon, *Sex among Allies: Military Prostitution in U.S.-Korea Relations* (New York: Columbia University Press, 1997), 50.

58. Bureau of Public Health, Ministry of Health and Social Affairs, "The V.D. Control Programmes (Proposed) in Tongduchon Area, Kyonggi-Do Province," February 1964, Kathy Moon Papers, WC.

59. Gyeonggi-do, "UNgun kani t'ǔksu ǔmsikchǒm yǒngǒp hǒga samu ch'wigǔp sebu kijun surip," 4.

60. Brazinsky, *Nation Building in South Korea*, 132–136.

61. Gyeonggi-do, *Gyeonggi t'onggye yǒnbo* (1971): 252.

62. Nam, *Hanmi kunsa kwan'gye sa*, 677.

63. Moon, *Sex among Allies*, 57–67.

64. Moon, *Sex among Allies*, 67–74.

65. Moon, *Sex among Allies*, 74–103.

66. Moon, *Sex among Allies*, 92.

67. Moon, *Sex among Allies*, 102.

68. Almost every conference of the Ad Hoc Subcommittee discussed how to improve the VD control program. In particular, the thirteenth conference, on March 16, 1973, clearly summarized what it had achieved from September 1971 to March 1973, when the campaign was conducted intensively. Joint Committee under the Republic of Korea and the United States Status of Forces Agreement, "Thirteenth Report of the Ad Hoc Subcommittee on Civil-Military Relations," March 16, 1973, Diplomatic Archives of the Ministry of Foreign Affairs (DAMFA), Seoul.

69. US-ROK Ad Hoc Subcommittee on Civil-Military Relations, "Eleventh Report of the Ad Hoc Subcommittee on Civil-Military Relations," July 31, 1972, 43, National Assembly Library (NAL), Seoul.

70. W. E. Sharp, "Report of the Fifth Korean-American Civil Affairs Conference," March 2, 1973, 2, DAMFA.

71. J. H. Allison, "Col J. H. Allison, USAF (Commander, 51st Air Base Wing, Osan)," March 2, 1973, 3, DAMFA.

72. MBC, "Seksŭ tongmaeng kijich'on," *Ije nŭn marhal su itta*, no. 61, February 9, 2003.

73. Kim Chŏng-Ja, *Migun wianbu kijich'on ŭi sumgyŏjin chinsil* (Seoul: Hanul ak'ademi, 2013), 246; and Sin Ŭn-Ju and Kim Hyŏn-Hŭi, "Gyeonggi-do kijich'on yŏsŏng noin silt'ae chosa," *Gyeonggi-do kijich'on yŏsŏng noin silt'ae chosa t'oronhoe* (October 24, 2008).

74. James Hathaway, "Trip Report," February 14, 1974, 17–18, SOFA-hanmi haptong wiwŏnhoe, *Kunmin kwankye imsi punkwa wiwŏnhoe, che 25-29 ch'a, 1974*, DAMFA.

75. Pogŏn sahoebu, "P'enisillin kwaminsŏng syokk'ŭ sago ch'ŏri e taehan hyŏpcho yoch'ŏng," *Pŏmnyŏng chamun* (1-1) (2-2), February 8, 1978, NAK (CA0026967).

76. Pŏmmubu, "P'enisillin kwaminsŏng syokk'ŭ sago ch'ŏri e taehan hyŏpcho yoch'ŏng," *Susa chihwi* (1) (3-2), March 4, 1978, NAK (CA0030059).

77. "WHO ŭi Dr. Antal ŭi ŭigyŏn," *Pŏmnyŏng chamun* (1-1) (2-2), NAK (CA0026967).

78. Kim Yeon-Ja, *Amerika t'aun wang ŭnni chukki obun chŏn kkaji ak ŭl ssŭda: Kim Yeon-Ja chajŏn esei* (Seoul: Samin, 2005), 141; and Kim, *Migun wianbu kijich'on ŭi sumgyŏjin chinsil*, 246.

79. Panel on Race Relations and Equality of Treatment, "First Report of the Panel on Race Relations and Equality of Treatment," December 6, 1971, DAMFA; and Moon, *Sex among Allies*, 77.

80. *Kyŏnghyang sinmun*, June 10, 1971.

81. KNP Yongsan Station and Headquarter US Army Garrison Yongsan, "Migun chŏpkaeŏp e chongsa hanŭn yŏrŏbun ege," June 14, 1971; I quoted an English translation of July 27, 1971, by the 24th Psychological Operations Detachment, Kathy Moon Papers, WC; and Moon, *Sex among Allies*, 28.

82. Moon, *Sex among Allies*, ch. 4.

83. VD Education Institute, "VD Case-Finding Manual for Use in Training Programs," May 1945, 44; Venereal Diseases; Office of Surgeon General (Army), WWII Administrative Records; RG 112, entry 31 (ZI), box 1266, NACP.

84. John Parascandola, "Presidential Address: Quarantining Women; Venereal Disease Rapid Treatment Centers in World War II America," *Bulletin of the History of Medicine* 83, no. 3 (Fall 2009): 457.

85. Kim, *Migun wianbu kijich'on ŭi sumgyŏjin chinsil*, 244–245; Sin and Kim, "Gyeonggi-do kijich'on yŏsŏng noin silt'ae chosa," 57; Chŏn Kyŏng-Ok, Pak Sŏn-Ae, and Chŏng Ki-Ŭn, *Han'guk yŏsŏng inmulsa* (Seoul: Sookmyung yŏja taehakkyo ch'ulp'anbu, 2005), 2: 140–141; and Saewumt'ŏ, *Kijich'on yŏsŏng munje haegyŏl ŭl wihan taean mosaek t'oronhoe*, November 27, 2008, 23.

86. Moon, *Sex among Allies*, 42; Park Sun-Sook, "Yŏsŏng ŭi sŏngsŏng (sexuality) ŭl chungsim ŭro pon maemaech'un ch'ŏngch'aek e kwanhan yŏngu" (master's thesis, Ewha Womans University, 1990), 38; and Min Kyŏng-Ja, "Han'guk maech'un yŏsŏng undong sa," in *Han'guk yŏsŏng inkwŏn undong sa*, ed. Han'guk yŏsŏng ŭi chŏnhwa (Seoul: Hanul ak'ademi, 1999), 278.

87. Enforcement Decree of the Yullak Prevention Act, enforced on February 20, 1962, Korea Law Information Center (KLIC), Sejong.

88. For instance, in 1975 the Seoul City government arrested 5,659 offenders against the act, of whom 3,225 were prostitutes serving Koreans and 562 comfort women. Since Seoul is the capital where the sex industry for Koreans was highly developed, and it hosted only one camptown at Itaewon, the number of arrested comfort women was less than the number of prostitutes serving Koreans. Seoul-si, *Seoul t'onggye yŏnbo* (1977): 213. Gyeonggi Province does not provide the statistics, but the province here seemed to crack down on comfort women as well, considering local governments' autonomy was very limited at that time under the military dictatorship.

89. Kim, *Amerika t'aun wang ŭnni chukki obun chŏn kkaji ak ŭl ssŭda*, 105.

90. Georgio Agamben, *State of Exception* (Chicago: University of Chicago Press, 2005), 4–7.

91. Georgio Agamben, *Homo Sacer: Sovereign Power and Bare Life* (Stanford, CA: Stanford University, 1998), 57.

92. Agamben, *State of Exception*, 3–4.

93. EUSA, "Circular No. 49: Preventive Medicine," 6; and EUSA, *Guide to a Healthful Tour in Korea*, August 1, 1960, 6; EUSA, Adjutant General Section, Pamphlets, 1958–63; RG 338, entry A1 269, box 21, NACP.

94. Woods, *Korea, Hills, Rice Patties, and Whores*, 11–12.

95. *Amerika kundae rŭl kisohanda: Chuhan migun pŏmjoe kŭnjŏl undong ponbu 15 nyŏn* (Seoul: Chuhan migun pŏmjoe kŭnjŏl undong ponbu, 2008); and *Gyeonggi-do kijich'on yŏsŏng saenghwal silt'ae mit chiwŏn chŏngch'aek yŏn'gu*, 62–68.

96. *Amerika kundae rŭl kisohanda*.

97. Following Michel Foucault and his characterization of biopolitics as a form of power that emerged in the late eighteenth century "to 'make' live and 'let' die." Michel Foucault, *"Society Must Be Defended": Lectures at the Collége de France,*

1975–76 (New York: Picador, 2003), 241. Foucault coined the concept "biopolitics" as a way to grasp the newly emergent aspects of the modern state such as economic liberalism, social security, and public health, as an expression of its interest in the new target, "population." The Korean government's control of camptown women seems very different from Western social policies that Foucault analyzed. Simultaneously, and illiberally, the control over camptown women had the aspects of biopolitics in that it persistently attempted to reproduce them as safe bodies by aggressively curing STIs. In this regard, the Korean government's prostitution policy can be considered a postcolonial illiberal version of biopolitics.

98. Agamben, *Homo Sacer*, 71.

99. Agamben, *Homo Sacer*, 97–99.

100. Kim, *Amerika t'aun wang ŭnni chukki obun chŏn kkaji ak ŭl ssŭda*, 98–99.

101. Kim, *Amerika t'aun wang ŭnni chukki obun chŏn kkaji ak ŭl ssŭda*, 123, 140.

102. Kim, *Migun wianbu kijich'on ŭi sumgyŏjin chinsil*, 165–168.

103. Tiffany A. Sippial, *Prostitution, Modernity, and the Making of the Cuban Republic, 1840–1920* (Chapel Hill: University of North Carolina Press, 2013), 7.

104. Kim, *Amerika t'aun wang ŭnni chukki obun chŏn kkaji ak ŭl ssŭda*, 113–114.

105. Pak Chŏng-Wŏn, "Munsan," *Sindonga* (September 1966): 288.

106. Kim, *Amerika t'aun wang ŭnni chukki obun chŏn kkaji ak ŭl ssŭda*, 152–158.

107. *Tonga ilbo*, July 5, 1960.

108. *Tonga ilbo*, November 8, 1967.

109. In court rulings, his name was deleted for privacy, but some Korean newspapers wrote his name in Korean as Stibŭn Alen Bawŏmaen. Therefore, his name can be assumed to be first name Steven or Stephen; middle name Allen, Alan, or Alen; and last name Bauerman(n) or Bowerman(n). Taebŏbwŏn, "P'an'gyŏl: Sarin hyŏnju kŏnjomul panghwa misu," September 11, 1979, *Chaep'ansŏ wŏnbon* (9), NAK (BA0220494).

110. I found this out through a telephone conversation with an NAK official in May 2014. He told me that "Stibŭn Alen Bawŏmaen" was on the list of a stay of execution of the sentence in 1983. I asked the NAK to release the related documents, but it refused to do so on the pretext of privacy.

111. Kim, *Amerika t'aun wang ŭnni chukki obun chŏn kkaji ak ŭl ssŭda*, 182–187.

3. "PIVOTAL WORKERS TO OBTAIN FOREIGN CURRENCY"

1. Kim Yeon-Ja, *Amerika t'aun wang ŭnni chukki obun chŏn kkaji ak ŭl ssŭda: Kim Yeon-Ja chajŏn esei* (Seoul: Samin, 2005), 123.

2. Kyot'ongbu, *Han'guk kyot'ong yŏn'gam* (1961): 233.

3. Kyot'ongbu, *Han'guk kyot'ong yŏn'gam*, 39.

4. Gregg Brazinsky, *Nation Building in South Korea: Koreans, Americans, and the Making of a Democracy* (Chapel Hill: University of North Carolina Press, 2007), 35–36.

5. *Tonga ilbo*, December 7, 1959.

6. *Han'guk kwan'gwang palchŏn sa* (Seoul: Han'guk kwan'gwang hyŏp'oe, 1984), 20.

7. Kyot'ongbu, *Han'guk kyot'ong yŏn'gam* (1961): 234.

8. *Tonga ilbo*, March 14, 1961.

9. Kyot'ongbu, *Han'guk kyot'ong yŏn'gam* (1964): 134.

10. Kyot'ongbu, *Kyot'ong paeksŏ* (1967): 232.

11. Kyot'ongbu, *Kyot'ong t'onggye yŏnbo* (1969): 256; and Kyot'ongbu, *Kyot'ong paeksŏ* (1967): 218.

12. Pak Tong-Ŭn, "Yanggongju wa honhyŏra," *Sindonga* (September 1966): 279–280.

13. Karl Marx, *Capital: A Critique of Political Economy*, vol. 1 (Middlesex: Penguine Books, 1982), pt. 8.

14. Silvia Federici, *Caliban and the Witch: Women, the Body and Primitive Accumulation* (New York: Autonomia, 2004), 85–97. I appreciate Prof. Takashi Fujitani for his comment that helped me dwell on Silvia Federici in this context.

15. Marx, *Capital*, 1: 926.

16. Kyot'ongbu, *Kyot'ong t'onggye yŏnbo* (1967): 159; Kyot'ongbu, *Kyot'ong t'onggye yŏnbo* (1972): 290–295; and Kyot'ongbu, *Kyot'ong t'onggye yŏnbo* (1979): 299, 312–313.

17. Brazinsky, *Nation Building in South Korea*, 132–136.

18. *Han'guk kwan'gwang ŭi onŭl kwa naeil* (Seoul: Han'guk kwan'gwang hyŏp'oe, 1975), 22; and In Tae-Jeong and Yhang Wii-Joo, "Segye ch'egye iron ŭl t'onghan han'guk kŭndae kungmin kwan'gwang ŭi hyŏngsŏng kwajŏng e kwanhan yŏn'gu: 1961–1979 sigi ŭi kukka chŏngch'aek ŭl chungsim ŭro," *Kwan'gwang rejŏ yŏn'gu* 18, no. 4 (2006): 177–178.

19. *Tonga ilbo*, May 28, 1951; and *Kyŏnghyang sinmun*, February 11, 1952.

20. Kang Chun-Man, *Rumsallong konghwaguk* (Seoul: Inmul kwa sasangsa, 2011), 17–48.

21. *Kyŏnghyang sinmun*, August 28, 1968.

22. *Maeil kyŏngje*, July 24, 1971.

23. "South Korea: The Seoul of Hospitality," *Time*, June 4, 1973.

24. Caroline Norma, "Prostitution and the 1960s' Origin of Corporate Entertaining in Japan," *Women's Studies International Forum* 34, no. 6 (2011): 509–519.

25. Kukche kwan'gwang hyŏp'oe, *Han'guk kwan'gwang t'onggye* (1978): 50–52; Kukche kwan'gwang hyŏp'oe, *Han'guk kwan'gwang t'onggye* (1980): 36; and Hisae Muroi and Naoko Sasaki, "Tourism and Prostitution in Japan," in *Gender, Work and Tourism*, ed. M. Thea Sinclair (London: Routledge. 1997), 179–185.

26. *Kwan'gwang chawŏn kaebal ŭi hyŏnhwang kwa kwaje* (Seoul: Taehan sanggong hoeŭiso, 1974), 59.

27. Yayori Matsui, "Sexual Slavery in Korea," *Frontiers: A Journal of Women's Studies* 2, no. 1 (1977): 23.

28. Yi Kyŏng-Min, *Kisaeng ŭn ŏttŏk'e mandŭrŏjyŏnnŭn'ga* (Seoul: Ak'aibŭ puksŭ, 2005); and Suh Ji Young, "Sangsil kwa pujae ŭi sigonggan: 1930 nyŏndae yorijŏm kwa kisaeng," *Chŏngsin munhwa yŏn'gu* 32, no. 3 (2009): 174–178.

29. Matsui, "Sexual Slavery in Korea," 24.

30. Kim Tong-Hyŏn, "Rŭppo ilbonin kwan'gwanggaek," *Sindonga* (January 1974): 221–222; and Sim Song-Mu, "Rŭppo 100 man myŏng tolp'a ŭi kwan'gwang han'guk," *Sindonga* (February 1979): 246.

31. *Han'guk kwan'gwang palchŏn sa*, 54.

32. Han'guk munhwa kwan'gwang yŏn'guwŏn, "Han'guk kwan'gwang suji," accessed April 9, 2021, https://know.tour.go.kr/stat/koreaTourIncomeDis19Re.do.

33. *Han'guk kyŏngje 60 nyŏn sa* (Seoul: Han'guk kaebal yŏn'guwŏn, 2010), 209.

34. Sim, "Rŭppo 100 man myŏng tolp'a ŭi kwan'gwang han'guk," 246–247.

35. Article 141 of the Local Tax Act, January 1, 1964, Korea Law Information Center (KLIC), Sejong; Naemubu changgwan, "Oegugin e taehan yuhŭng ŭmsikse kwase myŏnje e kwanhan chorye chunch'ik sidal," Gyeongsangbuk-do kihoekkwalli-sil pŏmmu tamdanggwan, *Chorye kongp'o wŏnbon*, National Archives Korea (NAK) (BA0181923), Daejeon; and Naemubu, "Oegugin e taehan yuhŭng ŭmsikse myŏnje e kwanhan chorye chung kaejŏng chorye sŭngin," Haengjŏng chojŏngsil che3 haengjŏng chojŏnggwan, *Seoul t'ŭkpyŏlsi chorye chejŏng kaejŏng* (7–12 wŏl), NAK (BA0083977).

36. *Kyŏnghyang sinmun*, October 5, 1972.

37. Kim, "Rŭppo ilbonin kwan'gwanggaek," 221–222.

38. Kim, "Rŭppo ilbonin kwan'gwanggaek," 221–222.

39. Thanh-dam Truong, *Sex, Money and Morality: Prostitution and Tourism in South-East Asia* (London: Zed Books, 1990), 116–118.

40. Luther H. Hodges, Foreword to *The Future of Tourism in the Pacific and Far East: A Report Prepared by Checchi and Company under Contract with the United States Department of Commerce and Co-Sponsored by the Pacific Area Travel Association*, ed. Harry G. Clement (Washington, DC: US Government Printing Office, 1961), iii.

41. Clement, ed., *Future of Tourism in the Pacific and Far East*, 286.

42. Morton D. Kauffman, *Tourism to Korea* (Seoul: United States Operations Mission to Korea, 1966), 133–134.

43. Kauffman, *Tourism to Korea*, 12.

44. Kukche kwan'gwang hyŏp'oe, *Han'guk kwan'gwang t'onggye* (1981–1983); and Han'guk kwan'gwang hyŏp'oe, *Han'guk kwan'gwang t'onggye* (1984–1989).

45. *Kyŏnghyang sinmun*, November 26, 1985.

46. The article introduces the author Jun Kanta as a "sexual adventurer and the moving force behind *Far East Video*," who "has made extensive tours of all the playgrounds of the Far East." Jun Kanta, "Hustler's Olympic-Goer's Guide to Korean Sex," *Hustler* (October 1988): 30.

47. Kanta, "Hustler's Olympic-Goer's Guide to Korean Sex," 32.

48. Pogŏn sahoebu, *Pogŏn sahoe paeksŏ* (1985): 98; and Pogŏn sahoebu, *Pogŏn sahoe t'onggye yŏnbo* (1989): 44–45; and "Chejŏng kaejŏng iyu," the Rule on Health Checkups of Employees in Sanitary Field, September 8, 1984, KLIC.

49. *Kwan'gwang pujori silt'ae mit pangji taech'aek* (Seoul: Pujŏng pangji taech'aek wiwŏnhoe, 1994), 66–70.

50. Yŏsŏng sinmunsa, "Yi U-Jŏng: Kisaeng kwan'gwang i aeguk imyŏn sŏnsaeng ttal put'ŏ kwan'gwang kisaeng mandŭsio," in *Iyagi yŏsŏngsa: Han'guk yŏsŏng ŭi sam kwa yŏksa* (Seoul: Yŏsŏng sinmunsa, 2000), 94–109.

51. Yi Hyŏn-Suk, *Han'guk kyohoe yŏsŏng yŏnhap'oe 25 nyŏn sa* (Seoul: Han'guk kyohoe yŏsŏng yŏnhap'oe, 1992), 82–92.

52. Cho Chun-Hyŏn, "Kin'gŭp choch'i," NAK, accessed January 13, 2023, www .archives.go.kr/next/search/listSubjectDescription.do?id=000947&sitePage=1-2-1.

53. Yi, *Han'guk kyohoe yŏsŏng yŏnhap'oe 25 nyŏn sa*, 93.

54. Yi, *Han'guk kyohoe yŏsŏng yŏnhap'oe 25 nyŏn sa*, 257–258.

55. *Maech'un munje wa yŏsŏng undong* (October 14, 1986); and *Kukche semina yŏsŏng kwa kwan'gwang munhwa* (April 20–23, 1988).

56. *Kwan'gwang pujori silt'ae mit pangji taech'aek*, 66–70.

57. The World Bank, "GDP (Current US$)—Korea, Rep," accessed April 2, 2021, https://data.worldbank.org/indicator/NY.GDP.MKTP.CD?locations=KR.

58. Yi, *Han'guk kyohoe yŏsŏng yŏnhap'oe 25 nyŏn sa*, 87–89.

59. Yi Mi-Gyŏng, "Maech'un munje e taehan yŏsŏng undongnonjŏk chŏpkŭn," *Maech'un munje wa yŏsŏng undong*, 60.

60. Son Tŏk-Su, "Sŏng chegukchuŭi ŭi hisaengjadŭl," *Maech'un munje wa yŏsŏng undong*, 39–56.

61. Han'guk yŏsŏng tanch'e yŏnhap, "Chegukchuŭi sŏng ch'imt'al kwa yŏsŏng," *Minju yŏsŏng* (June 1988); and *Kukche semina yŏsŏng kwa kwan'gwang munhwa*, 55.

62. Kong Tŏk-Kwi, "Kisaeng kwan'gwang silt'ae chosa pogosŏ rŭl naemyŏnsŏ," in *Kisaeng kwan'gwang: Chŏn'guk 4 kae chiyŏk silt'ae chosa pogosŏ* (Seoul: Han'guk kyohoe yŏsŏng yŏnhap'oe, 1983), ii, Korea Democracy Foundation (KDF) (00011045), Seoul.

63. Yun Chŏng-Ok, "Chŏngsindae wa uri ŭi immu," *Kukche semina yŏsŏng kwa kwan'gwang munhwa*; and Katharine H. S. Moon, "South Korean Movements against Militarized Sexual Labor," *Asian Survey* 39, no. 2 (1999): 310–327.

64. Yi, *Han'guk kyohoe yŏsŏng yŏnhap'oe 25 nyŏn sa*, 264.

65. Taehan ŏmŏnihoe, Kat'ollik yŏsŏng yŏnhap'oe, Han'guk kyohoe yŏsŏng yŏnhap'oe, Taehan YWCA yŏnhap'oe, "Kwan'gwang chŏngch'aek ŭn sijŏngdoeŏya handa," December 28, 1973, KDF (00443005).

66. Kong, "Kisaeng kwan'gwang silt'ae chosa pogosŏ rŭl naemyŏnsŏ," i.

67. *Kisaeng kwan'gwang*, 21.

68. Cho Ae-Sil, "Onŭl ŭl unda," in *Yŏsŏng kwan'gye yŏn'gu charyo 2: T'ŭkchip, maech'un* (Seoul: Han'guk kidok ch'ŏngnyŏn hyŏbŭihoe, 1983), 15, KDF (00198530).

69. Yi Yŏl-Hŭi, "Mŏrimal," *Maech'un munje wa yŏsŏng undong*, i.

70. Alan Hunt, *Governing Morals: A Social History of Moral Regulation* (Cambridge: Cambridge University Press, 1999), 147–149.

71. Cho, "Onŭl ŭl unda," 16.

72. This analysis was inspired by Ann McClintock. She criticizes the anti-sex work campaign for being internally contradictory: "On the one hand, prostitutes are patronized and silenced as having an inherent lack of agency—as coerced slaves and victims of 'false consciousness.' On the other hand, they are castigated for having an excess of agency, as irresponsibly trafficking in male fantasies and commodification." Ann McClintock, "Sex Work and Sex Workers," *Social Text* 37 (1993): 7.

73. Yi, *Han'guk kyohoe yŏsŏng yŏnhap'oe 25 nyŏn sa*, 267–268.

74. *Yŏsŏng kwa kwan'gwang munhwa: Jeju chiyŏk ŭl chungsim ŭro* (Seoul: Han'guk kyohoe yŏsŏng yŏnhap'oe), 32–37, KDF (00142569).

75. Cynthia Enloe, *Bananas, Beaches & Bases: Making Feminist Sense of International Politics* (Berkeley: University of California Press, 1990), 44.

76. Elaine H. Kim and Chungmoo Choi, eds., *Dangerous Women: Gender and Korean Nationalism* (London: Routledge, 1998); and Chŏng Hŭi-Jin, "Chugŏya sanŭn yŏsŏngdŭl ŭi inkwŏn: Han'guk kijich'on yŏsŏng undong sa," in *Han'guk yŏsŏng inkwŏn undong sa,* ed. Han'guk yŏsŏng ŭi chŏnhwa yŏnhap (Seoul: Hanul ak'ademi, 1999).

77. *Tonga ilbo*, May 31, 1973. The original version is as follows: "When Correspondent Chang asked three lovely kisaeng, who earn $500 per month, how they felt about the Japanese, one replied: 'It's hard for us to accept some—but we must work hard not only for ourselves and our families but for our country's future. Our country needs more money for its economic development.'" "South Korea: The Seoul of Hospitality," *Time*, June 4, 1973. It seems that this issue of *Time* was released a week earlier than the specified date, so the Korean newspaper could report on it on May 31, 1973.

78. *Kyŏnghyang sinmun*, August 14, 1981.

79. Hyŏndae han'guk kusul charyogwan, "*Yang Yun-Se kusul charyo*" (Seongnam: Han'guk'ak chungang yŏn'guwŏn, 2009), 305, 314.

80. The World Bank, "GDP per Capita (Current US$)—Korea, Rep.," accessed April 2, 2021, https://data.worldbank.org/indicator/NY.GDP.PCAP.CD?locations=KR.

81. Lee Sang Rok, "1970 nyŏndae sobi ŏkche chŏngch'aek kwa sobi munhwa ŭi ilsang chŏngch'ihak," *Yŏksa munje yŏn'gu* 17, no. 1 (2013): 137–182; and *Han'guk kyŏngje 60 nyŏn sa*, 117–119.

82. Paik Wook-inn, "Han'guk sobi sahoe hyŏngsŏng kwa chŏngbo sahoe ŭi sŏnggyŏk e kwanhan yŏn'gu," *Kyŏngje wa sahoe* 77 (2008): 199–225; and Jo Won Koang, "Han'guk sobi sahoe ŭi tŭngjang kwa misi kwŏllyŏk ŭi pyŏnhwa," *Han'guk sahoehak* 48, no. 1 (2014): 133–172.

83. In the 1980s, the real growth rate of the annual service sector was 9.7 percent, a bit lower than that the annual GDP, 10.0 percent. Han'guk ŭnhaeng, "Han'guk ŭnhaeng kyŏngje t'onggye sisŭt'em," accessed April 2, 2021, http://ecos.bok.or.kr.

84. Taegŏmch'alch'ŏng, *Pŏmjoe punsŏk* (December 1963): 181.

85. *Tonga ilbo*, December 13, 1968; and *Tonga ilbo*, December 13, 1969.

86. Jin-Kyung Lee, *Service Economies: Militarism, Sex Work and Migrant labor in South Korea* (Minneapolis: University of Minnesota Press), 99–100.

87. Article 9 of the Enforcement Decree of Food Sanitation Act, July 20, 1970, KLIC.

88. Pogŏn sahoebu, *Pogŏn sahoe t'onggye yŏnbo* (1961–1980).

89. Pogŏn sahoebu, *Pogŏn sahoe t'onggye yŏnbo* (1985–1991).

90. *Tonga ilbo*, January 19, 1985.

91. Lee Bong Soo, "Yuhŭng kinŭng chungsimji idong kwajŏng e kwanhan yŏn'gu" (master's thesis, Seoul National University, 1983), 14–30.

92. *Kyŏnghyang sinmun*, October 19, 1982.

93. Kim Hyŏn-Chang, "Sigol tabang ch'a rŭl p'alkka, yŏja rŭl p'alkka," *Saem i kip'ŭn mul* (June 1986): 67–68.

94. *Chosŏn ilbo*, July 11, 1962.

95. I have not found any materials to detail how STI testing was conducted on the women who sexually served Korean men at a local level. However, the women I interviewed for chapter 4 shared with me their experiences as a sex worker and a feminist activist, respectively. For instance, Han Min-Ju, who worked at a bar for Korean men, kisaeng houses, and clubs in camptown, recalled that the City of Incheon issued health certificates to sex workers catering not only to GIs but also to Korean men in the 1970s. She was apprehended and incarcerated in a female reformatory because she did not carry hers, as chapter 4 shows. In contrast, Lee Ock-jeong (Yi Ok-Chŏng), who established a shelter in Yongsan red-light district, recalled that regular STI testing was not conducted there until the late 1980s. In this way, STI testing for prostitutes or sex workers serving Korean men seemed to be carried out not extensively and somewhat haphazardly before the Seoul Olympic games.

96. Pogŏn sahoebu, *Pogŏn sahoe t'onggye yŏnbo* (1989): 44–45.

97. *Tonga ilbo*, August 11, 1980.

98. Shim Eun-jung, "Che 5 konghwaguk sigi p'ŭro yagu chŏngch'aek kwa kungmin yŏga," *Yŏksa yŏn'gu* 26 (2014): 197–238; and Lee Hyun Jin, "1980 nyŏndae sŏngae yŏnghwa chaep'yŏngga rŭl wihan sogo," *Hyŏndae yŏnghwa yŏn'gu* 18 (2014): 93–126.

99. Pogŏn sahoebu, *Pogŏn sahoe t'onggye yŏnbo* (1982–1991).

100. Choi Jai-Seuk, "Han'guk e issŏsŏ ŭi yullak yŏsŏng yŏn'gu ŭi chŏn'gae," *Asea yŏsŏng yŏn'gu* 20 (1981): 18, 24, 29–30; Choi Jae-Seuk, "Han'guk chŏptaebu ŭi yŏn'gu: Seoul-si ŭi chŏptaebu rŭl chungsim ŭro," *Asea yŏsŏng yŏn'gu* 22 (1983): 137, 140, 144; and Kim Yŏng-Mo, *T'oep'ye, yullak munje taeŭng pangan yŏn'gu* (Seoul: Hyŏndae sahoe yŏn'guso, 1984), 95–96, 105.

101. Nodongbu, *Maewŏl nodong t'onggye* (December 1985): 186–187.

102. Ch'oe Sŏng-Jae, "Yullak yŏsŏng munje silt'ae: Han'guk puinhoe silt'ae chosa rŭl chungsim ŭro," in *Yullak yŏsŏng mit mihonmo e taehan charyojip* (Seoul: Han'guk puinhoe ch'ongbonbu, 1985), 90; and Cho Sun-Gyŏng, "Han'guk yŏsŏng nodong sijang punsŏk ŭl wihan siron: Saengsanjik yŏsŏng nodongnyŏk pujok hyŏnsang ŭl chungsim ŭro," *Yŏsŏng* 3 (1989): 123.

103. Choi, "Han'guk chŏptaebu ŭi yŏn'gu," 144–145.

104. *Yoboho yŏsŏng silt'ae chosa pogosŏ* (Seoul: Pogŏn sahoebu, 1981), 53–54.

105. Eum Hye-Jin, "Sŏngmaemae tamnon ŭi pip'anjŏk koch'al: 1980 nyŏndae insinmaemae tamnon ŭl chungsim ŭro" (master's thesis, Seoul National University, 2006).

106. *Han'gyŏre sinmun*, December 11, 1988; *Kyŏnghyang sinmun*, December 13, 1988; and *Tonga ilbo*, December 14, 1988.

107. *Simin chagu undong II: Hyangnak munhwa ch'ubang kwa kŏnjŏn simin munhwa kakkugi simin undong* (Seoul: Seoul YMCA, 1995).

108. Han'guk yŏsŏng tanch'e yŏnhap, "Insinmaemae wa kwallyŏnhan han'guk yŏsŏng tanch'e yŏnhap ŭi sŏngmyŏngsŏ," December 14, 1988, KDF (00017428).

109. "Maech'un, insinmaemae kŭnjŏl ŭl wihan ch'immuk siwi," *Pet'ŭl* (April 1989): 15; Han'guk kyohoe yŏsŏng yŏnhap'oe, "89 nyŏn maech'un munhwa mit insinmaemae kŭnjŏl ŭl wihan t'ŭkpyŏl taech'aek wiwŏnhoe chunbi moim ŭl wihan pogosŏ," March 1989, KDF (00010190); and *Han'guk YWCA 80 nyŏn sa: Saengmyŏng ŭi param ŭro* (Seoul: YWCA, 2006), 284–285.

110. Yi Mi-Gyŏng, "Insinmaemae mit sŏngp'ok'aeng e taehan sahoe chŏngch'ijŏk paegyŏng," *Che 23 ch'a chŏngch'aek semina: Insinmaemae wa sŏngp'ok'aeng kŭnjŏl taech'aek* (February 2, 1989): 25, KDF (00073878).

111. Son Tŏk-Su, "Insinmaemae nŭn in'gyŏk p'agoe pŏmjoe ida: Kanggan insinmaemae ch'ŏbŏlpŏp kanghwahaeya," *Pet'ŭl* (July/August 1989): 2–3.

112. Kim Chin Kyun, ed., *1980 nyŏndae hyŏngmyŏng ŭi sidae* (Seoul: Saeroun sesang, 1999); Han'guk minjujuŭi yŏn'guso, ed., *Han'guk minjuhwa undong sa*, vol. 3 (Paju: Tolbege, 2010); and Barry Eichengreen, Dwight H. Perkins, and Kwanho Shin, *From Miracle to Maturity: The Growth of the Korean Economy* (Cambridge, MA: Harvard University Press, 2012).

113. *Simin chagu undong II*, 52–53.

114. Son, "Insinmaemae nŭn in'gyŏk p'agoe pŏmjoe ida," 2; Yun Yŏng-Ae, "Insinmaemae ŏttŏk'e kŭnjŏrhal kŏsin'ga," *Che 23 ch'a chŏngch'aek semina*, 40–41; and Yi Su-Yŏn, "Hyangnak sanŏp ŭi silt'ae wa kŭ wŏnin," *Kidokkyo sasang* (January 1989): 106.

115. *Insinmaemae ŭi silt'ae e kwanhan yŏn'gu* (Seoul: Han'guk hyŏngsa chŏngch'aek yŏn'guwŏn, 1993), 52–65.

116. Eum, "Sŏngmaemae tamnon ŭi pip'anjŏk koch'al," 34–36.

117. Son, "Insinmaemae nŭn in'gyŏk p'agoe pŏmjoe ida," 2–3.

118. *Taebŏmjoe chŏnjaeng paeksŏ* (Seoul: Kyŏngch'alch'ŏng, 1992).

4. LADIES AND GENTLEMEN (AND PROSTITUTES)

1. Kungnip yŏngsang chejakso, "Nae kojang sosik," *Daehan News*, October 12, 1963, accessed February 16, 2022, www.youtube.com/watch?v=3cZghqsBNpI.

2. Hŏnpŏp chaep'anso, "Kukyuji yangyŏ sinch'ŏng kŏbu ch'ŏbun wihŏn hwagin" (Chŏnwŏn chaep'anbu 2002-hŏn-ma-676, July 15, 2004), Korea Law Information Center (KLIC), Sejong; and Daejeon MBC News, "Pi maech'in tŭlp'an ŭi chinsil: Sŏsan kaech'ŏktan sakŏn," accessed Nov. 4, 2023, www.youtube.com/watch?v=w7sG4vtA6kQ.

3. Lee Sang Rok, "Kyŏngje cheil chuŭi ŭi sahoejŏk kusŏng kwa saengsanjŏk chuch'e mandŭlgi: 4.19-5.16 sigi hyŏngmyŏng ŭi chŏnyu rŭl tullŏssan kyŏnghap kwa chŏllyaktŭl," *Yŏksa munje yŏn'gu* 25 (2011): 147–153; Kim A-ram, "5.16 kunjŏnggi sahoe chŏngch'aek: Adong pokchi wa puranga taech'aek ŭi sŏnggyŏk," *Yŏksa wa hyŏnsil* 82 (2011): 351–355; and Lee Soyoung, "Kŏnjŏn sahoe wa kŭ

chŏktŭl: 1960–80 nyŏndae purangin tansok ŭi saengmyŏng chŏngch'i," *Pŏp kwa sahoe* 51 (2016): 35–38.

4. Park Chung Hee, *Kukka wa hyŏngmyŏng kwa na* (1963; Seoul: Kip'arang, 2017), 88.

5. Yi Sŭng-Ho, "Urinara poan ch'ŏbun ŭi yŏksajŏk chŏn'gae," *Hyŏngsa chŏngch'aek* 7 (1995): 75–77.

6. Hwang Jisung, "Changae yŏsŏng ŭi sisŏrhwa kwajŏng e kwanhan yŏn'gu: Seoul sirip punyŏ poho chidoso sarye rŭl chungsim ŭro" (PhD diss., Seoul National University, 2023).

7. Naemubu ch'ian'guk, *Kyŏngch'al t'onggye yŏnbo* (1964–1970).

8. Pogŏn sahoebu, *Punyŏ poho sisŏl hyŏnhwang*, 1985, National Archives Korea (NAK) (C11M30155), Daejeon; Pogŏn sahoebu, *Punyŏ haengjŏng 40 nyŏn sa* (Seoul: Pogŏn sahoebu, 1987), 111–115, 142–144; Pogŏn sahoebu, *Pogŏn sahoe t'onggye yŏnbo* (1971–1989); and Pogŏn pokchibu, *Pogŏn pokchi t'onggye yŏnbo* (1996): 212.

9. Chŏn Pyŏng-Sun, "Yullak yŏsŏng sŏndoso," *Yŏwŏn* (April 1965): 148; and Song Kŏn-Ho, "Tosi sahoe ŭi pyŏngni," *Yŏwŏn* (December 1962): 104.

10. The tentative title of Lee Ko Woon's documentary film is *Women of Breakwater*.

11. Kim Yeon-Ja, *Amerika t'aun wang ŭnni chukki obun chŏn kkaji ak ŭl ssŭda: Kim Yeon-Ja chajŏn esei* (Seoul: Samin, 2005), 67.

12. *Kyŏnghyang sinmun*, August 13, 1977.

13. Seoul-si, "Yun Ch'i-Yŏng Seoul sijang, punyŏ pohoso sich'al," Seoul Metropolitan Archives (IT4488).

14. Pogŏn sahoebu, *Pogŏn sahoe t'onggye yŏnbo* (1971): 310–311; and Pogŏn sahoebu, *Pogŏn sahoe t'onggye yŏnbo* (1974): 376.

15. Pogŏn sahoebu, *Pogŏn sahoe t'onggye yŏnbo* (1971): 310–311; Pogŏn sahoebu, *Pogŏn sahoe t'onggye yŏnbo* (1974): 376; Pogŏn sahoebu, *Pogŏn sahoe t'onggye yŏnbo* (1986): 212; and Pogŏn sahoebu, *Pogŏn sahoe t'onggye yŏnbo* (1990): 251.

16. Mun Sŏn-Hwa, "Han'guk yullak yŏsŏng sŏndo saŏp e taehan sogo" (master's thesis, Ewha Womans University, 1970), 41.

17. Pogŏn sahoebu, *Pogŏn sahoe paeksŏ* (1964): 186–188.

18. Kim Nak-Chung, "Haptong kyŏrhonsik sŏngkwa pogo," in *Yullak yŏsŏng e kwanhan yŏn'gu pogosŏ*, ed. Seoul t'ŭkpyŏlsi sirip punyŏ poho chidoso (Seoul: Seoul t'ŭkpyŏlsi sirip punyŏ poho chidoso, 1966), 90.

19. Kim, "Haptong kyŏrhonsik sŏngkwa pogo," 91.

20. Won Mi Hye, "'Sŏng p'anmae yŏsŏng' ŭi saengae ch'ehŏm yŏn'gu: Kyoch'ajŏk sŏng wigye ŭi sigongganjŏk chakyong ŭl chungsim ŭro" (PhD diss., Ewha Womans University, 2010), 122.

21. Hwang Jung-Mee, "Kaebal kukka ŭi yŏsŏng chŏngch'aek e kwanhan yŏn'gu: 1960–70 nyŏndae han'guk punyŏ haengjŏng ŭl chungsim ŭro" (PhD diss., Seoul National University, 2001), 104.

22. Won, "'Sŏng p'anmae yŏsŏng' ŭi saengae ch'ehŏm yŏn'gu," 121–129.

23. Kim Daehyun, "1950–60 nyŏndae 'yoboho' ŭi chaegusŏng kwa 'yullak yŏsŏng' saŏp ŭi chŏn'gae," *Sahoe wa yŏksa* 129 (2021): 37–38.

24. Kim Yong-A, "Yullak yŏsŏng e kwanhan silt'ae pogo: Sirip punyŏ poho chidoso wŏnsaeng ŭl chungsim ŭro," *Chibang haengjŏng* 143 (1965): 64–70.

25. Kim Young-Shik, Nam Taek-Sung, and Choi Jin-Hae conducted their research as the directors of Namgu Public Health Center (Daegu), Yongsan Public Health Center (Seoul), and Busan Jin-gu Public Health Center (Busan), respectively. Kim Young-Shik, "Tosi e issŏsŏ ŭi oegugin ŭl sangdaero han wianbu e taehan sŏngpyŏng kwalli," *Yebang ŭihak hoeji* 7, no. 2 (1974): 293–298; Nam Taek-Sung, "Urinara sŏngpyŏng kwalli e kwanhan yŏk'akchŏk koch'al," *Yebang ŭihak hoeji* 9, no. 1 (1976): 123–127; and Choi Jin-Hae, "Busan ilbu chiyŏk t'ŭksu ŏpt'aebudŭl ŭi sahoe ŭihakchŏgin chosa," *Yebang ŭihak hoeji* 10, no. 1 (1977): 125–133. In addition, the vast majority of the prostitution studies were conducted at the female reformatories or VD clinics, which might have been impossible without the permission and cooperation of the directors of those institutions.

26. For instance, Moon Koo Hyun, "Yullak yŏsŏng e taehan hyŏnhwang mit sŏngpyŏng e kwanhan yŏn'gu," *Kyungpook National University Nonmunjip* 8 (1964): 131–154; Kwŏn Kyu-Sik and O Yŏng-Gŭn, "Yullak yŏsŏng ŭi silt'ae," *Yŏsŏng munje yŏn'gu* 3 (1973): 149–171; and Yook Kil Sung, "Daejeon-si yullak yŏsŏng silt'ae e kwanhan yŏn'gu" (master's thesis, Hannam University, 1986).

27. Yi Ch'ŏl-Yong, *Ŏdum ŭi chasiktŭl* (Seoul: Saeum, 2015). This novel was written by Yi Ch'ŏl-Yong and revised by Hwang Sŏk-Yŏng in the late 1970s. On behalf of Yi, who was wanted by the police due to his activism for the poor, Hwang published the book in his name in 1980.

28. Michel Foucault, "Truth and Juridical Forms," in *Power: The Essential Works of Foucault, 1954–1986*, ed. James D. Faubion (New York: New Press, 2001), vol. 3: 11–15; and Michel Foucault, *Discipline and Punish: The Birth of the Prison* (New York: Vintage Books, 1991), 27–28.

29. Foucault, "Truth and Juridical Forms," 56–59; and Michel Foucault, *The Birth of Biopolitics: Lectures at the Collége de France, 1978–79* (New York: Palgrave Macmillan, 2008), 34–35.

30. I have collected the papers using Haksul yŏn'gu chŏngbo sŏbisŭ (Research Information Sharing Service, http://riss.kr).

31. Ha Sŏng-Hwan, "Kuktaean sakŏn ŭi kyoyuksajŏk hamŭi," *Chinbo p'yŏngnon* 69 (2015): 289–325.

32. Cheong Soo Bok, "Yi Sang-Baek kwa han'guk sahoehak ŭi sŏngnip," *Han'guk sahoehak* 50, no. 2 (2016): 1–40; and Kim Sungeun, "1950–60 nyŭndae miguk ŭi kyoyuk wŏnjo wa miguk yuhak sŏnho: Minnesota Project wa Fulbright Program ŭl chungsim ŭro," *Sahoe wa yŏksa* 122 (2019): 191–222.

33. Kim Bong Seok, "Yi Man-Gap ŭi sahoehak," *Han'guk sahoehak* 50, no. 2 (2016): 41–66; and Kim In Soo, "Nongsŏk Yi Hae-Yŏng ŭi sahoehak: 'Han'guk sahoe chosasa' ŭi ch'ŭkmyŏn esŏ," *Han'guk sahoehak* 50, no. 4 (2016): 27–66.

34. Kim, "Nongsŏk Yi Hae-Yŏng ŭi sahoehak," 36.

35. Sin Tong Yoll, "Ch'angnyŏ ŭi chinŭng kyesu: Sŏngpyŏng manyŏn ŭi wŏnch'ŏn ŭrosŏ" (master's thesis, Seoul National University, 1961), 2–3. This perspective was repeated in almost every study on STIs.

36. Kim, "Yullak yŏsŏng e kwanhan silt'ae pogo," 64.

37. Yi Ŭng-In, "T'ŭksu yullak yŏsŏng e taehan silt'ae chosa: Ilsŏn chigu chuhan migun sangdae yullak yŏsŏng ŭl chungsim ŭro," *Asea yŏsŏng yŏn'gu* 4 (1965): 193; Kim Myung Suk, "Yullak yŏsŏng e kwanhan chedojŏk koch'al" (master's thesis, Ewha Womans University, 1981), 3; and Yu Song-Ja, "Yullak yŏsŏng ŭi yoin punsŏk kwa sŏndo p'ŭrogŭraem e kwanhan yŏn'gu" (master's thesis, Ewha Womans University, 1974), 2.

38. Pogŏn sahoebu, *Pogŏn sahoe t'onggye yŏnbo* (1958): 213–214.

39. Article 16 of the Regulation of Brothel Owners and Prostitutes. Chōsen sōtokufu, *Chōsen sōtokufu kanbō* 1095 (1916): 446, National Library of Korea (NLK), Seoul.

40. Article 17 of the Regulation of Brothel Owners and Prostitutes. Chōsen sōtokufu, *Chōsen sōtokufu kanbō* 1095 (1916): 446.

41. Park Jung Ae, "Chosŏn ch'ongdokpu ŭi sŏngpyŏng yebang chŏngch'aek kwa hwaryupyŏng yebangnyŏng," *Sarim* 55 (2016): 308.

42. Yi, "T'ŭksu yullak yŏsŏng e taehan silt'ae chosa," 194.

43. Colin Gordon, "Governmental Rationality: An Introduction," in *The Foucault Effect: Studies in Governmentality*, ed. Graham Burchell, Colin Gordon, and Peter Miller (Chicago: University of Chicago Press, 1991), 8.

44. Lyo Kyung Goo, "Han'gugin sŏngpyŏng ŭi sahoe ŭihakchŏk chosa yŏn'gu" (master's thesis, Seoul National University, 1960); Yoon Bong Ja, "Chŏpkaek ŏpchadŭl e taehan sahoe ŭihakchŏk chosa yŏn'gu" (master's thesis, Seoul National University, 1963); Lee Tae Am, "T'ŭksu chiyŏk sahoein e taehan sahoe ŭihakchŏk chosa yŏn'gu" (master's thesis, Seoul National University, 1965); Kim, "Haptong kyŏrhonsik sŏngkwa pogo"; Kim Yŏng-Mo, *T'oep'ye, yullak munje taeŭng pangan yŏn'gu* (Seoul: Hyŏndae sahoe yŏn'guso, 1984); and Yŏn'gubu, "Hyangnak sanŏp ŭi p'aengch'ang wŏnin kwa taech'aek," *Sahoe chŏngch'aek yŏn'gu* 6 (1985): 140–170 (six). Sin, "Ch'angnyŏ ŭi chinŭng kyesu"; and Yi Mun-Ja, "Yullak yŏsŏng silt'ae e kwanhan yŏn'gu," in *Yullak yŏsŏng e kwanhan yŏn'gu pogosŏ*, ed. Seoul t'ŭkpyŏlsi sirip punyŏ poho chidoso (Seoul: Seoul t'ŭkpyŏlsi sirip punyŏ poho chidoso, 1966), 22–57 (two). Kang Il-Su, "MMPI e nat'anan yullak yŏsŏng ŭi sŏnggyŏk t'ŭkching," *Simnihak yŏn'gu* 14, no. 1 (1986): 53–62 (one).

45. Ian Hacking, "How Should We Do the History of Statistics?," in *The Foucault Effect: Studies in Governmentality*, ed. Graham Burchell, Colin Gordon, and Peter Miller (Chicago: University of Chicago Press, 1991), 182–183.

46. For notable exceptions, see Choi Jai-Seuk, "Han'guk e issŏsŏ ŭi yullak yŏsŏng yŏn'gu ŭi chŏn'gae," *Asea yŏsŏng yŏn'gu* 20 (1981): 9–52; and Choi Jai-Seuk, "Han'guk chŏptaebu ŭi yŏn'gu: Seoul-si ŭi chŏptaebu rŭl chungsim ŭro," *Asea yŏsŏng yŏn'gu* 22 (1983): 135–161.

47. Choi, "Han'guk e issŏsŏ ŭi yullak yŏsŏng yŏn'gu ŭi chŏn'gae," 17–18.

48. T'onggyech'ŏng, *In'gu ch'ongjosa* (1970), accessed January 10, 2023, https://kosis.kr/statHtml/statHtml.do?orgId=101&tblId=DT_1IN7002&vw_cd=MT_ZTITLE&list_id=A1181&scrId=&seqNo=&lang_mode=ko&obj_var_id=&itm_id=&conn_path=MT_ZTITLE&path=%252FstatisticsList%252Fstatistics

ListIndex.do; and T'onggyech'ŏng, *In'gu ch'ongjosa* (1975), accessed January 10, 2023, https://kosis.kr/statHtml/statHtml.do?orgId=101&tblId=DT_1IN7502& vw_cd=MT_ZTITLE&list_id=A11171&scrId=&seqNo=&lang_mode=ko&obj _var_id=&itm_id=&conn_path=MT_ZTITLE&path=%252FstatisticsList%252 FstatisticsListIndex.do.

49. Yi, "T'ŭksu yullak yŏsŏng e taehan silt'ae chosa," 195; and Park Tai Keun, "Wianbudŭl e taehan sahoe ŭihakchŏk chosa yŏn'gu: Gunsan chiyŏk ŭl chungsim ŭro" (master's thesis, Seoul National University, 1964), 17.

50. Sin, "Ch'angnyŏ ŭi chinŭng kyesu," 28; and Yi, "Yullak yŏsŏng silt'ae e kwanhan yŏn'gu," 49–51.

51. Chŏn, "Yullak yŏsŏng sŏndoso," 149.

52. Choi, "Han'guk e issŏsŏ ŭi yullak yŏsŏng yŏn'gu ŭi chŏn'gae," 29–30.

53. Yi, "Yullak yŏsŏng silt'ae e kwanhan yŏn'gu," 39.

54. Yi, "Yullak yŏsŏng silt'ae e kwanhan yŏn'gu," 39.

55. Kim, "Yullak yŏsŏng e kwanhan silt'ae pogo," 68.

56. Yi Mun-Ja asked her inmates why they ran away from home (and as a result, entered prostitution), and they replied "economic difficulties" (39.5%) and "conflicts with family members" (35.0%). Yi, "Yullak yŏsŏng silt'ae e kwanhan yŏn'gu," 38. Kim Yong-A's study was based on the same survey, while the categories were a little different. Kim, "Yullak yŏsŏng e kwanhan silt'ae pogo," 68.

57. Kim Yong-A, "Sisŏl kwalli e kwanhan sogyŏn: Kyodo rŭl chungsim ŭro," in *Yullak yŏsŏng e kwanhan yŏn'gu pogosŏ*, ed. Seoul t'ŭkpyŏlsi sirip punyŏ poho chidoso (Seoul: Seoul t'ŭkpyŏlsi sirip punyŏ poho chidoso, 1966), 6.

58. Yi, "Yullak yŏsŏng silt'ae e kwanhan yŏn'gu," 43–44; Mun, "Yullak yŏsŏng e taehan hyŏnhwang mit sŏngpyŏng e kwanhan yŏn'gu," 137–138; Yu, "Yullak yŏsŏng ŭi yoin punsŏk kwa sŏndo p'ŭrogŭraem e kwanhan yŏn'gu," 49–51; Rhee Se Young, "Yullak silt'ae e kwanhan yŏn'gu" (master's thesis, Kyunghee University, 1976), 58–59; and Yook, "Daejeon-si yullak yŏsŏng silt'ae e kwanhan yŏn'gu," 22–23.

59. Mun Su-Yŏng, "Yullak yŏsŏng sŏn'gyo: Yullak yŏsŏng silt'ae wa sŏn'gyo ŭi kanŭngsŏng e kwanhan yŏn'gu" (master's thesis, Seoul Theological University, 1977), 38.

60. Yu, "Yullak yŏsŏng ŭi yoin punsŏk kwa sŏndo p'ŭrogŭraem e kwanhan yŏn'gu," 45–47, 49–51.

61. Kim, "Yullak yŏsŏng e kwanhan silt'ae pogo," 65–66; Lee Yoo Sook, "Yullak yŏsŏng e kwanhan sahoe hwan'gyŏng chosa" (master's thesis, Seoul National University, [1962]), 9; Sung Yung Ja, "Wianbu e taehan sahoe ŭihakchŏk chosa yŏn'gu" (master's thesis, Seoul National University, 1966), 22; Yu, "Yullak yŏsŏng ŭi yoin punsŏk kwa sŏndo p'ŭrogŭraem e kwanhan yŏn'gu," 28–29; and Yi Myŏng-Ch'ŏl and Ch'oe Yŏng-Gyu, "Seoul sinae yullak yŏsŏng silt'ae chosa," *Sahoe pokchi yŏn'gu* 12, no. 1 (1978): 112–113 (limited number had both biological parents). Kim Ch'un, "Kijich'on chubyŏn yullak yŏsŏng e kwanhan silt'ae chosa: Pyeongtaek Paengseong-myeon Anjeong-ri rŭl chungsim ŭro," *Sahoe pokchi yŏn'gu* 9, no. 1 (1975): 70; Rhee, "Yullak silt'ae e kwanhan yŏn'gu," 50; and Kim Chŏng-Ok,

"Yullak yŏsŏng ŭi yullak yoin e kwanhan yŏn'gu: Busan t'ŭkchŏng chiyŏk ŭl chungsim ŭro," *Yŏsŏng munje yŏn'gu* 8 (1979): 181 (majority had both biological parents).

62. Yi, "Yullak yŏsŏng silt'ae e kwanhan yŏn'gu," 27–28; and Kim, "Yullak yŏsŏng e kwanhan chedojŏk koch'al," 32 (from cities). Lee, "Yullak yŏsŏng e kwanhan sahoe hwan'gyŏng chosa," 5; and Hong Jin Ok, "Urinara ŭi yullak yŏsŏng e kwanhan yŏn'gu" (master's thesis, Chunang University, 1968), 40 (from rural areas).

63. Joo Shinil, "Ilbu chiyŏk e issŏsŏ ŭi yullak yŏsŏng e kwanhan sahoe ŭihakchŏk chosa yŏn'gu" (master's thesis, Seoul National University, 1965), 8, 20; Kim, "Yullak yŏsŏng ŭi yullak yoin e kwanhan yŏn'gu," 180; and Choi, "Han'guk chŏptaebu ŭi yŏn'gu," 138 (majority had religious beliefs). Yoon, "Chŏpkaek ŏpchadŭl e taehan sahoe ŭihakchŏk chosa yŏn'gu," 17–18; Kwŏn and O, "Yullak yŏsŏng ŭi silt'ae," 153–154; and Kim, "Kijich'on chubyŏn yullak yŏsŏng e kwanhan silt'ae chosa," 67 (majority did not).

64. Choi, "Han'guk e issŏsŏ ŭi yullak yŏsŏng yŏn'gu ŭi chŏn'gae," 51.

65. Kim, "Yullak yŏsŏng e kwanhan silt'ae pogo," 70.

66. Sŏ Yŏn-Sun, "Yullak e issŏsŏ ŭi sisŏl poho wa Cottage System ŭi pigyo," *Sahoe saŏp* 9 (1975): 16.

67. Yu, "Yullak yŏsŏng ŭi yoin punsŏk kwa sŏndo p'ŭrogŭraem e kwanhan yŏn'gu," 47, 74.

68. Yi, "Yullak yŏsŏng silt'ae e kwanhan yŏn'gu," 56.

69. Mun, "Han'guk yullak yŏsŏng sŏndo saŏp e taehan sogo," 78, 86.

70. Kim, "Haptong kyŏrhonsik sŏngkwa pogo," 90.

71. Yi, "T'ŭksu yullak yŏsŏng e taehan silt'ae chosa," 196, 206.

72. Yang Chae-Bok, "Yullak yŏsŏng sŏngpyŏng e kwanhan sogo," in *Yullak yŏsŏng e kwanhan yŏn'gu pogosŏ*, ed. Seoul t'ŭkpyŏlsi sirip punyŏ poho chidoso (Seoul: Seoul t'ŭkpyŏlsi sirip punyŏ poho chidoso, 1966), 71.

73. Nam, "Urinara sŏngpyŏng kwalli e kwanhan yŏk'akchŏk koch'al," 124.

74. Hong, "Urinara ŭi yullak yŏsŏng e kwanhan yŏn'gu," 81, 117.

75. Kim Jo Young, "Kijich'on e kwanhan chirihakchŏk yŏn'gu: Gyeonggi-do Paju chibang ŭl chungsim ŭro" (master's thesis, Seoul National University, 1978); Kim Chae-Su, "Kijich'on e kwanhan sahoe chirihakchŏk yŏn'gu: Dongducheon ŭl sarye ro" (master's thesis, Korea University, 1979); and Hong Sŭng-P'yo, "Maech'un sahoe e kwanhan il yŏn'gu: Yeongdeungpo yŏk chubyŏn ŭi maech'un ŏpso esŏŭi ch'amyŏ kwanch'al" (master's thesis, Korea University, 1982).

76. Kim, *T'oep'ye, yullak munje taeŭng pangan yŏn'gu*; and Yŏn'gubu, "Hyangnak sanŏp ŭi p'aengch'ang wŏnin kwa taech'aek."

77. Kang Young Su, "Han'guk sahoe maemaech'un e kwanhan yŏn'gu: Yongsan yŏk chubyŏn maech'un yŏsŏng ŭl chungsim ŭro" (master's thesis, Ewha Womans University, 1989); Park Sun-Sook, "Yŏsŏng ŭi sŏngsŏng (sexuality) ŭl chungsim ŭro pon maemaech'un chŏngch'aek e kwanhan yŏn'gu" (master's thesis, Ewha Womans University, 1990); and Cho Hyoung and Chang Pil Wha, "Kuk'oe sokkirok e nat'anan yŏsŏng chŏngch'aek sigak: Maemaech'un e taehayŏ," *Yŏsŏnghak yŏn'gu* 7 (1990): 83–111.

78. Yi, "T'ŭksu yullak yŏsŏng e taehan silt'ae chosa," 205–206; Joo, "Ilbu chiyŏk e issŏsŏ ŭi yullak yŏsŏng e kwanhan sahoe ŭihakchŏk chosa yŏn'gu," 10–11; Hong, "Urinara ŭi yullak yŏsŏng e kwanhan yŏn'gu," 66–67; Chang Tong-Ch'il, "Yullak yŏsŏng ŭi silt'ae e kwanhan sogo: Jongno-gu wa Yeongdeungpo sŏndo chiyŏk ŭl chungsim ŭro," *Sahoe pokchi yŏn'gu* 2, no. 1 (1967): 128; Kwŏn and O, "Yullak yŏsŏng ŭi silt'ae," 161–162; and Kim, "Yullak yŏsŏng ŭi yullak yoin e kwanhan yŏn'gu," 185.

79. Son Chŏng-Mok, *Han'guk tosi 60 nyŏn ŭi iyagi* (Seoul: Hanul, 2005), 196.

80. Carol Smart, *Law, Crime and Sexuality: Essays in Feminism* (London: Sage, 1995), 192–195.

5. FEMINIST ATTEMPTS TO RECONSTRUCT A MORAL NATION

1. *Kyŏnghyang sinmun*, September 24, 2004.

2. Yi Kŭm-Hyŏng, "Sŏngmaemae t'ŭkpyŏlpŏp sihaeng hu sŏngkwa mit hyanghu ch'ian taech'aek" (presented at conference *Sŏngmaemae t'ŭkpyŏlpŏp sihaeng 3 chunyŏn, kŭ sŏngkwa wa kwaje*, September 17, 2007).

3. Michel Foucault defines "heterotopia" as "absolutely other emplacements" and "places that are outside all places, even though they are actually localizable." He enumerates several types of heterotopias, for instance, "heterotopias of crisis" for individuals in a state of crisis, "heterotopias of deviation" for individuals whose behavior is deviant, and so on. In common with many other countries, brothels, red-light districts, and other spaces common to the sex trade in Korea arguably offer a form of heterotopia. Michel Foucault, "Of Other Spaces," in *Heterotopia and the City: Public Space in a Postcivil Society*, ed. Michiel Dehaene and Lieven De Cauter (London: Routledge, 2008), 17–22.

4. Lee Ock-jeong and Yŏm Sang-Mi, *Maktallena, mak tallaena? Maktallena ŭi chip iyagi* (Seoul: Kaemagowŏn, 2005).

5. Mun Yŏng-Mi, *Amudo kŭnyŏ ŭi iyagi rŭl tŭrŏjuji anatta* (Seoul: Saemt'ŏ, 1999), 246–266.

6. Kim Yeon-Ja, *Amerika t'aun wang ŭnni chukki obun chŏn kkaji ak ŭl ssŭda: Kim Yeon-Ja chajŏn esei* (Seoul: Samin, 2005), 199–276.

7. Kim, *Amerika t'aun wang ŭnni chukki obun chŏn kkaji ak ŭl ssŭda*, 221.

8. Lee and Yŏm, *Maktallena, mak tallaena?*, 111.

9. Mun, *Amudo kŭnyŏ ŭi iyagi rŭl tŭrŏjuji anatta*, 233–235.

10. Lee and Yŏm, *Maktallena, mak tallaena?*, 79–80.

11. KBS, "'Wianbu' konggae chŭngŏn 30 chunyŏn: Kim Hak-Sun, tasi uri ap'e sŏda," *Sisa chikkyŏk*, August 13, 2021, accessed January 23, 2022, www.youtube.com/watch?v=1SjO4v7Ig8k.

12. *Tonga ilbo*, August 15, 1991; *Han'gyŏre sinmun*, August 15, 1991; *Chosŏn ilbo*, August 16, 1991; and Yoshiaki Yoshimi, *Comfort Women: Sexual Slavery in the Japanese Military during World War II* (New York: Columbia University Press, 2001).

13. Chung Chin Sung, "Kun wianbu/chŏngsindae ŭi kaenyŏm e kwanhan koch'al," *Sahoe wa yŏksa* 60 (2001): 34–59.

14. Kim Chung-kang, "'Wianbu' nŭn ŏttŏk'e it'yŏjyŏnna? 1990 nyŏndae ijŏn taejung yŏnghwa sok wianbu chaehyŏn," *Tongasia munhwa yŏn'gu* 71 (2017): 149–193.

15. Yi Hyŏn-Suk, *Han'guk kyohoe yŏsŏng yŏnhap'oe 25 nyŏn sa* (Seoul: Han'guk kyohoe yŏsŏng yŏnhap'oe, 1992), 385–390.

16. Yun Chŏng-Ok, "Chŏngsindae wa uri ŭi immu," *Kukche semina yŏsŏng kwa kwan'gwang munhwa* (April 20–23, 1988), 18–28.

17. Yi, *Han'guk kyohoe yŏsŏng yŏnhap'oe 25 nyŏn sa*, 398–399; and Han'guk chŏngsindae munje taech'aek hyŏbŭihoe 20 nyŏn sa p'yŏnch'an wiwŏnhoe, *Han'guk chŏngsindae munje taech'aek hyŏbŭihoe 20 nyŏn sa* (Seoul: Hanul Ak'ademi, 2014), 57–59.

18. Han Hye-In, "Chendŏ yusan ŭrosŏ ilbon'gun wianbu kirongmul," *Kirogin* 44 (2018): 112.

19. Han'guk chŏngsindae munje taech'aek hyŏbŭihoe 20 nyŏn sa p'yŏnch'an wiwŏnhoe, *Han'guk chŏngsindae munje taech'aek hyŏbŭihoe 20 nyŏn sa*, chs. 2 and 4.

20. *Uridŭl ŭi Kŭm-I* (Seoul: Chuhan migun ŭi Yun Kŭm-I ssi sarhae sakŏn kongdong taech'aek wiwŏnhoe, 1993).

21. Chŏng Hŭi-Jin, "Chugŏya sanŭn yŏsŏngdŭl ŭi inkwŏn: Han'guk kijich'on yŏsŏng undong sa, 1986–98," in *Han'guk yŏsŏng inkwŏn undong sa*, ed. Han'guk yŏsŏng ŭi chŏnhwa yŏnhap (Seoul: Hanul ak'ademi, 1999), 336–338; and *Amerik'a kundae rŭl kisohanda: Chuhan migun pŏmjoe kŭnjŏl undong ponbu 15 nyŏn* (Seoul: Chuhan migun pŏmjoe kŭnjŏl undong ponbu, 2008), 21–24.

22. *Chuhan migun ŭi Yun Kŭm-I ssi sarhae sakŏn charyojip* (Seoul: Chuhan migun pŏmjoe kŭnjŏl undong ponbu, 1994), 13; and *Amerik'a kundae rŭl kisohanda*, 97–98.

23. *Chuhan migun ŭi Yun Kŭm-I ssi sarhae sakŏn charyojip*, 8–14, 153–180.

24. Kim Hak-Sun, "Toep'uri hagi choch'a sirŭn kiŏktŭl," in *Kangjero kkŭllyŏgan chosŏnin kun wianbudŭl: Chŭngŏnjip*, ed. Chŏngsindae yŏn'guhoe (Seoul: Hanul, 1993), 1: 34–40.

25. Hyun Sook Kim, "Yanggongju as an Allegory of the Nation: Images of Working-Class Women in Popular and Radical Texts," in *Dangerous Women: Gender and Korean Nationalism*, ed. Elaine H. Kim and Chungmoo Choi (London: Routledge, 1998).

26. Chŏn Wu-Sŏp, "Yun Kŭm-I, kŭ nŭn nugu in'ga?," in *Uridŭl ŭi Kŭm-I* (Seoul: Chuhan migun ŭi Yun Kŭm-I ssi sarhae sakŏn kongdong taech'aek wiwŏnhoe, 1993), 6.

27. Chŏng, "Chugŏya sanŭn yŏsŏngdŭl ŭi inkwŏn," 338–345.

28. Kim, *Amerika t'aun wang ŭnni chukki obun chŏn kkaji ak ŭl ssŭda*, 252–253.

29. *Kyŏnghyang sinmun, Tonga ilbo, Maeil kyŏngje*, and *Hankyŏre sinmun*.

30. Katharine H. S. Moon, *Sex among Allies: Military Prostitution in U.S.-Korea Relations* (New York: Columbia University Press, 1997), 46.

31. Hŏnpŏp chaep'anso, "Yullak haengwi tŭng pangjipŏp che 7 cho tŭng e taehan hŏnpŏp sowŏn" (Chŏnwŏn chaep'anbu 91-hŏn-ma-178, January 25, 1996),

LAWnB, accessed January 23, 2022, https://academynext-lawnb-com-ssl.libproxy
.snu.ac.kr/Info/ContentView?sid=C000BEE1B8CFEA48.

32. Pogŏn sahoebu kajŏng pokchi simŭigwansil, "Pujŏng pangji taech'aek
wiwŏnhoe hoeŭi charyo: Yullak haengwi tŭng pangjipŏp kaejŏng kŏmt'o," April 28,
1994, *Yullak haengwi tŭng pangjipŏp kaejŏng charyo, 1994–1994*, 3, National Archives
Korea (NAK) (BA0760156), Daejeon; and Kajŏng pokchi simŭigwansil punyŏ pokchikwa, "MBC PD such'ŏp pangsong naeyong yoyak pogo (Yŏja kisurwŏn unyŏng
silt'ae)," February 1994, *Yullak haengwi tŭng pangjipŏp kaejŏng charyo, 1994–1994*, 6,
NAK (BA0760156).

33. Kajŏng pokchi simŭigwansil punyŏ pokchikwa, "MBC PD such'ŏp pangsong naeyong yoyak pogo," 5.

34. Han'guk kyohoe yŏsŏng yŏnhap'oe, "Yullak haengwi pangjipŏp kaejŏng
yŏn'gu moim t'oŭi naeyong," September 5, 1988, Korea Democracy Foundation
(KDF) (00011159), Seoul; and Han'guk kyohoe yŏsŏng yŏnhap'oe, "Yullak haengwi
pangjipŏp kaejŏng yŏn'gu moim," October 16, 1988, KDF (00011159).

35. Pogŏn pokchibu, *Pogŏn pokchi t'onggye yŏnbo* (1996): 212.

36. Pogŏn sahoebu, "Chungang yullak yŏsŏng sŏndo taech'aek wiwŏnhoe
(chuyo t'oŭi sahang)," April 30, 1992, in *Yullak haengwi tŭng pangjipŏp kaejŏng
charyo, 1993–1993*, 146, NAK (BA0760146).

37. Pogŏn sahoebu changgwan, "Yullak haengwi tŭng pangjipŏp e taehan
hŏnpŏp sowŏn simp'an yŏn'gi yoch'ŏng," October 18, 1993, *Yullak haengwi tŭng
pangjipŏp kaejŏng charyo, 1993–1993*, 233, NAK (BA0760145).

38. Hŏnpŏp chaep'anso, "Yullak haengwi tŭng pangjipŏp che 7 cho tŭng e
taehan hŏnpŏp sowŏn."

39. Pogŏn sahoebu, *Pogŏn sahoe t'onggye yŏnbo* (1971–1989); and Pogŏn pokchibu, *Pogŏn pokchi t'onggye yŏnbo* (1996).

40. Won Mi Hye, "'Sŏng p'anmae yŏsŏng' ŭi saengae ch'ehŏm yŏn'gu: Kyoch'ajŏk
sŏng wigye ŭi sigongganjŏk chakyong ŭl chungsim ŭro" (PhD diss., Ewha Womans
University, 2010), 120–128.

41. *Gyeonggi-do hyŏndaesa ŭi ŏduwun kŭnŭl* (Suwon: Gyeonggi munhwa chaedan, 2018), 158–176.

42. Kil Yun-Hyŏng, "Soe ch'angsal arae ungk'ŭrin sŏngpyŏng kwalliso,"
Han'gyŏre 21 695 (2008): 26; Paju-gun sŏngpyŏng kwalliso sŏlch'i chorye p'yeji
(March 1, 1996), Korea Law Information Center (KLIC), Sejong; and Uijeongbu-si
sŏngpyŏng kwalliso sŏlch'i chorye p'yeji (April 10, 2001), KLIC.

43. Kang Young Su, "Han'guk sahoe ŭi maemaech'un e kwanhan yŏn'gu:
Yongsan yŏk chubyŏn maech'un yŏsŏng ŭl chungsim ŭro" (master's thesis, Ewha
Womans University, 1989).

44. Won Mi Hye, "Han'guk sahoe ŭi maemaech'un yŏsŏng e taehan t'ongje
wa ch'akch'ui e kwanhan yŏn'gu" (master's thesis, Ewha Womans University,
1997).

45. Lee Hyo-Hee, "Siptae yŏsŏng ŭi sŏngchŏk sŏbisŭ kyŏnghŏm e kwanhan
yŏsŏngjuŭijŏk chŏpkŭn" (master's thesis, Ewha Womans University, 1998); Back
Jae Hee, "Oeguk yŏsŏng ŭi han'guk sŏng sanŏp yuip e kwanhan yŏn'gu: Kijich'on

ŭi p'ilip'in yŏsŏng ŭl chungsim ŭro" (master's thesis, Ewha Womans University, 2000); and Kathleen Barry, *Seksyuŏllit'i ŭi maech'unhwa* (Seoul: Samin, 2002).

46. On the division between the movement for Japanese military comfort women and the movement for camptown women, see Katharine H. S. Moon, "South Korean Movements against Militarized Sexual Labor," *Asian Survey* 39(2): 310–327.

47. *Kyŏnghyang sinmun*, February 10, 1997; and *Chosŏn ilbo*, April 15, 1997.

48. *Han'gyŏre sinmun*, June 19, 1998.

49. *Tonga ilbo*, September 3, 1998.

50. Min Kyŏng-Ja, "Han'guk maech'un yŏsŏng undong sa," in *Han'guk yŏsŏng inkwŏn undong sa*, ed., Han'guk yŏsŏng ŭi chŏnhwa (Seoul: Hanul academi, 1999), 287–288.

51. *Tonga ilbo*, November 9, 1991; *Kyŏnghyang sinmun*, November 9, 1991; and *Chosŏn ilbo*, November 13, 1991.

52. *Chosŏn ilbo*, January 19, 1968.

53. *Sinsang konggae taesang pŏmjoe charyo chonghap punsŏk* (Seoul: Han'guk hyŏngsa chŏngch'aek yŏn'guwŏn, 2004), 198–199.

54. *Kyŏnghyang sinmun*, August 26, 1998.

55. *Taehan min'guk nae roŭi kukche insinmaemae e kwanhan charyo kŏmt'o* (Seoul: Kukche iju kigu, 2002), 24–27.

56. *Oeguk yŏsŏng sŏngmaemae silt'ae chosa* (Seoul: Yŏsŏngbu, 2003), 71–72.

57. *Gyeonggi-do kijich'on yŏsŏng saenghwal silt'ae mit chiwŏn chŏngch'aek yŏn'gu* (Suwon: Gyeonggi-do yŏsŏng kajok chaedan, 2020), 33.

58. *2006 oegugin yŏnyein toip silt'ae chosa mit chŏngch'aek pigyo yŏn'gu* (Seoul: Munhwa kwan'gwangbu and Kukche iju kigu, 2006), 40–41.

59. Pŏmmubu, *Ch'uripkuk kwalli t'onggye yŏnbo* (1994–2002).

60. *Oeguk yŏsŏng sŏngmaemae silt'ae chosa*, 13–14.

61. *Oeguk yŏsŏng sŏngmaemae silt'ae chosa*, 200.

62. *Gyeonggi-do chiyŏk sŏngmaemae silt'ae chosa mit chŏngch'aek taean yŏn'gu* (Dongducheon: Saewumt'ŏ, 2001); *Sŏngsanŏp e yuiptoen oegugin yŏsŏng e kwanhan che 2 ch'a hyŏnjang silt'ae chosa pogosŏ* (Seoul: Han'guk kyohoe yŏsŏng yŏnhap'oe, 2002); and *Gyeonggi pukpu kijich'on chiyŏk sŏngmaemae kŭnjŏl ŭl wihan p'ihae yŏsŏng chiwŏn saŏp pogohoe charyojip* (Uijeongbu: Durebang, 2003).

63. Cheng Sealing, "Sarang ŭl paeugo, sarang e chukko," in *Yonggamhan yŏsŏngdŭl, nŭktae rŭl t'ago tallinŭn,* ed. Maktallena ŭi chip (Seoul: Samin, 2002); Back Jae Hee, "Sŏngmaemae konggan ŭi tamyŏnsŏng kwa salm ŭi kwŏlli," in *Kyŏnggye ŭi ch'ai, sai, t'ŭmsae: Sŏngmaemae konggan ŭi tamyŏnsŏng kwa salm ŭi kwŏlli,* ed. Kim Ae-Ryŏng (Seoul: Kŭrinbi, 2007); and Sealing Cheng, *On the Move for Love: Migrant Entertainers and the U.S. Military in South Korea* (Philadelphia: University of Pennsylvania Press, 2010), 27–28.

64. U.S. Department of State, "Victims of Trafficking and Violence Protection of 2000: Trafficking in Persons Report," 2001, accessed December 15, 2021, https://2009-2017.state.gov/j/tip/rls/tiprpt/2001/index.htm.

65. Pŏmmubu, "Mi kungmubu insinmaemae pogosŏ kŏmt'o mit hyanghu taech'aek," July 18, 2001.

66. *Sŏng ch'akch'wi mokchŏk ŭi insinmaemae hyŏnhwang kwa pŏpchŏk taeŭng pangan* (Seoul: Han'guk hyŏngsa chŏngch'aek yŏn'guwŏn, 2002), 97–99.

67. *Sŏng ch'akch'wi mokchŏk ŭi insinmaemae hyŏnhwang kwa pŏpchŏk taeŭng pangan*, 103–104.

68. U.S. Department of State, "Victims of Trafficking and Violence Protection of 2000: Trafficking in Persons Report," 2002, accessed December 15, 2021, https:// 2009-2017.state.gov/j/tip/rls/tiprpt/2002/index.htm.

69. *2006 oegugin yŏnyein toip silt'ae chosa mit chŏngch'aek pigyo yŏn'gu*, 85.

70. *Gunsan Daemyeong-dong Kaebok-dong sŏngmaemae chipkyŏlchi hwajae ch'amsa paeksŏ* (Jeonju: Jeonbuk yŏsŏng tanch'e yŏnhap, 2002), 19.

71. *Gunsan Daemyeong-dong Kaebok-dong sŏngmaemae chipkyŏlchi hwajae ch'amsa paeksŏ*, 215–222.

72. *Han'gyŏre sinmun*, September 22, 2000; *Kyŏnghyang sinmun*, September 27, 2000; *Kungmin ilbo*, January 30, 2002; and *Han'guk ilbo*, January 31, 2002.

73. *Gunsan Daemyeong-dong Kaebok-dong sŏngmaemae chipkyŏlchi hwajae ch'amsa paeksŏ*, 19–25.

74. *Han'gyŏre sinmun*, September 24, 2004.

75. *Kyŏnghyang sinmun*, May 18, 2004; *Han'gyŏre sinmun*, July 21, 2005; and *Chŏnbuk ilbo*, November 17, 2008.

76. *Tonga ilbo*, December 25, 2000.

77. Kim Hyŏn-Sŏn, "Sŏngmaemae pangji rŭl wihan kukche choyak mit kakkuk ŭi ippŏp sarye," '*Sŏngmaemae pangjipŏp' chejŏng* ŭl *wihan t'oronhoe* (October 23, 2001); and Kim Hyŏn-Sŏn, "Chŏn'guk sŏngmaemae p'ihae yŏsŏng silt'ae chosa kyŏlgwa palp'yo," *Han'guk chŏngbu ŭi sŏngmaemae pangji taech'aek ŏdi kkaji wanna* (July 15, 2002).

78. Kim Hyŏn-Sŏn, "Uri sahoe sŏngmaemae ŭi hyŏnsil kwa taech'aek pangan," *Gunsan hwajae ch'amsa rŭl t'onghae pon sŏngmaemae haegyŏl ŭl wihan t'oronhoe* (October 16, 2000); and Kim Hyŏn-Sŏn, "Han'guk sŏngsanŏp e yuiptoen iju yŏsŏng ŭi silt'ae wa haegyŏl pangan," *Asia sŏngsanŏp kŭnjŏl ŭl wihan net'ŭwŏk'ŭ kyŏlsŏng kwa sŏngmaemae pangji t'ŭkpyŏlpŏp chejŏng ŭl wihan kukche simp'ojiŏm* (October 19, 2001).

79. Jeong Mi Rye, "Insinmaemae pangji wa p'ihaeja poho rŭl wihan han'guk chŏngbu ŭi taech'aek e taehayŏ: Mi kungmubu insinmaemae pogosŏ e taehan pip'anjŏk kŏmt'o," *Migun kijich'on sŏngmaemae silt'ae wa sŏngchŏk insinmaemae kŭnjŏl ŭl wihan wŏnt'ak t'oronhoe* (August 29, 2002).

80. Kim, "Uri sahoe sŏngmaemae ŭi hyŏnsil kwa taech'aek pangan," 17–18; and Kim Hyŏn-Sŏn, "Uri sahoe ŭi simgak'an sŏngmaemae hyŏnsil kwa haegyŏl pangan," *Gunsan maemaech'un chiyŏk hwajae ch'amsa rŭl t'onghaesŏ pon sŏngmaemae hyŏnsil kwa taech'aek maryŏn ŭl wihan t'oronhoe* (December 6, 2000), 15–16.

81. Jeong Mi Rye, "Gunsan Daemyeong-dong ch'amsa ihu taech'aek hwaltong kwa ap'ŭro ŭi hwaltong kyehoek," *Gunsan maemaech'un chiyŏk hwajae ch'amsa rŭl*

t'onghaesŏ pon sŏngmaemae hyŏnsil kwa taech'aek maryŏn ŭl wihan t'oronhoe (December 6, 2000), 27.

82. Han'guk yŏsŏng tanch'e yŏnhap, "Sŏngmaemae alsŏn tŭng pŏmjoe ŭi ch'ŏbŏl mit pangji rŭl wihan pŏmnyuran," *Sŏngmaemae pangjipŏp chejŏng ŭl wihan t'oronhoe* (October 23, 2001).

83. Kathleen Barry, "International Human Rights and Sexual Exploitation," *Asia sŏngsanŏp kŭnjŏl ŭl wihan net'ŭwŏk'ŭ kyŏlsŏng kwa sŏngmaemae pangji t'ŭkpyŏlpŏp chejŏng ŭl wihan kukche simp'ojiŏm* (October 19, 2001), 66–69.

84. Han'guk yŏsŏng tanch'e yŏnhap, "Sŏngmaemae pangjipŏp chejŏng ŭl wihan t'oronhoe rŭl kaech'oehamyŏ," *Sŏngmaemae pangjipŏp chejŏng ŭl wihan t'oronhoe* (October 23, 2001).

85. Jeong, "Insinmaemae pangji wa p'ihaeja poho rŭl wihan han'guk chŏngbu ŭi taech'aek e taehayŏ," 23–24.

86. Han'guk yŏsŏng tanch'e yŏnhap, "Sŏngmaemae alsŏn tŭng pŏmjoe ŭi ch'ŏbŏl mit pangji rŭl wihan pŏmnyuran," 31, 36, 48–53.

87. Sheila Jeffreys, *The Idea of Prostitution* (North Melbourne: Spinifex, 1997), 5.

88. Kim, "Sŏngmaemae pangji rŭl wihan kukche choyak mit kakkuk ŭi ippŏp sarye," 11.

89. Kuk'oe samuch'ŏ, *Pŏpche sabŏp wiwŏnhoe hoeŭirok* (6) (July 1, 2003), 17.

90. Han'guk yŏsŏng tanch'e yŏnhap, "Sŏngmaemae alsŏn tŭng pŏmjoe ŭi ch'ŏbŏl mit pangji rŭl wihan pŏmnyuran," 38–39, 48–53.

91. Chŏng Sin-Muk, Kim Ae-Ran, and Kim Hyŏn-Sŏn, "Sŏngmaemae pangji t'ŭkpyŏlpŏp chejŏng e taehan ŏnnidŭl ŭi chujang," in *Sŏngmaemae alsŏn tŭng pŏmjoe ŭi ch'ŏbŏl mit pangji pŏmnyul chejŏng ŭl wihan charyojip* (Seoul: Han'guk yŏsŏng tanch'e yŏnhap, 2002), 85.

92. Park Jin-kyung, "Sŏngmaemae pangjipŏp chejŏng kwajŏng ŭi chŏngch'aek net'ŭwŏk'ŭ punsŏk" (master's thesis, Ewha Womans University, 2005), 48–52.

93. *Han'gyŏre sinmun*, November 18, 2002.

94. Park, "Sŏngmaemae pangjipŏp chejŏng kwajŏng ŭi chŏngch'aek net'ŭwŏk'ŭ punsŏk," 61–63.

95. Han'guk yŏsŏng tanch'e yŏnhap, "Sŏngmaemae pangji wa p'ihaeja inkwŏn poho kanghwa e kiyŏhal sŏngmaemae bangjipŏp ŭi kuk'oe t'onggwa rŭl hwanyŏng handa!," March 2, 2004, accessed December 20, 2021, http://women21.or.kr /statement/771.

96. Instead, if a foreign woman files a report on any offense or she is investigated as a victim of commercial sex acts, she will not be subject to compulsory deportation until related legal processes are initiated (Article 11 of the Act on the Punishment of Arrangement of Commercial Sex Acts). In addition, any claims that third parties have against prostitutes are invalid, as are any liabilities that prostitutes have to their employers or creditors (Article 10 of the same act), KLIC.

97. Kyŏngch'alch'ŏng, "Pŏmjoe palsaeng mit kŏmgŏ hyŏnhwang (chŏn'guk) (1990–2010)," accessed November 7, 2023, https://kosis.kr/statHtml/statHtml.do ?orgId=132&tblId=TX_132_2009_H1001&conn_path=I2.

98. Yi, "Sŏngmaemae t'ŭkpyŏlpŏp sihaeng hu sŏngkwa mit hyanghu ch'ian taech'aek," 63.

99. *Chŏn'guk sŏngmaemae silt'ae chosa* (Seoul: Han'guk yŏsŏng chŏngch'aek yŏn'guwŏn, 2007), 257–291.

100. *Sŏngmaemae silt'ae mit kyŏngje kyumo e kwanhan chŏn'guk chosa* (Seoul: Han'guk hyŏngsa chŏngch'aek yŏn'guwŏn, 2002), 369.

101. Pogŏn pokchibu, *Pogŏn pokchi t'onggye yŏnbo* (2006): 118–119.

102. *Han'gyŏre sinmun*, July 14, 2006.

103. Yŏsŏng kajokpu, "Sŏngpyŏng kwalli chedo nŭn saeroun sigak esŏ paraboaya: Sŏngmaemae kŭmji nŭn sŏngpyŏng yebang ŭi haepŏp" (July 14, 2006).

104. Hong Jia, "Midiŏ rŭl t'onghan sŏngmaemae ŭi ŭimi kusŏng: Chungang ilbo, Chosŏn ilbo, Kyŏnghyang sinmun, Han'gyŏre ŭi kisa punsŏk ŭl chungsim ŭro," *Han'guk yŏsŏnghak* 31, no. 3 (2015): 219–259.

105. I have not found any materials on what Hantŏ means. The literal translation is "wide vacant lot." What is clear is that the Hantŏ National Association did not seek to make clear its identity as a representative organization of brothel keepers through this vague title.

106. *Han'gyŏre sinmun*, October 19, 2019.

107. The term "solidarity" (*yŏndae*) has often been used in group names, in particular NGOs in Korea, such as People's Solidarity for Participatory Democracy (Ch'amyŏ yŏndae). It has meanings such as "alliance" or "collective." Chŏn'guk sŏng nodongja chunbiwi hanyŏyŏn, "Ch'ulbŏmsa," in *Sŏngmaemae ŭi chŏngch'ihak: Sŏngmaemae t'ŭkpyŏlpŏp chejŏng 1 nyŏn ŭi sichŏm esŏ*, ed. Yi Chae-In (Seoul: Hanul ak'ademi, 2005), 308–310; and Kook Kyung-Hee, "Han'guk sŏng nodongja undong e kwanhan yŏn'gu" (master's thesis, Chungang University, 2007), 50–53.

108. Minju sŏng nodongja yŏndae, "Ch'ulbŏm sŏnŏnmun: Chŏn'guk sŏng nodongja yŏndae hanyŏyŏn ŭl t'alt'oe hamyŏnsŏ," in *Sŏngmaemae ŭi chŏngch'ihak: Sŏngmaemae t'ŭkpyŏlpŏp chejŏng 1 nyŏn ŭi sichŏm esŏ*, ed. Yi Chae-In (Seoul: Hanul ak'ademi, 2005), 325–327; and Kook, "Han'guk sŏng nodongja undong e kwanhan yŏn'gu," 61–78.

109. Hwang Ho-T'aek, "Hwang Ho-T'aek kija ka mannan saram: Sŏngmaemae t'ŭkpyŏlpŏp chejŏng sanp'a Chi Ŭn-Hŭi yŏsŏngbu changgwan," *Sindonga* (November 2004).

110. Kim Sŏng-Jae, "Kongch'angje nŭn chinjŏnghan taean in'ga," *Han'gyŏre 21* (October 21, 2004).

111. Cho Yŏng-Suk, "Yŏsŏng e taehan sŏngchŏk ch'akch'wi pangji rŭl wihan han'guk yŏsŏng undong ŭi tojŏn kwa sŏngkwa," *Yŏsŏng e taehan sŏngchŏk ch'akch'wi kŭnjŏl ŭl wihan asia t'aep'yŏngnyang yurŏp ŭi kyŏnghŏm kwa kyohun* (September 21, 2005), 12.

112. Kook, "Han'guk sŏng nodongja undong e kwanhan yŏn'gu"; and Cho Eun-Joo, "Yŏsŏng hawi chuch'e esŏ sŏng nodongja undong ŭro: Sahoe undong esŏŭi kamjŏng kwa tongwŏn," *Kyŏngje wa sahoe* 78 (2008): 256–311.

113. Kook, "Han'guk sŏng nodongja undong e kwanhan yŏn'gu," 50–51.

114. Cho, "Yŏsŏng hawi chuch'e esŏ sŏng nodongja undong ŭro," 269.

115. Yi Chŏng-Ŭn and Hŏ Tʼae-Ju, "Sŏngmaemae kŭnjŏlchuŭi e pʼyoryuhanŭn chipkyŏlchi pʼŭrojektʼŭ," *Mal* (March 2005); Kim Yun-hee, "Incheon Sungui-dong sŏngmaemae chipkyŏlchi e taehan yŏnʼgu: Sŏngmaemae pangjipŏp kwa sibŏm saŏp e ŭihan pyŏnhwa rŭl chungsim ŭro" (masterʼs thesis, Seoul National University, 2006), 77–78; and Pogŏn pokchibu, "Chʼoejŏ saenggyebi kyechʼŭk chosa," accessed December 23, 2021, https://kosis.kr/statHtml/statHtml.do?orgId=117&tblId=DT _33104_N101.

116. Cho Soon ae, "Sŏngmaemae chipkyŏlchi pʼyeswae kwajŏng e natʼanan ʻchahwalʼ tamnon punsŏk" (masterʼs thesis, Sogang University, 2019), 88–93.

117. Minju sŏng nodongja yŏndae, "Yŏsŏng kajokpu nŭn chahwal sibŏm chiyŏk hwaktae rŭl chŭkkak chungji hara," in *Sŏngmaemae ŭi chŏngchʼihak: Sŏngmaemae tʼŭkpyŏlpŏp chejŏng 1 nyŏn ŭi sichŏm esŏ,* ed. Yi Chae-In (Seoul: Hanul akʼademi, 2005), 328–329.

118. *Sŏngmaemae pangjipŏp 1 nyŏn pʼyŏngga wa sŏng nodongja undong ŭi panghyang kwa chŏnmang* (September 23, 2005).

119. Won Mi Hye, "Yŏsŏngjuŭi sŏngjŏngchʼi: Sŏngmaemae kŭnjŏl undong ŭl nŏmŏsŏsŏ," in *Sŏngmaemae ŭi chŏngchʼihak: Sŏngmaemae tʼŭkpyŏlpŏp chejŏng 1 nyŏn ŭi sichŏm esŏ,* ed. Yi Chae-In (Seoul: Hanul akʼademi, 2005), 138–142.

120. *2019 sŏngmaemae siltʼae mit taeŭng pangan yŏnʼgu* (Seoul: Yŏsŏng kajokpu, 2019).

EPILOGUE

1. YTN, "ʻYŏngbo chaaewŏnʼ kangje ipsoja chinsang kyumyŏng chʼokku," November 15, 2021, accessed November 24, 2022, www.ytn.co.kr/_ln/0103_20211 1152233174741; and MBC, "[PD suchʼŏp] Silchong 24 nyŏn man e palgyŏndoen ŏmma, kŏri esŏ sarajin saramdŭl," October 4, 2022, accessed November 24, 2022, https://imnews.imbc.com/news/2022/society/article/6413946_35673.html.

2. Louis Althusser, "Ideology and Ideological State Apparatuses," in *Lenin and Philosophy and Other Essays* (New York: Monthly Review Press, 2001).

3. Kŏmchʼalchʼŏng, "Pŏmjoe palsaeng mit kŏmgŏ hyŏnhwang (chŏnʼguk) (2011– 2022)," accessed November 7, 2023, https://kosis.kr/statHtml/statHtml.do?orgId= 132&tblId=DT_13204_2011_211&conn_path=I2.

4. *Kungmin ilbo*, November 28, 2014. In July 2017, the Supreme Court decided that the government should compensate the victimʼs family with 5 million KRW (about US$5,000) for not providing appropriate protections for the victim, but the entrapment was legal. *Chungang ilbo*, July 4, 2017.

5. Since red-light districts are the most conspicuous manifestation of the sex industry, they offer the easiest targets for police crackdowns since the enactment of the Sŏngmaemae Prevention Acts. However, some red-light districts still survive today. The reason for this is that the police have argued that securing direct evidence of prostitution, such as used condoms or the scene of the criminal act of intercourse, is very difficult, even though it is easy to assume that prostitution is occurring in such

areas. The police also argue that staffing shortages prevent them from thoroughly investigating prostitution. *Pyŏlbyŏl chilmun sŏngmaemae e taehan 20 kaji iyagi* (Seoul: ELoom, 2013), 3–5.

6. *2010 sŏngmaemae silt'ae chosa* (Seoul: Yŏsŏng kajokpu, 2010), 48, 85–86.

7. *Sŏngmaemae silt'ae chosa kaesŏn pangan yŏn'gu* (Seoul: Han'guk yŏsŏng chŏngch'aek yŏn'guwŏn, 2015), 3; and Lee Soon Rae, Jeong Hey Won, and Park Cheol Hyun, "Pŏmjoe t'onggye wa yŏn'gu yulli: Sŏngmaemae silt'ae chosa ŭi sarye," *Konggong chŏngch'aek yŏn'gu* 32, no. 2 (2014): 1–16.

8. Sinbak Chin-Yŏng, "K'orona 19 wa yuhŭng chujŏm silt'ae mit yuhŭng chŏpkaegwŏn iranŭn il e taehayŏ," *Yuhŭng chujŏm mit yuhŭng chŏpkaegwŏn silt'ae chosa t'oronhoe* (September 30, 2021), 14.

9. E-narajip'yo, "Namsŏng taebi yŏsŏng imgŭm piyul," accessed November 5, 2023, www.index.go.kr/unity/potal/main/EachDtlPageDetail.do?idx_cd=2714.

10. Kim Joohee, *Reidi k'ŭredit: Sŏngmaemae kŭmyung ŭi ŏlgul ŭl hada* (Seoul: Hyŏnsil munhwa, 2020).

11. *2019 sŏngmaemae silt'ae mit taeŭng pangan yŏn'gu* (Seoul: Yŏsŏng kajokpu, 2019), 70–71, 217–334.

12. *2019 sŏngmaemae silt'ae mit taeŭng pangan yŏn'gu*, 522–523.

13. Kim Yŏn-Ju, "Ch'ŏngsonyŏn sŏngmaemae ŏttŏk'e pol kŏsin'ga," *Chinbo p'yŏngnon* 64 (2015): 276–278.

14. *Oegugin yŏsŏng sŏngmaemae silt'ae mit chedo kaesŏn pangan yŏn'gu* (Seoul: Yŏsŏng kajokpu, 2011), 10–11; and *Yesul hŭnghaeng pija soji ijumin inkwŏn sanghwang silt'ae chosa* (Seoul: Kukka inkwŏn wiwŏnhoe, 2014), 35–36.

15. Pŏmmubu, "Ch'uripkukcha mit ch'eryu oegugin t'onggye," accessed January 24, 2023, https://kosis.kr/statHtml/statHtml.do?orgId=111&tblId=DT_1B040A6.

16. *Oegugin yŏsŏng sŏngmaemae silt'ae mit chedo kaesŏn pangan yŏn'gu*, 42–44, 61–147.

17. Kim Ae-Ryŏng and Won Mi Hye, eds., *Pulgŭn pelbet aelbŏm sok ŭi yŏindŭl* (Seoul: Kŭrinbi, 2007); *Ch'ŏngnyangni: Ch'egyejŏk manggak, kiŏk ŭro yŏn'gyŏrhan yŏksa* (Seoul: ELoom, 2018); Kim Joohee, "'Irŏn saenghwal i innŭn chuldo mollassŏyo': Chungnyŏn yŏsŏng sŏngmaemae yuip ŭi chŏngch'i kyŏngje," *Han'guk yŏsŏnghak* 34, no. 1 (2018): 33–66; and *2019 sŏngmaemae silt'ae mit taeŭng pangan yŏn'gu*, 70–71.

18. Article 16 of the amended Enforcement Rule of Infectious Disease Prevention Act narrowed down the infections needing quarantine to scarlet fever and meningococcal meningitis; other third-class infectious diseases including STIs were excluded (enforced from January 17, 2006), Korea Law Information Center (KLIC), Sejong.

19. Pogŏn pokchibu, *Pogŏn pokchi t'onggye yŏnbo* (2006): 118–119; and Pogŏn pokchibu, *Pogŏn pokchi t'onggye yŏnbo* (2022): 164–165.

20. The Korea Center for Disease Control and Prevention (KCDC) declared the abolition of the system to register women who should be regularly examined for STIs from 2010 and to delete the category "recipients of regular STI testing" from the yearbooks of the Ministry of Health and Social Welfare. *2010 nyŏn sŏngpyŏng kwalli chich'im* (Seoul: Chilbyŏng kwalli ponbu, 2009), 3–4. Considering this point as the

abolition of mandatory regulation, I concluded in a 2019 paper that the toleration-regulation regime was finished and had given way to prohibition. Jeong-Mi Park, "Liberation or Purification? Prostitution, Women's Movement and Nation Building in South Korea under US Military Occupation, 1945–1948," *Sexualities* 22, nos. 7–8 (2019): 1066. However, I wondered how it was possible for the KCDC to conduct over one million STI examinations a year on women in the sex industry even after the registration system was abolished. In July 2021 I asked a staffer of the Korea Disease Control and Prevention Agency (formerly KCDC) about this, and he answered that health practitioners at public health clinics are recording the testing results of the "recipients of regular STI testing" using the "local health and medical information system." In other words, the category of recipients of regular STI testing continues to exist, and the government is still supervising them. For this reason, I now conclude that the toleration-regulation regime has not ended but has been reduced in scale.

21. *Chiyŏk sahoe kiban sŏngpyŏng yebang kwalli saŏp model kaebal mit chŏkyong* (Cheongju: Chilbyŏng kwalli ponbu, 2011), 79–83.

22. *Chiyŏk sahoe kiban sŏngpyŏng yebang kwalli saŏp model kaebal mit chŏkyong*, 14–17.

23. *Yŏsŏng, adong kwŏnik chŭngjin saŏp unyŏng chich'im* (Seoul: Yŏsŏng kajokpu, 2022), 287–288.

24. Starting with Chuncheon in 2013, by 2023 seventeen local governments have enacted ordinances to support the women working in red-light districts that are due to be shut down. KLIC.

25. Hwang Chŏng-Im, "T'al sŏngmaemae yŏsŏng ŭl wihan 'chahwal' chiwŏn chŏngch'aek i kŏrŏon kil, naagal kil," in *Kyŏngye ŭi ch'ai, sai, t'ŭmsae: Sŏngmaemae konggan ŭi tamyŏnsŏng kwa salm ŭi kwŏlli*, ed. Kim Ae-Ryŏng (Seoul: Kŭrinbi, 2007); Cho Soon ae, "Sŏngmaemae chipkyŏlchi p'yeswae kwajŏng e nat'anan 'chahwal' tamnon punsŏk" (master's thesis, Sogang University, 2019); and Hwang Kyoung-Lan, "Pan sŏngmaemae undong hwaltonggadŭl ŭi sŏngmaemae yŏsŏng chahwal chiwŏn il e kwanhan chedojŏk munhwa kisulchi" (PhD diss., Seoul Women's University, 2019).

26. E-narajip'yo, "Sŏngmaemae p'ihaeja chiwŏn hyŏnhwang," accessed November 5, 2023, www.index.go.kr/unity/potal/main/EachDtlPageDetail.do;jsessionid=bw47r6X8wn51WQJ1erZ4XKoxK6R0YI-DDtwtoh_x.node11?idx_cd=1592.

27. *2019 sŏngmaemae silt'ae mit taeŭng pangan yŏn'gu*, 344, 347, and 362.

28. Jeong Mi Rye, "Sŏngmaemae yŏsŏng pibŏmjoehwa ŭi kwanchŏm kwa p'iryosŏng e taehan yŏn'gu: T'al sŏngmaemae yŏsŏngdŭl ŭi moksori rŭl chungsim ŭro" (master's thesis, SungKongHoe University, 2010); Lee Na Young, "Sŏngp'anmaeja pibŏmjoehwa rŭl wihan siron: Sŏngmaemae t'ŭkpyŏlpŏp ŭl tullŏssan chaengchŏm kwa yŏsŏngjuŭi taean mosaek," *P'eminijŭm yŏn'gu* 15, no. 1 (2015): 211–247; Sinbak Chin-Yŏng, *Sŏngmaemae, sangsik ŭi p'ŭllaek'ol* (Seoul: Pomallam, 2020); Sŏngmaemae kyŏnghŏm tangsaja net'ŭwŏk'ŭ mungch'i, *Sŏngmaemae kyŏnghŏm tangsaja muhanbalsŏl* (Seoul: Pomallam, 2020); and Sŏngmaemae ch'ŏbŏlpŏp kaejŏng yŏndae, "Sŏngmaemae ch'ŏbŏlpŏp kaejŏng yŏndae palchok sŏnŏnmun" (March 22, 2022).

29. Kuk'oe, Ŭian chŏngbo sisŭt'em, accessed February 4, 2022, https://likms
.assembly.go.kr/bill/main.do.

30. *Yŏsŏng sinmun*, April 13, 2017.

31. *Chungang ilbo*, December 16, 2021.

32. Yŏsŏng munhwa iron yŏn'guso sŏng nodong yŏn'gut'im, *Sŏng nodong* (Seoul:
Yŏiyŏn, 2007).

33. Sa Mi-Suk, "Sŏng nodongja kwŏlli e kwansim ŏmnŭn sŏngmaemae
pangjipŏp," *Han'gyŏre sinmun*, October 8, 2013.

34. Milsa, Yŏnhŭi, and Chi Sŭng-Ho, *Sŏng nodongja, kwŏlli rŭl oech'ida: Milsa
wa Yŏnhŭi ŭi sŏng nodong iyagi* (Seoul: Ch'ŏlsu wa yŏnghŭi, 2015); and Chuhongbit yŏndae ch'ach'a, accessed February 5, 2022, https://sexworkproject.tistory.com/.

35. Kim Chi-Hye, "Yŏsŏng sŏng nodongja ch'ŏbŏl chohang wihŏn chech'ŏng
kwa sŏng nodongja ŭi kwŏlli," *Yŏ/sŏng iron* 28 (2013): 227–234; and Shin Sang-Sook,
"Chendŏ wa p'yŏngdŭng ŭi kwanchŏm esŏ pon sŏngmaemae ch'ŏbŏl ŭi p'ŭreim
kyŏnghap: Sŏngmaemae ch'ŏbŏlpŏp che 21 cho che 1 hang wihŏn pŏmnyul simp'an
ŭl chungsim ŭro," *Han'guk yŏsŏnghak* 33, no. 4 (2017): 1–37.

36. Oh Jaelim, Yoo Sook-Ran, and Ahn Jae-Hee, "Sŭweden ŭi sŏng kumaeja
ch'ŏbŏlpŏp chejŏng kwajŏng punsŏk," *Asia yŏsŏng yŏn'gu* 45, no. 2 (2006): 271–
312; and Huh Koung-Mi, "Norŭdik model sŏngmaemae chŏngch'aek ŭi tillema wa
sisachŏm," *Kyŏngch'arhak nonch'ong* 14, no. 2 (2019): 35–61.

37. E-narajip'yo, "Namsŏng taebi yŏsŏng imgŭm piyul,", accessed November 5,
2023, www.index.go.kr/unity/potal/main/EachDtlPageDetail.do?idx_cd=2714;
and OECD, "OECD Gender Wage Gap," accessed November 5, 2023, https://data
.oecd.org/earnwage/gender-wage-gap.htm.

38. Chuhongbit yŏndae ch'ach'a, accessed February 5, 2022, https://sexwork
project.tistory.com/111.

39. Julia O'Connell Davidson, "Prostitution and the Contours of Control," in
Sexual Cultures: Communities, Values and Intimacy, ed. Jeffrey Weeks and Janet
Holland (London: Macmillan, 1996), 193–194.

40. Kim, *Reidi k'ŭredit*, 191–193.

41. Julia O'Connell Davidson, "The Rights and Wrongs of Prostitution," *Hypatia* 17, no. 2 (2002): 85–86.

42. ELoom, "Sŏngmaemae yŏsŏng anjŏn ŭl marhal su innŭn'ga," June 28, 2012.

43. Maktallena ŭi chip, ed., *Yonggamhan yŏsŏngdŭl, nŭktae rŭl t'ago tallinŭn*
(Seoul: Samin, 2002).

44. Julia O'Connell Davidson, *Prostitution, Power and Freedom* (Ann Arbor:
University of Michigan Press, 1998), 121–122.

45. Karl Polanyi, *The Great Transformation: The Political and Economic Origins
of Our Time* (Boston: Beacon Press, 2001).

46. Kim and Won, *Pulgŭn pelbet aelbŏm sok ŭi yŏindŭl*; Hong Sŭng-Hŭi,
Pulgŭn sŏn: Na ŭi seksyuŏllit'i kirok (Seoul: Kŭrhangari, 2017); *Na to marhal su
innŭn saram ida: Sŏngp'anmae yŏsŏng annyŏngdŭl hasimnikka* (Seoul: Yŏiyŏn,
2018); Pomnal, *Kil hana kŏnnŏmyŏn pyŏrang kkŭt: Sŏngmaemae ranŭn ch'akch'wi
wa p'ongnyŏk esŏ saranamŭn han yŏsŏng ŭi yonggamhan kirok* (Seoul: Panbi, 2019);

Sŏngmaemae kyŏnghŏm tangsaja net'ŭwŏk'ŭ mungch'i, *Sŏngmaemae kyŏnghŏm tangsaja muhanbalsŏl*; and Chuhongbit yŏndae ch'ach'a, accessed February 6, 2022, https://sexworkproject.tistory.com/.

47. Pomnal, *Kil hana kŏnnŏmyŏn pyŏrang kkŭt*, 332–333.

48. Pyŏlli, "Pam ŭl hoengdanhanŭn mom ŭi kiŏk," Sŏng nodong p'ŭrojekt'ŭ che 1 hoe, accessed February 6, 2022, https://sexworkproject.tistory.com/12?category= 847381.

SELECTED BIBLIOGRAPHY

Only published freestanding materials, journal articles, and master's theses and PhD dissertations are included in the bibliography. Please refer to the endnotes of each chapter for other materials, such as articles from newspapers and other periodicals; online documents and articles; laws and regulations; statistics, yearbooks, and gazettes; documents housed at archives; and the brochures, pamphlets, and sourcebooks produced by social movement organizations.

ARCHIVES

Diplomatic Archives of the Ministry of Foreign Affairs (DAMFA), Seoul, Korea
Korea Democracy Foundation (KDF), Seoul, Korea
Korea Law Information Center (KLIC), Sejong, Korea
Library of Congress (LOC), Washington, DC, United States
National Archives at College Park, MD (NACP), United States (National Archives and Records Administration)
National Archives of Korea (NAK), Daejeon, Korea
National Assembly Library (NAL), Seoul, Korea
National Library of Korea (NLK), Seoul, Korea
Wilson Center (WC), Washington, DC, United States

NEWSPAPERS, MAGAZINES, AND PHOTOGRAPHS
Online Locations

Big Kinds (https://www.bigkinds.or.kr/)
Chungnam Institute of History and Culture (https://www.cihc.or.kr/)
Gyeonggi-do Multimedia Archives (https://exciting.gg.go.kr/)
Korean Newspaper Archives (https://nl.go.kr/newspaper/)

Naver News Library (https://newslibrary.naver.com/search/searchByDate.naver)
Seoul Metropolitan Archives (https://archives.seoul.go.kr/)

Newspapers and Magazines Cited

Chŏnbuk ilbo
Chosŏn ilbo
Chungang ilbo
Han'guk ilbo
Han'gyŏre sinmun
Han'gyŏre 21
Hansŏng ilbo
Hyŏndae ilbo
Kungmin ilbo
Kyŏnghyang sinmun
Maeil kyŏngje
Mal
Minju yŏsŏng
Pet'ŭl
Puin
Puin sinbo
P'yŏnghwa ilbo
Saem i kip'ŭn mul
Seoul sinmun
Sindonga
Tonga ilbo
Yŏsŏng sinmun
Yŏwŏn

OTHER SOURCES

Korean

Amerika kundae rŭl kisohanda: Chuhan migun pŏmjoe kŭnjŏl undong ponbu 15 nyŏn. Seoul: Chuhan migun pŏmjoe kŭnjŏl undong ponbu, 2008.

An Chin. *Migunjŏng kwa han'guk ŭi minjujuŭi.* Seoul: Hanul ak'ademi, 2005.

Back Jae Hee [Paek Chae-Hŭi]. "Oeguk yŏsŏng ŭi han'guk sŏng sanŏp yuip e kwanhan yŏn'gu: Kijich'on ŭi p'ilip'in yŏsŏng ŭl chungsim ŭro." Master's thesis, Ewha Womans University, 2000.

———. "Sŏngmaemae konggan ŭi tamyŏnsŏng kwa salm ŭi kwŏlli." In *Kyŏnggye ŭi ch'ai, sai, t'ŭmsae: Sŏngmaemae konggan ŭi tamyŏnsŏng kwa salm ŭi kwŏlli,* edited by Kim Ae-Ryŏng. Seoul: Kŭrinbi, 2007.

Barry, Kathleen. *Seksyuŏllit'i ŭi maech'unhwa.* Seoul: Samin, 2002.

Chang Tong-Ch'il. "Yullak yŏsŏng ŭi silt'ae e kwanhan sogo: Jongno-gu wa Yeong-deungpo sŏndo chiyŏk ŭl chungsim ŭro." *Sahoe pokchi yŏn'gu* 2, no. 1 (1967): 122–131.

Chang Wŏn-A. "Taranago ssaunŭn yŏjadŭl ŭi yŏksa ro pon pullidoen segye." In *Pulch'ŏbŏl: Sŏngmaemae yŏsŏng ŭl ch'obŏrhanŭn sahoe e tŏnjinŭn p'eminijŭm sŏnŏn*, edited by ELoom. Seoul: Hyumŏnisŭtŭ, 2022.

Cheng Sealing. "Sarang ŭl paeugo, sarang e chukko." In *Yonggamhan yŏsŏngdŭl, nŭktae rŭl t'ago tallinŭn*, edited by Maktallena ŭi chip. Seoul: Samin, 2002.

Cheong Soo Bok [Chŏng Su-Bok]. "Yi Sang-Baek kwa han'guk sahoehak ŭi sŏngnip." *Han'guk sahoehak* 50, no. 2 (2016): 1–40.

Chiyŏk sahoe kiban sŏngpyŏng yebang kwalli saŏp model kaebal mit chŏkyong. Cheong-gju: Chilbyŏng kwalli ponbu, 2011.

Cho Eun-Joo [Cho Ŭn-Ju]. "Yŏsŏng hawi chuch'e esŏ sŏng nodongja undong ŭro: Sahoe undong esŏŭi kamjŏng kwa tongwŏn." *Kyŏngje wa sahoe* 78 (2008): 256–311.

Cho Hyoung and Chang Pil Wha [Cho Hyŏng and Chang P'il-Hwa]. "Kuk'oe sok-kirok e nat'anan yŏsŏng chŏngch'aek sigak: Maemaech'un e taehayŏ." *Yŏsŏnghak yŏn'gu* 7 (1990): 83–111.

Cho Soon ae [Cho Sun-Ae]. "Sŏngmaemae chipkyŏlchi p'yeswae kwajŏng e nat'anan 'chahwal' tamnon punsŏk." Master's thesis, Sogang University, 2019.

Cho Sun-Gyŏng. "Han'guk yŏsŏng nodong sijang punsŏk ŭl wihan siron: Saengsanjik yŏsŏng nodongnyŏk pujok hyŏnsang ŭl chungsim ŭro." *Yŏsŏng* 3 (1989): 98–130.

Ch'oe Sŏng-Jae. "Yullak yŏsŏng munje silt'ae: Han'guk puinhoe silt'ae chosa rŭl chungsim ŭro." In *Yullak yŏsŏng mit mihonmo e taehan charyojip*. Seoul: Han'guk puinhoe ch'ongbonbu, 1985.

Ch'oe Ŭn-Gyŏng. "Ilche kangjŏmgi sŏngpyŏng e taehan ŭiryojŏk silch'ŏn: Ch'iryo wa yebang, tamnon ŭl chungsim ŭro." In *Yŏksa sok ŭi chilbyŏng, Sahoe sok ŭi chilbyŏng*, edited by Seoul taehakkyo pyŏngwŏn ŭihak yŏksa munhwawŏn. Seoul: Solbitkil, 2015.

Choi Jai-Seuk [Ch'oe Chae-Sŏk]. "Han'guk chŏptaebu ŭi yŏn'gu: Seoul-si ŭi chŏptaebu rŭl chungsim ŭro." *Asea yŏsŏng yŏn'gu* 22 (1983): 135–161.

———. "Han'guk e issŏsŏ ŭi yullak yŏsŏng yŏn'gu ŭi chŏn'gae." *Asea yŏsŏng yŏn'gu* 20 (1981): 9–52.

Choi Jin-Hae [Ch'oe Chin-Hae]. "Busan ilbu chiyŏk t'ŭksu ŏpt'aebudŭl ŭi sahoe ŭihakchŏgin chosa." *Yebang ŭihak hoeji* 10, no. 1 (1977): 125–133.

Chŏn Kyŏng-Ok, Pak Sŏn-Ae, and Chŏng Ki-Ŭn. *Han'guk yŏsŏng inmulsa*. Vol. 2. Seoul: Sookmyung yŏja taehakkyo ch'ulp'anbu, 2005.

Chŏn Wu-Sŏp. "Yun Kŭm-I, kŭ nŭn nugu in'ga?" In *Uridŭl ŭi Kŭm-I*. Seoul: Chu-han migun ŭi Yun Kŭm-I ssi sarhae sakŏn kongdong taech'aek wiwŏnhoe, 1993.

Chŏng Hŭi-Jin. "Chugŏya sanŭn yŏsŏngdŭl ŭi inkwŏn: Han'guk kijich'on yŏsŏng undong sa." In *Han'guk yŏsŏng inkwŏn undong sa*, edited by Han'guk yŏsŏng ŭi chŏnhwa yŏnhap. Seoul: Hanul, 1999.

Chŏng Pyŏng-Sŏl. *Na nŭn kisaeng ida: Sosurok ikki*. Seoul: Munhak tongne, 2007.

Chŏng Sin-Muk, Kim Ae-Ran, and Kim Hyŏn-Sŏn. "Sŏngmaemae pangji t'ŭkpyŏlpŏp chejŏng e taehan ŏnnidŭl ŭi chujang." In *Sŏngmaemae alsŏn tŭng pŏmjoe ŭi ch'ŏbŏl mit pangji pŏmnyul chejŏng ŭl wihan charyojip*. Seoul: Han'guk yŏsŏng tanch'e yŏnhap, 2002.

Ch'ŏngnyangni: Ch'egyejŏk manggak, kiŏk ŭro yŏn'gyŏrhan yŏksa. Seoul: ELoom, 2018.

Chŏn'guk sŏng nodongja chunbiwi hanyŏyŏn. "Ch'ulbŏmsa." In *Sŏngmaemae ŭi chŏngch'ihak: Sŏngmaemae t'ŭkpyŏlpŏp chejŏng 1 nyŏn ŭi sichŏm esŏ*, edited by Yi Chae-In. Seoul: Hanul ak'ademi, 2005.

Chŏn'guk sŏngmaemae silt'ae chosa. Seoul: Han'guk yŏsŏng chŏngch'aek yŏn'guwŏn, 2007.

Chuhan migun ŭi Yun Kŭm-I ssi sarhae sakŏn charyojip. Seoul: Chuhan migun pŏmjoe kŭnjŏl undong ponbu, 1994.

Chung Chin Sung [Chŏng Chin-Sŏng]. *Ilbon'gun sŏng noyeje: Ilbon'gun wianbu munje ŭi silsang kwa kŭ haegyŏl ŭl wihan undong*. Seoul: Seoul taehakkyo ch'ulp'anbu, 2004.

———. "Kun wianbu/chŏngsindae ŭi kaenyŏm e kwanhan koch'al." *Sahoe wa yŏksa* 60 (2001): 34–59.

Eum Hye-Jin [Yŏm Hye-Jin]. "Sŏngmaemae tamnon ŭi pip'anjŏk koch'al: 1980 nyŏndae insinmaemae tamnon ŭl chungsim ŭro." Master's thesis, Seoul National University, 2006.

Fujime Yuki. *Sŏng ŭi yŏksahak: Kŭndae kukka nŭn song ŭl ŏttŏk'e kwallihanŭn'ga*. Seoul: Samin, 2004.

Gunsan Daemyeong-dong Kaebok-dong sŏngmaemae chipkyŏlchi hwajae ch'amsa paeksŏ. Jeonju: Jeonbuk yŏsŏng tanch'e yŏnhap, 2002.

Gyeonggi pukpu kijich'on chiyŏk sŏngmaemae kŭnjŏl ŭl wihan p'ihae yŏsŏng chiwŏn saŏp pogohoe charyojip. Uijeongbu: Durebang, 2003.

Gyeonggi-do chiyŏk sŏngmaemae silt'ae chosa mit chŏngch'aek taean yŏn'gu. Dongdu-cheon: Saewumt'ŏ, 2001.

Gyeonggi-do hyŏndaesa ŭi ŏduwun kŭnŭl. Suwon: Gyeonggi munhwa chaedan, 2018.

Gyeonggi-do kijich'on yŏsŏng saenghwal silt'ae mit chiwŏn chŏngch'aek yŏn'gu. Suwon: Gyeonggi-do yŏsŏng kajok chaedan, 2020.

Ha Sŏng-Hwan. "Kuktaean sakŏn ŭi kyoyuksajŏk hamŭi." *Chinbo p'yŏngnon* 69 (2015): 289–325.

Han Hye-In. "Chendŏ yusan ŭrosŏ ilbon'gun wianbu kirongmul." *Kirogin* 44 (2018): 100–115.

Han Yong-Sŏp. "Han'guk kukpang chŏngch'aek ŭi pyŏnch'ŏn kwajŏng." In *Kukpang chŏngch'aek ŭi iron kwa silche*, edited by Ch'a Yŏng-Gu and Hwang Pyŏng-Mu. Seoul: Orŭm, 2002.

Han'guk chŏngsindae munje taech'aek hyŏbŭihoe 20 nyŏn sa p'yŏnch'an wiwŏnhoe. *Han'guk chŏngsindae munje taech'aek hyŏbŭihoe 20 nyŏn sa*. Seoul: Hanul ak'ademi, 2014.

Han'guk kwan'gwang palchŏn sa. Seoul: Han'guk kwan'gwang hyŏp'oe, 1984.

Han'guk kwan'gwang ŭi onŭl kwa naeil. Seoul: Han'guk kwan'gwang hyŏp'oe, 1975.

Han'guk kyŏngje 60 nyŏn sa. Seoul: Han'guk kaebal yŏn'guwŏn, 2010.

Han'guk minjujuŭi yŏn'guso, ed. *Han'guk minjuhwa undong sa*. Vol. 3. Paju: Tolbege, 2010.

Han'guk YWCA 80 nyŏn sa: Saengmyŏng ŭi param ŭro. Seoul: YWCA, 2006.

Han'gŭl Hak'oe. *Chosŏn mal k'ŭn sajŏn.* Seoul: Ŭryu munhwasa, 1957.

Hong Jia [Hong Chi-A]. "Midiŏ rŭl t'onghan sŏngmaemae ŭi ŭimi kusŏng: Chung-gang ilbo, Chosŏn ilbo, Kyŏnghyang sinmun, Han'gyŏre ŭi kisa punsŏk ŭl chungsim ŭro." *Han'guk yŏsŏnghak* 31, no. 3 (2015): 219–259.

Hong Jin Ok [Hong Chin-Ok]. "Urinara ŭi yullak yŏsŏng e kwanhan yŏn'gu." Master's thesis, Chunang University, 1968.

Hong Sŭng-Hŭi. *Pulgŭn sŏn: Na ŭi seksyuŏllit'i kirok.* Seoul: Kŭrhangari, 2017.

Hong Sŭng-P'yo. "Maech'un sahoe e kwanhan il yŏn'gu: Yeongdeungpo yŏk chubyŏn ŭi maech'un ŏpso esŏŭi ch'amyŏ kwanch'al." Master's thesis, Korea University, 1982.

Huh Koung-Mi [Hŏ Kyŏng-Mi]. "Norŭdik model sŏngmaemae chŏngch'aek ŭi tilema wa sisachŏm." *Kyŏngch'arhak nonch'ong* 14, no. 2 (2019): 35–61.

Hwang Chŏng-Im. "T'al sŏngmaemae yŏsŏng ŭl wihan 'chahwal' chiwŏn chŏngch'aek i kŏrŏon kil, naagal kil." In *Kyŏnggye ŭi ch'ai, sai, t'ŭmsae: Sŏngmaemae konggan ŭi tamyŏnsŏng kwa salm ŭi kwŏlli,* edited by Kim Ae-Ryŏng. Seoul: Kŭrinbi, 2007.

Hwang Jisung [Hwang Chi-Sŏng]. "Changae yŏsŏng ŭi sisŏrhwa kwajŏng e kwanhan yŏn'gu: Seoul sirip punyŏ poho chidoso sarye rŭl chungsim ŭro." PhD diss., Seoul National University, 2023.

Hwang Jung-Mee [Hwang Chŏng-Mi]. "Kaebal kukka ŭi yŏsŏng chŏngch'aek e kwanhan yŏn'gu: 1960-70 nyŏndae han'guk punyŏ haengjŏng ŭl chungsim ŭro." PhD diss., Seoul National University, 2001.

Hwang Kyoung-Lan [Hwang Kyŏng-Nan]. "Pan sŏngmaemae undong hwaltonggadŭl ŭi sŏngmaemae yŏsŏng chahwal chiwŏn il e kwanhan chedojŏk munhwa kisulji." PhD diss., Seoul Women's University, 2019.

Ilbon ŭi chŏnjaeng ch'aegim charyo sent'ŏ yŏn'gu samuguk. "Tokyo chaep'an esŏ simp'an padŭn ilbon'gun wianbu chedo." In *Ilbon ŭi kun wianbu yŏn'gu,* edited by Ilbon ŭi chŏnjaeng ch'aegim charyo sent'ŏ. Seoul: Tongbuga yŏksa chaedan, 2011.

Im Myŏng-Bang. "Injung sijŏl kwa t'aegŭkki e taehan kiŏk." *Hwanghae munhwa* 5 (1994): 156–163.

In Tae-Jeong and Yhang Wii-Joo [Yin T'ae-Jŏng and Yang Wi-Ju]. "Segye ch'egye iron ŭl t'onghan han'guk kŭndae kungmin kwan'gwang ŭi hyŏngsŏng kwajŏng e kwanhan yŏn'gu: 1961–1979 sigi ŭi kukka chŏngch'aek ŭl chungsim ŭro." *Kwan'gwang rejŏ yŏn'gu* 18, no. 4 (2006): 173–189.

Insinmaemae ŭi silt'ae e kwanhan yŏn'gu. Seoul: Han'guk hyŏngsa chŏngch'aek yŏn'guwŏn, 1993.

Jeong Mi Rye [Chŏng Mi-Rye]. "Sŏngmaemae yŏsŏng pibŏmjoehwa ŭi kwanchŏm kwa p'iryosŏng e taehan yŏn'gu: T'al sŏngmaemae yŏsŏngdŭl ŭi mokssori rŭl chungsim ŭro." Master's thesis, SungKongHoe University, 2010.

Jeong Young Sin [Chŏng Yŏng-Sin]. "Tong asia ŭi anbo punŏp kujo wa pan kiji undong e kwanhan yŏn'gu." PhD diss., Seoul National University, 2012.

Jo Won Koang [Cho Wŏn-Gwang]. "Han'guk sobi sahoe ŭi tŭngjang kwa misi kwŏllyŏk ŭi pyŏnhwa." *Han'guk sahoehak* 48, no. 1 (2014): 133–172.

Joo Shinil [Chu Sin-Il]. "Ilbu chiyŏk e issŏsŏ ŭi yullak yŏsŏng e kwanhan sahoe ŭihakchŏk chosa yŏn'gu." Master's thesis, Seoul National University, 1965.

Jung Keun-Sik [Chǒng Kǔn-Sik]. "Singminji wisaeng kyǒngch'al ǔi hyǒngsǒng kwa pyǒnhwa: Singminji t'ongch'isǒng ǔi sigak esǒ." *Sahoe wa yǒksa* 90 (2011): 221–270.

Kang Chun-Man. *Rumsallong konghwaguk.* Seoul: Inmul kwa sasangsa, 2011.

Kang Il-Su. "MMPI e nat'anan yullak yǒsǒng ǔi sǒnggyǒk t'ǔkching." *Simnihak yǒn'gu* 14, no. 1 (1986): 53–62.

Kang Jeong Sook [Kang Chǒng-Suk]. "Ilbon'gun 'wianbu'je ǔi singminsǒng yǒn'gu: Chosǒnin 'wianbu' rǔl chungsim ǔro." PhD diss., Sungkyunkwan University, 2010.

———. "Taehan cheguk ilche ch'ogi Seoul ǔi maech'unǒp kwa kongch'ang chedo ǔi toip." *Sǒurhak yǒn'gu* 11 (1998): 199–202.

Kang Young Su [Kang Yǒng-Su]. "Han'guk sahoe maemaech'un e kwanhan yǒn'gu: Yongsan yǒk chubyǒn maech'un yǒsǒng ǔl chungsim ǔro." Master's thesis, Ewha Womans University, 1989.

Kim A-ram. "5.16 kunjǒnggi sahoe chǒngch'aek: Adong pokchi wa puranga taech'aek ǔi sǒnggyǒk." *Yǒksa wa hyǒnsil* 82 (2011): 329–365.

Kim Ae-Ryǒng and Won Mi Hye [Wǒn Mi-Hye], eds. *Pulgǔn pelbet aelbǒm sok ǔi yǒindǔl.* Seoul: Kǔrinbi, 2007.

Kim Bong Seok [Kim Pong-Sǒk]. "Yi Man-Gap ǔi sahoehak." *Han'guk sahoehak* 50, no. 2 (2016): 41–66.

Kim Chae-Su. "Kijich'on e kwanhan sahoe chirihakchǒk yǒn'gu: Dongducheon ǔl sarye ro." Master's thesis, Korea University, 1979.

Kim Chi-Hye. "Yǒsǒng sǒng nodongja ch'ǒbǒl chohang wihǒn chech'ǒng kwa sǒng nodongja ǔi kwǒlli." *Yǒ/sǒng iron* 28 (2013): 227–234.

Kim Chin Kyun, ed. *1980 nyǒndae hyǒngmyǒng ǔi sidae.* Seoul: Saeroun sesang, 1999.

Kim Chǒng-Ja. *Migun wianbu kijich'on ǔi sumgyǒjin chinsil.* Seoul: Hanul ak'ademi, 2013.

Kim Chǒng-Ok. "Yullak yǒsǒng ǔi yullak yoin e kwanhan yǒn'gu: Busan t'ǔkchǒng chiyǒk ǔl chungsim ǔro." *Yǒsǒng munje yǒn'gu* 8 (1979): 175–190.

Kim Ch'un. "Kijich'on chubyǒn yullak yǒsǒng e kwanhan silt'ae chosa: Pyeongtaek Paengseong-myeon Anjeong-ri rǔl chungsim ǔro." *Sahoe pokchi yǒn'gu* 9, no. 1 (1975): 62–75.

Kim Chung-kang [Kim Chǒng-Gang]. "'Wianbu' nǔn ǒttǒk'e it'yǒjyǒnna? 1990 nyǒndae ijǒn taejung yǒnghwa sok wianbu chaehyǒn." *Tongasia munhwa yǒn'gu* 71 (2017): 149–193.

Kim Daehyun [Kim Tae-Hyǒn]. "1950–60 nyǒndae 'yoboho' ǔi chaegusǒng kwa 'yullak yǒsǒng' saǒp ǔi chǒn'gae." *Sahoe wa yǒksa* 129 (2021): 7–59.

Kim Gwi-ok [Kim Kwi-Ok]. "Ilbon singminjuǔi ka han'guk chǒnjaenggi han'gukkun wianbu chedo e mich'in yǒnghyang kwa kwaje." *Sahoe wa yǒksa* 103 (2014): 85–116.

Kim Hak-Sun. "Toep'uri hagi choch'a sirǔn kiǒktǔl." In *Kangjero kkǔllyǒgan chosǒnin kun wianbudǔl: Chǔngǒnjip*, Vol. 1, edited by Chǒngsindae yǒn'guhoe. Seoul: Hanul, 1993.

Kim In Soo [Kim In-Su]. "Nongsǒk Yi Hae-Yǒng ǔi sahoehak: 'Han'guk sahoe cho-sasa' ǔi ch'ǔkmyǒn esǒ." *Han'guk sahoehak* 50, no. 4 (2016): 27–66.

Kim Jo Young [Kim Cho-Yŏng]. "Kijich'on e kwanhan chirihakchŏk yŏn'gu: Gyeonggi-do Paju chibang ŭl chungsim ŭro." Master's thesis, Seoul National University, 1978.

Kim Jong-Geun [Kim Chong-Gŭn]. "Singmin tosi Kyŏngsŏng ŭi yugwak konggan hyŏngsŏng kwa kŭndaejŏk kwalli." *Munhwa yŏksa chiri* 23, no. 1 (2011): 115–132.

Kim Joohee [Kim Chu-Hŭi]. "'Irŏn saenghwal i innŭn chuldo mollassŏyo': Chungnyŏn yŏsŏng sŏngmaemae yuip ŭi chŏngch'i kyŏngje." *Han'guk yŏsŏnghak* 34, no. 1 (2018): 33–66.

———. *Reidi k'ŭredit: Sŏngmaemae kŭmyung ŭi ŏlgul ŭl hada.* Seoul: Hyŏnsil munhwa, 2020.

Kim Myung Suk [Kim Myŏng-Suk]. "Yullak yŏsŏng e kwanhan chedojŏk koch'al." Master's thesis, Ewha Womans University, 1981.

Kim Nak-Chung. "Haptong kyŏrhonsik sŏngkwa pogo." In *Yullak yŏsŏng e kwanhan yŏn'gu pogosŏ*, edited by Seoul t'ŭkpyŏlsi sirip punyŏ poho chidoso. Seoul: Seoul t'ŭkpyŏlsi sirip punyŏ poho chidoso, 1966.

Kim Sungeun [Kim Sŏng-Ŭn]. "1950–60 nyŭndae miguk ŭi kyoyuk wŏnjo wa miguk yuhak sŏnho: Minnesota Project wa Fulbright Program ŭl chungsim ŭro." *Sahoe wa yŏksa* 122 (2019): 191–222.

Kim Yeon-Ja [Kim Yŏn-Ja]. *Amerika t'aun wang ŭnni chukki obun chŏn kkaji ak ŭl ssŭda: Kim Yeon-Ja chajŏn esei.* Seoul: Samin, 2005.

Kim Yŏn-Ju. "Ch'ŏngsonyŏn sŏngmaemae ŏttŏk'e pol kŏsin'ga." *Chinbo p'yŏngnon* 64 (2015): 268–286.

Kim Yong-A. "Sisŏl kwalli e kwanhan sogyŏn: Kyodo rŭl chungsim ŭro." In *Yullak yŏsŏng e kwanhan yŏn'gu pogosŏ*, edited by Seoul t'ŭkpyŏlsi sirip punyŏ poho chidoso. Seoul: Seoul t'ŭkpyŏlsi sirip punyŏ poho chidoso, 1966.

———. "Yullak yŏsŏng e kwanhan silt'ae pogo: Sirip punyŏ poho chidoso wŏnsaeng ŭl chungsim ŭro." *Chibang haengjŏng* 143 (1965): 64–70.

Kim Yŏng-Mo. *T'oep'ye, yullak munje taeŭng pangan yŏn'gu.* Seoul: Hyŏndae sahoe yŏn'guso, 1984.

Kim Young-Shik [Kim Yŏng-Sik]. "Tosi e issŏsŏ ŭi oegugin ŭl sangdaero han wianbu e taehan sŏngpyŏng kwalli." *Yebang ŭihak hoeji* 7, no. 2 (1974): 293–298.

Kim Yun-hee [Kim Yun-Hŭi]. "Incheon Sungui-dong sŏngmaemae chipkyŏlchi e taehan yŏn'gu: Sŏngmaemae pangjipŏp kwa sibŏm saŏp e ŭihan pyŏnhwa rŭl chungsim ŭro." Master's thesis, Seoul National University, 2006.

Kisaeng kwan'gwang: Chŏn'guk 4 kae chiyŏk silt'ae chosa pogosŏ. Seoul: Han'guk kyohoe yŏsŏng yŏnhap'oe, 1983.

Kook Kyung-Hee [Kuk Kyŏng-Hŭi]. "Han'guk sŏng nodongja undong e kwanhan yŏn'gu." Master's thesis, Chungang University, 2007.

Kuwabara Shisei. *Naega parabon kyŏktong ŭi han'guk: Kuwabara Shisei han'guk sajin chŏnjip.* Seoul: Nunbit, 2008.

Kwan'gwang chawŏn kaebal ŭi hyŏnhwang kwa kwaje. Seoul: Taehan sanggong hoeŭiso, 1974.

Kwan'gwang pujori silt'ae mit pangji taech'aek. Seoul: Pujŏng pangji taech'aek wiwŏnhoe, 1994.

Kwǒn Hyǒk-Hŭi. *Chosǒn esǒ on sajin yǒpsǒ*. Seoul: Minǔmsa, 2005.

Kwǒn Kyu-Sik and O Yǒng-Gǔn. "Yullak yǒsǒng ǔi silt'ae." *Yǒsǒng munje yǒn'gu* 3 (1973): 149–171.

Lee Bong Soo [Yi Pong-Su]. "Yuhǔng kinǔng chungsimji idong kwajǒng e kwanhan yǒn'gu." Master's thesis, Seoul National University, 1983.

Lee Hyo-Hee [Yi Hyo-Hǔi]. "Siptae yǒsǒng ǔi sǒngchǒk sǒbisǔ kyǒnghǒm e kwanhan yǒsǒngjuǔijǒk chǒpkǔn." Master's thesis, Ewha Womans University, 1998.

Lee Hyun Jin [Yi Hyǒn-Chin]. "1980 nyǒndae sǒngae yǒnghwa chaep'yǒngga rǔl wihan sogo." *Hyǒndae yǒnghwa yǒn'gu* 18 (2014): 93–126.

Lee Im-ha [Yi Im-Ha]. "Migun ǔi tongasia chudun kwa seksyuǒliti." In *Tongasia wa kǔndae, yǒsǒng ǔi palgyǒn*, edited by Tongasia yugyo munhwakwǒn kyoyuk yǒn'gudan. Seoul: Ch'ǒngǒram, 2004.

Lee Na Young [Yi Na-Yǒng]. "Sǒngmaemae kǔnjǒlchuǔi undong ǔi yǒksajǒk hyǒngsǒng kwa pyǒnhwa." *Han'guk yǒsǒnghak* 25, no. 1 (2009): 5–34.

———. "Sǒngp'anmaeja pibǒmjoehwa rǔl wihan siron: Sǒngmaemae t'ǔkpyǒlpǒp ǔl tullǒssan chaengchǒm kwa yǒsǒngjuǔi taean mosaek." *P'eminijǔm yǒn'gu* 15, no. 1 (2015): 211–247.

Lee Ock-jeong [Yi Ok-Chǒng] and Yǒm Sang-Mi. *Maktallena, mak tallaena? Maktallena ǔi chip iyagi*. Seoul: Kaemagowǒn, 2005.

Lee Sang Rok [Yi Sang-Nok]. "Kyǒngje cheil chuǔi ǔi sahoejǒk kusǒng kwa saengsanjǒk chuch'e mandǔlgi: 4.19–5.16 sigi hyǒngmyǒng ǔi chǒnyu rǔl tullǒssan kyǒnghap kwa chǒllyaktǔl," *Yǒksa munje yǒn'gu* 25 (2011): 115–158.

———. "1970 nyǒndae sobi ǒkche chǒngch'aek kwa sobi munhwa ǔi ilsang chǒngch'ihak." *Yǒksa munje yǒn'gu* 17, no. 1 (2013): 137–182.

Lee Soon Rae, Jeong Hey Won, and Park Cheol Hyun [Yi Sun-Rae, Chǒng Hye-Wǒn, and Pak Ch'ǒl-Hyǒn]. "Pǒmjoe t'onggye wa yǒn'gu yulli: Sǒngmaemae silt'ae chosa ǔi sarye." *Konggong chǒngch'aek yǒn'gu* 32, no. 2 (2014): 1–16.

Lee Soyoung [Yi So-Yǒng]. "Kǒnjǒn sahoe wa kǔ chǒktǔl: 1960–80 nyǒndae purangin tansok ǔi saengmyǒng chǒngch'i." *Pǒp kwa sahoe* 51 (2016): 23–54.

Lee Tae Am [Yi T'ae-Am]. "T'ǔksu chiyǒk sahoein e taehan sahoe ǔihakchǒk chosa yǒn'gu." Master's thesis, Seoul National University, 1965.

Lee Yoo Sook [Yi Yu-Suk]. "Yullak yǒsǒng e kwanhan sahoe hwan'gyǒng chosa." Master's thesis, Seoul National University, 1962(?).

Lyo Kyung Goo [Yǒ Kyǒng-Gu]. "Han'gugin sǒngpyǒng ǔi sahoe ǔihakchǒk chosa yǒn'gu." Master's thesis, Seoul National University, 1960.

Maktallena ǔi chip, ed. *Yonggamhan yǒsǒngdǔl, nǔktae rǔl t'ago tallinǔn*. Seoul: Samin, 2002.

Migunjǒng pǒmnyǒng ch'ongnam [Yǒngmunp'an]. Seoul: Han'guk pǒpche yǒn'guhoe, 1971.

Milsa, Yǒnhǔi, and Chi Sǔng-Ho. *Sǒng nodongja, kwǒlli rǔl oech'ida: Milsa wa Yǒnhǔi ǔi sǒng nodong iyagi*. Seoul: Ch'ǒlsu wa yǒnghǔi, 2015.

Min Kyǒng-Ja. "Han'guk maech'un yǒsǒng undong sa." In *Han'guk yǒsǒng inkwǒn undong sa*, edited by Han'guk yǒsǒng ǔi chǒnhwa. Seoul: Hanul ak'ademi, 1999.

Minju sŏng nodongja yŏndae. "Ch'ulbŏm sŏnŏnmun: Chŏn'guk sŏng nodongja yŏndae hanyŏyŏn ŭl t'alt'oe hamyŏnsŏ." In *Sŏngmaemae ŭi chŏngch'ihak: Sŏngmaemae t'ŭkpyŏlpŏp chejŏng 1 nyŏn ŭi sichŏm esŏ*, edited by Yi Chae-In. Seoul: Hanul ak'ademi, 2005.

Moon Koo Hyun [Mun Ku-Hyŏn]. "Yullak yŏsŏng e taehan hyŏnhwang mit sŏngpyŏng e kwanhan yŏn'gu." *Kyungpook National University Nonmunjip* 8 (1964): 131–154.

Moon Sangseok [Mun Sang-Sŏk]. "Han'guk chŏnjaeng, kŭndae kungmin kukka hyŏngsŏng ŭi ch'ulbalchŏm: Chawŏn dongwŏnnon ŭi kwanchŏm esŏ." *Sahoe wa yŏksa* 86 (2010): 81–119.

Mun Kyŏng-Nan. "Migunjŏnggi han'guk yŏsŏng undong e kwanhan yŏn'gu." Master's thesis, Ewha Womans University, 1989.

Mun Se-Yŏng. *Chosŏnŏ sajŏn*. Keijō: Chosŏnŏ sajŏn kanhaeng hoe, 1938.

Mun Sŏn-Hwa. "Han'guk yullak yŏsŏng sŏndo saŏp e taehan sogo." Master's thesis, Ewha Womans University, 1970.

Mun Su-Yŏng. "Yullak yŏsŏng sŏn'gyo: Yullak yŏsŏng silt'ae wa sŏn'gyo ŭi kanŭngsŏng e kwanhan yŏn'gu." Master's thesis, Seoul Theological University, 1977.

Mun Yŏng-Mi. *Amudo kŭnyŏ ŭi iyagi rŭl tŭrŏjuji anatta*. Seoul: Saemt'ŏ, 1999.

Na to marhal su innŭn saram ida: Sŏngp'anmae yŏsŏng annyŏngdŭl hasimnikka. Seoul: Yŏiyŏn, 2018.

Nam Chŏng-Ok. *Hanmi kunsa kwan'gye sa*. Seoul: Kukpangbu kunsa p'yŏnch'an yŏn'guso, 2002.

Nam Hwa-Suk. "1920 nyŏndae yŏsŏng undong esŏŭi hyŏptong chŏnsŏnnon kwa kŭnuhoe." *Han'guksaron* 25 (1991): 201–249.

Nam Taek-Sung [Nam T'aek-Sŭng]. "Urinara sŏngpyŏng kwalli e kwanhan yŏk'akchŏk koch'al." *Yebang ŭihak hoeji* 9, no. 1 (1976): 123–127.

Oegugin yŏsŏng sŏngmaemae silt'ae mit chedo kaesŏn pangan yŏn'gu. Seoul: Yŏsŏng kajokpu, 2011.

Oeguk yŏsŏng sŏngmaemae silt'ae chosa. Seoul: Yŏsŏngbu, 2003.

Oh Jaelim, Yoo Sook-Ran, and Ahn Jae-Hee [O Chae-Rim, Yu Suk-Nan, and An Chae-Hŭi]. "Sŭweden ŭi sŏng kumaeja ch'ŏbŏlpŏp chejŏng kwajŏng punsŏk." *Asia yŏsŏng yŏn'gu* 45, no. 2 (2006): 271–312.

Paik Wook-inn [Paek Uk-In]. "Han'guk sobi sahoe hyŏngsŏng kwa chŏngbo sahoe ŭi sŏnggyŏk e kwanhan yŏn'gu." *Kyŏngje wa sahoe* 77 (2008): 199–225.

Pak Ch'an-P'yo. *Han'guk ŭi kukka hyŏngsŏng kwa minjujuŭi: Naengjŏn chayujuŭi wa posujŏk minjujuŭi ŭi kiwŏn*. Seoul: Humanit'asŭ, 2007.

Pak Ch'an-Sŭng. "Purŭjua minjokchuŭi, up'a minjokchuŭi, chwap'a minjokchuŭi." *Yŏksa pip'yŏng* 75 (2006): 286–290.

Pak Tong-Ch'an. *T'onggye ro pon 6.25 chŏnjaeng*. Seoul: Kukpangbu kunsa p'yŏnch'an yŏn'guso, 2014.

Park Chung Hee [Pak Chŏng-Hŭi]. *Kukka wa hyŏngmyŏng kwa na*. Seoul: Kip'arang, 2017. First published 1963.

Park Jeong-Mi [Pak Chŏng-Mi]. "Hasudo, p'ihaeja, wihŏm (e ch'ŏ) han yŏja: 19–20 segi ch'o 'ŭiryo-todŏk chŏngch'i' wa sŏngmaemae chŏngch'aek ŭi hyŏngsŏng." *Sahoe wa yŏksa* 120 (2018): 321–352.

———. "Kŭmyok esŏ yebang ŭro: 2 ch'a segye chŏnjaenggi migun ŭi sŏngpyŏng t'ongje, saengmyŏng kwŏllyŏk kwa chendŏ." *Kyŏngje wa sahoe* 113 (2017): 234–263.

———. "Migun chŏmnyŏnggi Okinawa ŭi kiji sŏngmaemae wa yŏsŏng undong." *Sahoe wa yŏksa* 73 (2007): 221–254.

Park Jin-kyung [Pak Chin-Kyŏng]. "Sŏngmaemae pangjipŏp chejŏng kwajŏng ŭi chŏngch'aek net'ŭwŏk'ŭ punsŏk." Master's thesis, Ewha Womans University, 2005.

Park Jung Ae [Pak Chŏng-Ae]. "Chosŏn ch'ongdokpu ŭi sŏngpyŏng yebang chŏngch'aek kwa hwaryupyŏng yebangnyŏng." *Sarim* 55 (2016): 299–326.

———. "Ilche ŭi kongch'angje sihaeng kwa sach'ang kwalli yŏn'gu." PhD diss., Sook-myung Women's University, 2009.

Park Sun-Sook [Pak Sŏn-Suk]. "Yŏsŏng ŭi sŏngsŏng (sexuality) ŭl chungsim ŭro pon maemaech'un ch'ŏngch'aek e kwanhan yŏngu." Master's thesis, Ewha Womans University, 1990.

Park Tai Keun [Pak Tae-Gŭn]. "Wianbudŭl e taehan sahoe ŭihakchŏk chosa yŏn'gu: Gunsan chiyŏk ŭl chungsim ŭro." Master's thesis, Seoul National University, 1964.

Pomnal. *Kil hana kŏnnŏmyŏn pyŏrang kkŭt: Sŏngmaemae ranŭn ch'akch'wi wa p'ongnyŏk esŏ saranamŭn han yŏsŏng ŭi yonggamhan kirok.* Seoul: Panbi, 2019.

Punyŏ haengjŏng 40 nyŏn sa. Seoul: Pogŏn sahoebu, 1987.

Pyŏlbyŏl chilmun sŏngmaemae e taehan 20 kaji iyagi. Seoul: ELoom, 2013.

Rhee Se Young [Yi Se-Yŏng]. "Yullak silt'ae e kwanhan yŏn'gu." Master's thesis, Kyunghee University, 1976.

Shim Eun-jung [Sim Ŭn-Chŏng]. "Che 5 konghwaguk sigi p'ŭro yagu chŏngch'aek kwa kungmin yŏga." *Yŏksa yŏn'gu* 26 (2014): 197–238.

Shin Kyu-hwan [Sin Kyu-Hwan]. "Kaehang, chŏnjaeng, sŏngpyŏng: Hanmal ilche ch'o ŭi sŏngpyŏng yuhaeng kwa t'ongje." *Ŭisahak yŏngu* 17, no. 2 (2008): 239–255.

Shin Sang-Sook [Sin Sang-Suk]. "Chendŏ wa p'yŏngdŭng ŭi kwanchŏm esŏ pon sŏngmaemae ch'ŏbŏl ŭi p'ŭreim kyŏnghap: Sŏngmaemae ch'ŏbŏlpŏp che 21 cho che 1 hang wihŏn pŏmnyul simp'an ŭl chungsim ŭro." *Han'guk yŏsŏnghak* 33, no. 4 (2017): 1–37.

Simin chagu undong II: Hyangnak munhwa ch'ubang kwa kŏnjŏn simin munhwa kak-kugi simin undong. Seoul: Seoul YMCA, 1995.

Sin Chu-Baek. "Hanbando esŏŭi ilbon'gun yŏksa (1904–1945)." In *Kundae wa sŏngp'ongnyŏk: Hanbando ŭi 20 segi*, edited by Song Yeon-ok [Song Yŏn-Ok] and Kim Yŏng. Seoul: Sŏnin, 2012.

Sin Tong Yoll [Sin Tong-Nyŏl]. "Ch'angnyŏ ŭi chinŭng kyesu: Sŏngpyŏng manyŏn ŭi wŏnch'ŏn ŭrosŏ." Master's thesis, Seoul National University, 1961.

Sinbak Chin-Yŏng. *Sŏngmaemae, sangsik ŭi p'ŭllaek'ol.* Seoul: Pomallam, 2020.

Sinsang konggae taesang pŏmjoe charyo chonghap punsŏk. Seoul: Han'guk hyŏngsa chŏngch'aek yŏn'guwŏn, 2004.

Sŏ Yŏn-Sun. "Yullak e issŏsŏ ŭi sisŏl poho wa Cottage System ŭi pigyo." *Sahoe saŏp* 9 (1975): 5–29.

Son Chŏng-Mok. *Han'guk tosi 60 nyŏn ŭi iyagi.* Seoul: Hanul, 2005.

———. "Kaehanggi han'guk kŏryu ilbonin ŭi chigŏp kwa maech'unŏp koridaegŭmŏp." *Han'guk hakpo* 6, no. 1 (1980): 98–112.

Sŏng ch'akch'wi mokchŏk ŭi insinmaemae hyŏnhwang kwa pŏpchŏk taeŭng pangan.
Seoul: Han'guk hyŏngsa chŏngch'aek yŏn'guwŏn, 2002.

Song Yeon-ok [Song Yŏn-Ok]. "Ilche singminjihwa wa kongch'angje toip." Master's
thesis, Seoul National University, 1998.

*Sŏngmaemae kyŏnghŏm tangsaja net'ŭwŏk'ŭ mungch'i. Sŏngmaemae kyŏnghŏm
tangsaja muhanbalsŏl.* Seoul: Pomallam, 2020.

Sŏngmaemae silt'ae chosa kaesŏn pangan yŏn'gu. Seoul: Han'guk yŏsŏng chŏngch'aek
yŏn'guwŏn, 2015.

Sŏngmaemae silt'ae mit kyŏngje kyumo e kwanhan chŏn'guk chosa. Seoul: Han'guk
hyŏngsa chŏngch'aek yŏn'guwŏn, 2002.

Sŏngsanŏp e yuiptoen oegugin yŏsŏng e kwanhan che 2 ch'a hyŏnjang silt'ae chosa pogosŏ.
Seoul: Han'guk kyohoe yŏsŏng yŏnhap'oe, 2002.

Suh Ji Young [Sŏ Chi-Yŏng]. "Sangsil kwa pujae ŭi sigonggan: 1930 nyŏndae yorijŏm
kwa kisaeng." *Chŏngsin munhwa yŏn'gu* 32, no. 3 (2009): 167–194.

———. "Singminji sidae kisaeng yŏn'gu (1): Kisaeng chiptan ŭi kŭndaejŏk chaep'yŏn
yangsang ŭl chungsim ŭro." *Chŏngsin munhwa yŏn'gu* 28, no. 2 (2005): 267–294.

Sung Yung Ja [Sŏng Yŏng-Ja]. "Wianbu e taehan sahoe ŭihakchŏk chosa yŏn'gu."
Master's thesis, Seoul National University, 1966.

Taebŏmjoe chŏnjaeng paeksŏ. Seoul: Kyŏngch'alch'ŏng, 1992.

Taehan min'guk nae roŭi kukche insinmaemae e kwanhan charyo kŏmt'o. Seoul:
Kukche iju kigu, 2002.

2019 sŏngmaemae silt'ae mit taeŭng pangan yŏn'gu. Seoul: Yŏsŏng kajokpu, 2019.

2006 oegugin yŏnyein toip silt'ae chosa mit chŏngch'aek pigyo yŏn'gu. Seoul: Munhwa
kwan'gwangbu and Kukche iju kigu, 2006.

2010 nyŏn sŏngpyŏng kwalli chich'im. Seoul: Chilbyŏng kwalli ponbu, 2009.

2010 sŏngmaemae silt'ae chosa. Seoul: Yŏsŏng kajokpu, 2010.

Uridŭl ŭi Kŭm-I. Seoul: Chuhan migun ŭi Yun Kŭm-I ssi sarhae sakŏn kongdong
taech'aek wiwŏnhoe, 1993.

Won Mi Hye [Wŏn Mi-Hye]. "Han'guk sahoe ŭi maemaech'un yŏsŏng e taehan t'ongje
wa ch'akch'ui e kwanhan yŏn'gu." Master's thesis, Ewha Womans University, 1997.

———. "'Sŏng p'anmae yŏsŏng' ŭi saengae ch'ehŏm yŏn'gu: Kyoch'ajŏk sŏng wigye ŭi
sigongganjŏk chakyong ŭl chungsim ŭro." PhD diss., Ewha Womans University, 2010.

———. "Yŏsŏngjuŭi sŏngjŏngch'i: Sŏngmaemae kŭnjŏl undong ŭl nŏmŏsŏsŏ." In
*Sŏngmaemae ŭi chŏngch'ihak: Sŏngmaemae t'ŭkpyŏlpŏp chejŏng 1 nyŏn ŭi sichŏm
esŏ,* edited by Yi Chae-In. Seoul: Hanul ak'ademi, 2005.

Yamashita Yŏng-Ae. "Han'guk kŭndae kongch'ang chedo silsi e kwanhan yŏn'gu."
Master's thesis, Ewha Womans University, 1992.

Yang Chae-Bok. "Yullak yŏsŏng sŏngpyŏng e kwanhan sogo." In *Yullak yŏsŏng e
kwanhan yŏn'gu pogosŏ,* edited by Seoul t'ŭkpyŏlsi sirip punyŏ poho chidoso.
Seoul: Seoul t'ŭkpyŏlsi sirip punyŏ poho chidoso, 1966.

Yang Dong Sook [Yang Tong-Suk]. "Haebang hu uik yŏsŏng danch'e ŭi chojik kwa
hwaltong yŏn'gu." PhD diss., Hanyang University, 2010.

Yesul hŭnghaeng pija soji ijumin inkwŏn sanghwang silt'ae chosa. Seoul: Kukka inkwŏn
wiwŏnhoe, 2014.

Yi Ch'ŏl-Yong. *Ŏdum ŭi chasiktŭl*. Seoul: Saeum, 2015.

Yi Hyŏn-Suk. *Han'guk kyohoe yŏsŏng yŏnhap'oe 25 nyŏn sa*. Seoul: Han'guk kyohoe yŏsŏng yŏnhap'oe, 1992.

Yi Kyŏng-Min. *Kisaeng ŭn ŏttŏk'e mandŭrŏjyŏnnŭn'ga*. Seoul: Ak'aibŭ puksŭ, 2005.

Yi Mun-Ja. "Yullak yŏsŏng silt'ae e kwanhan yŏn'gu." In *Yullak yŏsŏng e kwanhan yŏn'gu pogosŏ*, edited by Seoul t'ŭkpyŏlsi sirip punyŏ poho chidoso. Seoul: Seoul t'ŭkpyŏlsi sirip punyŏ poho chidoso, 1966.

Yi Myŏng-Ch'ŏl and Ch'oe Yŏng-Gyu. "Seoul sinae yullak yŏsŏng silt'ae chosa." *Sahoe pokchi yŏn'gu* 12, no. 1 (1978): 108–129.

Yi Nŭng-Hwa. *Chosŏn haeŏhwa sa*. Seoul: Tongmunsŏn, 1992.

Yi Ok-Sun. "Yullak yŏsŏng sŏndo." In *Yullak yŏsŏng mit mihonmo e taehan charyojip*. Seoul: Han'guk puinhoe ch'ongbonbu, 1985.

Yi Sŭng-Ho. "Urinara poan ch'ŏbun ŭi yŏksajŏk chŏn'gae." *Hyŏngsa chŏngch'aek* 7 (1995): 65–104.

Yi Sŭng-Hŭi. *Han'guk hyŏndae yŏsŏng undong sa*. Seoul: Paeksan sŏdang, 1994.

Yi Su-Yŏn. "Hyangnak sanŏp ŭi silt'ae wa wŏnin." *Kidokkyo sasang* (January 1989): 103–109.

Yi Ŭng-In. "T'ŭksu yullak yŏsŏng e taehan silt'ae chosa: Ilsŏn chigu chuhan migun sangdae yullak yŏsŏng ŭl chungsim ŭro." *Asea yŏsŏng yŏn'gu* 4 (1965): 193–207.

Yoboho yŏsŏng silt'ae chosa pogosŏ. Seoul: Pogŏn sahoebu, 1981.

Yŏn'gubu. "Hyangnak sanŏp ŭi p'aengch'ang wŏnin kwa taech'aek." *Sahoe chŏngch'aek yŏn'gu* 6 (1985): 140–170.

Yook Kil Sung [Yuk Kil-Sŏng]. "Daejeon-si yullak yŏsŏng silt'ae e kwanhan yŏn'gu." Master's thesis, Hannam University, 1986.

Yoon Bong Ja [Yun Pong-Ja]. "Chŏpkaek ŏpchadŭl e taehan sahoe ŭihakchŏk chosa yŏn'gu." Master's thesis, Seoul National University, 1963.

Yoon Eun-soon [Yun Ŭn-Sun]. "1920–30 nyŏndae han'guk kidokkyo chŏlche undong yŏn'gu." PhD diss., Sookmyung Women's University, 2001.

Yoon Hyaesin [Yun Hye-Sin]. "Ilche sidae kisaeng ŭi chŏgŭp'wa tamnon e taehan yŏn'gu." Master's thesis, Seoul National University, 2006.

Yŏsŏng, adong kwŏnik chŭngjin saŏp unyŏng chich'im. Seoul: Yŏsŏng kajokpu, 2022.

Yŏsŏng kwa kwan'gwang munhwa: Jeju chiyŏk ŭl chungsim ŭro. Seoul: Han'guk kyohoe yŏsŏng yŏnhap'oe.

Yŏsŏng kwan'gye yŏn'gu charyo 2: T'ŭkchip, maech'un. Seoul: Han'guk kidok ch'ŏngnyŏn hyŏbŭihoe, 1983.

Yŏsŏng munhwa iron yŏn'guso sŏng nodong yŏn'gut'im. *Sŏng nodong*. Seoul: Yŏiyŏn, 2007.

Yŏsŏng sinmunsa. "Yi U-Jŏng: Kisaeng kwan'gwang i aeguk imyŏn sŏnsaeng ttal put'ŏ kwan'gwang kisaeng mandŭsio." In *Iyagi yŏsŏngsa: Han'guk yŏsŏng ŭi sam kwa yŏksa*. Seoul: Yŏsŏng sinmunsa, 2000.

Yu Song-Ja. "Yullak yŏsŏng ŭi yoin punsŏk kwa sŏndo p'ŭrogŭraem e kwanhan yŏn'gu." Master's thesis, Ewha Womans University, 1974.

Yukkun ponbu. *Yugio chŏnjaeng hubang chŏnsa: Insap'yŏn*. Seoul: P'ungmunsa, 1956.

Agamben, Georgio. *Homo Sacer: Sovereign Power and Bare Life*. Stanford, CA: Stanford University, 1998.

———. *State of Exception*. Chicago: University of Chicago Press, 2005.

Althusser, Louis. "Ideology and Ideological State Apparatuses." In *Lenin and Philosophy and Other Essays*. New York: Monthly Review Press, 2001.

American Social Hygiene Association. *Digest of Laws Dealing with Prostitution and Other Sex Offenses*. New York: American Social Hygiene Association, 1942.

———. *Social Hygiene Legislation Manual, 1921*. New York: American Social Hygiene Association, 1921.

Bailey, Beth, and David Farber. *The First Strange Place: Race and Sex in World War II Hawaii*. Baltimore, MD: Johns Hopkins University Press, 1992.

Baldwin, Peter. *Contagion and the State in Europe, 1830–1930*. Cambridge: Cambridge University Press, 2004.

Balibar, Étienne, and Immanuel Wallerstein. *Race, Nation, Class: Ambiguous Identities*. London: Verso, 1991.

Ballantyne, Tony, and Antoinette Burton. *Bodies in Contact: Rethinking Colonial Encounters in World History*. Durham, NC: Duke University Press, 2005.

Barlow, Tani E. *The Question of Women in Chinese Feminism*. Durham, NC: Duke University Press, 2004.

Barry, Kathleen. *The Prostitution of Sexuality*. New York: New York University Press, 1995.

Bashford, Alison. *Imperial Hygiene: A Critical History of Colonialism, Nationalism and Public Health*. London: Palgrave Macmillan, 2004.

Bernheimer, Charles. *Figures of Ill Repute: Representing Prostitution in Nineteenth-Century France*. Durham, NC: Duke University Press, 1997.

Bishop, Ryan, and Lillian S. Robinson. *Night Market: Sexual Cultures and the Thai Economic Miracle*. New York: Routledge, 1998.

Brandt, Allan M. *No Magic Bullet: A Social History of Venereal Disease in the United States since 1880*. Oxford: Oxford University Press, 1987.

Brazinsky, Gregg. *Nation Building in South Korea: Koreans, Americans, and the Making of a Democracy*. Chapel Hill: University of North Carolina Press, 2007.

Chang, Kyung-Sup. *South Korea under Compressed Modernity: Familial Political Economy in Transition*. London: Routledge, 2010.

Cheng, Sealing. *On the Move for Love: Migrant Entertainers and the U.S. Military in South Korea*. Philadelphia: University of Pennsylvania Press, 2013.

Clement, Harry G, ed. *The Future of Tourism in the Pacific and Far East: A Report Prepared by Checchi and Company under Contract with the United States Department of Commerce and Co-Sponsored by the Pacific Area Travel Association*. Washington, DC: US Government Printing Office, 1961.

Corbin, Alain. "Commercial Sexuality in Nineteenth-Century France: A System of Images and Regulations." In *The Making of the Modern Body: Sexuality and Society in the Nineteenth Century,* edited by Catherine Gallagher and Thomas Laquer. Berkeley: University of California Press, 1987.

———. *Women for Hire: Prostitution and Sexuality in France after 1850.* Cambridge, MA: Harvard University Press, 1990.

Cowdrey, Albert E. *The Medics' War: United States Army in the Korean War.* Washington, DC: Center of Military History, US Army, 1987.

Cumings, Bruce. *The Origins of the Korean War.* Vol. 1, *Liberation and the Emergence of Separate Regimes, 1945–1947.* Princeton, NJ: Princeton University Press, 1981.

Ditmore, Melissa Hope, ed. *Encyclopedia of Prostitution and Sex Work.* Westport, CT: Greenwood Press, 2006.

Dower, John W. *Embracing Defeat: Japan in the Wake of World War II.* New York: W. W. Norton, 2000.

Eichengreen, Barry, Dwight H. Perkins, and Kwanho Shin. *From Miracle to Maturity: The Growth of the Korean Economy.* Cambridge, MA: Harvard University Press, 2012.

Enloe, Cynthia. *Bananas, Beaches & Bases: Making Feminist Sense of International Politics.* Berkeley: University of California Press, 1990.

Federici, Silvia. *Caliban and the Witch: Women, the Body and Primitive Accumulation.* New York: Autonomia, 2004.

Foucault, Michel. *The Birth of Biopolitics: Lectures at the Collège de France, 1978–1979,* edited by Michel Senellart. New York: Palgrave Macmillan, 2008.

———. *Discipline and Punish: The Birth of the Prison.* New York: Vintage Books, 1991.

———. *The History of Sexuality.* Vol. 1, *An Introduction.* New York: Random House, 1978.

———. "Of Other Spaces." In *Heterotopia and the City: Public Space in a Postcivil Society,* edited by Michiel Dehaene and Lieven De Cauter. London: Routledge, 2008.

———. "The Politics of Health in the Eighteenth Century." In *Power/Knowledge: Selected Interviews and Other Writings, 1972–1988,* edited by Colin Cordon. New York: Pantheon Books, 1980.

———. *Security, Territory, and Population: Lectures at the College de France 1977–1978,* edited by Michel Senellart. New York: Picador and Palgrave Macmillan, 2007.

———. *"Society Must Be Defended": Lectures at the Collège de France, 1975–1976,* edited by Mauro Bertani and Alessandro Fontana. New York: Picador, 2003.

———. "Truth and Juridical Forms." In *Power: The Essential Works of Foucault, 1954–1986,* Vol. 3, edited by James D. Faubion. New York: New Press, 2001.

Gandhi, Leela. *Postcolonial Theory: A Critical Introduction.* Crows Nest: Allen & Unwin, 1998.

Gordon, Colin. "Governmental Rationality: An Introduction." In *The Foucault Effect: Studies in Governmentality,* edited by Graham Burchell, Colin Gordon, and Peter Miller. Chicago: University of Chicago Press, 1991.

Hacking, Ian. "How Should We Do the History of Statistics?" In *The Foucault Effect: Studies in Governmentality*, edited by Graham Burchell, Colin Gordon, and Peter Miller. Chicago: University of Chicago Press, 1991.

Harsin, Jill. *Policing Prostitution in Nineteenth-Century Paris*. Princeton, NJ: Princeton University Press, 1985.

Henry, Todd A. *Assimilating Seoul: Japanese Rule and the Politics of Public Space in Colonial Korea, 1910–1945*. Berkeley: University of California Press, 2014.

———. "'In the Shadows of Women': Male-Bodied Service Labor, the Mass Media, and Gender Policing in Authoritarian South Korea." Presented at the 28th Colloquium of the Research Institute for Comparative Culture and Society, Yonsei University, February 23, 2021.

Hershatter, Gail. *Dangerous Pleasure: Prostitution and Modernity in Twentieth-Century Shanghai*. Berkeley: University of California Press, 1997.

Hicks, George. *The Comfort Women: Japan's Brutal Regime of Enforced Prostitution in the Second World War*. New York: W. W. Norton, 1997.

Hobson, Barbara Meil. *Uneasy Virtue: The Politics of Prostitution and the American Reform Tradition*. New York: Basic Books, 1987.

Hodges, Luther H. Foreword to *The Future of Tourism in the Pacific and Far East: A Report Prepared by Checchi and Company under Contract with the United States Department of Commerce and Co-Sponsored by the Pacific Area Travel Association*, edited by Harry G. Clement. Washington, DC: US Government Printing Office, 1961.

Howell, Philip. *Geographies of Regulation: Policing Prostitution in Nineteenth-Century Britain and the Empire*. Cambridge: Cambridge University Press, 2009.

———. "Prostitution and Racialised Sexuality: The Regulation of Prostitution in Britain and the British Empire before the Contagious Diseases Acts." *Environment and Planning D: Society and Space* 18 (2000): 321–339.

Huang, Hans Tao-Ming. "State Power, Prostitution and Sexual Order in Taiwan: Towards a Genealogical Critique of 'Virtuous Custom.'" *Inter-Asia Cultural Studies* 5, no. 2 (2004): 237–262.

Hunt, Alan. *Governing Morals: A Social History of Moral Regulation*. Cambridge: Cambridge University Press, 1999.

Jeffreys, Sheila. *The Idea of Prostitution*. North Melbourne: Spinifex, 1997.

Kauffman, Morton D. *Tourism to Korea*. Seoul: United States Operations Mission to Korea, 1966.

Kim, Elaine H., and Chungmoo Choi, eds. *Dangerous Women: Gender and Korean Nationalism*. London: Routledge, 1998.

Kim, Hyun Sook. "Yanggongju as an Allegory of the Nation: Images of Working-Class Women in Popular and Radical Texts." In *Dangerous Women: Gender and Korean Nationalism*, edited by Elaine H. Kim and Chungmoo Choi. London: Routledge, 1998.

Kim, Suzy. *Everyday Life in the North Korean Revolution, 1945–1950*. Ithaca, NY: Cornell University Press, 2016.

Koikari, Mire. *Pedagogy of Democracy: Feminism and the Cold War in the U.S. Occupation of Japan*. Philadelphia: Temple University Press, 2008.

Kovner, Sarah. *Occupying Power: Sex Workers and Servicemen in Postwar Japan*. Stanford, CA: Stanford University Press, 2012.

Kramm, Robert. *Sanitized Sex: Regulating Prostitution, Venereal Disease, and Intimacy in Occupied Japan, 1945–1952*. Oakland: University of California Press, 2017.

Langum, David J. *Crossing over the Line: Legislating Morality and the Mann Act*. Chicago: University of Chicago Press, 1994.

Legg, Stephen. "Governing Prostitution in Colonial Delhi: From Cantonment Regulations to International Hygiene (1864–1939)." *Social History* 34, no. 4 (2009): 447–467.

Lee, Jin-Kyung. *Service Economies: Militarism, Sex Work and Migrant Labor in South Korea*. Minneapolis: University of Minnesota Press, 2010.

Lee, Na Young. "The Construction of U.S. Camptown Prostitution in South Korea: Trans/formation and Resistance." PhD diss., University of Maryland, 2006.

Levine, Phillipa. *Prostitution, Race, and Politics: Policing Venereal Disease in the British Empire*. New York: Routledge, 2003.

Lim, Lin Lean, ed. *The Sex Sector: The Economic and Social Bases of Prostitution in Southeast Asia*. Geneva: International Labor Office, 1998.

Limoncelli, Stephanie. *The Politics of Trafficking: The First International Movement to Combat the Sexual Exploitation of Women*. Stanford, CA: Stanford University Press, 2010.

Luker, Kristin. "Sex, Social Hygiene, and the State: The Double-Edged Sword of Social Reform." *Theory and Society* 27, no. 5 (1998): 601–634.

Marshall, T. H. *Citizenship and Social Class and Other Essays*. Cambridge: Cambridge University Press, 1950.

Marx, Karl. *Capital: A Critique of Political Economy*. Vol. 1. London: Penguin Books, 1982.

Matsui, Yayori. "Sexual Slavery in Korea." *Frontiers: A Journal of Women's Studies* 2, no. 1 (1977): 22–30.

McClintock, Ann. *Imperial Leather: Race, Gender and Sexuality in the Colonial Contest*. New York: Routledge, 1995.

———. "Sex Work and Sex Workers." *Social Text* 37 (1993): 1–10.

Meade, Edward G. *American Military Government in Korea*. New York: Kings Crown Press, 1951.

Migdal, Joel S. *Strong Societies and Weak States: State-Society Relations and State Capabilities in the Third World*. Princeton, NJ: Princeton University Press, 1988.

Moon, Katharine H. S. *Sex among Allies: Military Prostitution in U.S.-Korea Relations*. New York: Columbia University Press, 1997.

———. "South Korean Movements against Militarized Sexual Labor." *Asian Survey* 39, no. 2 (1999): 310–327.

Moon, Seungsook. "Regulating Desire, Managing the Empire: U.S. Military Prostitution in South Korea, 1945–1970." In *Over There: Living with the U.S. Military*

Empire from World War Two to the Present, edited by Maria Höhn and Seungsook Moon. Durham, NC: Duke University Press, 2010.

Mort, Frank. *Dangerous Sexualities: Medico-Moral Politics in England since 1830*. London: Routledge, 2000.

Muroi, Hisae, and Naoko Sasaki. "Tourism and Prostitution in Japan." In *Gender, Work and Tourism*, edited by M. Thea Sinclair. London: Routledge, 1997.

Norma, Caroline. "Prostitution and the 1960s' Origin of Corporate Entertaining in Japan." *Women's Studies International Forum* 34, no. 6 (2011): 509–519.

O'Connell Davidson, Julia. "Prostitution and the Contours of Control." In *Sexual Cultures: Communities, Values and Intimacy*, edited by Jeffrey Weeks and Janet Holland. London: Macmillan, 1996.

———. *Prostitution, Power and Freedom*. Ann Arbor: University of Michigan Press, 1998.

———. "The Rights and Wrongs of Prostitution." *Hypatia* 17, no. 2 (2002): 84–98.

Parascandola, John. "Presidential Address: Quarantining Women; Venereal Disease Rapid Treatment Centers in World War II America." *Bulletin of the History of Medicine*, 83, no. 3 (Fall 2009): 431–459.

———. *Sex, Sin, and Science: A History of Syphilis in America*. Westport, CT: Praeger, 2008.

Park, Jeong-Mi. "Liberation or Purification? Prostitution, Women's Movement and Nation Building in South Korea under US Military Occupation, 1945–1948." *Sexualities* 22, nos. 7–8 (2019): 1053–1070.

Pickering, Michael. *Stereotyping: The Politics of Representation*. London: Palgrave, 2001.

Polanyi, Karl. *The Great Transformation: The Political and Economic Origins of Our Time*. Boston: Beacon Press, 2001.

Remick, Elizabeth J. *Regulating Prostitution in China: Gender and Local Statebuilding, 1900–1937*. Stanford, CA: Stanford University Press, 2014.

Rosen, Ruth. *The Lost Sisterhood: Prostitution in America, 1900–1918*. Baltimore, MD: Johns Hopkins University Press, 1982.

Sams, Crawford F. *Medic: The Mission of an American Military Doctor in Occupied Japan and Wartorn Korea*. New York: M. E. Sharp, 1998.

Scott, Joan Wallach. *Gender and the Politics of History*. New York: Columbia University Press, 1988.

Sippial, Tiffany A. *Prostitution, Modernity, and the Making of the Cuban Republic, 1840–1920*. Chapel Hill: University of North Carolina Press, 2013.

Smart, Carol. *Law, Crime and Sexuality: Essays in Feminism*. London: Sage, 1995.

Spivak, Gayatri C. "Subaltern Talk: Interview with the Editors." In *The Spivak Reader*, edited by Donna Landry. London: Routledge, 1995.

Stetz, Margaret, and Bonnie B. C. Oh, eds. *Legacies of the Comfort Women of World War II*. London: Routledge, 2001.

Stoler, Ann Laura. *Interior Frontiers: Essays on the Entrails of Inequality*. Oxford: Oxford University Press, 2022.

———. "Making Empire Respectable: The Politics of Race and Sexual Morality in 20th-century Colonial Cultures." *American Ethnologist* 16, no. 4 (1989): 634–660.

———. *Race and the Education of Desire: Foucault's "History of Sexuality" and the Colonial Order of Things*. Durham, NC: Duke University Press, 1995.

Sturdevant, Saundra Pollack, and Brenda Stoltzfus. *Let the Good Times Roll: Prostitution and the U.S. Military in Asia*. New York: New Press, 1992.

Suh, Sarah Chunghee. *The Comfort Women: Sexual Violence and Postcolonial Memory in Korea and Japan*. Chicago: University of Chicago Press, 2008.

Tilly, Charles. "War and the Power of Warmakers in Western Europe and Elsewhere, 1600–1980." CRSO Working Paper 287. 1983.

Truong, Thanh-dam. *Sex, Money and Morality: Prostitution and Tourism in South-East Asia*. London: Zed Books, 1990.

US Army Medical Department. *Preventive Medicine in World War II*. Vol. 5, *Communicable Diseases Transmitted through Contact or by Unknown Means*. Washington, DC: Department of the Army, 1960.

Walkowitz, Judith R. *Prostitution and Victorian Society: Women, Class and the State*. Cambridge: Cambridge University Press, 1980.

Woods, Mac E. *Korea, Hills, Rice Patties, and Whores*. N.p: n.p., [2001].

Yen, Wan-Chen. *Governing Sex, Building the Nation: The Politics of Prostitution in Postcolonial Taiwan (1945–1979)*. Newcastle upon Tyne: Cambridge Scholars Publishing, 2015.

Yoshimi, Yoshiaki. *Comfort Women: Sexual Slavery in the Japanese Military during World War II*. New York: Columbia University Press, 2001.

INDEX

pimps/pimping, 9, 60, 70, 122; abusing of prostitutes by, 123, 184, 192
Pinchbeck, Harriet Faye. See Mun Hye-Rim
Pocheon, 71
Polanyi, Karl, 192
procurers, 131, 132, 184; legal approach to, 7, 9, 10, 45; research on, 158
prohibition, of prostitution, 10, 37, 46, 79, 156; feminist campaign to prohibit prostitution, 160, 168–72; in post-colonial Korea, 7, 14, 45, 46, 47, 49, 71, 81, 108, 110, 143, 144, 147, 173, 174, 178, 233–4n20; in the United States, 9, 38, 80*tab*. See also Abolishment of the Public Prostitution Law (1948); Act on the Prevention of Commercial Sex Acts and the Protection of Victims (2004); Act on the Punishment of Arrangement of Commercial Sex Acts (2004); Sŏngmaemae Prevention Acts (2004); Yullak Haengwi Prevention Act ([Yullak Prevention Act] 1961)
prostitutes, 3–5; *ch'angnyŏ* (prostitutes for Korean men), 109; Cuban prostitutes, 84; conflicts among, 83–84; economic distress as a reason for becoming a prostitute, 138–39; education and intelligence of, 137–38; foreign women entering the Korean sex trade, 162–65, 185; legal approaches to in other states/empires, 8–13, 16–17; men who frequent prostitutes, 108–9, 173, 187–88; official term used by the Korean government to refer to (*yullak haengwija*), 5–7; the peculiarities of Korea's historical governmental approach to, 6–7; police crackdowns on, 110, 120–22, 146, 158, 177, 179, 182, 189, 232–33n5; "protection" of during incarceration, 143, 155, 157; "public prostitutes" (*kongch'ang*), 27; as refugees, 23, 50, 199–200n58; as social outcasts, 28, 78, 85, 151; as social pariahs confined in "states of exception" or "heterotopias," 147–48, 225n3; as "women needing protection" (*yoboho yŏja*), 6, 22, 117–18, 122, 132, 135, 143,

144, 145, 150, 156, 157, 180, 181, 187. See also "fallen women"; health certificates; licensed prostitutes; prostitutes, feminist shelters for; sex worker(s)
prostitutes, feminist shelters for, 2, 20, 147–50, 158, 159, 164, 168, 176, 187. See also Christian House; Durebang (My Sister's Place); Hansorihoe; Magdalena House (Maktallena ŭi chip); Saeumtŏ
prostitution: adolescent prostitution, 160–62, 184; and biopolitical states/empires, 8–12, 179–80, 212–13n97; current scale of the sex industry in Korea, 182–83; danger of as a profession, 191–92; explosive growth of in the 1980s, 108–14; and other forms of labor, 193–94; "public prostitution" (*kongch'angje*), 27, 29, 30*tab*.; the relationship of with Korea's post-colonial nation building, 13–17; three main forms of prostitution policy among states, 10. See also abolition, of regulation or prostitution; regulation of prostitution; prostitution studies; sex work
Prostitution of Sexuality, The (Barry), 159, 168
prostitution studies: flawed nature of, 140–41; and guidelines for "Protection and Guidance," 140–42; increase in from the 1960s on, 136; as power-knowledge, 132–33; and the state/social science coalition, 133–36; and statistics as a moral science, 136–40; and the transformation of knowledge, 158–59
Pyeongtaek, 71, 74, 87, 174, 175

queer sex work, 7

rapid treatment centers (United States), 35, 79, 80*tab*.
Recreation and Amusement Association (RAA, Japan), 34
red-light district(s), 5, 11–12, 28, 35, 80*tab*., 103, 105, 108, 110, 112, 136, 138, 148, 183, 184, 185, 225n3, 232–33n5; camptowns as, 64; closure of some red-light districts, 51, 178, 182, 187, 234n24; contemporary

red-light districts open today, 178; fires in, Gunsan, 160, 166–67; Jongno sam-ga district, 109, 144; "model project" for, 177; at Miari Texas, 146, 174; at Mukjeong-dong, 24; organization of women in, 174–76; police crackdowns on, 146, 174; in Pyeongtaek, 175; around train stations, Seoul, 109; in Yongsan, 20, 24, 109, 120, 148, 157, 158, 218n95
regulation, of prostitution, 7; French system (*réglementation*), 8–9; in other states/empires, 9–12, 16–17. *See also* abolition of regulation or prostitution; authorization-regulation, colonial; toleration-regulation, colonial; toleration-regulation regime, postcolonial
Regulation of Brothel Owners and Prostitutes (1916), 27, 30*tab.*, 45–46, 47
Regulation of Geisha, Barmaids, and Geisha Houses (1916), 27, 30*tab.*, 47
Regulation on Sexually Transmitted Disease Checkups (1969), 95–96
Remick, Elizabeth J., 12
"Resolution for Abolishing Public and Private Prostitution" (1946), 40
Rhee administration, 88
Rhee Syngman (Yi Sŭng-Man), 53, 64, 70
Roh Moo-Hyun (No Mu-Hyŏn), 171–72
"room salons," 109–10, 164, 178; Gangnam as the mecca of, 183; sex workers' income from, 183–84
Rule on Health Checkups of Employees in Sanitary Field (1984), 99, 110, 185
Rule on Health Checkups for STI and AIDS (2013), 185
Rule on Sexually Transmitted Disease Checkups (1978), 144
Russia, 9, 11, 163, 185

Saeumtŏ (Supporting Center for the Victims of Commercial Sex Acts), 164, 167, 168, 171
Sale or Contracts for Sale of Female Prohibited (Ordinance No. 70, 1946), 45, 46
Salvarsan, 30–31

Sams, Crawford F., 33–35
Scarlet ChaCha, 189, 192–93
Scott, Joan Wallach, 18
Second World War, 16–17, 38, 56, 71, 103, 133; defeat of Japan in, 12–13, 32–34; U.S. government's prostitution policy during, 35, 38, 79
Seoul: arrests of "comfort women" in, 212n88; prostitution venues in (Gangnam, Itaewon, Hyehwadong, Jongno sam-ga, Miari, Mukjeong-dong, Yongsan), 20, 24, 98, 109, 120, 142, 144, 146, 147, 174, 183, 212n88; as sex tourist spots, 89, 94, 101, 107; "South Korea: The Seoul of Hospitality," 93; special comfort troops in, 55; stationing of United Nations Command in, 65. *See also* Seoul City; Seoul Asian Games (1986); Seoul Olympic Games (1988), as the apogee of sex tourism
Seoul Asian Games (1986), 98, 101, 110
Seoul City, 24, 43, 49, 50, 141; lawsuits filed against the mayor of, 155–56
Seoul Municipal Reformatory to Protect and Guide Women. *See* Seoul Reformatory
Seoul National University, 132, 133
Seoul Olympic Games (1988), 101, 105, 110; as the apogee of sex tourism, 97–99
Seoul Reformatory, 115–16, 117, 119, 120, 130, 131, 132, 138, 139, 141; admission ceremony at, 121*fig.*; arranged marriages at, 128–30; embroidery class at, 127*fig.*; inmates' struggle against, 155–57
sex work, 7, 30, 131, 170, 186, 188; pro-sex work feminists, 178, 189, 190; Sex Work Project, 192–93. *See also* prostitution
sex worker(s), 3, 4, 5, 7, 8, 17, 184, 186–94; migrant sex workers, 185; as a new identity, 147, 176; as participants of their representation, 19; protests by, 16, 147, 156–57, 174–78, 175*fig.*, 189; serving American troops, 13, 154–55; serving Japanese tourists (tourist kisaeng), 88, 95; serving Korean men, 109, 110, 112, 114. *See also* prostitutes
"sexual imperialism" (Japanese), 21, 112, 151; critique of, 99–107; and the

Founded in 1893,
UNIVERSITY OF CALIFORNIA PRESS
publishes bold, progressive books and journals
on topics in the arts, humanities, social sciences,
and natural sciences—with a focus on social
justice issues—that inspire thought and action
among readers worldwide.

The UC PRESS FOUNDATION
raises funds to uphold the press's vital role
as an independent, nonprofit publisher, and
receives philanthropic support from a wide
range of individuals and institutions—and from
committed readers like you. To learn more, visit
ucpress.edu/supportus.

www.ingramcontent.com/pod-product-compliance
Lightning Source LLC
Chambersburg PA
CBHW030339270326
41926CB00009B/895